THE ORGANIZATION
OF POLITICAL PARTIES
IN SOUTHERN EUROPE

A volume in the Political Parties Series of the Workgroup on Elections and Parties of the Committee on Political Sociology, a Joint Committee of the International Political Science Association and the International Sociology Association.

Kay Lawson (ed.), *How Political Parties Work: Perspectives from Within* (1994)

THE ORGANIZATION
OF POLITICAL PARTIES
IN SOUTHERN EUROPE

EDITED BY

Piero Ignazi and Colette Ysmal

Foreword by Kay Lawson

PRAEGER

Westport, Connecticut
London

Library of Congress Cataloging-in-Publication Data

The organization of political parties in Southern Europe / edited by
   Piero Ignazi and Colette Ysmal ; foreword by Kay Lawson.
      p.   cm.
   Includes bibliographical references and index.
   ISBN 0–275–95612–1 (alk. paper)
      1. Political parties—Europe, Southern.   I. Ignazi, Piero.
   II. Ysmal, Colette.
   JN94.A979074   1998
   324.2'094—dc21   97–40888

British Library Cataloguing in Publication Data is available.

Library of Congress Catalog Card Number: 97–40888
ISBN: 0–275–95612–1

First published in 1998

Praeger Publishers, 88 Post Road West, Westport, CT 06881
An imprint of Greenwood Publishing Group, Inc.

Printed in the United States of America

The paper used in this book complies with the
Permanent Paper Standard issued by the National
Information Standards Organization (Z39.48–1984).

10 9 8 7 6 5 4 3 2 1

Contents

Figures and Tables   vii

Foreword   ix
Kay Lawson

Introduction   1
Piero Ignazi and Colette Ysmal

Part I. France

1. The Evolution of the French Party System   9
    Colette Ysmal

2. Conflict and Change in the Rassemblement pour la
    République   26
    Florence Haegel

3. The Front National: The Making of an Authoritarian Party   43
    Gilles Ivaldi

4. The Parti Socialiste: From a Party of Activists to a Party of
    Government   70
    Frédéric Sawicki

Part II. Italy

5. The Italian Party System: The Effective Magnitude of an
    Earthquake   91
    Luciano Bardi and Piero Ignazi

6. The Failed Renewal: The DC from 1982 to 1994   110
   Gianfranco Baldini

7. From Militants to Voters: From the PCI to the PDS   134
   Maria Pamini

8. MSI/AN: A Mass Party with the Temptation of the
   Führer-Prinzip   157
   Piero Ignazi

Part III.   Greece

9. The Political System in Postauthoritarian Greece (1974–1996):
   Outline and Interpretations   181
   P. Nikoforos Diamandouros

10. PASOK: The Telling Story of a Unique Organizational
    Structure   202
    Michalis Spourdalakis

11. Nea Demokratia: Party Development and Organizational
    Logics   221
    Takis S. Pappas

Part IV.   Spain

12. The Spanish Political Parties from Fragmentation to Bipolar
    Concentration   241
    Gabriel Colomé and Lourdes Lòpez-Nieto

13. The Organizational Dynamics of AP/PP   254
    Lourdes Lòpez-Nieto

14. The PSOE: The Establishment of a Governmental Party 270
    Gabriel Colomé

    Conclusion: Party Organization and Power—A Southern
    European Model?   281
    Piero Ignazi and Colette Ysmal

    Index   305

    About the Contributors   313

Figures and Tables

FIGURES

1.1   Family Tree and Evolution of the French Political Parties   12

3.1   The Structure of the National Front   53

TABLES

1.1   Results of the French General Elections, 1958–1993 (percentage of the vote cast)   15

2.1   RPR Offices Held by Federal Secretaries in 1993 (percentage values)   30

2.2   Turnover in National RPR Bodies, 1979–1993 (percentage of newly elected members)   37

4.1   Proportion of the PS Tendencies, 1971–1990 (percentages)   72

4.2   PS Membership, 1970–1991   74

4.3   Turnover of the PS Executive Bodies, 1973–1990 (percentages)   79

5.1   Percentage of Votes in the Chamber of Deputies, 1946–1996 (1994 and 1996 PR ballot votes)   93

5.2   Old and New Parties   102

6.1   DC Composition and Functions of the National Party Organs   116

6.2   Turnover of the DC National Executive from 1982 to 1993   117

6.3   DC Membership, 1982–1993   120

7.1   PCI/PDS Membership, 1976–1992   137

7.2   Turnover of the Central Committee/National Committee, 1979–1991   142

7.3	Turnover of the Executive Committee, 1979–1991	144
7.4	Parliamentarization Rate of the Executive Committee, Secretariat and CC/NC	146
8.1	Turnover in the MSI National Executive (*Direzione Nazionale*)	163
8.2	Membership of MSI/AN, 1960–1995	170
9.1	Results of National Elections, 1974–1996	184
10.1	PASOK Membership, 1977–1994	203
11.1	Intraparty Power Possessed by Each of ND's Subunits	231
11.2	Overall Assessment of Relative Distribution of Power within ND	233
12.1	Spanish Electoral Results, 1977–1996	248
13.1	AP/PP Members and Percentage of the Electorate	257
13.2	Distribution of Party Votes, Members, Delegates and Offices by Autonomous Communities, 1993	258
14.1	PSOE Members at Conference Year	272
14.2	PSOE Turnover within the Federal Executive Committee	275

Foreword

Kay Lawson

The *Organization of Political Parties in Southern Europe*, edited by Piero Ignazi, University of Bologna, and Colette Ysmal, Center for the Study of French Political Life, is the second volume published by Praeger in a series of volumes sponsored by the Work Group on Political Parties and Elections. The Work Group is a subgroup of the Committee on Political Sociology, one of the oldest and most distinguished international study groups, composed of the world's leading political scientists and sociologists, and affiliated with both the International Political Science Association and the International Sociology Association.

The first volume, *How Political Parties Work: Perspectives from Within*, edited by Kay Lawson, was published in 1994, and included the study of the internal life of parties from a wide range of nations (Germany, France, New Zealand, the United States, Norway, Japan, India, Belgium, Israel, the Czech and Slovak Republics, Poland, Great Britain and Spain). This eclectic volume has been well received, and has prompted the decision to publish further volumes dedicated to the parties of specific regions of the world. *The Organization of Political Parties in Southern Europe* continues the theme of the first volume, the internal dynamics of contemporary parties, and treats the major parties of France, Italy, Greece and Spain. A third volume, *Political Cleavages and Parties in the New Europe* (edited by Kay Lawson, Andrea Rommele and Georgi Karasimeonov), on the party systems of Bulgaria, the Czech Republic, Hungary, Poland and Romania, is now in press. As its title indicates, this volume will move away from the study of internal party life and concentrate on the question of how well the new parties represent the cleavages which are emerging in this transformed and still-transforming system.

Further volumes, one on Asian parties to be edited by Subrata Mitra of the University of Heidelberg, and another on Mid-Eastern parties, under the editorship of Gabriel Ben-Dor of Israel and Saad al Din Ibrahim of Egypt, are now being organized. Yet others, on African and Latin American parties, are on a more distant agenda, but the energies of the Work Group show no sign of flagging. Persuaded that academic irredentism is more often useful than dangerous, we boldly plan to cover the globe.

Meanwhile, here is volume two. As in all the Work Group's books, this one is written by indigenous scholars. Ignazi and Ysmal are well-known at home as well as in international scholarship for their penetrating studies of the changing politics of Italy and France, respectively, and they have brought together a team of authors with equally close familiarity with the subjects about which they write. The chapters are up-to-date, detailed, fully documented and accessible to all. Introductory chapters to each nation's parties provide the historical-constitutional background necessary to make the book useful not only to scholars working in the field of parties and organizations, but also as a possible text in a wide range of upper division or graduate courses in comparative politics. We look forward to its warm reception, and thank the editors for a job well done.

THE ORGANIZATION
OF POLITICAL PARTIES
IN SOUTHERN EUROPE

Introduction

————— *Piero Ignazi and Colette Ysmal*

The organization of political parties has come again to the core of the discipline: political scientists and political sociologists have been devoting more and more attention to this topic, which has been left unexplored for decades. The freezing in the discipline provoked by the majestic effort by Duverger in 1951 melted only at the turn of the 1970s and the 1980s.

William Crotty (1968), Samuel Eldersfeld (1964), Daniel Gaxie (1977, 1980), Robert Harmel et al. (1994, 1995), Kenneth Janda (1980, 1983), Kay Lawson (1976, 1994), Michel Offerlè (1991), Angelo Panebianco (1982), Joseph Schlesinger (1984), Kaare Strøm (1989), Spencer Wellhofer (1979), only to name a few (and pathbreaking) scholars, had provided some landmark contributions in the field. These theoretical analyses have been paralleled by a growing series of case studies[1] and by broad comparative analysis (Lawson, 1976, 1994; Lawson and Merkl, 1988; Katz and Mair, 1992, 1994; Harmel et al., 1995).

This book's scope falls in between two different approaches highlighted, respectively, by Lawson's (1994) recent editorial and Katz and Mair's majestic comparative study (1992, 1994).

The research coordinated by Katz and Mair attempted to identify an "evolutionary pattern" in the organizational story of parties—from the mass party to the catch-all and ultimately to the cartel party. This evolutionary approach is sustained by an innovative and adequate distinction of different "fields" of activity performed by the party itself: *the party on the ground*, the organizational territorial structure and the membership—the standard reference of the strength of parties; *the party in central office*, the national headquarters, with their staffs, bureaucracies, and financing; and *the party in public office*, the resources that parties possess as a result of their position in local and/or central government. The great value of this research resides in the massive amount of data that have been collected and analyzed within this framework. Thanks to this work we know a lot now about membership, territorial articulation, flanking organizations, membership in the collective bodies, party paid staff and finance. However, what is lacking in Katz and Mair's research is the assessment of power distribution within the party, beyond the statutory prescriptions and the formal rules.

While we acknowledge the importance of formal rules, the focus of our book, on the other hand, attempts to understand how parties "really" work: this means, *how actors within the party interact in order to get control of crucial resources and run the organization.* The intention of the present work is to highlight the intraparty conflicts in order to assess which are the *loci* of power, how the "dominant coalition" is composed and why and how it has changed over time, which organizational traits have been moulded by the different leadership and which style of leadership prevailed. Following this approach—which is indebted to Panebianco's (1982) framework integrated by the recent contribution by Harmel and Janda (1994), who have both brought into the party realm many hints of the organizational literature—we have reduced the basic information on parties (membership, local branches and so on) to the minimum and we have instead concentrated our attention on the power exchanges that occur within the party. The main questions we tried to answer concern: the general traits inherited by the party's originary model and the level of institutionalization and the style of leadership; the degree of factionalization and the means and resources of the dominant coalition to keep the rein of power; the turnover in the party executives and the modification of "composition and conformation" of the dominant coalition; the relationship between the party leadership and the flanking organization, between center and periphery, and between parliamentary party and party headquarters. This general framework flows across every contribution in this book, though with a different degree of emphasis.

In this sense, this book deviates from Lawson's collection of party studies. As the editor herself stresses in her conclusion, no explicit common framework has been "imposed" to any single party analysis since each contribution follows its own pattern. Lawson summarizes the set of contributions by highlighting four variables for the study of party organizations: motives, means, degree of closure and external situation (1994: 287). Motives comprise personal gains, devotion to a leader, devotion to an organization and commitment to policy; means are measured on the basis of the capacity to establish good relationships among various actors, efficient routine performance, and the responsiveness to external change; the degree of closure defines how neat the party boundaries are; the external situation links the party to the political system and analyzes the way in which system stability and power of the party in government interact with the internal life of parties. These variables (the first three more than the fourth one) capture some common elements of the collected chapters regarding the intraparty conflicts, the availability of resources, the leader-activists relationship. This approach has offered a variety of clues and hints as to the effective internal mechanics of the decision-making process and power relationship but has limited the assessment of generalizations about "how parties work." The various contributions (and the same conclusion by Kay Lawson) do not offer a new model or ideal-type of party.

The book has been conceived as an area study of a particular geopolitical region, Southern Europe, which comprises France, Italy, Greece and Spain. These countries are characterized by their common geographical position on the Mediterranean basin and consequently by the common cultural influences that this unifying element has provided through the centuries.[2] Common traits could be traced in the secular trade relationship, the catholic lineage (three countries out of four, Greece being of orthodox denomination and dominated for centuries by the Ottoman empire), the influence of Greek-Roman civilization, the late development of economy (with the exception of northern France), the period of authoritarian rule (limited to the 1940–1944 Vichy Republic for France), the emphasis on direct interpersonal relationship with strong ascriptive elements rather than formal and depersonalized attitudes (again with exception to northern France). These elements allow us, in a broad sense, to speak of the existence of a geopolitical area.

For each country only the most relevant and salient parties are analyzed: the Gaullists, the socialists and the frontists in France, the socialists and conservatives in Greece, the former Christian democrats, communists and neofascists (and their successors of the 1990s) in Italy, the socialists and the conservatives in Spain. Each country analysis is preceded by an introduction on the main institutional features and the evolution of the party system which could serve as a framework within which to insert the individual party study. This general overview of the party system and the institutional setting is intended to provide a better understanding of the various peculiarities inherent to single-party analysis. Finally, each party has a different time span of analysis. For the newest democracies (Greece and Spain) the analysis covers the whole period from the transition to democracy up until 1996. For Italy and France the time period varies from party to party according to key turning points in recent party history. For example, the Italian Christian Democracy has been studied in particular from the radical change in its "dominant coalition" provided by the secretary of Ciriaco de Mita in 1982 up until the transformation of the party into the Popular Party in 1994. Similarly, the Italian Communist Party is analyzed from the change of leadership in 1984 up until its transformation into the Democratic Party of the Left, while the neofascist party is scrutinized all along its history to control for the novelty introduced by its successor, the National Alliance. The French Socialist Party had its obvious starting point in 1971 with the refounding of the party under the leadership of François Mitterrand while the Gaullist RPR was radically renovated by Jacques Chirac in 1976. The Le Pen's Front National has been studied primarily after its emergence from total irrelevance after 1983–1984, though some mention is made of the previous decade, since its founding in 1972.

This project was conceived in 1992 by the two editors and strongly supported by the Work Group on Political Parties and Elections of the IPSA Committee on Political Sociology, chaired by Kay Lawson. The Italian CNR (Consiglio Nazionale delle Ricerche—National Research Council of Italy) generously supported this project with contribution n. 92.01682.CT09; and the University of Bologna's Dipartimento di Politica, Istituzioni, Storia hosted a final meeting of the various contributors in October 1995.

Many people have helped us in this project. First of all, we would like to thank Kay Lawson, whose friendly and constant support and encouragement helped us to overcome some critical junctures; moreover, she edited the English style of some chapters since none of the contributors in the book are native English-speaking but are political scientists from the various countries under study.

Crucial assistance in the editorial work has been provided by some graduate students at the Dipartimento di Politica, Istituzioni, Storia: Maria Pamini, Davide Pastore, Gabriella Russo and especially Gianfranco Baldini, who worked hard to provide a decent editorial manuscript. In addition, David Felsen, Thomas Gold, Tom Longo, visiting research fellow at the Dipartimento, provided language revision of some papers. Without their assistance the final stages of this project would have been much more difficult to realize.

NOTES

1. The case studies in party organization are now too numerous to give a complete or reliable account. Let's just quote the brilliant analysis by Schonfeld (1985) on the French RPR and PS.

2. Ferdinand Braudel's (1949) majestic research on the Mediterranean sea is the inevitable, classical reference.

REFERENCES

Braudel, Ferdinand (1949). *La Méditerranée et le Monde méditerranéen à l'epoque de Philippe II*. Paris: Colin.

Crotty, William (ed.) (1968). *Approaches to the Study of Party Organization*. Boston: Allyn and Bacon.

Eldersveld, Samuel (1964). *Political Parties: A Behavioral Analysis*. Chicago: Rand McNally.

Gaxie, Daniel (1977). "Economie des partis et retributions du militantisme." *Revue Française de Science Politique* 27: 123–154.

Gaxie, Daniel (1980). "Les logiques du recruitment politique." *Revue Française de Science Politique* 30: 5–45.

Harmel, Robert and Kenneth Janda (1994). "An Integrated Theory of Party Goals and Party Change." *Journal of Theoretical Politics* 6: 259–288.

Harmel, Robert, Uk Heo, Alexander Tan and Kenneth Janda (1995). "Performance Leadership, Factions and Party Change: An Empirical Analysis," *West European Politics* 18: 1–33.

Janda, Kenneth (1980). *Political Parties: A Cross National Survey.* New York: Free Press.

Janda, Kenneth (1983). "Cross National Measures of Party Organizations and Organizational Theory." *European Journal of Political Research* 11: 319–332.

Katz, Richard and Peter Mair (eds.) (1992). *Party Organizations: A Data Handbook on Party Organizations in Western Democracies, 1960–90.* London, Thousands Oaks, CA, and New Dehli: Sage.

Katz, Richard and Peter Mair (eds.) (1994). *How Parties Organize: Change and Adaptation in Party Organizations in Western Democracies.* London, Thousand Oaks, CA, and New Dehli: Sage.

Lawson, Kay (1976). *The Comparative Study of Political Parties.* New York: St. Martin's Press.

Lawson, Kay (1994). "Toward a Theory of How Political Parties Work." In Kay Lawson (ed.), *How Political Parties Work: Perspectives from Within,* pp. 285–303. Westport, CT: Praeger.

Lawson, Kay and Peter Merkl (eds.) (1988). *When Parties Fail: Emerging Alternative Organizations.* Princeton: Princeton University Press.

Offerlé, Michele. (1991). *Les partis politiques.* Paris: PUF.

Panebianco, Angelo (1982). *Modelli di Partito.* Bologna: Il Mulino [English translation: *Political Parties: Organization and Power.* Cambridge University Press, 1988].

Schlesinger, Joseph (1984)."On the Theory of Party Organization." *Journal of Politics* 46: 369–400.

Schonfeld, William (1985). *Ethographie du PS et du RPR.* Paris: Economica.

Strøm, Kaare (1989). "Intra Party Competition in Advanced Democracies." *Journal of Theoretical Politics* 1: 277–300.

Wellhofer, Spencer (1979). "The Effectiveness of Party Organization: A Cross-National Time Series Analysis." *European Journal of Political Research* 7: 205–224.

Part I

France

1

The Evolution of the French Party System

Colette Ysmal

Whereas a parliamentary Republic was established in 1875, political parties did not appear in France until the beginning of the twentieth century. The first permanent and centralized parties emerged in the left-wing part of the political spectrum with the formation in 1901 of the *Parti républicain radical et radical socialiste* (Republican, Radical and Radical-Socialist Party), commonly called the Radical Party, and of a Socialist Party named *Section française de l'Internationale ouvrière* (SFIO)—French Section of the Workers' International—in 1905.

In the conservative camp, mainly parliamentary groups, with little internal coherence, existed until the end of the Third Republic. Attempts to create parties did not really succeed, as right-wing leaders felt little need of a national organization with the constraints this implied. In 1944, after World War II, Catholic Resistance leaders formed the *Mouvement Républicain populaire* (MRP)—Popular and Republican Movement—which seemed at first to be a possible new home for the Conservatives. Its electoral success in the 1946 parliamentary elections (28.1 percent in June and 26.4 percent in November) made it the only party able to compete with the Communist and the Socialist parties. New cleavages appeared, however, in the late 1940s and in the early 1950s. Charles de Gaulle's dissatisfaction with the institutions of the Fourth Republic and its party system led him to launch a Gaullist Party in 1947: the *Rassemblement du Peuple français* (RPF)—Rally of the French People. Another part of the Conservative camp which, due to its compromising with the Vichy Regime, had lost credit with the electorate, reemerged in the late 1940s with the creation of the *Centre national des Indépendants et paysans* (CNIP)—National Center for Independents and Farmers. The RPF was a very organized party but its life span was very brief (Charlot, 1983). In the 1951 general elections, it took 21.8 percent of the vote but in 1953 it was dissolved by its leader, for whom it was no longer the appropriate vehicle for gaining power and for changing the political regime. The CNIP won 12.8 percent of the vote in 1951 and 14.5 percent in 1956. It was, nevertheless, little more than a label for what, in France, is called the *modérés* or for right-center candidates who shared a more or less common ideology but were unable to enter into a formal organization. Even within the National Assembly, these *modérés* lacked party discipline and did not always vote together.

PARTIES AND TRADITIONAL POLITICAL FAMILIES

Contrary to a common wisdom, the foundation of the Fifth Republic in 1958 did not lead to an important decrease in the number of parties and to a dramatic collapse of the "old" parties which existed before. In the 1990s, the party system might be still characterized by a proliferation of parties. According to the Ministry of Home Affairs, 55 "parties," groups and movements had candidates in the 1993 parliamentary elections. In 1994, 45 "parties" qualifed for the state financial aid to political parties, either by having elected deputies or senators or by having presented for the offices in the preceding (1993) elections in at least 50 constituencies. Of course, many of those organizations are limited in membership, in appeal or in territorial concern (parties in the Overseas Territories and Departments or in Corsica, for example). Many of them sprang up only at the whim of a single person and disappeared just after the election.

Even if one applies the term "party" only to those organizations which are the most important and constant organizers of French political life, one can still count, in the 1990s, some fifteen parties. From the extreme left to the extreme right, all the French traditional political families are represented. *Lutte Ouvrière*, Workers' Struggle (LO); the *Ligue communiste révolutionnaire*, Communist and Revolutionary League (LCR); and the *Parti communiste internationaliste*, Communist and Internationalist Party (PCI) are the heirs of different Trotskyist or Maoist factions. The Left, since the formation in 1920 of the French Communist Party (*Parti communiste français*, PCF), is divided between Communists and Socialists (Socialist Party, *Parti socialiste* or PS). Some Socialist dissenters formed the *Mouvement des Citoyens* (Movement for Citizens, MDC). The Greens (*Les Verts*) and *Génération Ecologie* (Ecological Generation) are two environmentalist parties. The *Parti radical socialiste* (PRS)—Radical-Socialist Party—and the *Parti radical* (Radicals) appeared as vestiges of the Radical tradition and of the party which "founded" the Third Republic and occupied, in the party system, a pivotal position until World War II. *Force Démocrate* (FD)—Democratic Force—consists of remnants of a Christian Democrat current never very firmly established in France. Two parties, the Republican Party (*Parti républicain*—PR) and the CNIP represent the Liberals. The *Rassemblement pour la République* (Rally for the

Republic—RPR) is the most recent offspring of Gaullism. Last is the *Front National* (National Front—FN), which occupies the extreme right part of the political spectrum.

In terms of number of parties, this description of French political parties in the 1990s makes clear the stability of a system mainly designed by the historical conflicts at work in the French society. The system is still determined not only by the *summa divisio* between the Left and the Right but also by the cleavages within each camp. Trotskyists, Maoists, Communists, Socialists and partially Radicals for the Left; Christian Democrats, Liberals, Gaullists for the Conservative camp. This stability is reinforced if we consider that many of the "new" parties are in fact "old" parties. Only the Radical Party, the Communist Party and the CNIP have continously kept the same name since, respectively, 1901, 1920 and 1948. Others have changed their labels to emphasize to the public that they have a new image and/or a new ability in shaping the political life. Here are the most important examples:

SFIO (1905) *Parti Socialiste*—PS (Socialist Party) (1969).

Mouvement des radicaux de gauche—MRG (Movement of Leftist Radicals) in 1972 named *Radical* in 1995 and *Parti radical-socialiste* in 1996 (Radical and Socialist Party).

Union pour la nouvelle République—UNR (Union for the New Republic) in 1958; *Union des démocates pour la Cinquième République*—UD Vè in 1967 (Union of Democrats for the Fifth Republic); *Union de défense de la République* in 1968—UDR (Union for the Defense of the Republic); then in 1976, *Rassemblement pour la République* or RPR (Rally for the Republic).

Fédération des Républicains indépendants—FNRI (Federation of Independant Republicans) in 1962–1977; *Parti républicain*—PR after 1997.

Mouvement républicain populaire—MRP until 1965; *Centre démocrate* (Democratic Center) from 1866 to 1986; *Centre des démocrates sociaux*—CDS (Center of Social Democrats) from 1986 to 1996 and *Force démocrate* (Democratic Force) "created" in 1996.

Figure 1.1 summarizes the evolution of the parties when one takes into consideration both the permanence of political families and change in parties' labels not really linked with a change in parties' organization and/or political ideologies, practices and policies. Few real "new" parties have appeared since 1958 with the notable exception of the Ecologists and of the National Front.

This is not to say that, in terms of parties' size, electoral fortune and political influence, the party system has not been modified since 1958 (Ysmal, 1989). The electoral law established in 1958—a two-ballot majoritarian system—has been reinforced by changes in the threshold qualifying candidates for the runoff (5 percent of the votes cast in 1958; 10 percent of the registered voters in 1966 and 12.5 percent of the registered voters in 1976). This system

Figure 1.1
Family Tree and Evolution of the French Political Parties

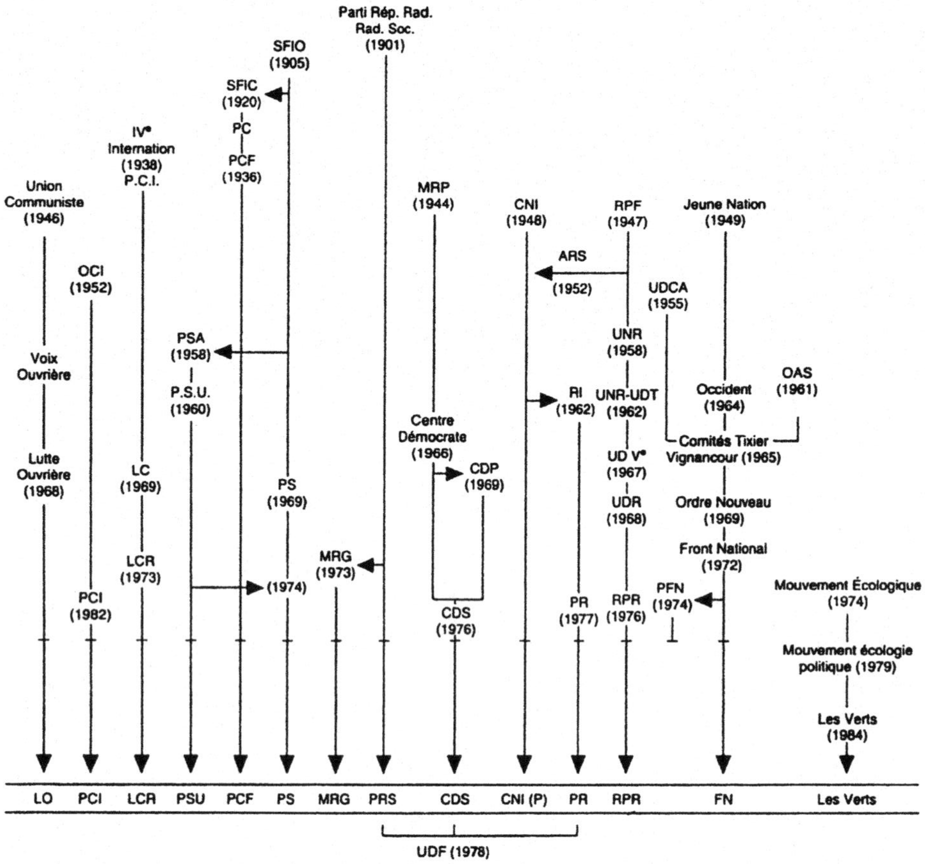

Parti Rép. Rad. Rad. Soc. (1901)

SFIO (1905)
SFIC (1920)
PC
PCF (1936)

IVe Internation (1938) P.C.I.

OCI (1952)

Union Communiste (1946)

Voix Ouvrière

Lutte Ouvrière (1968)

PSA (1958)
P.S.U. (1960)

LC (1969)
LCR (1973)

PS (1969)

MRG (1973)

(1974)

PCI (1982)

MRP (1944)
Centre Démocrate (1966)
CDP (1969)
CDS (1976)

CNI (1948)
ARS (1952)
RI (1962)
PR (1977)

RPF (1947)
UDCA (1955)
UNR (1958)
UNR-UDT (1962)
UD Ve (1967)
UDR (1968)
RPR (1976)

Jeune Nation (1949)
Occident (1964)
Comités Tixier Vignancour (1965)
Ordre Nouveau (1969)
Front National (1972)
PFN (1974)

OAS (1961)

Mouvement Écologique (1974)
Mouvement écologie politique (1979)
Les Verts (1984)

LO PCI LCR PSU PCF PS MRG PRS CDS CNI (P) PR RPR FN Les Verts

UDF (1978)

Source: Ysmal (1989).

pushed, first, parties to enter into electoral alliances which are in fact electoral and political coalitions. Alliances became more important than the individual future of each party. The fortune of parties was linked not only to their ability to maintain a party organization and a specific program but to use the electoral constraints as a way to maintain their influence. Second, and more important, the election of the President of the Republic by direct popular suffrage, adopted in 1962 and applied for the first time in 1965, changed the role and the nature of French political parties. As quoted by Tiersky (1994), "French political parties today are of two kinds: (1) the major parties that can hope to elect a president, and (2) the minor parties, which cannot." The establishment of the presidential election forced potential aspirants to the office to build broad partisan machines directed to the electorate at large; parties' strategies were no longer focused on the Parliament but on the conquest of the presidency.

It is important to note, however, that (1) this transformation of the party system linked to those institutional constraints was the result of a "long march" which concerned not only the Left (Johnson, 1981) but also the Right—the establishment of a new party system particular to the Fifth Republic was the result of a long process; and (2) that the efficiency of those institutional constraints was more evident in the 1970s than in the 1990s. Party realigments in the early years of the Fifth Republic as well as the bipolarization of the party system achieved in the 1970s did not survive when new conflicts and cleavages appeared within French society. Major parties, in Tiersky's terms, or "governing parties" in other terms are still the pillar of the party system. They are, however, more and more contested by the voters. Consequently, the party system tended, in the 1990s, to be more fragmented than it had been in the 1970s.

1958–1978: TOWARD A BIPOLARIZATION OF THE PARTY SYSTEM

When a new constitutional draft was submitted by General de Gaulle to a popular referendum in September 1958, the only major party that campaigned against ratification was the Communist Party. The SFIO, the Radical Party, the MRP and the CNIP decided, with more or less enthusiasm, to support the constitution, as did the followers of de Gaulle who formed the UNR in the fall of 1958. The result was a massive vote in favor of ratifying the 1958 Constitution (82.6 percent of the vote cast). Two months later, the first legislative elections of the Fifth Republic were characterized by the success of de Gaulle's backers. The UNR, not endorsed by de Gaulle but nonetheless an offspring of the RPF, gained 20.6 percent of the vote. The SFIO, the Radicals, the MRP and the CNIP benefited from their apparent Gaullism and kept their electoral influence. The main victim of the election was the Communists (18.9 percent against 25.9 percent in 1956). However, the party system remained organized around six main parties with a nearly equal electoral influence (see Table 1.1).

Compared to the 1958 election, the 1962 parliamentary elections were a watershed event. They followed a new referendum initiated by de Gaulle on a constitutional amendment providing for the direct election of the president by popular suffrage. This time, only the UNR supported de Gaulle's proposal. The antagonism was very strong between de Gaulle and the non-Gaullist parties but the latter were disowned by the voters. The amendment was popular and was ratified by 62.3 percent. Consequently, all the parties unified in the *Cartel des non* saw their share of the vote decreased in the legislative elections (Table 1.1). Moreover, as they contested not only de Gaulle but the principle of the election of the president by popular suffrage itself, the non-Gaullist parties were late in changing their organizations as well as their strategies to conform to the demands of the new system.

The Gaullists: From Dominance to Competition

In the 1962 general elections, the UNR increased its electoral influence dramatically as it gained 32.1 percent of the vote cast. Other groups participated in the Gaullist victory. Some leaders of the MRP chose to back de Gaulle but the main event was a split within the CNIP and the decision made by Valéry Giscard d'Estaing to support de Gaulle and to organize his followers under the label of *Républicains indépendants* (Independant Republicans). All in all, the "Gaullists" scored very high (36 percent of the votes). The MRP leaders joined the UNR; Giscard d'Estaing launched a party named FNRI (see Figure 1.1). As thus designed in the early 1960s, the Gaullist coalition assumed a dominant position in the party system, gaining 38.5 and 46.4 percent in 1967 and 1968, respectively.

With the election of Georges Pompidou to the presidency in 1969, the Gaullist coalition rallied other centrist leaders organized in a party named *Centre démocratie et Progrès* or CDP (Center for Democracy and Progress). Together they gained 37 percent of the votes in the 1973 legislative elections. One would emphasize three points, however. First, from 1962 to 1973, the balance of forces within the Gaullist bloc was asymmetric since the "pure" or orthodox Gaullists were dominant: the UNR, under its different names (see before) represented 89 percent of the Gaullist coalition in 1962, 82 percent in 1967, 80 percent in 1968 and 70 percent in 1973. Second, as these figures show, the influence of the Liberals (as represented by the FNRI) and of the Christian Democrats (via individual realignments sometimes more or less formally legitimized by an ad hoc party—as the CDP) was steadily increasing. Third, the incorporation of a new fraction of the center in Pompidou's majority did not allow the Gaullist bloc to increase its share of the vote. Therefore, the UDR (name of the UNR after 1968) was gravely weakened. In

Table 1.1
Results of the French General Elections, 1958–1993 (percentage of the vote cast)

	1958	1962	1967	1968	1973	1978	1981	1986	1988	1993
Extreme Left	1.6	2.0	2.2	4.0	3.2	3.3	1.2	1.5	0.4	1.8
Communist Party	18.9	21.9	22.5	20.0	21.4	20.6	16.3	9.7	11.2	9.1
Socialist Party	15.5	12.4	-	-	19.1	22.8	36.4	31.2	36.4	19.0
FGDS			18.9	16.5						
MRG	-	-	-	-	2.1	2.2	1.5	1.2	1.2	1.1
Radical Party	9.2	7.5	-	-	4.1	-	-	-	-	
MRP	11.1	7.9	-	-	-	-	-	-	-	
CNIP	14.2	7.3	-	-	-	-	-	-	-	
Modérés	5.8	4.2	1.9	1.2	3.4	1.9	0.9	1.6	2.0	3.2
Centre démocrate	-	-	15.4	11.2	9.2	-	-	-	-	
FNRI	-	2.3	5.5	8.4	7.2	-	-	-	-	
CDP	-	-	-	-	3.9	-	-	-	-	
UDF	-	-	-	-	-	22.0	20.8	16.0	17.6	20.7
Gaullists	20.6	33.7	33.0	38.0	25.9	22.8	21.2	26.9	20.9	20.2
Extreme right	2.6	0.7	0.6	0.1	-	0.5	0.1	0.3	0.1	0.2
Front national	-	-	-	-	0.5	0.3	0.2	9.8	9.7	12.7
Ecologists	-	-	-	-	-	2.0	1.1	1.2	0.4	7.8
Others	0.5	0.1	-	0.6	-	0.3	0.3	0.6	0.1	4.2

Source: Official sources of the Minister of Interior.

1973, the UDR gained only 25.9 percent of the vote and lost its position as main organizer of the party system.

The Gaullist Party's zenith appeared to have been linked to de Gaulle's personal position in French political life. Pompidou's presidency was characterized by a twilight of the "pure" Gaullists and the future of the party appeared to be linked to the conditions of the competition between Gaullism and the other components of the Conservatives. The election to the presidency of Giscard d'Estaing in 1974 was a turning point. At the first ballot, he overcame the Gaullist candidate (32.9 percent against 14.6) and took the presidency in the runoff (50.7 percent against 49.3 for François Mitterrand). In the 1978 general elections, the RPR formed by Jacques Chirac in 1976 and in competition with the Giscard coalition won only 22.8 percent of the vote.

The Non-Gaullist Right: From Collapse to Revenge

In 1962, due to the Gaullist electoral success, the MRP and the CNIP were the main victims of the general elections. The non-Gaullist right, named also "Centrists" or the "Center" thanks to its asserted position between the Left and the Gaullists, gained only 15.2 percent of the vote (25.3 percent in 1958).[1] Many attempts were made to unify this camp but they were unsuccessful both in terms of party organization and electoral appeal. First was the *Center démocrate* (Democratic Center), a party launched by Lecanuet in 1966, after his candidacy to the presidency in 1965, in order to organize the remnants of both the MRP and the CNIP. The Democratic Center scored, however, very poorly in the 1967 and 1968 elections: 15.4 percent in 1967 and 11.2 percent in 1968. Weakened by the reluctance of CNIP leaders to enter into a party organization and by the 1969 split among the Centrists (the CDP), it entered in 1973 into another electoral alliance named the *Mouvement réformateur* (Movement for Reforms), this time with the Radical Party. They gained, however, only 13.3 percent of the vote in the 1973 general elections: 4.1 percent for the Radicals and 9.2 percent for the *Centre démocrate*.

Such electoral showings made clear the collapse of the non-Gaullist right or of the Center in a party system mainly organized around the presidency in Gaullist hands from 1958 to 1974. With Giscard d'Estaing in the Elysée in 1974, new opportunities were provided for a reorganization of the party system and for the revenge of the non-Gaullist right. This reorganization did not, however, really change the concerned parties. In 1976, the *Centre des démocrates sociaux*—Center of Social Democrats (CDS) was little more than a regrouping of the *Centre démocrate* and of the CDP. In 1977, the change in the Giscardian party's name (from FNRI to PR) did not allow the president to launch the presidents' party normally required by the French institutions. The critical event was the creation of the *Union pour la Démocratie française* or UDF (Union for the French Democracy) in February 1978.

It is very difficult to qualify the UDF in terms of party organization. It was more than an electoral alliance and less than a party. More than an electoral alliance because the concerned parties entered into a coalition focused not only on the 1978 elections but on the support to a president elected in 1974 and not to be reelected, seven years later, without the support of a party of his own.[2] In this perspective, the UDF had a president, a General Secretary, a national apparatus with a National Council and a National Committee that appointed national delegates; it was seeking to develop a local organization. It was less than a party, however, since the UDF kept a confederal structure with parties remaining clearly identified and autonomous, able to have their own programs, leaders and strategies. The local organization of the UDF consisted merely of the local organizations of each of the parties in the confederation. It was very poor, as these parties were, in fact, "cadre-parties" organized around notables without any activist base at all.

The UDF electoral success in the 1978 general elections was not so evident: in 1973, all the parties unified in 1978 into the UDF had gained some 24 percent of the vote; in 1978, the UDF won about 22 percent of the vote. However, although the UDF did not increase the non-Gaullists' share of the vote, it did contribute to the new design of the party system in the 1970s. Very fragmented in the 1960s or in the early 1970s, the non-Gaullist right was now reunified under Giscard's leadership and could compete with the Gaullists.

The Left: The Rebirth of a Socialist Party

De Gaulle's return to power in 1958 produced a large shift from Left to Right. Having achieved 46.5 percent of the vote cast in 1956, the Right won 56.4 percent in 1958, 55.6 percent in 1962, 56.4 percent in 1967 and 58.9 percent in 1968. In 1958, the main victim was the Communist Party but, in the 1960s, it increased its share of the vote and, more important, kept its dominant position over the SFIO and its Radical allies (see Table 1.1). In 1958 and 1962, the electoral support of the SFIO and the Radical Party dropped continuously. Both parties could not prevent continuous splits and the formation of little parties or clubs made of elements systematically refusing to join the parties or of members having resigned for political reasons. The most important were the *Parti Socialiste Unifié* (Socialist Unified Party— PSU) formed in 1960[3] and the *Convention des Institutions Républicaines* (Convention for Republican institutions—CIR) launched by Mitterrand in 1964.

Many efforts were made, however, to modernize the SFIO and to unify the "non-Communist" left in 1963–1967. First was Defferre's candidacy for the presidency in 1963 and the attempt to create a Federation of the Socialists and of the Christian Democrats in 1965: the *Fédération des socialistes et des chrétiens démocrates*, named also *Grande fédération (Large Federation); sec-ond was Mitterrand's candidacy for the presidency in 1975 supported by a coalition of the SFIO, the Radicals and of many clubs (and by the Communists as well); third was the Fédération de la Gauche démocrate et socialiste* or FGDS (Federation of the Democratic and Socialist Left) launched by Mitterrand in 1966. All were unsuccessful in terms of party organization as well as in terms of electoral appeal. The FGDS was little more than an electoral coalition between the Socialists and the Radicals. In 1967 and 1968, they won 18.8 and 16.5 percent of the vote (19.9 for the two parties in 1962). The turning point was, however, the 1969 presidential election. The Socialist candidate gained only 5 percent of the vote (against 21.3 percent for the Communist candidate), the lowest score ever achieved by the Socialist Party since 1905. Such a collapse required the refoundation of the party.

Accordingly, the SFIO dissolved and, in the summer of 1969, a "new party" with a new leadership was formed: the *Parti Socialiste*—Socialist Party (PS). However, the "rebirth" of the PS began really in 1971 with the Epinay Congress. Three elements were crucial. First was the particular place of Mitterrand, elected leader of the party in 1971. His relatively successful candidacy in the 1965 presidential election (31.7 percent in the first ballot; 44.8 percent in the second round) had made him the symbol of both the leftists' fight against Gaullism and of the Union of the Left, including the Communist Party. This position legitimized his narrowly acquired but effective grip on a party he had joined very recently (1971) and on a party belonging to a political family which had never been his own (Cayrol, 1966; Nay, 1984; Pean, 1994). Mitterrand signified, first, the strong necessity for Socialist leaders, notables and members to change the party and to adapt it both to the institutional framework (in particular to the new mode of choosing the president) and the new course of French political life. He was the sole leader available for the PS in the early 1970s. Second and third, after the 1968 events, the French society asked for important economic or societal reforms (nationalizations; democratization of the social relations in the work places; feminism; abortion). The PS surfed on the wave (Capdevielle et al. 1978). The party's manifestos insisted on the specificity of a French Socialism based on the "rupture with capitalism" but also on *"changer la vie."* Mitterrand committed the PS to a strategy of Union of the Left interested not only in forming electoral alliances with the PCF, but also in finding programmatic grounds for this alliance. The "Common Program for Government" between the PS and the PCF was presented in 1972 as "the charter of a future government of the Left after its victory at the polls" (Ehrmann and Schain, 1992).

In many terms, the PS was the heir as well as the most accomplished product of the "long march" of the non-Communist left toward the redefinition of its organization, program and strategy. The formation of the PS had, however, effects on the other left-wing or center-left parties. In 1972, the Radical Party had to choose between an alliance with the PS (and support to the "Common Program") and integration into the Conservative camp. The result was a split within the party and the creation of the *Mouvement des Radicaux de gauche* (Movement of Leftist Radicals—MRG). Formed by notables whose principal aim was to secure their electoral positions, the MRG remained very weak and in an ancillary position vis-à-vis the Socialists. In 1974, the PS integrated a large part of the PSU led by Michel Rocard.

In the middle of the 1970s, there was, within the non-Communist left camp, no real room for another party. The PS unified, under Mitterrand's leadership, the vestiges of the SFIO, activists socialized in the SFIO but having opposed the party leaders (as the CERES—Centre for Socialist Studies and Researches led by Chevènement), old Mitterrand's companions of the CIR, leftists, Catholics and extreme left activists coming from the PSU). This hegemonic situation was reinforced by electoral success at the local and national levels. In the 1973 and 1976 departmental elections and in the 1977 municipal elections, the PS increased its share of the vote and its control over local government (Criqui, 1992). In the 1973 general elections, the PS and the MRG gained 21.2 percent of the vote; in 1978, they took together 25 percent and, for the first time since 1945, overcame the Communist Party (21.4 percent).

At the end of the 1970s, the party system was strongly polarized as it was divided between Left and Right, the organizing principle of French political life since 1789. The balance between the two camps changed, however, in the early 1970s to the benefit of the Left which increased its share of the vote (43.6 percent in 1967; 45.8 percent in 1973 and 50.2 percent in 1978). The 1978 elections made clear a new party system: two large electoral blocs (Left and Right) roughly equal in terms of electoral support, each consisting of two main parties (Communist and Socialist for the Left; RPR and UDF for the Right) also nearly equal at the polls: the PCF with 21.4, the PS with 25.1, the UDF with 22 and the RPR with 22.8 percent of the vote. Other parties remained in competition but the dynamics of the "*quadrille bi-polaire*" (Ysmal, 1989), that is, of the quadripartite structure, made them totally insignificant. In 1978, the four main parties, with their affiliates, gained some 95 percent of the vote.

THE FRAGMENTATION OF THE PARTY SYSTEM

In the 1980s and in the 1990s, the party system as established in the 1970s was seriously shaken. First were changes in the electoral fortune of the parties described as the pillars of the previous party system. Second was the emergence of new parties. Third, the dissatisfaction of the French people with political parties in general pushed them to vote for minor parties or for candidates without partisan affiliation.

The End of the "Quadrille Bipolaire"

The stability and the coherence of the party system, as established at the end of the 1970s, was questioned with Mitterrrand's successful bids for the presidency in 1981 and 1988. One can emphasize three elements.

First was the loss of electoral credit for the PCF which gained 15.4 percent in the 1981 presidential election; 9.6 in the general 1986 elections; 6.9 in the 1888 presidential election and 8.7 percent in the 1995 election. Even if the party scored generally better in general elections (see Table 1.1) thanks to the personal influence of its incumbent deputies and/or mayors, it was marginalized in terms of electoral support. Those electoral showings were the result of the erratic PCF strategy. In 1972, the Communists joined with the PS in the "Common Program for Government"; but, in 1977, they considered such tactics of "class cooperation" to have been damaging to the party. Therefore, they sabotaged a new agreement and turned back to isolation and strong polemics with the PS. In 1981, having helped elect Mitterrand, they were obliged to participate in the first cabinet; but, in 1984, they left the government.

The Communist organization was dramatically weakened: loss of party membership; decline of party activism; internal dissent (Hincker, 1995). More important was the electoral decline because it destabilized the left-wing camp and the party system. The PCF moved from a "major" to a "minor" party gaining less than 10 percent of the vote and unable to formulate a governing strategy. The PS was promoted as not only once again the main party of the Left (as it had been in the late 1970s) but as the sole leftist party able to govern and to represent the left-wing voters. And, in fact, in 1981, 1986 and 1988, with its MRG allies, it did take respectively, 37.9, 32.4 and 37.6 percent of the vote. The collapse of the party in the 1993 legislative elections (19 percent of the vote) as well as the score of Lionel Jospin in the 1995 presidential election (23.2 percent, better than in 1993 but far from the results achieved in the 1980s) make the present place of the PS in the party system dubious. It remains a "major" or a "governing" party but it seems unable, for the moment, to compete with the RPR and the UDF.

The late 1990s were characterized by a turn back to the dominance of the Conservatives. Since 1981 and the Socialist victory, the RPR and the UDF have continuously formed electoral and political alliances giving support to common candidates in the legislative and local elections (but not in the presidential race). Competition for supremacy within the right-wing camp was less important than the necessity to defeat the Socialists. As far as the presidential elections were concerned, in 1988 the Chirac (RPR) and Barre (UDF) candidacies were unsuccessful and had no effect on the RPR/UDF balance of forces. In 1995, Chirac (RPR) defeated Balladur (RPR but backed by UDF leaders and voters). Since the newly elected president decided not to organize anticipated general elections to ensure the continual dominance of the RPR, the balance of forces is frozen in a sort of "armed peace."

Consequently, it is not very interesting to deal with the respective electoral support of the RPR and the UDF, strictly linked to the pre-election bargaining for common candidacies. More important were the results of the RPR and UDF alliance in the late 1990s compared with their scores in the 1960s, in the late 1970s or the 1980s. In the 1978 general election, the RPR and the UDF took together 44.8 percent of the vote; the figures were 42 percent in 1981, 42.9 percent in 1986, 38.5 percent in 1988, 40.9 percent in 1993 (see Table 1.1). Thus, the RPR and the UDF won fewer votes in 1993 than in 1978 (a period of the Left's ascent) and, in the 1980s-1990s, the trend was toward a stabilization of their electoral influence around 40 percent of the vote. In the 1960s and in the early 1970s, the Conservatives (Gaullists and Centrists) won more than 50 percent of the vote (Table 1.1). In the late 1990s, the UDR and the UDF appeared to be dominant vis-à-vis the PCF and the PS; but they have lost their hegemony over the right-wing camp. This was the consequence of the institutionalization of the *Front national* (National Front—FN) in French political life.

The Consolidation of the National Front

The FN was not the first extreme Right party to have been formed in France but it was the first to gain so many votes and to succeed in maintaining/ increasing its electoral base. Until the 1980s, the extreme right organizations were "flash" parties appearing and disappearing according to the logics of the various "sentiments" at work in French society (anti-Semitism; support for fascism; colonial nostalgia). The most striking recent example was the Poujadists which gained 11.6 percent of the vote in 1956 and only 1.5 percent in 1958. In the 1965 presidential election, Jean-Louis Tixier-Vignancour won 5.6 percent of the vote but the party he launched in 1966 took 0.4 percent in the 1967 general elections before being shaken by internal splits and disappearing in the early 1970s.[4]

Formed in 1972, the FN gained, in the late 1970s, less than 1 percent of the vote and, in 1981, Jean-Marie Le Pen, its president, was not qualified to run for the presidency.[5] The turning point was the 1984 European elections: Le Pen's list took 11 percent of the vote. This success was confirmed in the 1986, 1988 and 1993 general elections: 9.8 percent in 1986, 9.7 in 1988 and 12.7 in 1993. In the 1988 and the 1995 presidential elections, Le Pen scored even better with respectively 14.6 and 15.3 percent of the electorate.

Many factors explained the FN's sudden emergence in the 1980s (Ignazi, 1996). First was proportional representation for the European elections but also for the 1986 legislative elections which allowed the party to gain seats both in the European Parliament (EP) and the National Assembly (AN).[6] On the one hand, voters knew that they were not about to cast a useless vote; on the other hand, seats in the EP but especially in the AN (35 in 1986) legitimized the party. Second was the takeover of the Left in 1981 which led to a radicalization of strong anti-Communist or anti-Socialist voters who moved from the RPR and the UDF to a more extremist vote. In the 1980s, more than 75 percent of the FN electorate were previous RPR/UDF voters. Third, and probably most important, was the electorate's move from leftist political orientations in the 1970s to "neo-conservative" positions (economic liberalism; individualism; law and order) in the 1980s. Unlike the RPR and the UDF, which were also concerned by such a change in ideology, the FN adopted a specific political line. It chose to make the immigrants the scapegoats for all the so-called French "disorders": unemployment, crime and violence, and loss of the French "national identity" due to the massive presence of non-Catholic people.

The FN thus made immigration a very important issue to which the other parties had to react in following, generally, the FN problematics. Thereby, the party gained legitimacy and increased its share of the vote. In the 1990s, the FN benefited also from the inability of the governing parties (PS, RRR and UDF) to solve the unemployment problem and from the involvement of those parties in either illegal financing of their activities or individual acts of corruption. Dissatisfaction with those parties increased and the FN used a populist, anti-elitist appeal which became more credible as the governing parties failed. In the 1995 presidential election, the FN gained new voters coming from the RPR and the UDF but mainly from the Left (Perrineau, 1995).

In terms of party system, one can conclude that the FN contributed, in the 1980s and the 1990s, to the RPR and UDF loss of hegemony over the right-wing camp. In the 1990s, it also interfered with a possible electoral recovery by the Socialist Party and, therefore with its ability to recover its pivotal position in the party system.

The Ecologists: From Nothing to Nothing

The environmental issue has never been very important in France. In 1974, René Dumont, candidate to the presidency, was the first to put issues linked to the use of natural resources on the political agenda and to attempt to demonstrate that the developed countries' model of development had had terrible costs in terms of environment. He gained, however, only 1.3 percent of the vote. Many ecologist groups proliferated in the late 1970s, finding it unnecessary to launch a centralized and organized party. Candidates to European or presidential elections took 4.5 percent of the vote in the 1979 European elections and 3.9 percent in the 1981 presidential election.

In 1984, the *Verts, Parti écologiste* (Greens, Ecological Party) was formed but did not change the Ecologists' poor electoral support: 3.9 percent in the 1984 European elections; 3.8 percent in the 1988 presidential election. In the 1989 European elections, the Greens suddenly increased their share of the vote to 10.6 percent. Such a success inspired the creation in 1990 of a second Ecologist Party labelled *Génération Ecologie* (Ecological Generation—GE) by Brice Lalonde, a former leader of one of the most important Ecological groupings in the 1970s (*Les amis de la Terre*—Friends of the Earth—but also a member, in the same years, of the PSU and, in the 1980s, an ally of the Socialists). In the 1992 regional elections, GE took 7.1 percent of the vote

(7.5 percent for the Greens). Due to the electoral law, the two parties entered into an alliance for the 1993 general elections and took together 7.8 percent of the vote. This score was interpreted as an electoral defeat by both parties and created a crisis in the Ecological organizations (Boy, 1993; Roche 1995).

The GE, which had been little more than Lalonde's party and a vehicle for securing his personal political influence, was wasted as many of its activists and official-elected left. The Greens, shaken by many splits, were weakened: in the 1995 presidential election, they gained only 3.4 percent of the vote. Internal crisis within the Ecologist parties could not, however, explain alone the collapse of both the parties. Such an evolution also questioned the significance of the Ecologists' success in 1992–1993 which, now, appeared to have been based less on concern for environmental issues than on voter dissatisfaction with the Socialist Party. In 1992, 75 percent of the Ecologist voters were previously PS voters. In 1993, the Ecologist electorate appeared to be divided into two components: "true" but minority Ecologists for whom "defense of the environment" was the main issue and the main reason for explaining their electoral choice; "disappointed Socialists"—the most important part—for whom the environment was less important than the opportunity to cast an anti-PS vote without moving to the right-wing parties. The Greens attempted to elaborate a new program in which environmental preoccupations would be linked with more general orientations: attacks on the capitalist system and on the "mondialization" of the economy; defense of the welfare state; fight against unemployment by a decrease in the work week (from 39 to 32 hours). Such a strategy was, however, not very efficient in the 1995 presidential election.

CONCLUSION

In the early 1990s, the institutionalization of the National Front and the sudden appearance of the Ecologists destabilized the party system. In the late 1970s, it was structured around "major" parties quite equal in terms of electoral and political influence; in 1993, three "major parties" (PS, UDF and RPR) and four "minor" parties (PCF, FN, Greens and GE) coexisted. The ability of the three "governing parties" to gain extensive electoral support dramatically decreased: they took together 78 percent of the vote cast in the 1981 general elections, 75 percent in 1988 but only 60 percent in 1993. Even the presidential election is no longer an exception: in 1995 the three "*presidentiable*" candidates (Jospin, Balladur and Chirac) won 62 percent of the vote (75 and 70 percent for their counterparts in 1981 and 1988 presidential elections).

One can object that the three largest parties are quite hegemonic on the second ballot and are the only parties able to gain seats in the National Parliament as well as the presidency. Such a situation does increase their significance within the party system. However, they can no longer be said to represent well the entire electorate nor to establish their governments in accordance with a *national* (as opposed to a *governing*) majority (Lawson, 1997). Therefore these political parties lose credit with the voters and dissatisfaction with all parties as well as with the political system dramatically increases. In October 1996, only 27 percent of those interviewed thought "that they felt to be well represented by a political party" and 26 percent "by a political leader"; 43 percent thought that "democracy does not work well in France" (compared to 53 percent in 1985). In March 1997, only 34 percent said that the PS "could solve the problems that France has to face." The figures were 31 percent for the RPR and 17 for the UDF.

NOTES

1. The "Centrists " were defined by themselves as occupying an intermediate place on the political spectrum between the "Collectivist Left" (Communists and Socialists) and the Gaullists which were said to be "Conservatives." In fact, the analysis of parties' manifestos as well as surveys among both members and voters showed that the Centrists were more conservative than the Gaullists.

2. The UDF unified not only the CDS and the PR but also the Radical Party, the Giscardian Club *Perspectives et Réalités* (Prospects and Realities), a very little grouping made of previous members of the SFIO labelled *Parti Social-Démocrate* (Social Democrat Party) and finally direct members not affiliated to any of the quoted parties.

3. Formed in 1960, the PSU was composed of members having left the SFIO in 1958 and of leftist activists—Catholics, Marxists, ex-Communists—having been, in particular, involved in all the movements against the Algeria War. Then, it was active in the 1968 events. After 1969, many of its members moved to the PS and the PSU turned into an extreme Left party. It disappeared in 1989 (see Hauss, 1978).

4. The party was named *Alliance pour le progrès et les libertés* (Alliance for Progress and Freedom).

5. Every candidate for the presidency must be supported by 500 local and/or national elected officials in at least 30 departments.

6. In 1985, Mitterrand decided to move from the majoritarian system adopted in 1958 to proportional representation. The majoritarian system was reintroduced in 1986 by the victorious right-wing coalition.

REFERENCES

Boy, Daniel (1993). "Ecologistes: retour sur terre." In Pascal Perrineau and Colette Ysmal, *Le vote sanction. Les élections législatives de mars 1993*, pp.161–184. Paris: Presses de Sciences po.

Capdevielle, Jacques, Elisabeth Dupoirier, Gérard Grunberg, Etienne Schweisguth and Colette Ysmal (1978). *France de gauche, Vote à droite*. Paris: Presses de Sciences po.

Cayrol, Roland (1966). *François Mitterrand*. Paris: Presses de Sciences po.

Charlot, Jean (1983). *Le gaullisme d'opposition 1946–1958*, Paris: Fayard.

Criqui, Etienne (1992). "Le pouvoir départemental. L'hégémonie des droites." In Philippe Habert, Pascal Perrineau and Colette Ysmal (eds.), *le vote eclaté. Les elections regionales et eautouales de 1992*, pp. 289–305. Paris: Deportement d' Etudes Politiques du Figaro et Presses de Sciences Po.

Ehrmann, Henry W. and Martin A. Schain (1992). *Politics in France*. New York: HarperCollins.

Hauss, Charles (1978). *The New Left in France: The United Socialist Party*. Westport, CT: Greenwood.

Hincker, François (1995). " Le PCF devant l'échéance présidentielle." In Pascal Perrineau and Colette Ysmal, *Le vote de crise: L'élection présidentielle de 1995*, pp. 47–60. Paris: Presses de Sciences po.

Ignazi, Piero (1996). "Un nouvel acteur politique." In Nonna Mayer and Pascal Perrineau, *Le Front national à découvert*, pp. 63–80. Paris: Presses de Sciences po.

Johnson, Richard,W. (1981). *The Long March of the French Left*. London: MacMillan.

Lawson, Jay (1997). "In Defense of a Multi-party System." In John Green and Paul Herrnson, *Minor Parties in US Politics*, New York: Rowman and Littlefield.

Nay, Catherine (1984). *Le Noir et le Rouge ou l'histoire d'une ambition*. Paris: Grasset.

Péan, Pierre (1994). *Une Jeunesse française: François Mitterrand 1934–1947*. Paris: Fayard.

Perrineau, Pascal (1995). "La dynamique du vote Le Pen: le poids du gaucholepéniste." In Pascal Perrineau and Colette Ysmal (eds.), *Le vote sanction, Les élections législatives de mars 1993*, pp. 243–262. Paris: Presses de Sciences po.

Roche, Agnès (1995). "Les candidatures écologistes: la chasse aux signatures." in Pascal Perrineau and Colette Ysmal (eds.), *Le vote sanction, Les élections législatives de mars 1993*, pp. 81–93. Paris: Presses de Sciences po.

Tiersky, Ronald (1994) *France in the New Europe*. Belmont: Wadsworth.

Ysmal, Colette (1989). *Les partis politiques sous la Vème République*. Paris: Domat/ Montchrestien.

2

Conflict and Change in the Rassemblement pour la République

─────────────────────────── *Florence Haegel*

The *Rassemblement pour la République* (Rally for the Republic—RPR) was founded in December 1976 and for nearly 20 years, its president, Jacques Chirac, tried to win the presidency. In May 1995, he succeeded and the RPR occupied a position it never had before: to be the president's party. As heir of former Gaullist organizations, the RPR simply returned to the Gaullist sources, however. The main feature of all Gaullist parties lay, in fact, in their position as founders of the institutions of the Fifth Republic. As such, they occupied a specific place in the party system. As their successive names illustrate (*Union pour la nouvelle République*, Union for the New Republic—UNR; *Union de défense de la République*, *Union for the Defense of the Republic*—UDR and now RPR), their first concern was to promote, then defend, institutions questioned not only by left-wing parties but also by a part of the right-wing camp.

Two major changes occurred in the 1970s, however. One was the gradual rallying of left-wing political forces to these institutions (a shift that took place during Pompidou's presidency). More crucial was the loss of power positions: the presidency in 1974, the post of Prime Ministership in 1976—both to those political forces which would be unified in the UDF in 1978; and the National Assembly in 1981 with the Socialist victory. For nearly 20 years the RPR was either in outright opposition to or supported a prime minister not issued from the party itself: Barre in 1976–1981 or, even, Balladur in the 1993–1995 period of divided government.

The consequence was a genuine identity crisis (Schonfeld, 1986). The RPR needed to remodel its identity and to change at the ideological, programmatic (Haegel, 1990; Baudouin, 1984, 1990) and organizational levels as well. This last dimension is the one we will analyze here by examining three aspects in turn: the organization of activists, the organizational features and specifically the question of the leadership, and finally the rationale behind leadership selection.

THE PARTY STRUCTURES

By creating the RPR, its leaders sought to transform the UDR into a mass party with a large activist force and characterized by a centralized party structure. The RPR wanted to establish an organization based on the mobilization and the maintainance of a large set of activists. In this perspective, ideas such as modernization, efficiency and will to create an "electoral machine" after the American model were emphasized (Crisol and Lhomeau, 1977). It is true that the RPR, compared to its *Union pour la Démocratie française* (Union for French Democracy—UDF) counterpart, is unique with respect to the type of networks and structures constituted in order to shore up its audience. At the heart of this scheme are the federations which ensure the link between the activist network and the party leadership.

Activists' Organization and Networks

The "transformation of the UDR political entreprise" (Offerlé, 1984) and its reincarnation as the RPR prompted a change in leadership symbolized by Chirac's taking power but also a general reorganization. The main issue of this transformation was to reinforce membership and to increase militantism. From 1958 to 1976, Gaullist organizations were not built on activist structures since they were virtually limited to a "ministerial circle and a parliamentary group" (Charlot, 1970a). In fall 1974, Chirac conquered, in fact, the UDR by pitting these organs against each other. To become General Secretary, he initially drew support from the parliamentary group against the leaders who enjoyed governmental legitimacy. Then, later, he strengthened the body of activists with the tactical concern of "circumventing the political bosses" (Offerlé, 1984). This choice sounded, however, like an attempt to renew the party organization and to change a right-wing party culture little inclined to rely on activist participation. From then on, self-celebration of the party strength, campaigning for membership recruitment and the rapid propagation of an activist culture became elements of party life. At the same time, party rallies glorified the activist masses and celebrated these troops that were ready to enter the election battle.[1]

The statutory changes in 1976 roughly boiled down to two innovations. The first and main modification was the creation of the position of president occupied by Chirac; the second concerned the organization of activists.

The territorial structures of the RPR mirrors the French administrative organization, widening out from cantons to voting districts, departments and regions. In this pyramid, the decisive level remains the department federation. The regional structure does not really have any significant influence[2]; activity at the level of the cantons and electoral constituencies is restricted to membership recruitment and activist meetings. In 1987, the idea of improving the organization of the activist base and strengthening the RPR's local networks did lead to creating a new office: the canton delegate. In each canton, that is at a very low level of the country's administrative organization, he/she represents the party. At first appointed by the department secretary, these delegates, since 1989, are elected by the members. Their presence helps reinforce the activist structure, and consequently constitutes a backbone for a network that is often slack. It, nevertheless, remains true that, in many places, the existence of this link is merely a formal one, and that, in others, the post is not even filled.

At the electoral constituency level, a secretary is elected every three years by the district committee.[3] Even if, in certain cases, this election proves to be genuinely competitive, it is often limited by the presence of an official candidate backed by local elected officials (deputies, mayors, general councillors).

The RPR also wanted to strengthen various groups—"sectors"—inside the party such as women and youth. In each department, specific delegates responsible for youth and women's activities have been established. To underline this effort, representation of these categories in the National Council has recently been reinforced by instituting a quota reserved for them in this organ.[4] In the same way, the *"Femme-Avenir"* movement—Women for the Future—has set itself the objective of rallying women close to the RPR.[5] An attempt was also made to reactivate party activity in the workplace but was quite unsuccessful

Last, two largely RPR-dominated associations are worth mentioning for the role they play in establishing and diffusing projects or propaganda themes. The first is the *Club 1989* founded in July 1981. This rather selective club was to stimulate debates in the perspective of designing a political platform for the 1986 parliamentary elections. In quite a different fashion, the *Union nationale universitaire*, National University Union (UNI), a determined right-wing association including students, teachers and interested individuals, acted as a pressure group in university spheres but also as an ideological propaganda group that, without being entirely dominated by the RPR, has consistently supported Chirac.

Maintaining ties with "associated movements" remains officially on the agenda even though, on a practical level, there has been a noticeable decrease in the impact of such satellite organizations. It corresponds both to the idea of developing the RPR's influence in specific sectors and social groups and to the concern with establishing a pluralist and diversified image of the movement. In accordance with a common political practice, the variety of types of support are plainly displayed so as to soften the image of most organizations as monolithic and closed.

The Federations' Degree of Autonomy

Determining the degree of autonomy granted to or gained by the federations is a difficult task. According to party statutes, hierarchical control remains strong since federal secretaries are appointed by the General Secretary. The central leadership's power of appointment is increased by the fact that the General Secretary cannot only relieve a person of his function but also dissolve a federation. The reality appears more complex, however.

The federal secretary is unquestionably a representative of the central office: the renewal rate of those occupying this position provides convincing evidence. In 1994, for instance, only about one-third of the RPR's department secretaries had been appointed before Juppé took over in 1988. And of about 90 department secretaries, 25 of them were appointed during the year 1993. Election years would seem to be privileged moments for remodeling local party leadership and reinforcing the party cohesion. This high renewal rate attests to the control exercised by the national leadership, the repercussion of changes at the top on the selection of department officials and the impact of the election calendar.

With the exception of federations in serious and public crisis where an emissary from Paris is named, the department secretary is rarely an outsider, parachuted leader, however. According to the statutes, department secretary appointments must be ratified by the Federal Committee. With only a few exceptions, this approval procedure seems a mere formality; the department committee and local elected officials were in most cases consulted beforehand, or the the choice was made on their own initiative. In fact, the RPR's department leaders are essentially recruited among local elected officials: only 22 percent in 1993 held no elected position. In general, they acquired their position thanks to a combination of party and local electoral office resources, mainly at the municipal and cantonal level. They have also "more prestigious" mandates at the national level and, in many cases, hold a plurality of offices either at the local level (most typically mayor and general councillor) or at the local and national levels (see Table 2.1).

The control exercised by the national leadership over the federations is confirmed when one examines the party's candidate selection process. The statutes stipulate that nominations at the canton and municipal levels (in towns with a population of less than 30,000 inhabitants) are in the hands of the departmental committee, which has a right of veto. Regarding parliamentary elections, the competent body is officially the National Council which "decides on candidate nominations and withdrawals on the basis of proposals made by the federations and the delegation of these powers." Thus, the texts seem to emphasize the importance of the central authority in the process of designating candidates for the general elections. The actual method of designating candidates suggests that more diverse mechanisms are at work behind the official centralized process (Schonfeld, 1985). Under

Table 2.1
RPR Offices Held by Federal Secretaries in 1993 (percentage values)

Offices	%
Members of the European Parliament	2
Members of the National Assembly	32
Members of the Senate	3
Regional Councillors	27
General Councillors	42
Mayors	30
Town Councillors	43
No elected office	22

The total is higher than 100 percent because many people hold a plurality of offices.
Source: RPR headquarters.

normal circumstances (that is, when elections occur as scheduled), the search for candidates is undertaken two years before the given election and involves numerous consultations and negotiations. This back-and-forth between the various local representatives (department secretary and elected officials of the department) is conducted under the aegis of the election board.[6] In case of discord, or even more open conflict between the central and the local level or within either, various arguments can be deployed such as the supposed preference of the activists or allies (in this case the UDF counterparts). The argument used most often remains the voters' opinion in the given district and consequently, the alleged chances of winning the election. The RPR makes a wide use of opinion polls which, in many cases, act as arbitrator to designate "the best candidate."

The RPR: A Voters' or an Activists' Party?

The terms proposed by Charlot (1970a and 1970b) to describe the organization of Gaullist parties have emphasized a dual characteristic of these groups. One concerns their definition as voters' parties, the primary purpose of which is to win votes and increase their electoral audience by sweeping as widely and thus as diversely as possible. On the other hand, as "dominant parties," they also differ by the central position they occupy in the political system or their hegemony over their opponents. Even if it gained an enviable position in the French party system both in terms of membership size and degree of activism, the RPR, designed to win votes and help its leader rise to the presidency, had, until the 1995 presidential election, failed to fulfill its ambition.

In the first ballot of the 1981 presidential election, Chirac scored 18 percent of the vote; in 1988, he did not increase significantly his share of the vote

(19.9 percent); on April 23, 1995, he won only 20.8 percent of the votes cast. Compared to de Gaulle's or Pompidou's era, when the UNR and the UDR were in an uncontested hegemonious position, the RPR and its leader have patent difficulties in conquering the lead. Basically, the stability of the electoral base of "presidential Chiraquism" can be identified in terms of strongholds (greater Paris and the Massif Central, particularly the Limousin region) organized around the personal influence of the RPR's president, mayor of Paris and department councillor in Corrèze. The electoral force of Gaullism has, however, survived thanks to "the strength of its organization and the density of its network of elected officials and activists solidly implanted throughout the country which are weakened in the case of presidential elections when the party is marginalized and when a more competitive political offer gave voters a choice among the various right-wing political families" (Habert, 1988).

If this analysis is given credence, it reveals a paradox: despite the RPR's vocation to be a voters' party, its maintains its electoral influence mainly due to its activists and finds itself, to some extent, trapped in this role. The paradox is all the more striking since the widespread and long-standing mistrust of political parties in France is fed, in the case of a Gaullist-inspired organization, by a reinforced wariness toward these ferments of division of the national community.

Assessing RPR membership is not an easy task as the party does not provide continuous and serious series of data. In 1994 the figures, according to the RPR's membership board, were 148,000 people, a membership size deemed credible by Knapp (1994). In 1996, according to the same board, the figures are 102,000 people; 1976 and 1981 seemed to mark a double turning point. In the two years following its creation, the RPR experienced a period of membership expansion; then after 1981 the decline of left-wing activism was balanced by a renewal of right-wing activist structures, from which the RPR benefited considerably (Ysmal, 1994). After 1988, the situation was less glorious and official figures even acknowledged a drop in membership between 1988 and 1996. The evolution of the RPR membership also can be appreciated through the surveys conducted among party delegates. In 1984, 30 percent of the delegates had joined the party between 1976 and 1980 while 50 percent had joined after the defeat in 1981 (Brechon et al., 1987). In 1990, 20 percent of the delegates declared themselves to have been members of the UDR; 70 percent to have been members of the RPR between 1976 and 1988 while only 10 percent have done so since 1988 (Habert, 1991).

THE ENTRENCHMENT OF THE HIERARCHICAL SYSTEM AND ATTEMPTS AT DEMOCRATIZATION

The RPR stands out by the frequency of statutory reforms: three overhauls have been undertaken since its creation, in 1978, 1984 and 1989. In fact, the party has a particular relationship with its statutes since it uses statutory change as an instrument, a resource in the hands of leaders to channel opposition or diffuse criticism and even marginalize individual members.[7]

The more recent statutory reform (1989) occurred after Chirac's defeat in the 1988 presidential election. His failure led to questioning certain traditional elements of the RPR's identity. The offensive involved the party's system of alliances with the UDF, the internal life of the movement and its ideological orientations as well (Haegel, 1991). A survey conducted by SOFRES during the February 11, 1990 party conference confirmed the persistence of discontent or disarray among party middle-level elites, elected officials and activists who seemed fearful of the future of their party.[8] An analysis of responses (Habert, 1991) to open-ended questions revealed the nature of the complaints: a lack of communication and democracy, the Paris-centered and technocratic quality of the leadership. Likewise, a majority of the delegates—whatever their level of responsibility—insisted on their lack of influence in the decision-making process[9] and hoped that internal reforms would go further, leading to selection by election of leaders at all levels.[10]

Competing Selection Procedures

In the organizational history of the RPR, three selection procedures have long coexisted: a hierarchical principle based on nomination, a representation principle based on elections and a *de jure* principle for elected officials. Changes over time have gradually reduced, at least formally, the hierarchical principle, maintained *de jure* representation and increased the share of elected members.

The party's executive body in fact long exercised direct power in shaping national and local bodies. Originally, a large proportion of members were named directly by the president. Half the members of the Political Council were thus chosen by the president who nominated also a large part of the Central Committee and Department Committee members. Following the same rationale, a short-lived consultative body of about 200 members entirely designated by the president was created in 1984. In the 1990s, this direct and acknowledged power of the president to shape all the party organs is no longer statutory. Since 1984, only the General Secretary and the Executive Committee are directly appointed by the president. The 1989 revision of the statutes improves internal democracy: the General Secretary and the federal secretaries as well must submit an annual report to the vote of the respective bodies: the National Council and the Federal Committees. If defeated in the vote, they have to resign.

Reverence of legitimate authority, touchstone of the political culture of Gaullist-inspired parties, is, however, reinforced by the positions given to *de jure* members in the governing bodies at the local and national level.

At the local level, the only function subject to direct election, that of canton delegate, has very little influence. The composition of constituency and federal executive committees attests to the importance of *de jure* members, mainly local elected officials. Since 1989, to create a more balanced representation, the role of *de jure* members has been restricted while representatives elected by the members must be at least twice as large as the number of *de jure* members.

This dichotomy between *de jure* members and members' representatives is also found at the national level. First, in the Political Board (new name for the Political Committee since 1984), 30 members are elected by the National Council and 13 are *de jure* members.[11] Within the National Council, *de jure* members (parliamentarians, European deputies, members of the Political Board and members of the Executive Committee appointed by the president; regional delegates, department secretaries; former Gaullist prime ministers, former party secretaries and presidents of parliamentary groups) constitute an overwhelming majority. In a body of about 700 people, only 270 seats are reserved for elected representatives of federations and persons elected from a national list during party conferences.

Nevertheless, it would be naive to think that reverence of authority emerges only by examining the party's statutes. Real practices and procedures make clear that the principle of elections as implemented by the RPR grants a decisive role to co-optation. The phenomenon of heading off competition can be seen both in the number of candidates that run and the persistence of the practice of tightly controlling internal candidacies. As far as the control of appointed bodies by the membership is concerned, the vote is kept under the leaders' close supervision and unanimity remains the rule. In 1993, Juppé's report was approved by 97 percent of those voting.

Entrenchment of Hierarchical Authority and Leadership Crisis

The principles that governed the creation of the RPR in 1976 created an organization centered on the authority of its president who himself benefited from popular legitimacy since he was directly elected by the delegates during the party conference. The president's authority was originally founded on a considerable power of appointment (cf. Panebianco, 1988). In the 1990s, this power remains partially intact since the president appoints the General Secretary and, on the latter's recommendation, the 20-odd national secretaries that make up the Executive Committee. Of course, this prerogative alone does not define his leadership. Panebianco (1988), Collsvald (1994), analyzing the type of authority and the specific methods of establishing leadership which would characterize Gaullist organizations, have stressed the routinization process of a charismatic leadership. The internal crisis that the RPR went through after its leader was defeated in the 1988 presidential race led to dealing with the permanence of this model.

Naturally, clans, networks and "currents of opinion" had never been absent from the party life of Gaullist movements since 1958. The protest movement which emerged at the end of the 1980s took another dimension, however. It led, in particular, to the official (though short-lived) recognition of different "sensibilities." The effects on the leadership of such an institutionalization of internal dissent should not be underestimated.

Faced with this internal yet public competition that is so unusual for the RPR, Chirac adopted a tactic that demonstrates well the entrenchment of the principle of authority. The RPR president committed himself directly and personally to the defense of his General Secretary; linking his fate (to remain or not as president) to a large approval of the motion he advocated, he posed a question of confidence to the 1990 conference delegates. For once, this episode did not produce the RPR's characteristic unanimity: the Chirac-Juppé motion culled a large majority of the votes (68.6 percent) but the competing motion received the approval of 31.4 percent of the delegates, despite the president's direct engagement.

The official life span of these "sensibilities" was no more than eighteen months. During the summer of 1991 they were put to rest. The return to unanimous voting testifies to the reluctance to allow divergent tendencies to be expressed. The difficulty of accommodating such a practice was moreover indicated by the adoption, in May 1990, of a code of good conduct that corseted the expression of the different "tendencies." The tendencies could benefit from the RPR administrive structure; but their spokesmen had to subscribe to three pledges: to refrain from any personal attack against a member of the RPR; not to develop these currents at a regional, department or local level; and to submit all their propaganda activities to the National Executive Committee. Behind the adoption of such regulations was also the crucial question of the use of party logos, a monopoly reserved to the majority and more or less denied to the leaders of tendencies. This episode confirmed the existence of deep-rooted norms that exclude expression of organized and long-life factions and tend to marginalize any subleaders who contest the party leadership or threaten the collective identity of the party.

CHANGES IN LEADERSHIP SELECTION

At the time of the 1995 presidential election, it was all the more difficult to try to describe the RPR leadership, as the context within the party was anything but ordinary. Serious turmoil did arise from the competition in which the RPR's two presidential candidates, Jacques Chirac and Edouard Balladur, were engaged. To attempt an accurate definition of the logic of how the RPR leadership works, one should analyze three different phenomena: potential differences between formal and informal rules for the selection of the leadership; renewal of the governing bodies; channels for and patterns of recruitment of the leaders.

Official and Informal Structures

RPR statutes provide for the coexistence of numerous official structures and of more or less informal and intertwined structures. Apart from the president and the General Secretary, the party is "led" by an Executive Committee that in the 1990s is made up of deputy General Secretaries, national secretaries, deputy national secretaries and national delegates (42 people in 1990). Alongside this body is a Political Board composed of 39 members. The third institution is the National Council. In addition to these three organs, which are provided for in the statutes, are high consultative committees, constituted by theme (overseas departments and territories, local democracy, sports, participation and work, etc.). On the whole, the most striking characteristic is the overlapping of party and elected positions. The party elite draws considerably from the population of its elected officials. On a other hand, the analysis of power and decision-making in the RPR clearly and logically indicates that the larger a body is, the less power it has (Knapp, 1994).

In the RPR, like anywhere else, official organizational charts say little about the actual exercise of power. Chirac's closest advisors, for example, have never occupied formal party positions. This was the case for Pierre Juillet and Marie-France Garaud until 1979 and for Edouard Balladur until 1993. Similarly, it is significant that, on the fringe of the official organization, a small governing body has been constituted, known as the "steering group" (and nicknamed "mammoths" by the press as a parallel to the "elephants" of the Socialist Party). This group, formed around Jacques Chirac, meets on a weekly basis and varies in size.[12] Finally, the short-circuiting of official organs is also made clear by the fact that the leadership does not consult party bodies when strategic decisions are to be made. In the case of the Maastricht Treaty, for example, appeal to a "yes" vote in the 1992 referendum was decided by the "Mammoths." As the National Council, reflecting the majority of RPR voters and members, was fairly hostile to the treaty, it was not consulted.

The second phenomenon characterizing the RPR is the traditional concentration of power at the level of the president and/or the secretariat, concentration reinforced under Juppé leadership first as General Secretary and then as president. A permanent team of approximately 100 members acts within the six major boards.[13] At the heart of this structure is Juppé's chief of staff who is more powerful than any deputy General Secretary since, prior to May 1995, he was simultaneously head of all six boards, including the decisive sector of political affairs.

This high concentration of power can probably be explained by the fear of fragmentation within the RPR's governing bodies themselves. It did not succeed in avoiding the development of centrifugal forces, however. Some of them were linked to the particular context of the 1995 presidential campaign and to Chirac's desire not to be only a RPR candidate. Thus in preparing his campaign, his first concern was to establish think tanks and advisory boards parallel to the RPR. The mobilization of experts responsible for drawing up campaign themes was undertaken under the authority of a high-level civil servant, deputy secretary of the Paris City Hall; the campaign staff was made up of personalities that occupied no position within the party.

Risks of fragmentation appear to be long-lived, however. Teams within the RPR multiply as do competing clans that become institutionalized by creating parallel structures. After 1988, Balladur launched the *Association du Libéralisme populaire* (which can be translated as Association for Liberalism, aimed at incorporating popular classes into the economic system). Officially dissolved, the Pasqua-Seguin current was transformed into an association named *Demain La France*—Tomorrow France. Moreover, sector-oriented associations have been founded recently by members of the RPR's governing bodies. They generally are not located in the national party headquarters and they publish their own newsletters, allowing the subleaders to conduct their own activities outside the party. The "currents of opinion" are no longer officially visible, but external expression of clans and tendencies remains. Juppé's answer to a reporter regarding the difficulty of "grafting on currents"—"It is not part of our culture. In fact, in the Socialist Party, the currents legitimize presidential teams. In the RPR the president's legitimacy is strong"[14]—seems far too definitive. In recent years, the development of organizations parallel to the party attests, in fact, to a more or less clear desire for independence from the RPR leadership.

The Renewal of Governing Bodies

Analyzing in the 1970s the executive bodies of the different Gaullist organizations, Schonfeld (1980) emphazised high replacement levels in the party leadership. From 1967 to 1977, the mean rate of turnover was 41 percent for the Central Committee and 40 percent for the Political Council and Executive Committee. Once Chirac assumed party leadership, there was even more change in the three bodies both in 1975 and 1976 (UDR) or in 1977 after the creation of the RPR. According to him, this high mobility, considered too hastily as a guarantee of a democratic internal life, was more due to the president's strong power of appointment which characterized a "monocratic" type of leadership.

If one looks to the life span of the successive heads of the organization (president; General Secretaries), one can note a tendency to a certain slackening of the top RPR leadership turnover and to a normalization of its profile. For nearly 20 years, Chirac was president; General Secretaries have enjoyed increasing longevity. Whereas the first two, Monod and Devaquet, were in office for less than two years, their successors were much more stable: five years for Pons; slightly less than four years for Toubon; seven years for Juppé before being elected as RPR president in 1995. This evolution toward greater

Table 2.2
Turnover in National RPR Bodies, 1979–1993 (percentage of newly elected members)

Offices	1979	1981	1982	1984	1986	1987	1988	1990	1992	1993
Central Committee/National Council	-	-	53	49	-	53	-	53	-	49
Political Council/ Political Board	73	-	60	55	-	30	-	77	-	23
Executive Committee	42	36	-	59	43	-	44	27	48	72

Source: Knapp (1994).

stability is due to both the organization's institutionalization and a greater standardization of profiles of those holding office. The first two General Secretaries appeared to be atypical. Top civil servant or scientist respectively, they held no elected office and benefited from no real party experience before their appointment. Their successors better fit the profile of political professionals: long careers within the party; elective positions; ministers' entourages or cabinets; posts in government.

Behind these data, Table 2.2 shows continued high turnover of the representative or executive bodies, however, and the influence of the top leadership over the renewal process. For a large part the apparent renewal of the Central Committee /National Council and of the Political Council/Political Board is linked to a dramatic increase in the number of seats. Within the first one, membership has risen by a factor of seven (100 members in 1974 but 700 in 1991). Such a multiplication of positions attests to the president's payroll, however, and allows him to reward his supporters or exclude those deemed inadequate and, therefore, to shape the governing bodies. Change in the composition of the Executive Committee appears to be first linked to the appointment by the president of new General Secretaries-General (1979, 1984, 1988) and to a reorganization of the leadership. It is clear, however, that the RPR president may, at any moment, decide to modify the most important RPR governing body on his own responsibility for political reasons (e.g., to strenghten party cohesion on the eve of decisive elections as in 1992) or other criteria.[15]

Recruitment Channels

In Chirac's own political career, as well as in the RPR's history, the conquest of the Paris mayorship in 1977 was critical. At a time when the Gaullist Party had lost power over the state and all the resources on which it had founded its organization, its new president was elected mayor of Paris. He thus became the head of a staff of 40,000 civil servants which, from a financial and administrative but also from a symbolic point of view, rivalled the state administration (Haegel, 1994). Therefore, the Paris City Hall occupied a central position within the RPR organization. It worked as a privileged channel for recruiting RPR leaders.[16] Four out of the six successive RPR secretaries-general have worked in close collaboration with the mayor of Paris. In 1993, 12 out of the 42 members of the Political Board were Parisians and 8 came from the Parisian region departments (Knapp, 1994).

As pointed out by Jacob (1988), the supremacy of the Parisian network within the RPR was, among others, an element of the crisis the party went through after its president was defeated in the 1988 presidential election. The so-called "Rénovateurs" (Renovators) led their battle in the name of "youth" and to accelerate generational renewal. Their discontent was also linked to the underrepresentation of "provincials" in the executive bodies. The leaders of the movement were indeed these new young "notables" whose successes in cities or local constituencies would have, if Chirac had won the presidency, opened for them positions in the government. Having accumulated political resources, they hoped to gain, at least, leadership positions within the RPR.

Such an importance of the Parisian network and of the president's power of appointment did not avoid, however, a process of "notabilization" of the party elites linked to RPR's electoral successes, in the late 1980s and in the early 1990s, in local elections. As a consequence, the party's governing bodies granted greater importance to local officeholders: in the 1990s, nearly all of them were elected at the national and/or regional or departmental level. If the president's appointment powers do not change, the reservoir from which he/she has to draw is more and more autonomous vis-à-vis the leader since its political resources are linked to popular suffrage rather than to party legitimacy.

Therefore, relations between the party and its elected officials have become a critical issue. Since 1984, the RPR created diverse coordination structures to maintain cohesion among local elective officials. As far as the parliamentary party is concerned, its relative independance, even as the "party of the president," can be illustrated by rules for designating the group's president, the special position occupied by Seguin, and by reluctance to back the governement under all circumstances.

CONCLUSION

How should the various definitions proposed to describe the RPR from an organizational point of view be evaluated? Knapp (1994) tests five main party models (cadre versus mass party, catch-all party and stratarchic versus monocratic leadership) to conclude that these notions all provide relevant elements of analysis but that they remain inadequate. He leaves out the concept of "charismatic party model" tendered by Panebianco (1988) to characterize, among others, Gaullist-inspired movements. In conclusion, we would like to put this last qualification to the test.

This notion, derived from Weber's analysis of charismatic types of domination, is suggested in order to define a type of organization that refers to a precise "genetic model." This is characterized by common features such as the absence of factions or more precisely the fact that they are restricted to the upper strata and have little impact on the periphery, a weak bureaucracy (the division of labor being constantly redefined by the leader), a high degree of centralization, the variety of ties made with outside groups, attachment to a subversive ideology that would tend to question the status quo, and lastly a fragile degree of institutionalization. On this final item, he grants, however, a separate status to Gaullist organizations considered as the only ones that have managed to actually be institutionalized.

Such an analysis raises at least two questions. The first is the validity of the "charismatic party" concept to qualify all Gaullist organizations. This is not to deny the charisma of the Head of Free France during World War II (founder of the Fifth Republic) but to test this passage from a form of authority to a model of organization. To illustrate the limits of this explanatory model, it should suffice to recall that General de Gaulle created two successive party organizations: the RPF, founded in 1947, and the UNR in 1958. Although these two formations had the same "charismatic leader" they displayed very different organizational features. Should these two parties be qualified using the same term "charismatic"?

The second question concerns the evolution of Gaullist-inspired organizations. If one agrees to qualify the UNR as a "charismatic party," how should the RPR be defined? Can it still be considered to represent this model? Or should more emphasis be placed on the institutionalization process it has undergone? A Weberian interpretation would in fact lead to stressing "routinization of charisma" of which it would be the result. On this point Weber wrote:

In its pure form charismatic authority has a character specifically foreign to everyday routine structures. The social relationships directly involved are strictly personal, based on the validity and practice of charismatic personal qualities. If this is not to remain a purely transitory phenomenon, but to take on the character of a permanent relationship, a "community" of disciples or followers or a political party organization or any sort of political or hierarchical organization, it is necessary for the character of charismatic authority to become radically changed. Indeed, in its pure form charismatic authority may be said to exist only *in statu nascendi.* It cannot remain stable, but becomes either traditionalized or rationalized [legalized], or a combination of both. (Weber, 1968)

As the only charismatic type of party organization that has become institutionalized and has simply managed to endure, the RPR would then be an illustration of the process of routinization.

What conclusions can be drawn from these various interpretations? We must first emphasize that the evolution of operational methods within the

RPR provides a useful means of identifying the persistence of organizational mechanisms that are characteristic of the charismatic party model. The organization's obvious centralization, the sense of discipline and the practice of unanimity, as well as the difficulty of officially grafting on various currents would lend credence to this interpretation. One can in contrast stress the relative local autonomy of officials in their departments, the challenge to the leadership that broke out after the defeat of 1988, the expression of real currents in years 1989–1990 and the competition at the top between Chirac and Balladur in the 1995 presidential election.

As for the theme of "routinization," it would lead to emphasizing the tendency of the organization to become bureaucratized. It is true that contrary to early formations inspired by Gaullism, the RPR stands out by its organized party leadership. The presence of a party administration located in Paris could indicate a process of bureaucratization. But the scope and influence of this bureaucracy must not be overestimated. The process of bureaucratization remains minimal and we should instead place greater emphasis on the margins of autonomy of certain sectors of party organization with regard to the central administration. Thus the most recent studies on the internal operation of the RPR emphasize, for instance, the growing importance of elected officials in the organization, even the continual tendencies of teams to fragment. Beyond typologies that sometimes lead to masking changes, it is thus important to remain attentive to the complexity of relational systems that characterize party organizations.

NOTES

1. RPR leaders make frequent use of military metaphors. See Haegel (1987).

2. According to Article 5 of its statutes, "the Rally's regional committee coordinates the Federation's ideas and proposals regarding the economic and social development of each region."

3. This committee, like most RPR organs, reflects a duality between *de jure* members (all RPR members who are elected officials in that district) and members elected by their peers.

4. Among the 700 members that make up the National Council, 26 are elected among department delegates for youth and the same number among department delegates for women's activities.

5. The Centre de Formation d'Etudes et d'Information, Center for Training and Information (CFEI), founded in 1965 was rechristened *Femme-Avenir* like the name of its newsletter. It claims that in the 1990s it has 50,000 members and sympathizers.

6. The election board is a committee convened by the General Secretary-General. It includes the National Secretary for elections, important party leaders and some electoral specialists.

7. This was the case of the 1978 reform. Suppressing the *de jure* membership of the presidents of the National Assembly and the Senate as well as government ministers to the executive bodies helped to eliminate Jacques Chaban-Delmas, who had

been elected president of the National Assembly without the official party support but with the help of the Giscardians.

8. Forty-eight percent of the middle-level elites (and 62 percent of the RPR sympathizers) agreed with the proposal, "Some say that the RPR has been on decline for the past few years."

9. Sixty-four percent (compared to 34 percent) felt that "members have a very weak or rather weak influence over the RPR major policy decisions."

10. Seventy-five percent (compared to 23) wanted to see "the RPR go further in reforming its statutes (for instance, election of leaders at every level)."

11. President, General Secretary, former prime ministers and incumbent Prime Minister, presidents of National Assembly, Senate European Parliament groups, deputy General Secretary (ies), Treasurer, National Assembly President, President of Association of French Mayors, and an honorary member in the person of Maurice Schumann, former spokesman for Free France.

12. After 1993, it included Jacques Chirac, Alain Juppé, Jean-Louis Debré, Charles Pasqua, Philippe Séguin, Bernard Pons and Pierre Messmer.

13. Political affairs, studies, administrative and financial, training, membership and press relations departments.

14. *La Croix*, 6 March 1993.

15. Claims for rejuvenation and feminization increased in the RPR in the 1980s. The appointment of Fabius as Socialist Prime Minister in 1984 pushed the RPR toward a generational replacement symbolized by the nomination of Toubon as General Secretary in 1984 and the marginalization not only of the old Gaullists (the WWII generation) but also of the "Fathers" of the Fifth Republic. Feminization of the leadership remains limited. The more a body has real power, the less women are represented. In 1995, the Executive Committe is only 10 percent women.

16. The Paris City Hall served also as a place where defeated deputies or ex-members of ministers' staffs could be reemployed.

REFERENCES

Baudoin, Jean (1986). "Gaullisme et 'Chiraquisme': Réflexions autour d'un adultère." *Pouvoirs* 28: 53–56.

Baudoin, Jean (1990). "Le Moment Néolibéral' du RPR: Essai d'Interprétation." *Revue Française de Science Politique* 40: 830–843.

Brechon, Pierre, Jacques Derville and Patrick Lecomte (1987). *Les cadres du R.P.R.* Paris: Economica.

Charlot, Jean (1970a). *Le Phénomène Gaulliste*. Paris: Fayard.

Charlot, Jean (1970b). "Du Parti dominat." *Projet* 18: 941–952.

Collovald, Annie (1994). *Jacques Chirach ou les conditions d'appropriation de l'héritage gaulliste. Contribution à l'analyse de la routinisation du charisma*. Thèse de doctorat de Science Politique, Université de Paris.

Crisol, Patrick and Jean Yves Lhomeau (1977). *Le Machine RPR*. Paris: Intervalle Fayolle.

Habert, Philippe (1988). "Jaques Chirac: La Logique d'une Défaite." In Philippe Habert and Colette Ysmal (eds.), *L'Election Présidentielle*. Paris: Le Figaro/Etudes Politique, pp. 14–16.

Habert, Philippe (1991). "Les cadres du RPR. L'empire éclaté." In Sofres, *L'Etat de l'Opinion*, pp. 199–219. Paris: Le Seuil.

Haegel, Florence (1987). "Le RPR: les Contraintes d'une Machine Partisane." *Etudes*: 601–608.

Haegel, Florence (1990). "Mémoire, Héritage, Filiation. Dire le Gaullisme et Se Dire Gaulliste au RPR." *Revue Française de Science Politique* 40: 864–878.

Haegel, Florence (1991). "La recomposition de l'Opposition: Propédeutique de la Compétition Politique." In D. Chagnollaud (ed.), *Bilan Politique de la France*, pp. 185–190. Paris: Hachette.

Haegel, Florence (1994). *Un maire*. Paris: Presses de la Fondation Nationale des Sciences Politiques.

Jacob, Jean (1988). "Les Rénovateurs au RPR." *Revue Politique et Parlamentatire* 938: 27–35.

Knapp, Andrew (1994). *Gaullism since De Gaulle*. Aldershot: Dartmouth.

Offerlé, Michel (1984). "La Transformation d'une Entreprise Politique." *Pouvoirs* 28: 5–26.

Panebianco, Angelo (1988). *Political Parties: Organization and Power*. Cambridge: Cambridge University Press.

Schonfeld, William (1980). "La Stabilité des Dirigeants des Parties Politiques." *Revue Française de Science Politique* 30: 477–505.

Schonfeld, William (1985). *Les Eléphants et l'Avengle*. Paris: Economica.

Schonfeld, William (1986). "Le RPR et l'UDF à L'Epreuve de l'Opposition." *Revue Française de Science Politique* 36: 14–28.

Weber, Max (1968). *Economy and Society: An Outline of Interpretative Sociology*. New York: Bedminster Press.

Ysmal, Colette (1994). "Transformations du Militantism et Déclin des Partis." In Pascal Perrineau (ed.), *L'Engagement Politique*, pp. 41–66. Paris: Presses de la Fondation Nationale des Sciences Politiques.

3

The Front National: The Making of an Authoritarian Party

Gilles Ivaldi

INTRODUCTION

Since its emergence in the mid-1980s, the *Front National*—National Front
(FN) has gained a sizeable number of votes in almost all major elections,
becoming one of the main actors of political life in France. The FN was
founded in 1972, and during the 1970s and the early 1980s the party remained
politically irrelevant. The FN suffered severely from the factionalism endemic
in the extreme Right and it did not succeed in gaining votes either in local
or in national elections. In 1974, Jean-Marie Le Pen received less than 1
percent of the vote at the first ballot of the presidential election. The same
Le Pen did not take part in the 1981 contest since he was unable to find the
500 signatures of local councillors necessary for him to stand in the first
round.

In the early 1980s the National Front started to increase its support by
exploiting the immigration issue. The party enjoyed its first success at the
local level in 1983, obtaining 16.7 percent in a municipal by-election in the
city of Dreux. The FN accompanied this performance by winning 11 percent
in the 1984 European elections emerging from the political wilderness. Two
years later, the FN went on to score 10 percent, with 35 of its candidates
elected in the parliamentary elections of March 1986. More recently, in 1995,
Le Pen achieved his highest score on the national level—15 percent of the
national electorate—in the first round of the presidential election. On that
occasion, in particular, the FN increased its support in the urban-working
and lower-middle classes, the groups most affected by economic recession,
social disintegration and the crisis of "community consciousness" (Wieviorka, 1990, 1994).

Since the early 1990s the contemporary FN's electorate appears to have a higher degree of identification with the party. Voting for the FN now tends to be permanent and less volatile. Le Pen's voters not only protest against the system and the established parties, as they did in the mid-1980s, but totally agree with the nationalist-populist political agenda of the party (Perrineau, 1995).

Meanwhile, Le Pen has managed to turn the FN into an effective nationwide organization in order to compete in both local and national elections. The years 1978–1990 have thus witnessed the development and reinforcement of the whole party apparatus, which is now rigorously organized as an instrument for mobilizing political support. The present strategy of the FN is to turn the organization into a new party of government or, at least, into an ultimate arbiter of elections, a dominant partner in future national coalitions and a main challenger to the Left.[1]

By the mid-1990s, the FN had become institutionalized within French politics. On the one hand the actual party's strength is clearly assessed by existing organizational data: individual membership—estimated at about 15,000 in 1986 (Ysmal, 1989)—had risen to 40,000 in 1993 (*Liberation*, 21 September 1993). In 1994, the *Bleu-Blanc-Rouge* yearly festival regrouped nearly 50,000 party activists, members and sympathizers. In 1995, Jean-Marie Le Pen began his campaign with a claimed 45,000 fully paid members. The FN leader knows that he can depend on a small but dedicated grass roots membership, which is usually involved in vigorous local campaigning. An important change occurred in the late 1980s and the early 1990s, when, as a result of its increasing electoral success,[2] the FN set up a broad organizational system and developed its apparatus on a large scale at every level. In spite of its highly centralized organization and the presence of top-level functionaries who control party communication, the National Front gives a key role to its high-ranking party expert members and activists as "ambassadors" for their movement to the community. In exploring the reasons for the success of the FN, a great part has been played by grassroots campaigning by local party activists in influencing election outcomes and mobilizing the vote for the far Right at constituency or cantonal levels.

On the other hand, Le Pen's movement has largely failed to renew its image and still remains a party outside of the mainstream which doesn't stand a realistic chance of attaining the position of a governmental party. Despite successive attempts to change its image, Le Pen's movement is still clearly identified with the extreme Right. Opinion polls show that 73 percent of the interviewees think that the FN is a danger to democracy (*Le Monde*, 4 February 1994), and in July 1995, only 22 percent agreed with Le Pen's criticism of the "establishment" (*Le Monde diplomatique*, March 1996). Since the 1995 presidential elections, the FN has been credited with 15 to 20 percent of national electoral support (*Le Monde*, 12 February 1996).

The main purpose of this chapter is to examine the FN's organization, elites, internal strains and conflicts, together with the strategies of the party and its factions. The relevant changes that have occurred in the various facets of party organization over time will be analyzed, such as the creation and definition of its overall structure, development of basic structures inside the party, relationships between the different units, flanking organizations, the structure of the headquarters, nomination of the executive bodies and the delegates at the party conferences, and the generational and political turn-over and circulation of elites.

CIRCULATION OF ELITES AND ITS EFFECTS ON THE REDEFINITION OF PARTY STRATEGY AND IDEOLOGY: HISTORICAL DEVELOPMENT OF PARTY FACTIONS WITHIN THE NATIONAL FRONT

Generational and political turnover inside Le Pen's movement is important in explaining successive (re)definitions of the party's dual strategy and ideology, development of the organization, actual strains and divisions within the leadership, and how the various subgroups of elites interact inside the party to achieve power.

The FN was founded in October 1972 as an attempt to unify the various families of the French far Right. The movement was born out of a tiny neo-fascist organization, *Ordre Nouveau*, New Order (ON), and was intended to serve both as the strategic vehicle for revolutionary nationalist activism and as a means of entering the legitimate political space by competing in the elections and fielding candidates in the 1973 legislative elections. The aim of this dual strategy was to pull the extreme Right from political isolation by promoting nationalist values and concealing the FN's "true" orientations behind a pseudo-democratic manifesto (Camus, 1985, 1989; Rollat, 1985; Chebel d'Apollonia, 1988; Taguieff, 1985). The 1972 FN's initial leadership appears to have been very heterogeneous, bringing together three main components: the "conservative," poujadist and anti-Gaullist fringe embodied by Jean-Marie Le Pen and former members of the *Organisation Armée Secrète*, Secret Armed Organization (OAS), such as Roger Holeindre; the neofascist tendency incarnated by Alain Robert, Pascal Gauchon, François Brigneau and the activists of *Ordre Nouveau*; and the group aligned with the newspaper *Militant* edited by the former SS Officer Pierre Bousquet.

The FN faced its first electoral failure in March 1973 with less than 1 percent of the total vote. The movement remained weakened by internal factions, which led to a confrontation between Le Pen and the members of *Ordre Nouveau* and provoked a schism between the fascists and those who wanted to "modernize" the party. The leaders and a great part of the members of ON left the party and formed a rival group in 1974—*Parti des Forces Nouvelles*, Party of New Forces (PFN). This first phase in the FN's evolution clearly shows the fundamental antagonism between different types of elites inside the party over strategies necessary for the party to leave the small world of the extreme Right. It also explains the necessity of Le Pen to balance the claims of the internal strains in order to maintain his leadership.

While the moderate wing of the FN was publicly trying to distance itself progressively from fascism, a strong neofascist contingent continued within the party until the late 1970s. In 1974, Le Pen's movement welcomed pro-Nazi extremists such as François Duprat and his *Groupes nationalistes-révolutionnaires*, National Revolutionary Group (GNR), or the *Fédération d'Action Nationale et Européenne*, Federation for National and European Action (FANE).[3] Moreover, Bousquet and the *Militant*'s editors didn't leave the organization. In the mid-1970s, the neofascist elites acquired a great importance inside the organization. Alain Renault, who was the co-director of Duprat's *Cahiers Européens*, was nominated as secretary-general of the FN. In terms of ideology, the fascist political agenda was implemented around new themes: racism, militarism, anti-Democracy, anti-Semitism and anti-Zionism.

The FN performed very badly in the 1978 legislative election and the party was coming close to extinction. Aware of the electoral damage caused by the links with radical far-Right activists and ideology, Le Pen and the "electoralist" fringe forced them to leave the party (Camus and Monzat, 1992). The split with the neofascists was precipitated mainly by two events. First, the sudden death of François Duprat in March 1978 deprived the revolutionary nationalists of their leader and led to a split with the GNR, the FANE and *Militant*. Second, the FN welcomed another stream of the French neofascism, embodied by Jean-Pierre Stirbois and the members of the *Solidariste* movement.[4]

The years 1977/1978 therefore must be seen as an important turning point in the construction of FN's ideological and organizational structure. The schism allowed Le Pen to temper the ideological stands of his party and to fashion a new identity for the FN. Even when immigration was by no means a new concern on the French far Right, the purpose of the new General Secretary Stirbois was to make the defense of national identity against foreigners a key issue of the FN's political agenda. Under the aegis of Stirbois the organization of the party structure was carried out by the new leadership with a substantial degree of professionalism. Finally, the *Solidaristes* emerged as an extremely influential group within the party and, as will be shown later, some of the companions of Stirbois still belong to a well-identified faction within today's FN (Michel Collinot, Marie-France Stirbois, Roland Gaucher, Bruno Gollnisch). This particular group represents a clearly defined tendency, which continues to influence the party's politics.

At the beginning of the 1980s, there were favorable conditions for the FN to try to seek new alliances both on its Left and on its Right. The new partners of Le Pen's party absorbed the traditionalist Catholics, and a part of what has been called the *Nouvelle Droite*, New Right. Both these groups entered the

FN and started to influence its ideology and strategy. First, the FN allied with the far-Right Catholics of the *Comités Chrétienté-Solidarité*, Committee for Christianism and Solidarity (CCS), adopting some of their views on family, abortion, Christian identity and religious nationalism. The party also benefited from the support of the traditionalist newspaper *Présent.*[5]

Second, in the mid-1980s the party attempted to integrate into the moderate Right political space when nontraditional actors, operating outside the far Right, rose to prominence within the party. By establishing links with the *Club de l'Horloge*, the FN tried to develop a strategy of "respectability," seeing the opportunity to promote the FN as an established party. Before the legislative election of March, the movement thus opened itself to a new generation of elites, which came from the *Nouvelle Droite* (Jean-Yves Le Gallou) and the traditional right-wing parties (Bruno Mégret). This group of "modern" elites—in the sense that they were not "historical" members of the far-Right family—formed a third influential faction within the party's leadership, the *Horlogers*, advocating neoliberal thought and free market economic principles, as well as a more consensual approach supportive of cooperation between Le Pen's movement and the mainstream right-wing parties. The composition of the 1986 parliamentary group reflects the strategy of internal moderation with an ideological reorientation and renewal among the FN elites. There were fifteen old party members (those who joined the party before 1984), seven who joined in 1984/1985, and "respectability" and "modernity," which expressed twelve 1986 newcomers drawn from the "modern elite."

In sum, since 1986, patterns of elite recruitment at the national level have changed considerably. Political turnover inside the FN's leadership may be summed up as follows: (1) recruitment within the FN is largely closed and the highest levels of the party's hierarchy are no longer accessible to people from the outside; (2) most of the people who rise to prominence within the national staff (such as Carl Lang, for example) come from the inner circle and are filtered by a long *cursus honorem* to ensure their total identification with the strategy, the ideology and the interests of the party; (3) two major types of resources are necessary for access to the national leadership: first, the linkage with one of the main party factions identified; second, one's "symbolic" election as a party representative (see the cases of Yann Piat and Marie-France Stirbois in 1989).

POWER RELATIONS AND EVOLUTION OF PARTY STRUCTURE

As mentioned above, the traditional turnover inside the far Right is not only important in explaining changes in the party's strategy and ideology, but also in understanding the successive phases of development of the FN as an organized political force. Conceiving the party as an arena—that is, an environment where rival groups of individuals interact to achieve power—one has to stress the fact that the circulation of elites since the late 1970s has had a significant influence on the party structure and, more importantly, on how this structure works *in situ*. As we shall see, organizational changes are tightly linked to changes in power relations.

In the mid-1980s, the executive bodies at the national level remained under the firm and exclusive leadership of Le Pen and Stirbois. Thus, authority was concentrated in the chairman and the Secretary General, who both decided party policy. The 1984 Political Bureau, which was the FN's central office, can properly be described as the personal machine of Le Pen and Stirbois. Recruitment of a new member was based upon co-optation and had to gain the agreement and the acceptance of the chairman. The access to the party's hierarchy is strictly limited to the "long-standing followers," those who took part in the creation of the movement in the early 1970s.

The first electoral success of the far Right in the European election of 1984 did not imply any substantial redefinition of the autocratic power relationships within the organization. Because of FN's origins, the structure of the party was still underdeveloped, both territorially and functionally. For the most part, the candidates elected in the European Parliament had been selected by Le Pen from among the members of the Political Bureau, which appears to be an almost exclusive source of recruits for elective positions at the national level. Unlike other parties, the FN thus avoided any potential clash between the party apparatus and the "party in office" constituted by the group of MEPs. The national headquarters controlled the departmental federations which had no freedom at all in defining policy and party strategy at the constituency level. Le Pen and his personal staff in the Political Bureau established definite priorities of policy and strategy and communicated them downward through the regional structures. Federal and Regional secretaries were nominated by the party's headquarters in Paris and remained under the complete control of Stirbois. Moreover, there were no horizontal connections between local units of the FN but only vertical relationships between the national and the local levels. Considering the lack of structured organizations at constituency and municipal levels in the early 1980s, individual initiatives often played a great role in the organization of the departmental federations, and thus contributed to the development of new basic party structures.

In 1985, a few changes occurred in political recruitment. Since the FN was competing in the cantonal elections, it needed to find hundreds of potential candidates for elective positions, to enlarge its political base throughout the country. In the 1985 cantonal elections, the FN was able to field 1,521 candidates, occupying three-quarters of the cantons (Mayer and Perrineau, 1989). For a great part of them, these candidates were not original followers of the far Right but came from the mainstream right-wing parties (RPR and UDF). Rapid access to an elective position or a function within the local structures of the FN evidently represented in the eyes of these people a major factor for mobilization. From the point of view of the party, such an opening, in order to be viable, involved establishing a national control upon FN representatives elected to local office. New committees were thus created to publish documents and communicate information about the party's strategy, ideology and political agenda. More fundamentally, these committees aimed to ensure internal discipline and ideological orthodoxy within the organization.

In 1986 a new electoral system was introduced, moving toward proportional representation on a departmental basis. This fundamental change in the electoral rules allowed the FN a key opportunity to enter the French Assembly, as the likelihood of being elected increased. The FN funnelled many more resources to the newcomers. Parliamentary candidates were still selected by the national headquarters and the local structures did not have much power. Potential candidates had to be approved by the FN's leadership, and in several cases, this selection "by the top" produced conflicts within the local federations of the party because of the way some candidates were imposed by Paris. However, the renewal of national and local elites was in process. Among the ranks of the 35 deputies and the 140 regional councillors elected in 1986, we find individuals from various professional sectors of society. On the other hand, Le Pen's movement did not really succeed in attracting well-entrenched local political notables. Well-rooted local candidates were relatively rare within this new generation of FN elites.

Even when the renewal led to a circulation of elites, this process did not imply any significant redefinition of the power relationships within the FN. Among people who were recruited for the 1986 election, only a few individuals really entered the decision-making bodies of the FN. In fact, in the composition of the Political Bureau of the party, 17 out of 21 were original companions of the FN; and only four emerged from the newcomers. If we look at the central structure of the headquarters, which consists of five main elements—the Political Bureau, the group of European deputies, the members of Parliament, the campaigning staff together with the support committee—we see that the old FN elites were overrepresented. Therefore, the circulation of elite was very limited.

The late 1980s represent a major turning point in the FN's ideological and organizational structuration. First, the years 1986–1988 can be seen as a period of probation for individuals who recently joined the party and had been elected as party representatives. Because of their "moderate" political profile, these people were clearly the most committed to the party's strategy which aimed at extricating the FN from its political isolation by establishing links with mainstream right-wing organizations. Second, the modern elites played their role in a dual strategy which involved both the leaning toward the moderate Right and ideological radicalization. Previous research has shown that the FN leadership does well when it addresses unspeakable but meaningful signals to the virulently anti-Semitic neofascist wing. The latter appears to pay attention to what is left unsaid in allusions, innuendoes and verbal abuses such as Le Pen's coded sentiments on the gas chambers—when he described the Nazi persecution of the Jews as a "detail"—or his attacks on the power of "the international Jewish organization" (*Le Monde*, 7 December 1989).

Behind the official discourse, friendly signals to the radical fringe of the French extreme Right are sent, which also aim to preserve the party's political identity and distinction (Buzzi, 1994; Taguieff, 1986). While anti-Semitism is not an overt theme, there is little doubt that Le Pen is always prepared to inveigh against Jews in his speeches. In spite of their political origins, the 1986 newcomers were largely involved in this dual strategy and never hesitated to promote extreme standings (Birenbaum, 1992: 67). In November 1991, the FN published 50 proposals for the immigration policy, which advocated resistance to racial integration and called for racial segregation.[6]

As a consequence of their growing involvement in complex party strategies, the "modern elites" progressively increased their power within the FN. Changes that occurred in the party's national structure in 1988 illustrate this phenomenon. In September 1988, a General Delegation (*Délégation générale*) was created to organize the communication of propaganda and ideological formation of party members and cadres. Conceived as a "think tank" within the FN, the Delegation was mainly concerned with creating and promoting new ideas. The nomination of Mégret as head of the delegation clearly provides a counterweight to the old orthodox guard and its leader Jean-Pierre Stirbois. Both Mégret's access to the party's national leadership and the role he was expected to play in establishing tactical contacts with the mainstream Right were already attested by his appointment as the manager of Le Pen's 1988 presidential campaign.

The death of Stirbois in November 1988 partly modified the balance of power within the national elite. Although the faction, of which the former General Secretary was the leader, still remained as an informal but very influential group within the party, significant changes occurred in the distribution of responsibilities. Stirbois's successor, Carl Lang, was the former chairman of the *Front National de la Jeunesse*, National Front Youth (FNJ), and had no linkage with the traditional factions. The same goes for all the new members of the Political Bureau appointed by Le Pen. All those who entered leadership positions in 1988 came from within the organization. They are, in fact, labelled "FN," since they can be totally identified with the party, its ideology and its chairman's views.

Deprived of a leading figure such as Stirbois, the general secretariat appeared to be subject to control by Le Pen himself. Moreover, the body was substantially restructured to ensure Le Pen's monopoly and control. "Fidelity" and "modernity" were the key principles upon which the changes were based. The new structure was thus staffed by old members of the FN together with FN's young internal elite which has pursued its whole political career within the party.

By 1989, in an attempt to establish lists of potential candidates in the municipal elections, people were drawn from among local activists and notables, but none of them were selected without permission from the regional and national staffs. Most of the national leaders were put forward as candidates. The FN finally managed to present 663 lists and elected 1,336 municipal councillors. In order to coordinate and control activities of local FN representatives, the general secretariat was subdivided into three departments, the heads of which were directly accountable to the political bureau and the party chairman: the *secrétariat aux élus* (officeholders secretariat), which is in charge of the FN representatives at the local level and diffuses basic documents for the training and the formation of the party candidates; the *secrétariat aux elections* (electoral secretariat), who takes care of all the organizational aspects of the elections; the *secrétariat national à l'encadrement* (membership secretariat), who establishes links with local members and activists. With such an increasingly complex structure, the autocratic functioning inherited from the initial system was largely tempered. In practice, these measures aimed principally to undermine the personal power of the General Secretary and simultaneously to reinforce Le Pen's total authority and control. At the beginning of the 1990s, the FN had a complex nationwide network of structures, from the Political Bureau down to the departmental federations and sections at the constituency level. Table 3.1 details the present organization of Le Pen's party.

Since the late 1970s, authority has been concentrated in the party chairman, Jean-Marie Le Pen, who sets out the political agenda directing party policy and strategy. "When Le Pen speaks everybody is silent; when Le Pen decides no-one dares to advance the least bit of an objection. . . . Nothing confronts the king at the risk of infuriating him and making him angry," as Roger Holeindre confirmed in 1985 (Birenbaum, 1992: 53).

At the March 1990 and February 1994 congresses, Le Pen remained the charismatic, legitimate and undisputed leader of the FN, by winning a "Soviet" overwhelming majority of 100 percent among the party delegates. In both cases, he was actually the only candidate. The "popularly elected" party chairman thus provides the post hoc legitimation needed for the party leadership's initiatives.

Several reasons can help to account for this firm and uncontested leadership at the head of the party. First, the early electoral successes of the far Right were due to Le Pen's personal appeal and not to the party itself. His personality represents a substantial component of the FN's power of attraction. Second, his absolute legitimacy at the head of the FN allows him to maintain the internal coherence of the organization. Today Le Pen probably remains the only guarantee of unity against the power of conflicts within the FN's leadership. Considering this ideological heterogeneity, Le Pen's charisma ensures union within the party's members at the national and local levels.

Finally, most FN national leaders are largely indebted to Le Pen for having provided them with power and responsibilities within the party's executive organs. The party chairman is in a decisive position to influence personnel recruitment. He plays a critical role in both the mobility of cadres and structuration of their career aspirations. Le Pen's supremacy over the whole executive apparatus and the making of party policy is thus accepted by all.[7] Le Pen's access to information and his monopolistic ability to comment on all policy matters in the mass media make him the central actor in the FN's broad political communication.

In describing the overall structure of the party, one probably has to stress the predominance of the executive bodies. Although it elects the chairman and the Central Committee, the Congress is not a governing body (see Figure 3.1). It consists of representatives from all departmental federations, who are elected by party members at the local level and are basically expected to "applaud at the conference." Therefore, the FN National Congress is more an exhibition of enthusiasm and solidarity with the leadership than a vehicle for the expression of dissent among the membership. In fact, the ex-officio party delegates are quite numerous. Central Committees and National Councils have been established in order to support rather than control the party leadership. They both exercise a purely advisory role.

The FN's executive bodies are ruled by a small cohort of Le Pen's close colleagues. In the last decade, a series of internal changes in party organization have weakened the Political Bureau's influence and redistributed power and responsibilities among other top-level party organs (such as the Executive Bureau or the vice-presidency). In 1990, the list of 30 members for the Political Bureau was submitted by Le Pen to the Central Committee for the formal agreement and was unanimously approved. For the most part, those elected are members of the previous bureau, whose composition reflects the distribution of the various tendencies within the party.

As a matter of fact, general policy-making and supervisory power are now vested within the Executive Bureau. Among its members are the top officials drawn from the highest levels of the party hierarchy, the *crème de la crème* of the party apparatus. Although it is not officially stated in the party's statute, the Executive Bureau appears to be the top decision-making body, and Le Pen is the natural leader of such body.

Finally, the executive bodies include the General Secretariat and the General Delegation, which are conceived as interconnected bodies although they possess separate domains of responsibility and clear assignments: ideology and propaganda are the responsibility of the Delegation, while party organization is that of the Secretariat. Dualism between the Delegation and the Secretariat weakens the power of both the General Secretary and General Delegate while strengthening Le Pen's personal position. National secretaries

Figure 3.1
The Structure of the National Front

National Level--Executive Bodies			
Party Chairman (Jean-Marie Le Pen since 1972) Elected by the Congress. He determines the Congress schedule and decides when to convene meetings of the Political Bureau.			
Cabinet Director	Treasurer	Executive Bureau	Vice-Chairmen
Jean-Marie Le Chevallier	Jean-Pierre Reveau	Top decision-making body. (Not specified in the party statute) Le Pen and close colleagues (Mégret, Lang, Chaboche, Gollnisch, Reveau).	Vice-Chairmen (Dominique Chaboche) (Martine Lehideux since 1994) Vice-Chairman in charge of social affairs (Carl Lang). Vice-Chairman in charge of international affairs (Gollnisch nominated in 1994).
		Political Bureau: representation of party tendencies. Headed by Le Pen. Appoints the regional and departmental secretaries.	
General Secretariat (Lang, 1988-1995; Gollnisch since 1995)		General Delegation (Mégret since 1988)	
Activities of the National Secretariats: control over federations, party representatives, membership; administration, finances and campaigning. Publishes *Les Nouvelles du Front*.		Activities of the National Delegations: propaganda, studies, formation, party manifestations, international relations. Publishes the *Circulaire de la délégation générale*.	

National Level--Representative Organs		
Central Committee: "Parliament" with advisory role (100 members). It endorses with the Political Bureau nominated by the party chairman.	National Council: advisory role, with no real power. 300 members selected from the Political Bureau, the central committee and the party representatives.	Scientific Council: internal party think tank. Founded in 1989 by Mégret and Le Gallou.
Congress: delegates elect the Party chairman and the Central Committee. No real power, with a symbolic function (1,002 delegates in 1990; 1,650 in 1994).		

Regional Level	
Regional Secretaries. Appointed by the Political Bureau, to supervise the departmental secretaries.	Regional Councillors Group

Departmental Level					
Departmental Secretaries and Assistants. Appointed by the national political bureau.					
Bureau					
Secretary in charge of membership	Treasurer	Propaganda	Press	Administration	Security-*Direction protection sécurité* (DPS).
Local party representatives, supervised by the National Secretariat.					
Party Membership					
Elect delegates at the national congress					

control party basic structures, and at the same time coordinate and transmit information up and down the hierarchy. Regional secretariats carry out their functions by creating a channel of communication between local leadership and the central headquarters. At the departmental level the organization of the party's structure is a virtual copy of the existing national model of executive bodies. Federal secretaries are asked to act as "administrative prefects" for their party within the local community.

The new *Institut de formation nationale*, National Institute for Training (IFN), whose fundamental principles derive from the communist model of making propaganda, disseminates ideas through the publication of basic documents and by providing a forum for discussion and training of the personnel of the party. Publications such as *Militer au Front* (1991) or the *Guide du responsable* (1993) contribute to the formation of guidelines for local activism and concurrently encourage ideological commitment on the part of newcomers. By 1993, the FN issued 17 million booklets and brochures, to which were added 2.5 million stickers, 250,000 copies of the *Lettre de Jean-Marie Le Pen* and 500,000 posters.

To a certain extent, FN local officials have indirectly benefited from this broad policy of political education. The ideological formation provided and supervised by the national headquarters makes them well-tutored activists. Since they consequently acquire greater legitimacy in commenting and analyzing local events in the scope of FN's orthodoxy, they have more influence in making decisions which affect their membership and potential electorate at the constituency level. Local leadership is also bolstered to help stimulate ground-level mobilization for the FN, by organizing their own campaign activities.

The 1994 congress of the FN took place in a general context of demobilization, which required organizational changes in the national leadership. Some of the "first-generation" actors and remnants of the old guard were thus removed from the ruling elite. Others, such as Gollnisch, appointed party Vice-Chairman and member of the Executive Bureau, used associations with factions as a resource for climbing the party ladder. Since the new Vice-Chairman finds his support within the "Stirbois faction," his internal promotion can be seen as an effort to counter Mégret's influence and alter the balance of power among elite elements within the central leadership. Concurrently, ten new members were added by Le Pen to the existing Political Bureau, as an attempt by the party chairman to restrict the Bureau's power.

The composition of the list presented by the FN in the 1994 European election reflected the new balance of power and the greater part played by Gollnisch. Selection was made by the Executive Bureau. The candidates were drawn mainly from the Political Bureau, according to their linkages to the various internal factions or tendencies. If there were significant changes in the distribution of positions, personnel turnover and renewal nevertheless remained limited, since most of the candidates had already stood for the 1989 European elections.

The FN penetration at the local level is assessed by the 1994 cantonal elections, when the FN managed to run candidates in 1.848 of the 1.922 cantons where contests took place. The FN obtained about 10 percent of the total vote in the first round, but suffered from the strategy of the mainstream right-wing parties which were not inclined to ally with Le Pen's organization at either the national and local level, and thus contributed to its political marginalization. With 90 candidates contesting for the second ballot, only four FN general councillors were elected.[8]

By 1994, however, the major task assigned to the entire FN apparatus was related to Le Pen's candidacy in the forthcoming 1995 presidential election. A support committee was formed in order to supervise campaign activities. Top-level leaders of the party appeared to be largely involved in this process, with their own areas of responsibility.

Even though the good performance of Le Pen at the first ballot demonstrated that alternation of power would be a possibility in the future, on the other hand, the FN still needs an alliance with the mainstream right-wing parties. In the June 1995 municipal elections, the FN was driven into a more relaxed attitude, seeking tactical alliances with the Right. Its second-ballot strategy openly demonstrated that candidates of the party were asked to carry on at the local level the alliance rejected by the RPR/UDF at the national level. Extreme Right lists were formed in all the communes where the FN was able to achieve a 10 percent threshold at the first ballot. Although at the moment it has only 1,100 municipal councillors, the FN managed to field about 25,000 candidates across the country. Several top-level leaders were put forward as party representatives. As a general guideline, the FN will stand down its candidates in the municipalities where local leaders of the Right agree to make pacts with them. In the places where the mainstream Right refuses alliance, the far Right will contest the second ballot independently.

In spite of the success of Le Pen's party in the first round, there were very few deals made with the RPR/UDF at the local level. In the second ballot, its candidates therefore stood in 108 communes with more than 30,000 inhabitants and finally obtain almost 2,000 seats in city councils; the FN won the control of three towns in the south of France: Toulon (Jean-Marie Le Chevallier), Orange (Jacques Bompard, former member of the OAS and the neofascist group *Occident*) and Marignane (Daniel Simonpieri, close colleague of the far-Right local prominent figure Ronald Perdomo). For the first time, Le Pen's party thus experienced the exercise of municipal power. The three mayors' tasks were mainly directed toward the building of a local "FN system" through the control of municipal services and associations. Since French law has considerably increased the executive power of local authorities in a wide range of spheres, the communes' own competence and resources are largely used to spread the influence of the party in almost all the sectors of municipal activities (allocation of housing and jobs, city council grants to local associations, direct aid and assistance, employment of permanent party staff). However, the lack of substantial electoral support—the FN candidates' scores averaged 35 percent of the votes cast—prevents the mayors from openly proclaiming important changes in municipal policies, and leads to a discreet strategy of "soft" control and "entryism." To a certain extent, they have fallen back to their earlier objectives in favor of a more consensual approach.

The electoral success stimulated further party organization. In December 1995, two new national delegations were created under the responsibility of Mégret: *actions catégorielles* and *édition*. Lang, who resigned from the General Secretariat in September 1995, was nominated as party Vice-Chairman in charge of social affairs. As a consequence of his growing influence within the national leadership, Gollnisch was appointed as General Secretary. Internal restructurating of the leading executive bodies involved shifting some responsibilities for treasury, administration and personnel away from the Secretariat to Le Pen himself. The FN leader thus received additional executive powers as the president, clearly making him even more powerful.

A WORLD APART? EXTREME RIGHT PRESS AND FN FLANKING ORGANIZATIONS

The last decade has thus witnessed the development of the FN's basic structures and the reinforcement of the whole party apparatus at both the local and national levels. Since the mid-1980s the FN has accompanied its internal development with the formation of a large number of peripheral organizations and the promotion of several associated newspapers. Unlike the French Communist Party, which attempted to create a "counter-community" and an all-embracing world, the FN's strategy is predominantly based upon "entryism." The aim of spreading ideological influence within the whole community through existing structures is a very interesting feature of the contemporary far Right attempt at outward diffusion. However, FN flanking groups and extreme Right newspapers play different parts in this strategy: the role assigned to the former is to disseminate FN ideology in a wide range of professional sectors and associations, while the latter are involved mainly in maintaining the "umbilical cord" with the extreme fringe of the French far Right. The main publications of the FN are *Identité* and *La Lettre de Jean-Marie Le Pen*.

Led by party intellectuals, *Identité* is conceived as a more theoretical review and as a forum for ideological debates on main contemporary issues. The party's body of intellectuals, mainly the former members of the *Club de l'Horloge* and the liberal-nationalist New Right stream such as Mégret, Le Gallou or Blot, make regular contributions to this journal. *La Lettre de Jean-*

Marie Le Pen, created in 1985 by Jean-Marie Le Chevallier, gives news, reports the leadership's opinions and presents the party line.

More interesting is the role played by the extreme Right press not directly owned by the party. The Catholic and ultra-Conservative stream of the far Right is incarnated by the fundamentalist daily newspaper *Présent,* which was founded by Bernard Antony, François Brigneau, Pierre Durand (royalist activist, former member of the Poujadist movement and supporter of *Algérie française* within the OAS) and Jean Madiran (present director, former activist of the royalist organization *Action Française*). Its neo-Vichy ideology is clearly stated by the overt references to the major doctrinal elements of Pétain's regime—God, patriotism, family, duty to work—which situate *Présent* in the forefront of the defense of the ultra-Conservative National Revolution. Its principal themes are inspired by the French anti-revolutionary tradition: moral and spiritual decadence, plots by the freemasons, the Jews and high finance, anti-communism, anti-democracy, inclination toward monarchy and a strong rejection of the political establishment.

With a readership of 31,000, *Minute-La France* is probably the most important FN-associated newspaper. It is headed by Serge Martinez (former member of the RPR) and Serge de Beketch. *National Hebdo,* which currently sells over 15,000 copies, was created in 1984 by Roland Gaucher, a former leader of a fascist movement founded by Marcel Déat in the interwar years, and Michel Collinot. Considering the extreme ideological stance taken by its publishers, *National Hebdo* undoubtedly plays a prominent role in the development of the relationship between the FN and the more radical groups on its right.

This kind of press speaks to the activists of the extreme Right rather than the general public. In particular, newspapers such as *Présent* or *National-Hebdo* willingly promote the anti-Semitism and "revisionism" of the far-Right groups, which deny or minimize the Nazi genocide of World War II.[9] Since the extreme Right newspapers are not officially affiliated with the FN, Le Pen and his colleagues often argue that they cannot be held responsible for what is said in them, and deny their participation in the promotion of anti-Semitic and racist values. Behind these tactical attempts to fashion a respectable identity, the nature of the relationship between the far-Right press and the FN is clear. First, the national leaders of the FN rarely condemn the outrageous articles published by the associated newspapers; second, today's extreme Right publishers are closely involved in the FN's organization and play a prominent role within its central leadership. Durand (co-director of *Présent*) and Gaucher (previous director of *National-Hebdo*) are members of the FN's Political Bureau, while Serge Martinez (*Minute-La France*) is a member of the Central Committee.

Since the mid-1980s, the structural changes within the FN have also been associated with the development of numerous flanking organizations, circles and clubs. The aim is to create a nationwide network which can coordinate the work of existing associations, encourage the formation of new ones and widely disseminate FN propaganda. The party started to practice "entryist" tactics through associated organizations in 1985. Development of flanking structures and FN-related trade unions is now among the major goals of the national leadership's strategy. The main targets of the party's mobilization strategy include social groups which are traditionally most susceptible to the appeal of the extreme Right: policemen, small business traders and shopkeepers. Moreover, the FN aims to spread its influence as well within left-wing trade unions.[10]

As by-products of both FN organizational reinforcement and individual initiatives, large numbers of flanking groups and clubs have come into existence during the last decade. Their main purpose is lobbying within specific areas of concern or particular social and professional sectors. Various spheres are now subject to attempts by the FN to influence their policies and ideologies. The *Front national de la jeunesse*, the FN youth movement (FNJ), was founded in 1974 to recruit young people into the party. Since the party has not been very successful in attracting young people, the FNJ has largely retained its independent status. Significant changes have occurred in the early 1990s when the FN started to achieve significant scores among those voting for the first time (especially young men). The structure dedicated itself to the task of promoting the FN within universities and secondary schools. In 1990–1991, the FNJ supervised the creation of two more student unions: the *Renouveau étudiant* (RE), and the *Renouveau lycéen* (RL). Support among school teachers is sought through the *Mouvement pour un enseignement national*, Movement for a National Teaching (MEN). Aware of the necessity to recruit more young members in the near future, the central leadership has recently established direct and official links between the youth organization's leaders and the party's presidency. Today's FNJ claims 15,000 members across the whole country and plays a greater role within the party as a locus for "orthodox" political socialization of a new generation of activists. Training of young party members and cadres is thus among the major responsibilities assigned to the revitalized structure. During the recent years, however, the FNJ has been radicalized by revolutionary extremists such as the activists of the Skinhead movement, or the ultra-Nationalists.

Youth, veterans, *rapatriés*, army officers, and members of the police are all among the main target areas of the FN's entryist strategy. The *Cercle national des combattants*, Veterans' National Circle (CNC) was founded in 1985 in order to increase support for the party among the veterans. By 1994, the circle claimed a membership of 5,000. To the CNC may be added the *Cercle national des officiers et sous-officiers de réserve*, National Circle of Lieutenant Reserve (CNOSOR), conceived of as a forum for army officers, and the *Cercle national des gens d'armes*, Circle of Army Members (CNGA). Two former home commandants of the OAS are in charge of the *Cercle national des rapatriés*. Because many of today's FN elites were closely involved in the

Algérie française struggle, Le Pen's party traditionally enjoys widespread sympathy among the French people who left Algeria and resettled in France after independence in 1962 (see the importance of the *rapatriés* group within the FN membership).

In recent years, the FN has concentrated much of its efforts to both the French justice system (with the association of judges and magistrates' *Droit et Liberté*, Right and Freedom) and the police. Le Pen's party achieved success first by infiltrating the *Fédération professionnelle indépendante de la police*, Police Professional Independent Federation of (FPIP), and then by promoting its own union of policemen through the *Front national de la police*, National Front of Police (FNP). The FPIP was predominantly seen as an FN-associated union in the sense that the organization shared most of the party's views on immigration and law-and-order policies, although there are no actual official links between the two organizations. In 1995, the FN split with the union and launched the FNP, which won 7.4 percent of the votes in the election for the representative bodies of the uniformed police officers (for its part, the FPIP obtained 5.8 percent).

The FN is represented in professional sectors and business groups largely through its association *Entreprise moderne et libertés*, Modern Enterprise and Freedom (EML). Formed in 1984, the EML is an "umbrella" organization which includes various associated professional circles: companies, public transportation, taxi services, building trades, commerce, industry, health, banking, and law. At the 1996 Congress of EML, the whole structure was reorganized according to different sectors of activity. There is also an organization of farmers—the *Cercle national des agriculteurs de France*, National Circle of Farmers (CNAF)—which was created in November 1990 and published the monthly *Lettre aux Paysans* (Peasants Newsletter).

An important function of the EML structure is that of fund-raising, even if control over party finance is another area where Le Pen's monopoly is virtually absolute. At the beginning, the FN benefited from Le Pen's personal fortune, largely due to the Lambert inheritance.[11] Now, both organizational and electoral activities require new sources of party finances. Other than membership subscriptions (the party also charges for admission to its rallies) and voluntary donations, there are refunds of election expenses and a proportion of the salaries that the FN representatives (MEPs, councillors) receive from the state. Contributions by firms make up a part of the party's income (*Liberation*, 3 January 1996). According to the newspaper *Le Monde* (8 February 1992), financial linkages have also been established, since 1984, between the FN and the Reverend Moon's organization. Recent development in FN tactics suggests increasing importance of professional sectors and business companies as targets for far-Right lobbying.

In addition, there are other associations such as CNFE or the *Fraternité française*, French Fraternity. These campaign groups, with their emphasis on family, abortion, religion or poverty, are active over the whole range of

FN policy. They organize single-issue campaigns within their own field of social concern. With a claimed membership of 5,000, the *Cercle national de femmes d'Europe*, National Circle of European Women (CNFE), is a women's organization involved in the promotion of traditional family values. The FN is also linked to various anti-abortion and so-called "rights of the child" groups, such as *Laissez-les vivre*, Let Them Live, whose leadership includes several members of the FN; or *SOS-Tout-Petits*, headed by a member of the National Front and Le Pen's personal political staff. Recently, this association has resorted to illegal methods, and its members have been involved in violent action against hospitals and physicians who legally carry out abortions. Direct action groups have thus emerged alongside moderate anti-abortion associations such as the FN-affiliated *Cercle Renaissance*, Renaissance Circle, whose head is an FN regional councillor for Ile-de-France and former activist of the neofascist group *Occident*. Some of these groups are linked to associations of the fundamentalist Catholics, such as the *Comités Chrétienté-Solidarité*, Christiany-Solidarity Committees, the *Fraternité Saint-Pie X* or the *Alliance générale contre le racisme et pour le respect de l'identité française et chrétienne*, General Alliance Against Racism and for the Respect of the French and Christian Identity (AGRIF). FN "religious" groups include the *Cercle des juifs de France*, French Jewish Circle (CJF), which claims 1,000 members (mostly *séfarades*, Jewish people coming from North Africa). The circle is often used by the party to deny accusations of anti-Semitism.

Other social categories are among the potential targets of FN strategy. Le Pen's party aims to attract retired people through its *Cercle national des retraités et préretraités*, National Cicrle of Retired and Pre-Retired, with a claimed 3,000 members in 1994 (Le Monde, 6 December 1994). *Fraternité française* was founded in 1988 and relaunched by Mégret in the early 1990s. This association already possesses 45 regional delegations throughout the whole country. Local structures are organized to mobilize the disadvantaged French people by providing food, advice, or personal and administrative assistance. Unemployed people are also represented within the *Front anti-chômage*, Anti-Unemployment Front created in 1987. In February 1994, Samuel Maréchal, leader of the FNJ, founded the *Association de recherche pour l'emploi des jeunes*, Association for the Research of Youth Employment (AR-PEJ), which is particularly concerned with young, unemployed people. Both these structures exist to create a network of contacts between those looking for work and employers wishing to skirt the existing anti-discrimination laws and practice a covert policy of "French first."

This picture highlights that the development of flanking organizations is now among the main goals of FN policy and strategy. In describing this growing network of far-Right associations, we have to stress the important role played by local activists in attracting potential voters and members through FN-affiliated structures. Furthermore, the actual social organization within the FN may be described as a small private world with its own activities, protecting its members from the outside. Anne Tristan, in her eyewitness account of life in the FN, paints a very interesting picture of the activities of FN members. Her work points out the emotional fervor of being admitted to a world of total certainty and all-demanding dedication. Previous research has shown that the FN achieves its highest polls in deprived urban areas where there are no active associations or organizations able to integrate the inhabitants and work to improve the neighborhood (Mayer and Perrineau, 1989). Assistance, help or information are among the most important functions which the FN grassroots members fulfill in these areas, by promoting new structures which can surround those most likely to commit themselves to far-Right subgroups. A great strength of the party lies in the existence of this core of dedicated activists—the lifeblood of the party machine—trained and disciplined, capable of working in an efficient and organized manner.

POWER CONFLICTS WITHIN THE FN

This last section seeks to describe and explain the main power conflicts within the FN. Although the FN appears to the outside world as a highly centralized organization united around a single and well-defined ideological line, it experiences, like other French parties, real internal conflicts which regularly lead to overt struggles among the leaders. As mentioned previously, the streams within the FN had originally represented differing ideological traditions and political styles of behavior, which derived their strength from a large range of historical references. Conflict initially had taken place in the party between the violent neofascist activists and those who wanted to promote the party on the electoral scene. In 1973, the latter provoked a split over neo-Conservative ideology. No less important was the 1978 clash between Le Pen and the revolutionary nationalists' views over the new ideological orientations imposed by Stirbois and the *Solidaristes*. Because of the political irrelevance of the FN in that period, changes and conflicts occurred within the small marginal world of the extreme right wing

In the 1980s, conflicts over party policy, identity and strategy reflected a crucial division between an old orthodox guard and a group of "reformists." The former claimed to preserve the old-fashioned identity of the FN in spite of its electoral achievement, whereas the latter called for significant changes in party strategy, implying a shift toward the Conservative right wing which would allow, in their view, an increase in support from the RPR/UDF electorate. Substantial evidence suggests that, since the early 1990s, factions have increasingly become mere vehicles for the leadership ambitions of rival groups operating within the party elite. However, unity has been guaranteed by intraparty discipline, even at the cost of expulsions.

Such personal conflicts and attempts to maintain iron discipline can be examined within the FN leadership, with varying levels of intensity in different periods. The party's evolution can be seen as a series of alternating "hard-line" and "conciliatory" phases. The first attempt to integrate the party into the moderate Right political space in 1986, by establishing links with the national-conservative fringe of the New Right, provoked bitter conflicts between the newcomers and the old guard. Although the old FN elites were still overrepresented within the executive bodies, the leadership had become less homogeneous. Some of the new prominent figures such as Mégret, Le Gallou or Blot were uneasy with the muscular authoritarianism that characterized Stirbois's attitudes toward party organization. These internal divisions between the "notables" and the "believers" were, for example, responsible for some resignations. In 1986, the FN leadership incorporated a variety of conflicting policy and strategy perspectives that created serious struggles over power and intraparty organization. The FN was also riven with conflicts at the local level, since many of the candidates fielded by the party in the parliamentary election were drawn from among the ranks of the newcomers. For instance, the party suffered severe internal problems in Marseille, where Pascal Arrighi (who joined the FN in 1986) and Ronald Perdomo (original member since 1972) competed in a battle over control of the departmental federation.

Even if an MEP like Olivier d'Ormesson resigned in protest to what appeared to be a process of ideological radicalization within the national leadership, most of the old guard's prominent representatives supported the party's chairman. Similarly, in 1988 another contrast emerged among the modern elites who had joined the FN in the mid-1980s over the "Durafour-crématoire" controversy.[12] On the other hand, Le Pen found once again unconditional support from the members of Stirbois's faction. In part, these resignations/expulsions reflected the impact of intraparty fragmentation and showed that dissidents are not tolerated by the party. However, they were less the product of fundamental ideological divisions than of power conflicts within the FN's leadership.[13]

By 1988, it was clear that a sizeable segment of the party's leadership and activists did not accept Stirbois's hegemony over the movement. Intraparty tensions festered and the General Secretary met growing opposition from Mégret between the two rounds of the 1988 presidential election. Le Pen's score in the first ballot produced new quarrels on the party's second-ballot strategy. Mégret called for the endorsement of Chirac in the second ballot, expressing the fears that a division of the ranks of the Right would lead to a second victory for Mitterrand. Stirbois's attitude to the second ballot was completely different: the FN Secretary-General was quite willing to contribute to the defeat of the RPR candidate with the old far-Right tradition of anti-Gaullist hostility. Moreover, Stirbois secretly recommended a tactical "revolutionary vote" (i.e., a second-ballot vote for Mitterrand). He argued that the FN would benefit electorally from a victory of the Left and the resulting Socialist government, which could potentially provoke a radical shift toward the FN among the right-wing electorate.

With the death of Stirbois, there occurred a shift in the balance of power within the FN national leadership. Faced with its political isolation, the party's immediate task was to distance itself from the radical strategy of the old guard and to seek alliances with the mainstream Right in the forthcoming 1989 municipal elections. Mégret's strategy thus grew in importance. The composition of the list put forward by the FN in the 1989 European election clearly showed that party leadership had fallen increasingly into the hands of the *Horlogers*. Some of Stirbois's closest friends were not even put forward as candidates, while others were not elected because of their low positions on the list. This outcome provoked virulent criticism and several prominent figures of the original far Right organized a vigorous anti-*Horlogers* campaign, urging a tough line against the new neoliberal orientations of the party. Simultaneously, they argued for the necessity of the FN to return to the original social and populist themes of the far Right in order to gain greater support among the working-class electorate. In the years 1989–1991, it was not just Mégret who was subjected to criticism from the FN leadership. Lang's position as the head of the General Secretariat also came under systematic attack from opponents of his reorganization policy. Criticism of the organization and demands for more intraparty democracy arose. But, once again, the dissenters had other choices than to "exit" from the party.

Struggles between rival factions remain a typical feature of today's FN. The nomination of Gollnisch as party Vice-Chairman and member of the Executive Bureau in 1994 shows a significant change in strategy and the increasing influence of the hard and uncompromising Stirbois's function within the central headquarters. His rise can be seen as a tactical way of countering Mégret's power. Gollnisch thus proves to be a figure who can mobilize wide support among the original members, by linking together the various factions of the orthodox old guard into an opposition to Mégret. The internal debate concerns party strategy and some of the differences separating the two groups have clearly been magnified, mainly as a result of the recent evolution in the social composition of the FN's electoral support. A tradition of revolutionary politics persists within the FN and periodically erupts into the intraparty political scene. The old guard, which is determined to make the party a vehicle for the maintenance of a separate extreme Right identity, stresses "revolutionary" vanguard activity and calls for the abandonment of the neo-Conservative, ultra-Liberal economic policy embodied by the *Horlogers*. Such an ideological shift toward "left-wing" social-populist themes is seen as a means of increasing the FN's electoral success, by enlarging its political base among the lowest social categories and acting as the spokesman of the "laboring classes." On the other hand, Mégret's biggest challenge lies in constructing a new reformist identity as the only winning strategy. Supported by some of the cadres of the new generation, he champions the policy of a broad union of the Right which would imply a significant transformation from a radical to increasingly moderate government party, similar to the change undergone by the MSI in Italy. The struggle between Mégret and Gollnisch for control of FN executive bodies in order to replace Le Pen is manifest within the Executive Bureau which now appears to be the main locus of political dissent. The ideological divides and rivalries within the ranks of the FN have not stopped and many defections of top-level party representatives occurred during 1994.

The unprecedented good score obtained by Le Pen in the first round of the 1995 presidential election among the working class and unemployed voters, with respectively 30 and 25 percent of the vote, raised, however, doubts about party strategy, and forced Le Pen to agree with the idea of the FN adopting a new ideological line.[14] The FN thus seems to be radicalizing further its position by reverting to the tough line of the remnants of the old guard. The FNJ activists and the Stirbois faction had launched the idea of a *Front populiste* which would aim to develop the FN's appeal to the left-wing electorate, whereas Mégret and his close colleagues seemed to be more pre-occupied with the mobilization of the conventional right-wing voters. In July 1995, the debate within the party took place around the new FNJ slogan: "neither right nor left, but French" (*Ni droite, ni gauche, Français*). But this attitude provoked violent reactions among the main figures of the party, showing once more the basic split between radical and reformist leaders.

In relation to these existing divisions over which strategy to adopt, the FN is also confronted by the problem of the relationship between the party and its three mayors who were elected in Toulon, Orange and Marignane in the June 1995 municipal contest. During the weeks following the elections, the "low profile" taken by the mayors in the implementation of FN policy at the local level led to a public quarrel with their party chairman. Arguably, they were preoccupied with the maintenance and enlargement of the electoral support in their communes rather than the FN management of municipal policies. As they were experiencing for the first time the problems of power, the mayors deliberately talked down programmatic ambition in the name of local political realities. They were much more inclined to cool down their ideology and temporarily jettison a part of their extreme Right doctrinal baggage. For instance, they opposed the FN policy of the implementation of the *Préférence nationale* (French first). At one point that they were asked by the national headquarters to carry out their municipal policies in accordance with the FN's basic principles and official politics. The mayors' affair raises problems of strategy and identity; first, the ideological rigidity of Le Pen, and the authoritarian manner with which he responds to intraparty dissent, which is explained by reference to the FN's recent willingness to fashion its orthodox political identity. This was clearly stressed by Le Pen when he said that the party "should demonstrate that the FN mayors are different from the other mayors," that is, the FN is not a party like the others. Second, the electoral success of FN municipal leaders was to a large degree a product of their own popularity and local reputations. As they establish themselves, they seek above all to maintain a personal vote at the local level, which is incompatible with the high degree of centralization within the FN.

As in the 1980s, today's changes in party structure correspond to the redefinition of the power relationships between the various FN executive bodies. Since 1995, personal strategies have played a great role in the tensions between the General Delegation and the General Secretariat. Mégret and Dubois (EML) are currently in conflict concerning the control over the development of FN-affiliated associations among the professional sectors. Mégret first challenged Dubois's power by creating a new *coordination des actions catégorielles* (coordination of professionals' actions) within his own structure. At the same time, Mégret, weakened by his defeat in the municipal election in Vitrolles, was the victim of a sustained, and highly personalized, vendetta by his opponents among the fundamentalist Catholics. The latter, who for the most part support Gollnisch, call for the suppression of the General Delegation and protest against Mégret's monopolistic control over FN propaganda policy. In June 1995, the newspaper *Présent* launched its own association (*Présent-Militants*). As a result of these tensions at the highest level of party hierarchy, the FN now faces several resignations by activists throughout the country.

The preceding discussion has led us to stress the role played by Le Pen in maintaining the internal coherence of the FN. It has been argued that Le Pen's overall control allows him to balance the claims of the various tendencies to ensure his own leadership. In reality, however, Le Pen has, since the late 1970s, been able to control the leadership ambitions of rival groups within the FN. His strategy of "divide and rule" has involved taking great care to appoint prominent figures to executive bodies, allowing factional fights to fester and ensuring his ultimate authority at the head of the organization. The leaders of the FN are never appointed to unite the various factions but, to a certain extent, to maximize party in-fighting, now a common feature of contemporary FN life. Over the last ten years, Le Pen's attitudes have evolved according to the specific contexts in which individual battles took place. After the "Mégret vs Stirbois" war in the late 1980s, Le Pen now seems to favor Gollnisch as a counterweight to Mégret's personal influence within the National Executive body.

CONCLUSION

The early 1990s have witnessed the end of what has been called the "Le Pen phenomenon" dynamics, and the emergence of a *National-frontisme*, which refers to the party itself and not just its charismatic leader (Wieviorka, 1995). In the last decade, the FN has succeeded in offering a political outlet to various kinds of sentiments within the French electorate. Le Pen's party has grown and prospered in a way that earlier manifestations of the extreme Right in France—such as the Poujadism in the mid-1950s—did not. There is now a permanent far-Right electorate which is not concerned so much with expressing its disaffection and exasperation toward the established parties, but rather with displaying a stronger identification with and commitment to the FN. In that sense, the FN has partly ceased to exist as a single-issue movement or a protest force, drawing from a wide range of policies and issues other than immigration and security.

In spite of its unprecedented electoral achievement, the FN remains isolated on the far Right of the French political spectrum and doesn't stand a realistic chance to exercise power at the governmental or presidential levels (Perrineau, 1993). The public image of the party is undoubtedly hurt by the identification of the FN with the extreme Right, which remains a source of fear for a majority of the French. Politically, tactical alliances between the FN and the established parties of the Right have come under strain. In 1993 and 1995 the latter achieved electoral success and came to power without needing to ally with Le Pen's party. Given this political isolation, the FN is now confronted with the problem of its role in the forthcoming 1998 legislative election. Although the far-Right leaders claim to have a "majority vocation," debate within the party continues to address the question of which strategy is necessary to avoid being condemned to perpetual opposition. A main area of controversy is whether the party should work to reestablish contacts with the mainstream Right. On this issue, political cultures still shape attitudes and styles of behavior among the FN's prominent figures, leading to intraparty dissent.

A second question for the future is whether the FN will be able to maintain its share of the vote without Le Pen. Although the party did—and still does— largely benefit from the charisma of its chairman, FN should be able to survive the political retirement of Le Pen. On the other hand, however, the party will have to surmount the crisis of finding a successor to its chairman, and to draw up rules of succession which will be legitimate in the eyes of its members. No leader capable of asserting authority over the leadership and appealing to Le Pen's electorate has yet emerged in either group. As mentioned above, the FN puts a high premium on party loyalty but largely remains subject to intense faction fights. The recent evolution within the FN leadership shows that the "war of succession" has already started. The deep-seated rivalry between Mégret and Gollnisch continues to poison relations between the various streams. Both the General Delegate and the General Secretary try to establish themselves as "natural" leaders of the FN. However, a "nationalist compromise" built round Le Pen ensures a minimum of unity within the party. Despite this convergence, the separate identities remain in place. The various ideologies and belief systems within the FN over the last decade have led to the development of party factions and to patterns of competing strategies. Now, in the late 1990s, the FN national leadership is still marked by tensions and conflicts between those who complain about the outdatedness of the party profile and those who seek to conserve its long-standing strategy of intransigence.

Considering the actual power conflicts inside the organization, a period of uncertainty will probably be occasioned by the political retirement of Le Pen. On the other hand, the existence of internal dissidence is counterbalanced by the success of the FN in turning itself into a powerful machine, whose importance should not be underestimated. Since the early 1980s, the party has managed to consolidate its electoral results by setting up an effective organization with established local and national elites, and a growing nationwide network of circles which aim to spread the influence of the FN in all sectors of society. Under the aegis of Lang and Stirbois, Le Pen's movement has carried out a successful program of organizational modernization. The contemporary FN can thus be described as an "institutionalized" party, since it is structured with the aim to exercise power within the political system. This has contributed to an increase in its degree of depersonalization which indubitably constitutes an essential condition for the continuity of the organization, allowing it to outlive the life span of its founder (Charlot and Charlot, 1985).

Finally, one has to stress the impact of the FN on present-day French politics. Since it has managed to open up its own space for political debate and to put its main issues onto the political agenda, Le Pen's party is now part of the French political map. The favorable opportunity-structure afforded by the political system between 1984 and 1986, through proportional representation, has largely benefited the FN by allowing the far Right to win seats in both the European and national parliaments. In the 1980s, the ideas of the FN have been given credence and have thus been allowed to enter the orbit of mainstream political space. The appropriation of FN themes by the conventional Right further confirmed the legitimacy of Le Pen and produced a new political configuration. Between 1986 and 1993, French right-wing parties and governments have been affected by the electoral rise of the FN, and have changed policies in order to claim far-Right credentials for themselves. Although some of the FN's major issues, such as race or law and order, have partly remained outside the mainstream parties' political agenda in the 1995 presidential election, it seems clear that the extreme Right has largely succeeded in projecting its own set of nationalist and xenophobic values onto the French political scene, and has therefore profoundly penetrated the public's consciousness.

NOTES

Special thanks to Edward Welch for his help in the revision of this chapter.

1. The 1995 FN's manifesto stressed this new "majority vocation" of the party and called similarly for *"un septennat Le Pen: soit à l'Elysée, soit pour résister à la tête du mouvement national"* (*Libération*, 14–15 January 1995).

2. For example, 91 departmental secretaries took part in the 1990 Congress (there are 95 departments in metropolitan France).

3. In 1974, the FN's strategy of "multiple memberships" allowed the activists of other far-Right groups—such as the GNR or the FANE—to join the party.

4. French *Solidarisme* was first incarnated by the *Mouvement Jeune Révolution* (MJR), which was a subgroup of the *OAS Métro-Jeunes*. In the early 1970s most of its activists took part in the creation of the *Groupe Action Jeunesse* (GAJ), a violent, ultra-Nationalist organization. In the mid-1970s the GAJ split over the anti-American and anti-Zionist ideology. Those who supported a tough anti-Semitic stance joined Duprat's GNR and formed the *Mouvement nationaliste révolutionnaire* (MNR), whereas Stirbois created the *Union Solidariste* which merged with the National Front in 1977.

5. For example, in 1995, Le Pen adopted a strong anti-abortion position under the pressure of the Catholics.

6. "*Pourquoi se battre pour la préservation des espèces animales et accepter, dans le même temps, le principe de disparition des races humaines par métissage généralisé?*" declared Mégret, showing that he does not shy away from making racist statements.

7. "*Le FN s'est constitué par le sommet, autour d'un homme,*" said Lang in September 1993 (*Libération*, 21 September 1993).

8. Fernand Le Rachinel (Manche), Marie-France Stirbois (Dreux, Eure-et-Loire), Eliane Guillet de la Brosse (Toulon, Var) and Jacques Peyrat (who was elected in a by-election in 1993).

9. In 1978, after the death of fascist leader Duprat, *Le National* (the early FN official newspaper) wrote about the *ennemi apparent avec son mufle hideux*, the *tabous hérités de la Seconde guerre mondiale*, the *lobbies* and their *mensonges nourriciers*. *Présent* regularly emphasises the influence of the *lobbies cosmopolites*. Its director, Madiran, skillfully weaves together anti-Semitic and Nationalist themes, by attacking the *Juifs puissants et agissants . . . que l'on n'a pas empêchés de nuire à la France* (*Le Monde*, 29 May 1990).

10. Apparently, by 1995 party activists had been secretly asked to infiltrate organizations such as *Force Ouvrière* or the communist *Confédération générale du travail* (CGT)(*Libération*, 3 January 1996).

11. Hughes Lambert was a rich elderly who left Le Pen an important fortune in 1976.

12. In reference to the Nazi death camps, Le Pen made a distasteful pun on Michel Durafour, minister in the government, whose name contains the syllable *four*, the French word for *oven* (*Durafour-crématoire*). Bachelot, Arrighi and Yann Piat (the only MP) were thus expelled from the party because of their public criticism of Le Pen and his *calembour inadmissible et odieux* (*Le Monde*, 8 September 1988, and 12 October 1988).

13. The eviction of Piat by the Political Bureau must principally be regarded as a consequence of her deep-seated personal rivalry with Le Pen. Arrighi used defection as a means of protesting against the appointment of Gabriel Domenech (local representative of the Stirbois line) as Federal Secretary in Marseille. Similarly, his failure to control the FN federation in Paris led to frustration on the part of Bachelot, who took the initiative to leave the party, thus avoiding the weakening of his position within the national leadership (Birenbaum, 1992).

14. It seems clear that the appointment of Gollnisch as General Secretary in 1995 is part of this broad strategy.

REFERENCES:

Birenbaum, Guy (1992). *Le Front national en politique.* Paris: Editions Balland.
Buzzi, Paul (1994). "Le Front national entre national-populisme et idéologie d'extrême-droite." *In* Pierre Bréchon (ed)., *Le discours politique en France: Evolution des idées partisanes*, pp. 15–36. Paris: Les Etudes de la Documentation française.
Camus, Jean-Yves (1985). "Les familles de l'extrême-droite." *Projet* 193: 29–38.
Camus, Jean-Yves (1989). "Origine et formation du Front national (1972–1981)." In Nonna Mayer and Pascal Perrineau (eds.), *Le Front national à découvert*, pp. 17–36. Paris: Presses de la FNSP.
Camus, Jean-Yves and Renè Monzat (1992). *Les droites nationales et radicales en France. Répertoire critique.* Lyon: Presses universitaires de Lyon.
Charlot, Monica and Jean Charlot (1985). "Les groupes politiques dans leur environnement." In Jean Leca and Madeleine Grawitz (eds.), *Traité de science politique*, vol: 3. Paris: PUF.
Chebel d'Apollonia, Ariane (1988). *L'extrême-droite en France: de Maurras à Le Pen.* Paris: Editions Complexe.
Mayer, Nonna and Pascal Perrineau (dir.) (1989). *Le Front national à découvert.* Paris: Presses de la Fondation Nationale des Sciences Politiques.
Perrineau, Pascal (1993). "Le Front national, la force solitaire." In *Le vote sanction: les élections législatives des 21 et 28 mars 1993*, pp. 137–160. Paris: Département d'Etudes politiques du Figaro et Presses de la FNSP.
Perrineau, Pascal (1995). "La dynamique du vote Le Pen: le poids du gaucholepénisme." In *Le Vote de Crise: l'élection présidentielle de 1995*, pp. 243–262. Paris: Département d'Etudes politiques du Figaro et Presses de la FNSP.
Rollat, Alain (1985). *Les hommes de l'extrême-droite: Le Pen, Ortiz et les autres.* Paris: Calmann-Lévy.
Taguieff, Pierre-André (1985). "Les droites radicales en France: nationalisme révolutionnaire et national-libéralisme [Réflexions sur les nouveaux espaces de l'autoritarisme en France]." *Les Temps Modernes* 465: 1780–1842.
Taguieff, Pierre-André (1986). "L'identité nationale saisie par les logiques de racisation. Aspects, figures et problèmes du racisme différentialiste." *Mots* 12, Numéro spécial "Droite, nouvelle droite, extrême droite. Discours et idéologie en France et en Italie."
Tristan, Anne (1987). *Au Front.* Paris: Gallimard.
Wieviorka, Michel (1990). "La crise du modèle français d'intégration." *La Documentation française* 161: 3–16.
Wieviorka, Michel (1994). *Racisme et xénophobie en Europe. Une comparaison internationale.* Paris: Editions La Découverte.
Wieviorka, Michel (1995). "Les trois mues du FN." *Libération*, 4 August.
Ysmal, Colette (1989). *Les partis politiques sous la Vème République.* Paris: Montchrestien.

4

The Parti Socialiste: From a Party of Activists to a Party of Government

──────────────────────── *Frédéric Sawicki*

When describing the organization of the *Parti Socialiste* (Socialist Party—PS), political scientists followed two distinct alternatives. The first is to emphasize the permanence of the structures, a permanence that party spokesmen themselves assert by constantly referring to the same label,[1] the same forefathers and the same historical events. The second, in contrast, involves emphasizing change, by drawing parallels between, on the one hand, internal party conflicts and the resulting shift in the balance of power and rules of the game, and, on the other hand, transformations in the political and social environment (Lagroye, 1989). Scholars who defend the thesis of historical continuity in French socialism stress its structural difference with the major northern European Social Democratic parties as well as the British Labor Party. This difference is said to be due to the lack of organic ties with trade unions and the entrenchment of French Socialism in the rural population or among low- and middle-level civil servants (Portelli, 1980; Bergounioux and Grunberg, 1992). The Socialist Party thus appears to be, if not since its origins at least since the creation of the *Parti Communiste Français* (French Communist Party—PCF) in 1920,[2] mainly focused on securing electoral offices, and a party where politicians were as important as activists. According to Bergounioux and Grunberg, the lack of linkage with the working class combined with competition from a strong Communist Party, has caused French socialism to "remain true to its origins, even when the conditions that presided over its formation have changed significantly and when other socialist parties have abandoned their initial goals" (1992: 15). Suffering a deficit of working-class and activist legitimacy, Socialist leaders have been reluctant to abandon a class-based, anti-capitalist discourse and to assume their vocation to exercise power (Sadoun, 1993).

Without denying the relevance of this approach, which is somewhat reminiscent of Panebianco's analysis (1988), we would instead emphasize changes undergone by the PS since its "rebirth" in 1971. Three elements are central: Mitterrand's election as First Secretary; the change in statutes that introduced, in particular, designation of the leadership by proportional representation; the electoral and programmatic alliance with the Communist Party known as *Union de la Gauche* (Union of the Left).[3] The importance of the 1971 watershed must not be overestimated (Rey and Subileau, 1991). Nevertheless, the PS has developed a new party model structured around its members, activists and the organization of diversified networks attempting to extend the party's influence.

Since the beginning of the 1980s, the party has had to face an unprecedented series of transformations, however. In part, these were related to its rise to national power and exercise of it for ten years (1981–1986, then 1988–1993). The institutions of the Fifth Republic, the power conferred to the president, the status reserved to any "president's party," all these factors have combined to weaken the autonomous activity of the party and, as a consequence, the membership and the forms of militantism which had been developed in the 1970s. Changes in Socialist links with the "civil society" were also due to the weakening of those networks on which the party built its influence in the same years, however. Christian Left associations, the "laïque movement"[4] no longer have, due to the evolution of the society, the same importance as they had, and, therefore, are no longer either a reservoir for Socialist recruitment (thereby, increasing the risks of a professionalization of the party) or a channel for spreading the PS program. Change within the PS, including organizational change, cannot be interpreted without consideration not only of the political but also the social environment (Sawicki, 1997).

STRENGTH AND WEAKNESS OF THE EPINAY SOCIALIST PARTY

The Socialist Party: An Aggregation of Tendencies?

The process of PS renewal began well before 1971 and has extended well beyond. As such, the Epinay Congress (11–13 June 1971), presented in retrospect as a critical event, was a new stage in a process of aggregation of various left-wing parties and clubs born in the 1960s. The first step was the *Fédération de la Gauche Démocrate et Socialiste* (Federation of the Democratic and Socialist Left) created just after the 1965 presidential election. The second, which occured in 1969, was the transformation of the SFIO into a new organization named the PS (Hurtig, 1970; Estier, 1970; Loschak, 1971; Pudlowski, 1975; Kesler, 1995). In 1969, the party leadership was largely renewed: 48 percent of the Executive Committee and 69 percent of Executive Board were new members (Schonfeld, 1980). Among the federal cadres there

Table 4.1
Proportion of the PS Tendencies, 1971–1990 (percentages)

Year	CERES*	Poperen	Mitterrand	Mauroy	Rocard	Mollet
1971	8.5	11.9	15.8	28.5	-	33.5
1973	21	5	65	-	-	8
1975	25	-	68	-	-	3
1977	24	-	75	-	-	-
1979	15	-	46	16	20	-
1983	18.1	-	77	-	4.7***	-
1985	-	-	71	-	28.5	-
1990	8.5	7.2	28.9/28.4**	-	24	-

*CERES was renamed *Socialisme et République* in 1985.
**The Mitterrand tendency broke up into Jospin and Mauroy supporters and Fabius's followers.
***Rocard's Tendency Dissidents.
Source: data provided by the PS National Bureau.

was also considerable rejuvenation (Bacot, 1979; Poperen, 1975). The third stage was, in 1971, Mitterrand's and his little party's (*Convention des Institutions Républicaines*—Convention for Republican Institutions—CIR) incorporation into the PS. Even if, in 1969 and 1971, some *Parti socialiste unifié* (Unified Socialist Party—PSU) leaders and followers had joined the party, the PS status as the sole or hegemonic party of the "non-Communist Left" was only achieved in 1974 when Rocard and the majority of PSU activists and members joined.[5]

In 1971, Mitterrand and his backers owed their success to their acceptance of a statutory reform that was to prove of capital importance. Article 5 of the statutes stipulated that "at the local, federal, and national level, proportional representation is applied according to the vote on political motions put to the National Congress." As a result, proportional distribution of leadership positions was introduced at all levels of party organization for any motion that received at least 5 percent of the members' vote. This regulation has recognized and legitimized tendencies within the party; it has also contributed to a sort of "congealing" of balance of power among them. The 5 percent threshold, the requirement that each motion submitted to the Party Conference be accompanied by a list of candidates to the Steering Committee (*Comité directeur*), equal to the total number of seats to be filled and to be backed by at least one member of the incumbent Executive Committee, explain why since 1971 no new tendencies have emerged. The sole exception was the Rocard tendency but it was constituted within the PSU. Alliances to form the internal "dominant coalition" have always been negotiated at the top of the party. They have varied according to circumstances but Mitterrand's tendency remained, untill 1988, the PS central pillar (Table 4.1).

Since affiliation with an organized tendency has become imperative for anyone claiming control over the party, whatever the level (national, federal, local) and for anyone aspiring to an elective office as well, tendencies have become more organized. They made strong efforts to mobilize members and establish their ideological identity through, in particular, an abundant production of programs and doctrines. However, the PS is not a federation of tendencies. First, some federations are not organized around tendencies either because of individual resources of their leaders or due to historical habits pushing toward unanimity. Second, the tendencies differ in their degree and means of organization. Even the CERES, which in the 1970s drew its inspiration from a "Leninist-style" hierarchical and disciplined organizational mechanism, and which developed its own press and training programs, only succeeded to impose its organizational model in a small number of federations (Hanley, 1982, 1986). As far as Rocard's tendency is concerned, it was not actually structured until 1978, when Rocard decided to challenge Mitterrand's presidential leadership. After this attempt failed, it remained dormant from 1980 to 1985. The Mitterrand tendency has always been basically a conglomerate of teams and old notables coming from the CIR or the SFIO and of a new generation of elected officials that gradually conquered cities, cantons and districts throughout the 1970s. Its coherence resides mainly in benefits expected from or granted by Mitterrand's status first as PS First Secretary, then as President of the Republic

Generally speaking, all the tendencies have been fairly indulgent to the ideological loyalty of their supporters, especially when they were party officeholders and/or elective officials, that is when they might be relatively autonomous thanks to their personal resources. Futhermore, the implementation, in 1975, of a centralized system for financing party activities limited the development of peripheral organizations. Lastly, electoral success in the 1970s, largely ascribed to Mitterrand and the strategy he represented, ensured, over affiliation to any tendency, a predominant sense of belonging to a sole party. Therefore, though tendencies play a crucial role in party life, they are not "proto-parties" or "factions."

The Activist Revival

As a result of the Epinay Congress there was an increase in the membership. As shown by Table 4.2, the PS was to double its membership in ten years: from 80,300 in 1971 to 196,501 in 1981 after electoral successes in presidential and parliamentary elections [6]. This development of party members was combined with a territorial redistribution of PS influence. In new towns or neighborhoods, and in traditionally catholic and conservative regions such as Brittany, previously anemic sections or federations considerably developed whereas the old strongholds in the Nord-Pas-de-Calais, the South West and South East regions stagnated and lost the dominant influence

Table 4.2
PS Membership, 1970–1991

Year	Members	Year	Members
1970*	70,400	1981	196,500
1971	80,300	1982	213,600
1972	92,200	1983	203,500
1973	107,800	1984	189,300
1974	137,000	1985	176,900
1975	149,600	1986	177,300
1976	159,500	1987	183,200
1977	160,000	1988	202,100
1978	180,000	1989	204,200
1979	159,000	1990	165,200
1980	189,000	1991	155,000

*Data refers to SFIO members.
Source: data provided by the PS National Bureau.

they had enjoyed within the SFIO. It was in "greater Paris" (10 percent of party members) and the Rhône-Alps region (7 percent), both representative of "modern" France, that the PS's expansion was the strongest (Portelli, 1980: 123). Although the strongholds did not change (Nord, Pas-de-Calais, Bouches-du-Rhône), their relative weight decreased. Moreover, the designation of leaders by proportional representation prevented the old strongholds from controlling the party as they did in the SFIO when alliances between the Pas-de-Calais and Nord federations were enough to determine the party leadership.

The high degree of renewal in membership was accompanied by strong appeals to activism. PS members were asked to participate in the "social movement" issued from the 1968 events (e. g., feminism; housing; teaching). Efforts were made to organize the party in the workplace: in the 1970s, 230 corporate sections and 809 corporate groups were formed (Cayrol, 1978b).[7] Socialist activists could again be seen distributing tracts at factory gates and PS-elected officials again carried banners in demonstrations. PS activists' affiliation with trade unions and voluntary associations was strongly encouraged: according to article 12 of the 1974 statutes, "Party members must belong to a trade union . . . , to a cooperative if there is one where they live and to a consumers' association." A new style of activism has developed as shown by a 1972 survey in a Socialist federation: 44 percent of the members described themselves as "active members"; 57 percent declared they regularly attended party meetings; 25 percent devoted most of their time to putting up posters and distributing tracts, and 45 percent to meetings and individual contacts; last, 40 percent claimed to spend over an hour per week in union activities and 75 percent in voluntary association activities (Lagroye et al., 1976).

Activist legitimacy was restored in contrast with the democratic legitimacy of the elected officials. The SFIO "notable," presented as a readily compromising clientelist boss out of touch with the working class, acted as a foil. Statutes adopted in 1974 (modified in 1975, 1977, 1979, 1982 and 1990) and the 1978 internal chart specified the respective roles of activists and elective officeholders. Members were given critical importance in elaborating the party's manifestos, in fixing political alliances and in nominating leaders at every level of the organization. Article 49 of the statutes specified that, in all electoral districts, candidates are selected by members. Other rules limited the freedom and the powers of elected officials: written engagement from any of them to resign if they left the party; mandatory payment of dues, the amount of which being set by the Congress; subordination of the parliamentary group to the party; discipline of vote for deputies and senators. Furthermore, the creation of the *Fédération Nationale des Elus Socialistes et Républicains* (National Federation of Socialist and Republican Elective Officials) worked both to bring together Socialist elected officeholders or those close to the party and to transmit the party's message and directives through training brochures and sessions. The "internal chart" adopted in 1978 again specified that no party body can be composed of a majority of members of Parliament. This rule has been violated in practice, however. In 1977, it had been decided that their participation in the National Secretariat, Executive Board and Steering Committee should not exceed 20 percent of those bodies' members[8]; in 1978, the threshold was increased to 50 percent since over a third of the members of the governing bodies were deputies or senators.[9] The statutes also limited the leadership role that elected officials could exercise at the local level: Federal First Secretaries were not at the same time to be members of Parliament, presidents of departmental or regional councils; section secretaries were not to be mayors in large cities. Old and powerful federations were long reluctant to enforce these rules. When they were gradually implemented after 1979, they did not prevent elected officials from finding ways to circumvent them by putting their henchmen in key positions.

The renewal of activism must not be exaggerated, however. With less than 200,000 members for over 7.5 million voters on the first ballot of the 1981 presidential election (i.e., 2.5 members for 100 voters), the PS remained well behind other Social Democratic parties where this rate varies between 20 and 30 percent. PS electoral influence was largely due to its elected officials. From 1971 to 1995, 55 federations out of 95 in metropolitan France have had continuously less than 1,000 members; only ten federations regularly exceeded 3,000 members. Efforts to create sections and groups in the work place remained limited since they never had, in the 1970s, really existed outside the public sector (Cayrol, 1978b). Members coming either from workers' unions or from associations did not find their place in a party where the majority of activists were more interested in ideological debates and/or in electoral strategies than in day-to-day problems affecting the working class. With the exception of teachers' unions, links with workers' unions were often either weak or conflictual. The youth and students remained so strange for the party that obstacles were put by the leadership in the way of a possible development of the *Jeunesses Socialistes* (Movement of Young Socialists— MJS).[10] In 1975, Mitterrand decided that the MJS could have no autonomy vis-à-vis the party. It became a simple sector of activity with no permanent staff or headquarters, and is now entirely supervised by party leaders. Even if the PS is relatively bureaucratized, it is still far from matching the archetype of a mass party (Duverger, 1951).

The Mitterrand Leadership

Many of such organizational traits were, in fact, linked to the social composition of the party or to the domination of "intellectuals" (teachers; high civil servants) as well as to a political culture more Republican than properly Social democratic, for not making reference to Marxism.[11] The domination at all party levels of leaders with intellectual resources was reinforced by the absence of any real training policy or affirmative policies of promoting less-educated activists. Meager funds and a small national staff—some 100 people worked at party headquarters in the mid-1970s and 150 at the end of the 1980s—alone do not explain the lack of training sessions similar to the Communist model. Mitterrand's personality combined with his fear that party sectors devoted to actions in the workplace or to training might fall under the control of the party's Left led him to rely on local elected officials, his old companions and experts recruited among high-level civil servants, rather than on PS activists. Mitterrand's triple authority, as the "First of the Socialists," the acknowledged negotiator with the Communist Party and moreover the party's candidate to the presidency, enabled him to impose a presidential style of government.

Therefore, he could import to the PS the leadership style he had developed within the CIR. In the 1970s, the large staff he hired had, in many cases, no positions in the PS. The "experts committee" and specialized commissions (100 in mid-1970s, according to Cayrol (1978a)) he settled did not exist in party statutes; the party could not control their recruitment or their political orientations (Dagnaud and Mehl 1982). Although they had no formal decision-making power, they contributed largely to elaborating the 1981 Mitterrand program and the first Socialist government's projects; they also served as recruiting grounds for ministers or ministers' staffs (cabinets) as well.[12] A strict division of tasks and a low degree of collegial administration characterized Mitterrand's staff as leader of the PS: by preferring to listen separately to the opinions of each of his advisors, he managed to maintain total control over decision-making circuits and to create relationships with his collaborators that were as effective as they were functional.

His leadership was not "monocratic," however (Schonfeld, 1980). First, Mitterrand's power was based on a large network of local elected officials to whom he granted a large degree of freedom in local party organization, electoral alliances and ideological orientations. Even reluctance to left-wing unity, a central facet of Mitterrand's image, was tolerated within limits. Thus, whereas he had threatened to expel any incumbent mayors not having implemented alliances with the PCF in the 1977 municipal elections, united leftist lists were formed in only 52 percent of large cities (with 9,000 inhabitants and over) and none of the reluctants were sanctioned (Lacorne, 1980). Similarly, Mitterrand was always careful to limit national party leaders' parachuting into electoral districts against the advice of federations and sections. Second, as free as his personnal staff was from the party, Mitterrand's leadership was always limited by the party's ability to change the leader himself or to contest his power. Tendencies might back Mitterrand or not. Party conferences were, in fact, conflictual and unanimity was not the rule.

TRANSFORMATION OF INTERESTS, POSITIONS AND ASSETS IN THE PS AFTER 1981: FROM A MILITANT PARTY TO A PARTY OF PROFESSIONAL POLITICIANS

In the late 1970s, both memberhip renewal and activist revival appeared relatively limited. The formation of both local and national leadership remained under the "notables' " control. The national leadership worked as a presidential team not really interested in developing the party's strength when it did not attempt to impede the party's development. Generally speaking, the PS was already prepared for the changes which occurred in the 1980s or the early 1990s: the move to a "government party"; the drying up of recruitment channels and the move to a professionalization of party elites.

A Government Party

Access to government, at least at the local level, was experienced in the late 1970s when the party won many mayorships, gained positions in cities ruled by the Communist Party (thanks to the Union of the Left) and increased its influence in departmental and regional councils.[13] The PS thus became a "government party" in the broad sense of the term, because internal power struggles, particularly for party and elected positions, took on increasing importance. In many cases, local party sections came under the control of elected officials who could neutralize possible internal opposition or rivalry. Even in cases where young mayors attempted to implement a new style of relationship between City Hall and Socialist sections, the latter were, more or less quickly, used at the sole benefit of those in office (Dion, 1986). Well before the 1981 victory, many enthusiastic activists became "notables." The lack, at section or federation level, of a strong party organization gave the local notables more autonomy vis-à-vis party rules. Access to party positions, in particular, was no longer decided upon the basis of the balance among tendencies.

This trend was accentuated with Mitterrand's election to the presidency in 1981 and with the PS victory in the June 1981 general elections. The Socialist group suddenly increased from 113 (in 1978) to 265 deputies. Only a small minority were already solidly established locally.[14] Consequently, to ensure their political future, most of them devoted more time to consolidating their electoral positions and to gaining mandates at the local level than to party activities. The election to the National Assembly of 20 percent of incumbent Federal First Secretaries contributed to the weakening of the party, particularly in areas where the PS was not well established and where few trained candidates were interested in occupying this relatively thankless office.

The party "devitalization" was even more striking in the national governing bodies whose members were literally sucked into ministries and ministers' staffs. Not only did party ex-numbers one and two (Mitterrand and Mauroy) became President and Prime Minister, but all the influential leaders were granted portfolios in the government or occupied offices within the Parliament. Forty percent of the Executive Board members elected in 1979 had to quit their offices within the party where Jospin, made responsible for perpetuating Mitterrand's legacy, organized a new leadership.

The renewal of the party elite was less important than in 1979 when Rocard's failed attempt to unseat Mitterrand led the latter to promote a new generation of elites (75 percent of newly elected to the National Secretariat and 55 percent to the Executive Board). As shown by Table 4.3, "new members" were only 50 percent and 44 percent, respectively. Moreover, the percentage of "freshmen" who were not former members of executive bodies (called "first-time members" in Table 4.3) is particularly low (25 percent for the Secretariat and 30 percent for the Executive Board). In the 1980s, the PS's national elite was particularly stable. The apparent 1987 turnover of "new" members was due to the return of deputies and ministers defeated in the 1986 general elections as indicated by the figures of first-time members.

Such a low degree of real renewal was a consequence of the continuous control over the party by Mitterrand via Jospin. As president of the Republic, Mitterrand favored party leadership subordinated to him. No party leaders could oppose a party or electoral legitimacy. The party had, on an other hand, no programmatic initiative. In 1987, only when the party had returned to opposition and on the eve of the 1988 presidential election, experts' committees and specialized commissions were reinstalled.

Relations between the parliamentary group, the party and the Mitterrand's cabinet, all three controlled by the president's loyal followers or the president himself, were uneven. From 1981 to 1986, meetings between both Mitterrand

Table 4.3
Turnover of the PS Executive Bodies, 1973–1990 (percentages)*

Year	National new members (%)	Secretariat first time members (%)	Executive new members (%)	Board first time members (%)
1971	46.6	46.6	37.0	33.3
1974	18.7	18.7	7.4	7.4
1979	75.0	68.7	55.5	51.8
1981	50.0	25.0	44.4	29.6
1983	31.2	25.0	29.6	25.9
1985	33.3	33.3	22.2	7.4
1987	56.2	25.0	37.0	11.1
1990	75.0	56.2	55.5	48.1

*Deputy Secretaries and substitute members not included.
First column (new members) refers to all those who had not served in the immediately preceding NEC. The second column includes members with no previous experience in whatever NEC.
Source: computed by the author on data provided by the PS National Bureau.

and the party leadership and between the president and subleaders of his tendency sought to ensure the party and the deputies' loyalty. As pointed out by Portelli (1992: 114), those meetings were "mainly a means in Mitterrand's hands for an apparent bargaining power when the Elysée's control over the principal governing bodies of the State was total."

As a consequence, the rare expressions of public dissatisfaction with the government's policies came from the parliamentary group, without any success, however. Organized protest within the party received low support: at the 1983 Party Conference, the Chevènement's motion against the economic policies of austerity received 18 percent of the delegates' vote. Neither the departure of the Communists from the government in 1984 nor the withdrawal of some symbolic Socialist issues were discussed within the party. Significantly, the most important conflict between the government and the party arose in 1985, around an apparently secondary issue: should the Prime Minister or the PS First Secretary organize the electoral campaign for the 1986 parliamentary election? By claiming this responsibility, the leadership attempted to challenge the party's last remaining area of power: recruiting candidates and conducting electoral campaigns.

A Party of Professional Politicians

The multiplication of positions the PS had to offer, directly or indirectly, changed the party profile. On the local level, along with the increase in elected offices (mayorships; urban districts, departmental and regional councils), was the development of advisors and representatives in numerous public and semi-public bodies (e.g., housing offices, town planning offices, boards of associations linked to city halls) and in firms contracted by local governments. On the national level, the French administrative organization offers for those who control the government many positions including those available through co-optation or by appointment of *de jure* members in the High Administration, consultative bodies and state-owned companies. The number of the latter increased dramatically in the early 1980s with the process of "nationalizations" initiated by the Socialist government. Therefore, activist and ideological resources lost much of their importance. Activists were no longer "useful" in party life. First, they were discredited through the increasing use of municipal employees and professional public relations agencies for campaigning. Second, they were marginalized by elected officials in their statutory power over both candidate recruitment and Socialist policy elaboration.

Dissatisfaction with the PS organization was unlikely to arise since the networks on which it had built its influence in the 1970s were also in crisis. First, there was a change in recruiting teachers and in teaching unions which reduces the influence of traditional channels of PS recruitment. In 1973, 15 percent of the PS members were teachers (Hardouin, 1978) but they were only 9 percent in 1990 (IFOP, 1991). Among the conferences delegates, their proportion varied from 36 percent in the 1970s to 21 percent in the 1990s (Perrineau, 1991). As far as the catholic left circles are concerned, they were weakened by the general movement of de-Christianization. Catholic youth movements, Third World associations, environmental groups, from which a great many PS members came, introducing new concerns and new methods to the Left, have not yet really been replaced. Significantly, new PS leaders in the 1980s and the 1990s came either from the High Administration or from Trotskyist parties or anti-racist associations. Those two channels of recruitment did not have the same social influence, however. Last, the PS has also been affected by changes in sociocultural associations (e.g., youth clubs, neighborhood associations, movements for popular education, community educational projects, community centers) which had provided many PS activists in the 1970s. Very successful, these associations became used by local government for public policies (Balme, 1989). Therefore they moved into virtual enterprises with sizable budgets and management constraints requiring special skills. They gradually called on professional staffs rather than on volunteer activists. Conflicts arose between associations' executives and volunteers who felt excluded and denounced the new direction, due, according to them, to the politicians' grip on the associations.

The stability, or even slight increase in PS membership in the 1980s masks, in fact, a large transformation of the party which had turned into a party of politicians and managers. The percentage of professional politicians, that is, those who "live mainly from politics," is difficult to assess. The figures usually given, 40,000 elected officials and their 20,000 direct collaborators, seem to attest that the PS has been transformed into an electoral machine. Such a hypothesis is confirmed by the fact that a large majority of members are little involved in associations or trade unions. According to an IFOP survey, in the 1990s, 40 percent of party members belonged to no association and 52 percent to no trade union, contrary to what is required by the statutes.[15] This phenomenon seems to be linked to the departure of many trade unions and voluntary associations activists, replaced by new members less involved in social movements. According to the same survey, 44 percent of PS members joined after 1981, which represents approximately 90,000 new recruits. However, during the same time period, total membership remained virtually stable (+7,600). Assuming that few of the newcomers had been PS members before, one can estimate that 40 percent of those who were party members in 1981 had quit by 1990.

This change in membership did not lead to a rejuvenation of the members nor to a renewal of party elites. Bergounioux and Grunberg (1993) reported that in 1990, no more than 31 percent of members were under 40 years old; they were 37 percent in 1973 (Hardouin, 1978). The same trend is found among national Congress delegates: in 1973, 58 percent were under 40 years old compared to 33 percent in 1990 (Perrineau, 1991). New members are excluded from party positions and elected offices. Our own research into three PS federations shows, for instance, that in none of them does the percentage of leaders and officeholders who joined after 1981 exceed 5 percent (Sawicki, 1997). The same occurred at the highest levels of PS leadership. Very few new leaders have emerged in 1981–1990. From 1973 to 1990, 90 people sat either on the Executive Board or the National Secretariat: 37 (41.1 percent) were in place for only two years; at the other extreme, 18 (20 percent) had been in office for at least ten years [16]. These data (see also Table 4.3) do not qualify the PS as an "oligarchic" party, however; they indicate the party's inability to have a united and coherent leadership, independent from both the government and the parliamentary group. It would seem that involvement in the executive and parliamentary arena, as well as in local government, appealed much more to the majority of Socialist middle-level elites and elected officials than does involvement in the party. This was the case, at least until Jospin left his position as First Secretary and the question of Mitterrand's succession after 1988 whetted appetites once again!

The weakening of the party and its social base can also be measured by members' participation in party activities. The adoption of the "one vote=one mandate" rule in 1990[17] provides some indication of the actual degree of mobilization within the party. When, in December 1991, debates were organized on the Socialist "Program for the Year 2000," voters were estimated at 60,000, that is, less than one in two members. Membership decreased in the 1990s: 165,186 in 1990, 155,000 in 1991 and 103,000 in late

1993, following the PS's collapse in general elections. Members' dues only represented 10 percent of the party budget in 1992, or 20 million francs out of a total budget of 203 million.

Instrumentalization of the Tendencies and Return to a Territorial Logic

As a logical consequence of all these changes, new interests and new constraints appeared. The increasing importance of "power issues" (local and national government and party leadership as well) blurred, if not destroyed, former loyalties, and made the reasons for affiliation with various tendencies more complex. The evolution of the Mitterrand tendency since 1981 has been particularly significant. As the threat from the Rocardian "right" and Chevènementist "left"—both strong factors of Mitterrandists' homogeneity—slowly vanished, the tendency first changed, then split up in 1990. Given its inability to unite durably elected officials involved in territorial battles of influence and leaders divided by their unequal access to state resources, the former Mitterrand movement split into Fabius's backers and Jospin's supporters. Fabius, due to his relationship with Mitterrand and his ties with the high-level civil service and state enterprises, mobilized most of the influential ministers and parliamentary members as well as young mayors and departmental councillors, all of whom were interested in control over the party at the national and/or local level; Jospin, First Secretary in 1981–1888, received support from all those who had not benefited from a ministerial or electoral promotion when they felt they had made great sacrifices for the party.

Despite the absence of ideological or sociological cleavage dividing Fabius followers from the Jospin-Mauroy tendency, the debates, before the 1990 Rennes Congress, reached a degree of vehemence unequaled since the Metz Congress in 1979 when Mitterrand and Rocard fought for the presidential nomination. In fact, internal issues had become preponderant, if not vital, for most of the delegates present. In early 1990, several factors contributed to exacerbating party issues. First, tensions emerged between well-established local officials and the party's national and federal executive bodies over the role of national leadership over selection and electoral alliances. The ambitions of the newcomers to play a greater role in the party's governing bodies clashed with the monopolization of these positions by the generation that rose to power in the 1970s. Since most of the party's local and national leaders who were promoted in the 1970s were between 30 and 40 years old, the process of internal party mobility was slowed. This was resented all the more since the electoral influence of the PS continued to decline. Second, the appointment to government, after 1988, of Centrist leaders, personalities coming from the "civil society" and of "experts" who had previously served in Mitterrand's staffs in the Elysée limited the number of available ministries for the PS and the party leadership influence as a channel of recruitment for offices in government. In the Cresson (1991–1992) and Bérégovoy (1992–1993) governments, seven ministers were former members of Mitterrand's cabinet during his first term and all the key posts (e.g., Foreign Affairs, Defense) were held by the president's long-term political allies. None of the large cities' Socialist mayors elected or reelected in 1989 entered the government in the 1988–1993 period. Relations between the party leadership and the Elysée went from bad to worse. Third, Mitterrand's succession was now open. Mitterrand clearly chose to back Fabius in his diverse and unsuccessful attempts to win the PS leadership. Such a strategy led to the making of an unstable "anti-Fabius" coalition composed of former backers of Mitterrand exasperated by this "latecomer," national party cadres with often lower socioeconomic backgrounds and Rocardians interested in preserving their leader's opportunity to be the PS candidate for the 1995 presidential election.[18]

The traditional tendencies fell apart. Important was the split within the CERES (*Socialisme et République* since 1985), a part of which left the PS in 1993. In turn, a new leftist tendency tried to organize around former Trotskyist and/or anti-racist activists: it did not have any influence, however, except in a few federations. Without forming a tendency, Delors's followers organized activities outside the party by creating clubs to support first his candidacy for the 1995 presidential election; and second, after Delors's refusal to be the Socialist candidate, to elaborate social and economic proposals. Generally speaking, new leaders appeared with low party skills.

CONCLUSION

In the early 1990s, the PS was not the party it had been in the 1970s. Access to government as well as changes in reservoir of recruitment converted the PS away from emphasizing, even if only symbolically so, membership, party activism, involvement in unions and associations, control over the leadership (at all levels) by the membership. As a "government party," the PS tended to become a party where the presidency and national and local government became such important issues that activists were marginalized. After 1988, party life was structured around Mitterrand's relations with the party and internal conflicts among national leadership, national subleaders and local party officeholders as well as national and local elected officials raised to control Mitterrand's succession. Membership dramatically decreased (Table 4.1) along with the PS's ability to avoid the development of parties' competing with it as the left-wing "dominant party" in the political system.[19] Changes in the statutes including direct election of all candidates for party offices, including the presidency, by the members were internal reforms that cannot resolve all the problems the PS has to face in the late 1990s: the drying up of its activist network; the professionalization of its elites as well as internal conflicts.

NOTES

1. "Parti Socialiste" has been the name generally used for the *Section Française de l'International Ouvrière*, French Section of the Workers' Internationale (SFIO) since its creation in 1905.

2. The creation of the PCF did sever the links of the SFIO with the largest workers' union, the *Confédération générale du Travail*, General Confederation of Workers (CGT).

3. The Union of the Left also included a fraction of the former Radical Party which split to form the MRG (*Mouvement des Radicaux de Gauche*, Leftist Radicals). This union led to the signature, in 1972, of a Common Government Program. It was denounced by the Communist Party just a few months before the March 1978 parliamentary election. In practice, for both municipal and parliamentary elections, the Socialists and the Communists have practiced "Republican discipline," in other words, withdrawal in favor of the left-wing candidate leading the race on the first ballot as well as joint management of local institutions.

4. Behind the expression "laïque movement" one can refer to a nebula made up of public sectors of Education: *Fédération de l'Education Nationale* (FEN) activists, particularly its main union, the *Syndicat National des Institutueurs et des Professeurs de Collège* (SNI-PEGC) for teachers, those of the *Fédération de Conseils de Parents d'Elèves* (FCPE) for parents; circles united nationally into the *Ligue de l'Enseignement.* It includes also associations devoted to popular education or Freemasons belonging to the *Grand Orient de France* (GOF). This nebula is characterized by plurality of positions of the activists in various organizations. Although no organic or exclusive ties link these activists with the Socialist Party, a significant percentage of these organizations' national and local leaders are nevertheless close to, or members of, the PS (Aubert et al., 1985)

5. For more details, see Ysmal in this book, Chapter 1.

6. These figures must be corrected in two directions, however. First, the figure that indicates that PS membership was 80,000 in 1971 was an agreement between the SFIO and Mitterrand establishing together a balance of members: 70,000 for the SFIO; 12,000 for the CIR. The actual membership in 1971 was lower: 50,000 members according Ysmal (1989); second, a great many SFIO members left the PS due to the alliance with the Communist Party . Therefore, one can guess that the evolution and the renewal of the PS membership was more important than indicated in Table 4.2.

7. The corporate section is directly linked to a departmental federation and has deliberation powers and the right to vote. The corporate group is a simple meeting level for activists belonging to the same company. They remain members of a local section.

8. The National Secretariat and the Executive Board (National Board since 1990) form the party's executive bodies. The Executive Board "handles Party administration and management" (Article 40 of the statutes). It is made up of 27 permanent members and the same number of substitutes and is elected by the Steering Committee (131 members until 1990) by proportional representation of the tendencies. Within the

Secretariat, there are only representatives of the "dominant coalition." It is generally made up of sixteen members—including the First Secretary—to which can be added a variable number of deputy secretaries.

9. The percentage was even as high as 48 percent in the Executive Board. After the 1981 legislative elections, the 50 percent limit was passed in the National Secretariat which then had as many as 13 members of Parliament out of its 15 members, as opposed to 6 out of 15 in 1979 (Hamon, 1986: 93).

10. The MJS membership was only 10,000. The PS leadership controlled the membership to avoid "Leftist" orientations developing as they had within the German Socialist Party with the Jusos.

11. The literature concerning the social bases of the PS is abundant. See in particular, Garraud (1989), Rey and Subileau (1991), Sawicki (1997). As far as the political orientations of Socialist members are concerned, see Portelli (1980) and Rey and Subileau.

12. 42 percent of Mitterrand's staff and experts in commissions became members of ministerial cabinets and some important ministers had belonged to these structures even if, before 1981, they received formal party legitimacy via, under Mitterrand's umbrella, brief election to the PS governing bodies.

13. In 1977, 81 (out of 241) cities with 30,000 inhabitants and over had a Socialist mayor; Socalists were deputy-mayors in the 72 large cities ruled by the PCF. Department councillors went from 424 in 1973 to 558 in 1979 and the PS controlled 30 departments (out of 95). It also ruled 7 out of the 22 regions in Metropolitan France.

14. Among those elected in 1981, 48 percent were already mayors and 43 percent departmental councillors, but these figures were only 40 and 41.5 percent, respectively, among those newly elected. Twenty-one percent of new Socialist deputies had no local mandates (Collovald, 1985 : 32).

15. Survey realized by IFOP for the daily newspaper *Libération* (March 14, 1990).

16. Twelve (13.3 percent) were in office for four years, 16 (17.7 percent) for six years and seven (7.7 percent) for eight years.

17. Until then, for the party Congress, sections had one mandate for 25 members who had paid their dues, as long as at least a quarter of them had actually voted; voting by proxy was not allowed (articles 16 and 17 of the statutes).

18. He is perceived as overprivileged thanks to his bourgeois and Parisian social origins as well as to his education—he was a graduate of both *"grandes écoles"* (the Ecole Normale and the *Ecole Normale d'Administration (ENA)*)—he is a member of the High Administration (*Conseil d'Etat*). He appears also less as a party activist than a "careerist" whose party positions were due to Mitterrand's fatherly protection.

19. In the 1993 general elections, the ecologists won 7. 8 percent of the vote (19 percent for the PS); in the 1994 European elections, the PS list gained only 14 percent of the vote when a Leftist radicals list won 12 percent of the vote cast.

REFERENCES

Aubert, Veronique et al. (1985). *La fortresse enseignante. La Federation de l'éducation nationale.* Paris: Fayard.

Bacot, Paul (1979). *Les dirigeants du parti socialiste.* Lyon: Presses Universitaires de Lyon.

Bailey, Frederick G. (1969). *Stratagems and Spoils: A Social Anthropology of Politics*. Oxford: Basil Blackwell.

Balme, Richard (1989). "L'Association dans la Promotion du Pouvoir Municipal." In Albert Mabileau and Claude Sorbets (eds.), *Gouverner les Villes Moyennes*, pp. 81–107. Paris: Pedone.

Bell, David S. and Byron Criddle (1984). *The French Socialist Party: Resurgence and Victory*. Oxford: Clarendon Press.

Bergounioux, Alain and Bernard (1979). *La Social-Démocratie ou le Compromis*. Paris: PUF.

Bergounioux, Alain and Gérard Grunberg (1992). *Le Long Remords du Pouvoir. Le Parti Socialiste Français 1905–1992*. Paris: Fayard.

Cayrol, Roland (1978a). "La Direction du Parti Socialiste." *Revue Française de Science Politique* 28: 201–219.

Cayrol, Roland (1978b). "Le Ps à l'Enterprise." *Revue Française de Science Politique* 28: 296–312.

Cole, Alistair M. (1989). "Factionalism. The French Socialist Party and the Fifth Republic: An Explanation of Intra-Party Divisions." *European Journal of Political Research* 17: 77–94.

Collovald, Annie (1985). "La République du Militant. Recrutement et Filières de la Carrière Politique des Députès Socialistes en 1981." In Pierre Birnbaum (ed.), *Les Elites Socialistes au Pouvoir, 1981–1985*, pp. 11–52. Paris: PUF.

Dagnaud, Monique and Dominique Mehl (1982). *L'Elite Rose. Sociologie du Pouvoir Socialiste*. Paris: Ramsay.

Derville, Jaques (1976). "La Fédération Socialiste de l'Isère depuis 1969. Contribution à l'Etude de l'Evolution du Parti Socialiste." *Revue Française de Science Politique* 26: 558–99.

Dion, Stéphane (1986). *La Politisation des Mairies*. Paris: Economica.

Duverger, Maurice (1951). *Les Partis Politiques*. Paris: A. Colin.

Estier, Claude (1970). *Journal d'un Fédéré. La Fédération de la Gauche au Jour le Jour: 1965–1969*. Paris: Fayard.

Feretti, Raymond (1975). "Le Militants de la Fédération du Ba-Rhin du PS." *Nouvelle Revue Socialiste* 14: 8–15.

Garraud, Philippe (1989). *Profession: Homme Politique. La Carrière Politique des Maires Urbains*. Paris: l'Harmattan.

Guidoni, Pierre (1973). *Histoire du Nouveau Parti Socialiste*. Paris: Tema.

Hamon, Philippe (1986). *Le Groupe Parlementaire Socialiste à l'Assemblée Nationale de 1973 à 1981*, Thèse de troisième cycle de science politique, Université Paris I.

Hanley, David (1982). "The Ceres in two Départements—Political Compromise on Aude and Ille-et-Vilaine." In David Bell (ed.), *Contemporary French Political Parties*, pp. 123–137. London: Croom Helm.

Hanley, David (1986). *Keeping Left? Ceres and the French Socialist Party. A Contribution to the Study of Fractionalism in Political Parties*. Manchester: Manchester University Press.

Hardouin, Philippe (1978). "Les Caractéristiqus Sociologiques du Parti Socialiste." *Revue Française de Science Politique* 28: 220–256.

Hurtig, Christiane (1970). *De la Sfio au Nouveau Parti Socialiste*. Paris: Armand Colin.

IFOP (1990). *Les Militants du Parti Socialiste*. Sondage IFOP-Libération, Etude: 1.134.

Kesler, Jean-François (1990). *De la Gauche Dissidente au Nouveau Parti Socialiste. Les Minorités qui ont Rénové le PS*. Toulouse: Privat.

Lacorne, Denis (1980). *Les Notables Rouges. La Construction Municipale ae L'union de la Gauche*. Paris: Presses de la FNSP.

Lagroye, Jaques (1989). "Change and Permanence in Political Parties." *Political Studies* 37: 362–375.

Lagroye, Jaques, Guy Lord, Lise Mounier-Chazel and Jaques Palard (1976). *Les Militants Politiques dans Trois Partis Français (PC, PS, UDR)*. Paris: Pedone.

Loschak, Danièle (1971). *La Convention des Institutions Républicanes: François Mitterand et le Socialisme*. Paris: PUF.

L'Ours Cahier et Revue (1991). *Juin 1971. Le Congrès d'Epinay. Extraits des Débats du Congrès*, n° 199, mai-juin.

Montcourtois, Florence (1992). *Le Mouvements des Jeunes Socialistes*. Mèmoire de DEA de Science Politique, Université de Paris I.

Panebianco, Angelo (1988). *Political Parties. Organization and Power*. Cambridge: Cambridge University Press.

Perrineau, Pascal (1991). "Les Cadres du Parti Socialiste: la Fin du Parti d'Epinay." In Olivier Duhamel and Jérome Jaffre (eds.), *Sofres. L'Etat de Opinion 1991*. Paris: Le Seuil.

Poperen, Jean (1975). *L'Unité de la Gauche. 1965. 1973*. Paris: PUF.

Portelli, Hugues (1980). *Le Socialisme Français tel qu'il est*. Paris: PUF.

Portelli, Hugues (1985). "Le Proportionelle et les Partis. Etude de Cas." *Pouvoirs* 32: 83–94.

Portelli, Hugues (1992). *Le Parti Socialiste*. Paris: Montchrestien, coll.Clefs.

Pudlowski, Gilles (1975). *Jean Poperen et l'UGCS*. Paris: Editions Saint-Germain-des Prés.

Rey Henri and Françoise Subileau (1991). *Les Militants Socialistes à l'Epreuve du Poivoir*. Paris: Presses de la FNSP.

Sadoun, Marc (1993). *De la Démocratie Française: Essai sur le Socialisme*. Paris: Gallimard.

Sawicki, Frédéric (1994). "Configuration Sociale et Genèse d'un Milieu Partisan. Le Cas du Parti Socialiste en Ille-et-Vilaine." *Sociétés Contemporaines* 20: 83–110.

Sawicki, Frédéric (1997). *Le Rescau du Parti Socialiste. Sociologie du Milieu Partisan*. Paris: Belin.

Sawicki, Frédéric (1994). "Laurent Fabius: du Giscard de Gauche' au "Socialiste Moderne." *Pole Sud*, n° 1.

Schonfeld, William R. (1980). "La stabilité des Dirigeants des Partis Politiques: le Personnel des Directions Nationales du Parti Socialiste et du Mouvement Gaulliste." *Revue Française de Science Politique* 30: 477–505.

Schonfeld, William R. (1985). *Ethnographie du PS et du RPR: les éléphants et l'Aveugle*. Paris: Economica.

Ysmal, Colette (1989). *Les Parties Politiques sous la V République*. Paris: Montchrestien.

Part II

Italy

5

The Italian Party System: The Effective Magnitude of an Earthquake

─────── *Luciano Bardi and Piero Ignazi*

INTRODUCTION

The Italian party system has undergone a rather dramatic transformation in recent years. The change has been quite abrupt because, up to the late 1980s and early 1990s, the party system exhibited a remarkable stability in terms of number and relative size of the political actors (i.e., relevant political parties); direction of political competition; and format and dynamics of the relationship between government and opposition. In fact, contrary to a widely shared common wisdom, the Italian party system was not *unstable*; and, even more paradoxically, also the government was not *unstable*, as we will try to demonstrate, stressing the distinction between cabinet survival and government composition. This interpretation of prevailing stability of the Italian party system is in contrast with the magnitude of change that has occurred in the last few years. All the parameters of stability collapsed starting from the early 1990s: number and size of parties radically changed, the government/opposition relationship became conflictual rather than bargain-oriented and the format of the government was totally reverted.

The first section will deal with the "setting," the basic elements of the party system until the great transformation; the second will focus on the elements which introduced the change; the third will describe the new features of the party system.

THE STABILITY OF THE SYSTEM UP TO THE 1990s

The first legislative parliament, elected in 1948 (the first general election, in June 1946, concerned the two-year-term constitutional assembly), presented some traits which moulded the system up to recent times.

Since the recovery of democracy, Italy has exhibited a highly fragmented party system, with at least eight, but often more, national parties represented in Parliament at any given time (Table 5.1). This came as a natural consequence of the proportionality of its electoral systems at all levels. *Only four parties*, however, had consistently relevant electoral support: the *Democrazia Cristiana*—Christian Democracy (DC), the system's dominant party since 1948; the *Partito Comunista Italiano*—Italian Communist Party (PCI), the strongest opposition party; the *Partito Socialista Italiano*—Italian Socialist Party (PSI); and the neofascist *Movimento Sociale Italiano*—Italian Social Movement (MSI); all the other parties usually obtained less than 5 percent of the vote.

More specifically, the dominant party, the DC, with 35–40 percent of the vote, was representative of the Catholic "component of the Italian society" and of the moderate, bourgeois, pro-American and anti-Communist electorate. Second, there was a strong Communist Party, collecting regularly around 25 percent of votes and capable of attracting students and educated voters as well as lower-income voters. Third, there was a Socialist Party, highly factionalized, medium-sized (ranging betweeen 10 and 15 percent of the votes) and subordinated to the PCI up to the late 1950s. Fourth, a sizeable nondemocratic Right, composed of monarchists (up to the 1960s) and neofascists that, even if highly marginalized, was able to attract, especially in the southern regions, relevant popular consents. Finally, the last feature of the Italian party system concerned a set of minor pro-government parties: the *Partito Repubblicano Italiano*—Italian Republican Party (PRI), the *Partito Liberale Italiano*—Italian Liberal party (PLI) and the *Partito Socialista Democratico Italiano*—Italian Social Democratic party (PSDI) (a splinter faction of the PSI) appealing to nonconfessional, non-Communist voters, heirs to the Risorgimento tradition.

The *format of the party system*, based on eight parties, maintained itself with minor variations up to the late 1980s. These regarded: (a) the Socialist family which experienced a series of splits, attempts at reunification and further splits; (b) the neofascists which absorbed the monarchists in 1972; (c) the rise of very minor New Left/Ecologist/Left-Libertarian parties (*Democrazia Proletaria*, Proletarian Democracy (DP), *Partito Radicale*, Radical Party (PR) and *I Verdi*, The Greens) which obtained some (few) seats starting from 1976. These newcomers, however, never played any significant role in the parliamentary arena (except, in some particular circumstances, the PR, thanks to its ability to raise new political issues in a provocative style). Therefore, in terms of party actors the Italian system proved to be amazingly stable as only one party (the monarchist) had completely disappeared, and the newcomers that appeared in the mid-1970s did not gather all together more than 5 percent of the votes, with the exception of the 1987 elections when they obtained 6.8 percent of the votes.

Furthermore, the *stability of the party system* appears quite remarkable

Table. 5.1
Percentage of Votes in the Chamber of Deputies, 1946–1996 (1994 and 1996 PR ballot votes)

PARTY	1946	1948	1953	1958	1963	1968	1972	1976	1979	1983	1987	1992	1994	1996
Extr. Left[1]						4.4	1.9	1.5	1.4	1.5	1.7			
RC												5.6	6.0	8.6
PCI-PDS[ii]	18.9	31.0	22.6	22.7	25.3	26.9	27.2	34.4	30.4	29.9	26.6	16.1	20.4	21.1
Greens											2.5	3.0	2.7	2.5
La Rete												1.9	1.9	
PR[iii]												1.2	3.5	1.9
PSI-SI[iv]	20.7		12.7	14.2	13.8	14.5	9.6	9.6	9.8	11.4	14.3	13.6	2.2	
PSDI[v]		7.1	4.5	4.6	6.1		5.1	3.4	3.8	4.1	2.9	2.7		
PRI	4.4	2.5	1.6	1.4	1.4	2.0	2.9	3.1	3.0	5.1	3.7	4.4		
DC-PPI	35.2	48.5	40.1	42.3	38.3	39.1	38.7	38.7	38.3	32.9	34.3	29.7	11.1	6.8
Italy's Pact													4.6	
Dini's List														4.3
CCD-CDU														5.8
PLI[vi]	6.8	3.8	3.0	3.5	7.0	5.8	3.9	1.3	1.9	2.9	2.1	2.8		
Monarchist	2.8	2.8	6.8	2.2	1.7	1.3								
North Leag.											0.5	8.7	8.6	10.1
Forza Italia													21.0	20.6
MSI-AN		2.0	5.8	4.8	5.1	4.4	8.7	6.1	5.3	6.8	5.9	5.4	13.5	15.7
Others	11.2	2.3	2.9	6.3	1.3	1.6	2.0	0.7	2.6	3.2	3.4	4.9	4.7	2.7
Total	100.0	100.0	100.0	100.0	100.0	100.0	100.0	100.0	100.0	100.0	100.0	100.0	100.0	100.0

Notes: (i) In 1968 and 1972 PSIUP (Socialist Party for the Proletarian Unity); in 1979 PDUP (Party of Proletarian Unity); in 1976, 1983 and 1987 DP (Proletarian Democracy); (ii) in 1948 the PCI polled together with the PSI in the Popular Front; PDS since 1992; (iii) Lista Pannella since 1992; (iv) SI (Italian Socialists) since 1994; (v) the PSDI polled together with the PSI in the 1968 election; (vi) in 1946 UDN (National Democratic Union), in 1948 National Bloc.

Source: official data provided by the Ministry of Interior.

looking at the relative electoral strength of individual parties. After the stabilization occurred in 1953 (the first legislative election in 1948 was quite exceptional in many respects), the parties maintained more or less their original electoral size and oscillated in a range of 2–3 percentage points with few exceptions: MSI in 1972 +4.2 percent, PCI in 1976 +7.2 percent, DC in 1983 −5.4 percent. Total volatility in fact proved to be quite limited, fluctuating around the European mean (Gallagher et al., 1995: 233; Bardi and Ignazi 1996).

The direction and the style of the competition were interpreted, according to Sartori's scheme (1976, 1982) as centrifugal and ideological. The parties were distributed along the Left–Right continuum occupying also the extreme positions at the two poles of the axis: the PCI was located at the left-end pole and the MSI at the right-end pole. The large distance between the most distant parties determined the polarization of the system. Even more: the type of conflict that prevailed in Italy in the first postwar decades was ideological as opposed to pragmatic. Political discourse was moulded on contrasting and opposite *Weltanschaaungen* rather than policy issues. Therefore, the two anti-system parties (MSI and PCI) forced a centrifugal drive, through overpromising and outbidding, in order to enfeeble the center of the political spectrum. These connotations reflect Sartori's model of polarized pluralism. Opposed to this interpretation stood the one known as "imperfect bipartism" (Galli, 1966). According to this view, the Italian party system had experienced since 1946 a process of concentration around the two main parties (DC and PCI) at the expenses of the other medium-sized and smaller parties. This trend should have led, in principle, to a bipartisan and bipolar configuration of the system. However, the PCI's lack of legitimacy inhibited a real alternation in government producing therefore an "imperfect" bipartisanism. This competing, somewhat less sophisticated, interpretation seemed to be supported by empirical evidence when the two main parties collected in the 1976 election 73.1 percent of the votes (and 68.3 percent in 1979). At the same time the PCI started to move away from its anti-system standing. Moreover, the *direction of competition*, as argued by Farneti (1983), changed from a *centrifugal* drive in the 1950s and the 1960s to a *centripetal* drive; and after the highly ideological 1970s (which even fostered a long season of political violence and terrorism) the style of political conflict became much more bargain-oriented, tolerant and pragmatic. However, it should be stressed that *only the style* of political competition changed while the distance between the poles remained constant, therefore keeping alive the connotation of polarized pluralism. A massive survey conducted by the Istituto Cattaneo suggests in fact that in 1990 the distance between PCI and MSI supporters (see Schadee 1995: 83) was even larger—6.4 points—compared to the one assessed in 1975—5.8 points—by Sani and Sartori (1983: 323).

Finally, there was the *government/opposition relationship*. Up to the 1994 earthquake the pattern is defined by four elements: (a) the pivotal role of the DC always present in each government coalition up to 1993 and holding the prime ministry continuously up to 1981 and then from 1987 to 1992; (b) the flanking role of the minor parties *vis-à-vis* the DC in the various government formats (*centrismo*: PLI, PRI and PSDI from 1947 to 1962; *centro-sinistra*: PRI, PSDI and PSI from 1962 to 1979; *pentapartito*: PLI, PRI, PSDI and PSI from 1980 to 1993); (c) the exclusion from government of the bilateral oppositions, the PCI (and later the minor new Left groups) on the Left side, and the MSI on the Right side; (d) a tendency toward bargain and compromise in the parliamentary arena, particularly in committee work, between government and (especially Left) opposition.

Actually, during a three-year period (1976–1979), DC-led cabinets were supported also by the Communist Party, that abstained or voted with the governmental coalition *without* taking ministerial positions. Indeed, the PCI's lack of legitimacy, which prevented it, like the extreme Right MSI, from acquiring an open governmental role, caused a stalemate in the party system which permitted the survival of DC-axed coalitions, albeit with some (minor) changes in their party composition. At any rate, the format of the governmental coalition remained stable, inhibiting any radical alternation in government (Mershon 1996) and thus contributing to the government's lack of responsiveness. On the other hand, the presence of the same parties in the various cabinets contrasts with the high mortality rate of postwar governments: 11.3 months in the 1945–1994 period (Vassallo, 1994). Cabinet turnover, however, is quite a primitive measure. In fact, in order to affirm the effective existence of government instability one should rather control for the change in cabinets' party compositions and for the turnover of political personnel in ministerial posts. First, in the Italian case, the absence of a competing alternative coalition enabled the same parties to occupy, in various combinations, the ministries. Second, the same pattern emerges as far as political personnel is concerned. Governmental personnel viscosity is striking in comparative perspective (Calise and Mannheimer, 1982: 109–141). This latter aspect is represented at best by the curriculum of Giulio Andreotti, very young undersecretary of the first DC Prime Minister, Alcide de Gasperi, in 1947, then member of government many times and seven times Prime Minister up to 1992: *a 45-year-long career.*

The rather large cabinets (almost half of them—26 out of 51—were "surplus majority" coalitions [Gallagher et al., 1995: 319]) were supported for most of the postwar period by four- or five-party, Center or center-left, coalitions, normally including the Christian Democrats, the Liberals, the Republicans, the Social Democrats, and, since the early 1960s, the Socialists. As already stated, the DC was throughout the period the relative majority party, that is, the largest in terms of electoral support, and the indispensable cornerstone of any governmental coalition. This attribute gave the party a dominance that went beyond the levels one could have expected in consideration of its actual electoral strength. After the first short-lived postwar government led by the Liberal-Radical Resistance leader Ferruccio Parri (May-December 1945) only two prime ministers were non-DC: the Republican Giovanni Spadolini (June 1981–November 1982) and the Socialist Bettino Craxi (August 1983–March 1987). Moreover, the presence and role of the DC ministries were dominant (Leonardi and Wertman, 1989). However, the bulk of DC power did not reside in the governmental sphere but in its absolute control of the policy-making and of high officials' appointments. The "party governmentness" (Katz, 1986: 45–46) feature of Italian governments, that is, the capacity to appoint officials in the governmental-bureaucratic structures and state-controlled agencies, was first very high and second, almost monopolistically controlled by the DC until the mid-1970s. This characteristic of party penetration in civil society (known in Italian as *partitocrazia*), was then shared by the other governmental parties. Until the mid-1970s the DC, which invented, theorized and practiced the party encroachment and control of any sector of the political system, society and even the economy, "kept the reins of 80 percent of the power with 40 percent of the votes" as a charismatic industrialist figure such as Fiat's president Giovanni Agnelli said. Only after that period, a weakened DC shared part of the power developing the so-called *lottizzazione*, which indicates party practices to respectively appropriate and parcel out all top decision-making and managerial positions in the administration at all levels and in the public or semi-public sectors of industry and finance. The Socialist Party, in particular, became the beneficiary of the *lottizzazione*, obtaining in the 1980s a larger and larger share of positions. On the other hand, it should be noted that the public sector of the economy is anomalously large for a capitalist country. The portion of total GNP produced by the state-owned or state controlled industry oscillated between one quarter and one fifth. Moreover, the Ministry of Treasury had the right to appoint (until 1993) the president (and sometimes the boards of directors) of almost all banks (which are subject to state control with very very few exceptions). Therefore, party ability to appoint officials and direct policies was overwhelmingly superior to all the other Western countries.

Besides this peculiar structure of the economic sector, which by itself favored a certain degree of party penetration, Italian parties could pervade civil society, thanks to the high legitimacy they acquired for their role in the postwar democratization process. In fact, all the postwar governmental parties plus the leftist ones (PCI and PSI) were the protagonists of the Resistance war against Nazi fascism in 1943–1945. Italian democracy was set up by the six parties which had formed the Comitato di Liberazione Nazionale—National Liberation Committee (CLN) and which controlled almost the totality of seats in the Constitutional Assembly in 1946–1948.

Moreover, during the early years of the Italian Republic, political parties had established solid links with organized interest groups (industrialists, agricultural and retail associations, trade unions) in order to influence their policy (Morlino, 1991b). This was made possible by the intrinsic weakness of Italian civil society (Pasquino, 1985) and more importantly, by the absence of a hegemonic class, a role never acquired by the Italian bourgeoisie. Parties were blamed, as they were the regulators (Pasquino, 1989) and gatekeepers (Morlino, 1991a; Morisi, 1991) in the system. The corruption and inefficiency of government favored, especially from the 1970s onward, the growth of a huge public debt and consistently high budget deficits, but also the state's inability to fight (or even the willingness to connive with) organized crime. This created a growing gap between discontented groups in society and the traditional parties, regardless of whether they had constantly been part of the governmental coalition, such as the DC, the PLI, the PRI, the PSDI, and the PSI since 1963, or were always confined in the opposition, like the PCI and its offspring, the PDS. Even the latter was in fact blamed for its acquiescence and inability to prevent a degeneration of the system.

In conclusion, the number and size of the relevant parties (eight parties with: two pivotal, two medium-sized and four minor), the style and direction of the competition (centrifugal) and the (large) ideological distance, the government/opposition relationship (bargaining and consensual), the format of government in terms of coalitions and political personnel; all (with the exception of the style and direction of political competition) offered a picture of amazing stability. Moreover, parties had become more and more powerful, penetrating civil society, draining resources from the public sector of the economy and managing a very wide area of patronage.

ORIGINS AND FACTORS OF PARTY SYSTEM CHANGE

The collapse of Italy's historic parties was rather sudden, but a certain malaise had been affecting them at least since the early 1960s (Bardi and Morlino, 1994). All parties, irrespective of their size, were organized along the "standard" mass party model: open and massive recruitment, emphasis on militantism, diffusion of local branches, network of flanking organizations, formal bottom-top decision-making process and leaders' selection, prevalence of collective executive bodies over the secretary, preeminence of the party executives over the parliamentary fraction. However, throughout that period, societal changes undermined traditional parties' structuring and way of functioning. The attempt by Italian parties to undergo a process of organizational adaptation with the declared intent to "open up" to the needs and requests coming from an evolving society was in most cases very superficial and did not represent a proper response. In fact, at the same time, parties developed to its fullest extent the *partitocrazia* system with the clear effect of *making society and the state adapt* to their needs (Bardi and Morlino, 1994). With one exception, the modification which the parties accomplished prior to 1992 concerned the party system more than the parties as such: in fact, with the (relevant) exception of the 1991 radical change (and split) of the PCI (Ignazi, 1992), the other changes concerned the composition of the party system. These include: the emergence of new actors such as the *Partito radicale*—Radical Party (PR), the *Verdi*—the Greens, and *La Rete*—the Network, all of which organized according to nontraditional models; and finally, the eruption of the *Lega Nord*—Northern League, with its charismatic profile. Each of these new actors (and later again, *Forza Italia*—Go Italy!) seemed better able than many of its traditional counterparts to respond to the widespread unsatisfaction of part of civil society (Morlino and Tarchi, 1996). After 1992, the "Clean Hands" investigations had devastating effects on the political parties and their organizations (for one, the complete disruption of the illegal system of party financing made the old party models obsolete), and, most of all, they tried to cope with the new context of manifest expression of anti-party sentiment enforcing some internal changes (which led in certain cases, such as for the DC, to the breakdown of the party: see Chapter 6, this volume)

It would then appear that the parallel process of organizational adaptation and societal encroachment by political parties had the dual effect of delaying the crisis of party in Italy while at the same time deepening the separation between the parties themselves and important sectors of civil society, especially those that did not benefit directly from the *partitocrazia* system. Indeed, the amount of resources drained by the *partitocrazia* system had reached enormous proportions. The reality of Italian party organizations can be grasped only by exploring the complex, and often illegal, system of relationships between political parties and organized or even individual interests. Italian party organizations certainly were enormously expensive machines, even if scarce availability and unreliability of financial data makes accurate assessments very difficult. Official party finance data are available only from 1974 on, when party budgets first became public and standardized according to the law on the public funding of political parties. The new law was also intended to discourage illegal contributions, but failed to curb political corruption as well as the involvement of public companies in illegal party financing. The cost of party politics in Italy has increased enormously since the mid-1970s as a result of the "media revolution" and the "office revolution," which required huge investments, increasing paid staff and salary expenditures. Parties could therefore hardly afford to give up funding from public companies, despite its becoming illegal; hence the explosion of the *tangenti* system since the 1970s. The total amount illegally obtained by Italian political parties was estimated at more than 3,000 billion lire a year, at least *ten times* the total official income of *all* Italian political parties (Bardi and Morlino, 1994).

A further change involved parties' relationship with the civil society. The de-ideologization and secularization of the 1960s strongly affected the relations between the parties and their flanking organizations. As the traditional flanking organizations—youth and women, sport and leisure, professional and trade union—declined, failing to guarantee a solid and faithful electoral and militant reservoir, the parties tried to develop new means in order to cope with new social movements and actors in civil society as a whole (Della Porta, 1996). In particular, the firm grip that the most important parties had on the trade unions changed after the momentous social unrest of the late 1960s. As a result, the unions sought and obtained more autonomy from the political parties. Party hegemony over the unified workers' movement was definitively broken during the 1980s. Furthermore, other sectorial/professional trade unions, totally independent from any party, emerged in the 1980s, collecting in some areas and in some circumstances a sizeable support from the concerned categories.

In front of the decline of membership and militants in the flanking organizations too, parties made every effort to obtain control of mass-communication media and expand their reach beyond the fading subcultural confines. Already in the 1950s, in addition to their official newspapers, the larger parties deeply influenced some important "independent" newspapers through the party-sponsored appointment of editors and journalists. The DC, as the cornerstone of every governmental coalition, had a very strict control of the public radio and television (RAI) until the late 1970s, and only in 1976 did a Constitutional Court ruling put an end to state monopoly of radio and television broadcasts. The ruling permitted private broadcasts at the local level. But by the mid-1980s, many of the newly created local television stations were concentrated into three national networks owned by Silvio Berlusconi. On the other hand, in the same period, the RAI was managed accordingly by the three main parties. The DC controlled the most popular channel, the PSI controlled the second one in terms of share, and the PCI the least popular state channel. Such partition provoked an increasingly strong reaction by the public and was very effectively exploited by the opponents of the *partitocrazia*.

Everything changed in few months, thanks to the mutual reinforcing actions of two set of events: the Clean Hands investigation and the electoral referenda of 1991 and 1993.

The Clean Hands investigation, contrary to many previous inquiries on single phenomena of corruption, involved first the entire political-economical elite of the most advanced and prosperous major Italian city, Milan, and then spread out all over the country. The first move of the magistrates in Milan, the so-called "industrial capital" of Italy, demonstrated that all parties, both in government and in opposition in local government, were involved in the inquiries. To give an account of the extent of the inquiries, after the first arrest in February 1992 more than 25,000 were investigated in one year and many thousands were sentenced. In Milan the procurers, until June 1994, investigated 2,928 persons, with 874 sentenced for corruption, bribery, illegal party financing and so on (Magatti, 1996: 36–37). The crucial importance of this investigation lies in the "discovery" by the mass public of the diffusion and extent of the political corruption. The continuous, daily flow of information, reinforced by dramatic events such as the suicide of Raul Gardini, the very popular former president and executive manager of Italy's second major Italian industrial group (Ferruzzi), provoked a further decrease in the (already quite low) level of confidence in democracy (Morlino and Tarchi, 1996). In other terms, Clean Hands, on one side, produced a widespread anti-party sentiment with a demand for radical renewal and, on the other side, hit the leadership and the political class of the governing parties (DC, PSI, PLI, PRI and PSDI): the general secretaries of all these parties were forced to resign by the early 1993. The investigations, rather, served as a catalyst for changes which the party leaderships had been trying, successfully up to then, to postpone indefinitely, even if pressures for extensive reform had been building up for almost 30 years. To be sure, the discovery of *tangentopoli* and the consequent public outcry against the political parties and "their system" constituted a (one of the) final blow(s) for the transformation.

The growing dissatisfaction with the governing parties was already in the making at the beginning of the 1990s: well beyond the survey data which highlight this pattern, the result of the 1991 electoral referendum proved the irritation/distrust vis-à-vis the governing parties, in particular the PSI[1]. In that circumstance almost the totality of the voters (95.6 percent) agreed to the proposed (minor) modification of the electoral system, conceived to prevent bribery, while the PSI leader and former prime minister Bettino Craxi, and more cautiously the DC, had opposed it. Voters proved to be disloyal to their parties. This disloyalty was not novel, as also in former referenda voters swung from their parties (Uleri, 1994: 417–422). But while on previous occasions the voters had returned to their parties in the following elections, in this circumstance some switches appeared to be definitive.

The first partial move was highlighted in the 1992 parliamentary election when total volatility increased from 8.4 in 1987 to 14.2, and a brand new party broke into the frozen party system and entered Parliament with more than 50 deputies: the *Lega Nord*—Northern League. For the first time since 1948 a genuinely new party, that is *not the by-product of a split from a previous party* (as in the case of *Rifondazione Comunista*—Communist Refoundation [RC] in 1991, of the *Partito Socialista di Unità Proletaria*—Italian Socialist Party Proletary Union [PSIUP] in 1964 and of the PSDI in 1947 and again 1969), gained a sizeable amount of seats jumping from 0.5 percent in 1987 to 8.7 percent of the vote in 1992. If we consider that the party is present in the northern regions (23 percent in Lombardy, 18 percent in Venetia,16 percent in Piedmont and 14 percent in Liguria), its overall performance is quite astonishing.

Lega Nord found its origin in demands for the affirmation of local culture and dialects and therefore was considered as a new expression of the center/periphery cleavage; however, it gained momentum as an expression of protest against the inefficiency and corruption of the central government and should more correctly be interpreted as a challenger to the traditional parties (Diamanti, 1995). The eruption of the *Lega Nord* into the Italian political scene was perhaps the decisive factor in surfacing mass anti-party sentiment. Anti-partyism had remained underground until the *Lega Nord* successfully channelled mass dissatisfaction and anti-establishment attitudes toward the system's custodians, the traditional parties.

The traditional parties' weakening hold over the party system is further manifested by both the election in May 1992, a few weeks after the general elections, of Oscar Luigi Scalfaro as the president of the Republic—a DC outsider unsupported by the main DC factions and oddly promoted by the anti-clerical Radical leader Marco Pannella—and the appointment of an independent nonmember of Parliament and governor of the Bank of Italy, Carlo Azeglio Ciampi, as Prime Minister in April 1993.

The final assault against the old system was provided by the 1993 electoral referenda (promoted by the same group that had promoted the 1991 referendum) which imposed a new electoral system: a single ballot majority system for 75 percent of the seats and a proportional system with a 4 percent threshold for the remaining 25 percent (D'Alimonte and Chiaramonte, 1995). This referendum was approved with a massive 82.7 percent of the votes.

The Clean Hands investigation and electoral referenda paved the way for the change: the *Lega Nord* breakthrough was the first visible sign of change but only with the enforcement of the new electoral system and the coming of the 1994 legislative elections when the party system completely changed actors, relative parties' strength, type of competition, government composition and relationship with the opposition.

THE NEW PARTY SYSTEM

The 1994 elections represented a watershed in the evolution of the party system (Table 5.2) (Bartolini and D'Alimonte, 1995). The traditional parties either disappeared or were drastically reduced: of the five governing parties—DC, PSI, PSDI, PRI, PLI—only the DC, *while split in three separate groups*, maintained a certain continuity. The bulk of the DC transformed itself into *Partito Popolare*—Popular Party (PPI) at the beginning of 1994. A conservative splinter group left the party and founded the *Centro Cristiano Democratico*—Christian Democratic Center (CCD). A further component of the old DC had already left the year before under the leadership of Mario Segni—the promoter and foremost spokesman of the 1991 and 1993 electoral referenda initiatives—forming an embryonic party called *Patto Segni*—Segni Pact. The other four governmental parties totally collapsed: at the 1994 legislative elections the PSI, after a series of spits and defections, collected 2.2 percent (−11.0 percent) and the PRI, the PLI and the PSDI were even unable to present autonomous party lists at the elections; some of the previous lead-

Table 5.2
Old and New Parties

Traditional Parties

Old Names *New Names*

DC *Partito Popolare Italiano*—Italian Popular Party (PPI) (January 1994)

splinters:
La Rete—The Net (1991)
Patto Segni—Segni Pact (1993)
Cristiano Sociali—Social Christians (CS) (1993)
Centro Cristiano Democratico—Christian Democratic Center (CCD) (January 1994)
Cristiani Democratici Uniti—United Christian Democrats (CDU) (1995)

PCI Partito Democratico della Sinistra—Democratic Party of the Left (PDS) (1991)

splinter:
Rifondazione Comunista—Communist Refoundation (RC) (1991)

PSI Socialisti Italiani—Italian Socialists (SI) (1994)

splinters:
Rinascita Socialista—Socialist Rebirth (1993)
Alleanza Democratica—Democratic Alliance (AD) (1993)
Federazione liberal-socialista—Liberal-Socialist Federation (1993)
Laburisti—Labour (1994)

MSI Alleanza Nazionale—National Alliance (AN) (1995)

splinter:
Movimento Sociale-Fiamma Tricolore—Social Movement Tricolour Flame (MS-FT) (1995)

PRI Partito Republicano Italiano—Italian Republican Party (PRI)

splinter:
Alleanza Democratica—Democratic Alliance (AD) (1994)

PLI Federazione dei Liberali Italiani—Federation of the Italian Liberals (1994)

splinter:
Unione di Centro—Center Union (1994)

PSDI Partito Socialdemocratico Italiano—Italian Social Democratic Party (PSDI)

splinter:
Movimento di Rinascita Socialdemocratica—Movement of Social Democratic Rebirth (1994)

PR Lista Pannella—Pannella List (1992)
Lista Pannella—Riformatori-Pannella List-Reformers (1994)

New Parties

Liga Veneta—Venetia League (1983)
Lega Lombarda—Lombard League (1987)
merge in:
Lega Nord—Northern League (1991)

Verdi (sole che ride)—Greens (smiling sun) (1985)
Verdi arcobaleno—Rainbow Greens (1987)
merge in:
Verdi—Greens (1990)

Forza Italia (1994)

Rinnovamento Italiano—Italian Renewal (RI) (1996)

ers ran as candidates (and few were elected) on different party lists. Of the ex-DC components, the moderate wing, the CCD, entered the electoral alliance with the right-wing parties gaining a fair amount of seats—29 (4.6 percent)—without presenting its own separate list; the *Patto Segni* collected almost two million votes (4.7percent); and the PPI more than four million, that is 11.1 percent. However, the plurality rule for three-quarters of the seats penalized the latter two parties, that obtained 15.7 percent of the votes and got only 7.3 percent of the seats in the Chamber of Deputies.

On the Left, a coalition of different parties and movements was formed: the progressive alliance. This alliance comprized the renewed ex-Communist Party PDS, the hard-line Communists RC, the Greens, the populist anti-Mafia movement La Rete, the very minor Left catholic group *Cristiano Sociali—*Social Christians (CS), the liberal *Alleanza Democratica—*Democratic Alliance (AD) and the remnants of the PSI. The alliance obtained 34.3 percent of the votes and 33.8 percent of the seats in the Chamber, and 32.9 percent of the votes and 38.7 percent of the seats in the Senate. With 20.4 percent, the PDS recovered more than 4 points with respect to the previous election and also RC with 6.0 percent gained some votes; all the other parties of the coalition failed to pass the four percent threshold in the PR election and therefore contributed to the Left's poor showing.

The right wing consisted of three main parties plus three minor ones. The three main parties were Berlusconi's brand new *Forza Italia*, the *Lega Nord*, and the neofascist MSI which contested the election under the name of *Alleanza Nazionale—*National Alliance (AN); the three minor ones were the Radical Party leader Marco Pannella's list, the DC moderate splinter group CCD, and the PLI's splinter group *Unione di Centro—*Center Union. The first three parties established two twin coalitions: the *Polo della Libertà* (Freedom Pole) between *Lega* and *Forza Italia*, which presented candidates in the northern regions; and the *Polo del Buon governo* (Pole of Good Government), between *Forza Italia* and AN, in the center-south. This twofold alliance was necessary because of the League's refusal to participate in an alliance with the "neofascists" of AN. Therefore, the only unitary element of the right-wing front was offered by Berlusconi's *Forza Italia* which bridged two mutually hostile parties (League and AN): in fact, in the north AN presented lists against the *Polo della Libertà* candidates. The two alliances together got 46.4 percent of the votes and 58.1 percent of the seats in the Chamber, that is, a comfortable majority; but with 42.7 percent of the votes in the Senate they got just 49.5 percent of the seats, thus failing to reach the absolute majority. As Italy is a system of "perfect bicameralism," the government has to receive the vote of confidence from both chambers: this unbalance was easily redressed owing to the some centrist MPs who joined the right-wing front. *Forza Italia*'s 21.0 percent made it the most voted party but, on the basis of an agreement with the League which allotted to the latter two-thirds of the constituencies of the north, it got a lower parliamentary representation: 15.7 percent of the seats in the *Camera*. On the contrary, the League greatly benefited from this pact, as with 8.4 percent of the votes (it presented candidates only in the northern regions) it obtained 18.6 percent of MPs, which made it the largest group in Parliament. The MSI/AN almost tripled its share of votes—13.5 percent (+8.1)—corresponding to 17.3 percent of MPs, the second largest group, on the same level as the PDS.

Consistently with the earthquake in the party system, MPs turnover was dramatic. In the 1994 Parliament, 71 percent MPs had no previous parliamentary experience and only 12 percent, with three or more terms in their curricula, could be described as veterans.

One of the most striking features of the 1994 elections was the success of a brand new party such as *Forza Italia*. This party, officially launched on January 26, 1994 (seven weeks before the election date), although covertly prepared since the previous summer, was founded and led by the Milanese entrepreneur Silvio Berlusconi. With 21.0 percent of the vote in the March parliamentary election and 30.6 percent in the June European election, *Forza Italia* proved to be Italy's first party. This unprecedented outcome is related to three main factors: the collapse of the traditional governing parties (in particular DC and PSI); the skillful (and abundant) use of the mass media; the novelty of political supply in terms of candidates and issues.

The new party, the new set of alliances, Berlusconi's being depicted as a newcomer and outsider, in spite of his close relationship with former PSI leader Bettino Craxi; all provided him with a novel political image: exactly what was needed to respond to the peculiar anti-party sentiments unleashed by *Tangentopoli*. This image, expression of a new political dimension, "new versus old," was skilfully advertised thanks to his quasi-monopoly of private television broadcasting (Berlusconi's three networks gather almost half of the total national audience). Berlusconi's own television campaign coupled with coverage given by the state-owned channels rapidly pushed him to the center of the electoral contest. Finally, his political proposals were particularly innovative: the party presented a *Manifesto* with a clear neo-Conservative Liberal approach, proposing limitations on welfare provisions, a reduction of income taxes, and an emphasis on free market, that constituted a radical innovation in the Italian political context. Ample access to the media, communication skills, novelty and centrality of political issues, all made Berlusconi the magnet of the electoral campaign.

The progressive alliance, on the other hand, was presented by the opposite front as the true interpreter of the old regime, the so-called "First Republic." In reality, the Left front did nothing to avoid this stigma: in fact, it declared the intention to continue the economic path designed by the previous government led by the former Central Bank governor Carlo Azeglio Ciampi. Therefore, the progressives offered the image of continuity, while a breakup with the past was clearly sought by public opinion. Notwithstanding the transformation from PCI to PDS in 1991 with the consequent ideological revision and the moderation of its electoral *Manifesto,* the PDS was charged, other than being "old," with still being "Communist" and a danger for Democracy. Moreover, the Left alliance was burdened with the nostalgic Communists of *Rifondazione Comunista* that hammered the middle-class electorate with frightening proposals to tax Treasury Bonds, admiring statements about Castro's regime, and the like.

The 1994 party system's radical transformation involved changes in the actors and in parties' relative strength: some traditional parties disappeared (PLI, PRI and PSDI); the two major governing parties (DC and PSI) collapsed; absolute (as *Forza Italia,* CCD and the Segni Pact) or relatively newcomers (*Lega Nord* and *Rifondazione*) made their breakthrough, and—oddly enough in the light of the introduction of a majority rule for 75percent of the seats—a plethora of minor parties survived. The only "traditional" parties to increase their votes were the PDS and, more spectacularly, the MSI/AN. Party system change did not reduce fragmentation, as might have been expected, as the number of the parties that obtained seats even increased, jumping from 16 in 1992 to an even more remarkable 20 in 1994. These changes were coupled with changes in the direction and style of competition and in the government relationship with the opposition.

The new electoral system imposed a new style in the political competition. After a period of de-radicalization of the political conflict, more issue-oriented and pragmatic, the collapse of the Center parties (DC and PSI) enforced a new polarization in the system (Morlino, 1996: 23). The 1994 electoral campaign was in fact the most conflictual and harsh since the 1950s. Partly as a by-product of this steep radicalization and of the majoritarian electoral system, the bargaining attitude, which had characterized the government/opposition relationship, was replaced by an adversarial style. On the other hand, the electoral law (and the re-radicalization process) enhanced the formation of two competing coalitions leading in turn toward a bipolar type of conflict. Campaign rhetoric aside, the two coalitions' electoral strategies and issue priorities followed a centripetal logic. In fact, the Berlusconi government—*all but one composed of freshmen*—enforced a more adversarial standing. The break both in terms of parties' composition and of political personnel was remarkable compared to the previous governments. Finally, the Berlusconi government was completely novel as made up by three parties that had never had access to government before, either because they were previously anti-system (MSI/AN) or brand new (*Forza Italia*) or a mixture of the two (*Lega Nord*).

All that, however, did not produce definitive transformations in some features, such as cabinet stability. The Berlusconi government survived for slightly more than seven months, even less than the average for pre-plurality cabinets, due to the *Lega Nord*'s defection from the majority in December 1994. The following government, headed by Lamberto Dini, former Ministry of Treasure in the Berlusconi cabinet, but self-declaredly politically independent, lasted for over a year, but could not rely on an organic political majority in Parliament. It was a so-called "technical" government entirely composed of non-MPs without any previous governmental experience (except Dini himself), invested with a limited and specific mandate, with the understanding that it would resign after the mandate was completed. During his office, Dini managed to obtain stable support from center-left parties and, directly or through abstention, from the *Lega Nord*. But any attempt to transform the cabinet into one with a political majority or otherwise prolong its existence failed in early 1996 when the two opposed coalitions, recast as the center-right *Polo per le Libertà*—Freedom Pole (*Forza Italia*, AN and CCD-CDU) and the center-left *L'Ulivo*—Olive Tree (PDS, PPI, Greens, Dini's *Rinnovamento* lists and other minor groups comprising a large part of the former socialists) proved unable to reach a compromise even on the general principles of a projected institutional reform. The outcome was that, less than two years after the elections that were supposed to give Italy a heretofore unknown stability, the President of the Republic was forced to dissolve Parliament and call new elections.

The renewal of the party system has come to a partial rest with the 1996 elections. Compared to the previous legislature the parties with at least one seat in Parliament were reduced to fourteen (instead of 20) and the volatility was halved (Bardi and Ignazi, 1996). Three new parties contested the 1996 elections while one disappeared. The new parties were: Prime Minister Lamberto Dini's electoral cartel *Rinnovamento*; the moderate *Cristiani Democratici Uniti*—United Christian Democrats (CDU), yet one more Catholic splinter group from the PPI; the minor splinter faction which opposed the MSI transformation into a more mainstream and ostensibly respectable *Alleanza Nazionale* in January 1995, the die-hard *Fiamma Tricolore*—Three-Colored Flame. On the other hand, the Segni Pact dissolved and the leadership itself decided not to contest the elections.

Parties' vote shares did not differ much compared to 1994. The PDS made a small gain which, together with a slight decrease of *Forza Italia*, projected the former to the first position. AN had a further increase, but well below its hopes, as much as *Rifondazione* and the *Lega Nord*. The PPI suffered the split of the CDU and reached a minimum of 6.8 percent, notwithstanding the support of the center—left's leader candidate, Romano Prodi, and of other Centrist leaders. The other two moderate catholic groups—CCD and CDU—presented common candidates, challenging the PPI with 5.8 percent. And finally, the Dini list barely passed the 4 percent threshold. All the other parties confirmed the modest results of 1994. However, thanks to the single-member candidacies many more parties/groups entered Parliament such as, for one, the Greens.

Fragmentation remains quite high but the tendency toward a bipolar configuration has strengthened, as the only remaining Center party, the PPI, was forced to join the center-left even at the expense of a further split by the

CDU. On the other hand, the *Lega Nord* remained outside the two coalitions and ran the elections alone claiming to represent different interests (the regional, northern ones) not taken into consideration by all the other parties. Thanks to its geographically concentrated strength, especially in the northern areas of Venetia and Lombardy, the *Lega* managed to elect 59 MPs (9.3 percent).

Radicalization and polarization are still relevant even if the Prodi government might contribute to relaxation of the tensions between the two blocks. But, as is evident from the above discussion, Italy's recent political changes have involved almost exclusively parties and the party system. Not much has changed in the way Italian government actually works: cabinets still have to rely on composite and unstable majorities and the first legislature elected during this period was not even able to survive for half a term. Moreover, as the *Ulivo* coalition did not get the majority in the Lower Chamber it avails itself of the parliamentary support of *Rifondazione comunista* which, however, does not take part in the cabinet.

In sum, fragmentation is high while decreasing, the parties seem to have consolidated their constituencies, the government is profoundly renewed both in terms of parties and of political personnel, and the relationships between *Ulivo* and *Polo* keep an adversarial style.

CONCLUSIONS

The extent of the change in the party system is revealed by the fact that none of the ten major competitors in the 1996 Chamber of Deputies' proportional election (accounting for almost 97 percent of the votes and all but a handful of seats) were present with the same names and symbols as in the 1987 election. Moreover, all but two of them, the Democratic Party of the Left and the Party for Communist Refoundation, experienced important formal or even substantial changes since the 1992 election; all the others, most notably those resulting from the Christian Democratic diaspora, changed name or symbols since the 1994 election or emerged during that time, such as *Forza Italia*, while Lamberto Dini's *Rinnovamento Italiano*—Italian Renewal (RI) came in 1996. The sheer number of these changes, albeit formal and superficial in some cases, reveals the magnitude of the party system transformation. Moreover, by 1996 even Italy's surviving historical parties had adopted new organizational models. The PDS, on one side, and AN, on the other side, experienced quite different organizational reforms, ranging from adaptation to "electoral professional party" in the former case, to the furthering of a "fuher-prinzip" style in the latter. Finally, the new electoral law, which was introduced to respond to demands for more stable majorities and more effective government, failed to produce conditions for an alternation in power between relatively homogenous coalitions and ultimately a radical reduction in the number of parties in the system. The evidence provided by the two elections (1994 and 1996) held under the new electoral law is far from being conclusive, and the law's effectiveness cannot be properly assessed, also because other institutional changes seemed necessary for a more consistent and far-reaching reform of the political system were never undertaken. What can be definitively asserted is that the ongoing evolution has already produced a different party system, certainly in terms of its actors.

NOTE

1. The referendum was called by a group of backbenchers coming from different parties in order to reduce the preferential vote in the ballot sheet from four to just one. This was meant to reduce briberies in the ballot spoil. The PSI leadership in particular opposed the proposal and provocatively invited the citizens "to go to the beach" instead of polling.

REFERENCES

Bardi, Luciano and Piero Ignazi (1996). "The Italian Party System: Still a Case of Polarized Pluralism?" Paper presented at the APSA Congress, San Francisco, August 29–September 1.

Bardi, Luciano and Leonardo Morlino (1994). "Italy: Tracing the Roots of the Great Transformation." In Richard Katz and Peter Mair (eds.), *How Parties Organize*, pp. 242–277. London: Sage.

Bartolini, Stefano and Roberto D'Alimonte (1995). *Maggioritario Ma Non Troppo*. Bologna: Il Mulino.

Biorcio, Roberto and Renato Mannheimer (1995). "Relationship between Citizens and Political Parties." In Hans Dieter Klingemann and D. Fuchs (eds.), *Citizens and the State, Beliefs in Government Series*, pp. 206–226. Oxford: Oxford University Press.

Calise, Mauro and Renato Mannheimer (1982). *Governanti In Italia*. Bologna: Il Mulino.

D'Alimonte, Roberto and Alessandro Chiaramonte (1995). "Il nuovo Sistema Elettorale Italiano: le Opportunità e le Scelte." In Stefano Bartolini and Roberto D'Alimonte, *Maggioritario ma non Troppo*, pp. 37–84. Bologna: Il Mulino.

Della Porta, Donatella (1996). *Movimenti Collettivi e Sistema Politico In Italia. 1960–1995*. Bari: Laterza.

Diamanti, Ilvo (1995). *La Lega. Geografia, Storia e Sociologia di un Soggetto Politico*. Roma: Donzelli.

Farneti, Paolo (1983). *Il Sistema dei Partiti In Italia 1946–1979*. Bologna: Il Mulino.

Gallagher, Michael, Michael Laver and Peter Mair (1995). *Representative Government in Western Europe*, 2nd ed. New York: McGraw-Hill.

Galli, Giorgio (1966). *Il Bipartitismo Imperfetto. Comunisti e Democristiani In Italia*. Bologna: Il Mulino.

Ignazi, Piero (1992). *Dal Pci al Pds*. Bologna: Il Mulino.

Katz, Richard (1986). "Party Government: A Realistic Conception." In Francis G. Castles and Rudolf Wildenmann (eds.), *The Future of Party Government. Volume 1: Visions and Realities of Party Government*, pp. 31–71. Berlin: De Gruyter.

Leonardi, Robert and Douglas Wertman (1989). *Italian Christian Democracy. The Politics of Dominance*. London: Macmillan.

Magatti, Mauro (1996). *Corruzione Politica e Società Italiana*. Bologna: Il Mulino.

Marletti, Carlo (1987). "Partiti ed Informazione Televisiva. La Nomina di Enrico Manca a Presidente della Rai." In Piergiorgio Corbetta and Robert Leonardi (eds.), *Politica In Italia 1987*. Bologna: Il Mulino.

McCarthy, Patrick (1992). 'The Referendum of 9 June." In Stephen Hellman and Gianfranco Pasquino (eds.), *Italian Politics: A Review* 7: 11–29. London: Pinter.

Mershon, A. Carol (1996). "The Costs of Coalition: Coalition Theories and Italian Governments." In *American Political Science Review* 3: 534–554.

Morisi, Massimo (1991). "Il Parlamento tra Partiti e Interessi." In Leonardo Morlino (ed.), *Costruire la Democrazia*, pp. 367–446. Bologna: Il Mulino.

Morlino, Leonardo (1991a). "Introduzione." In Leonardo Morlino (ed.), *Costruire la Democrazia*, pp. 9–39 Bologna: Il Mulino.

Morlino, Leonardo (1991b). 'La Confagricoltura dell'Attesa al Compromesso', In Leonardo Morlino (ed). *Costruire la Democrazia*, pp. 127–206. Bologna: Il Mulino.

Morlino, Leonardo (1996). "Crisis of Parties and Change of Party System In Italy." *Party Politics* 2: 5–30.

Morlino, Leonardo and Marco Tarchi (1996). "The Dissatisfied Society: the Roots of Political Change In Italy." *European Journal of Political Research* 30: 41–63.

Pasquino, Gianfranco (1985). *Il Sistema Politico Italiano*. Bari: Laterza.

Pasquino, Gianfranco (1989). "Unregulated Regulators: Parties and Party Government." In Peter Lange and Marino Regini (eds.), *State, Market and Social Regulation. New Perspectives on Italy*. Cambridge: Cambridge University Press.

Sani, Giacomo and Giovanni Sartori (1978). "Frammentazione, Polarizzazione e Cleavages: Democrazie Facili e Difficili." *Rivista Italiana di Scienza Politica* 8: 339–362.

Sartori, Giovanni (1976). *Parties and Party Systems: A Framework for Analysis*. Cambridge: Cambridge University Press.

Satori, Giovanni. (1982). *Teoria lei partiti e caso italiano*. Milano: Sugorco.

Schadee, Hans (1995). "Destra, Sinistra, Centro: Etichette Partitiche e Contenuti Politici." In Arturo M.L. Parisi and Hans M.A. Schadee, *Sulla Soglia del Cambiamento. Elettori e Partiti alla fine della Prima Repubblica*, pp. 75–104. Bologna: Il Mulino.

Uleri, Pier Vincenzo (1994). "Dall' Instaurazione alla Crisi Democratica. Un'analisi del Fenomeno Referendario In Italia (1946–93)." In Mario Caciagli and Pier Vincenzo Uleri (eds.), *Democrazie e Referendum*, pp. 390–430. Bari: Laterza.

Vassallo, Salvatore (1994). *Il Governo di Partito In Italia*. Bologna: Il Mulino.

6

The Failed Renewal: The DC from 1982 to 1994

Gianfranco Baldini

INTRODUCTION

The study of the organization of political parties should start, following the seminal work of Panebianco (1988), from the analysis of the origins of the party (the genetic model), taking into account also the main lines of its historical evolution, and, last but not least, the role and functions played by the party in the political system. This general *caveat* becomes a rule if the case study is the *Democrazia Cristiana* (Christian Democracy—DC), that has been the majority party in all the postwar Italian governments uninterruptedly from 1945 to 1993. These dates almost correspond to the party's birth and collapse, as it transformed itself into the *Partito Popolare Italiano* (Popular Party—PPI). The adoption of this name recalled the former pre-fascist party that had formed the core of the rising DC, formally constituted in 1942.

The main focus of this chapter will be on the last twelve years of existence of the DC as such (1982–1993), starting from the long secretaryship of Ciriaco De Mita (1982–1989) and analyzing the organization of the party until the early 1990s. The significance behind this choice lies in the interesting attempts of De Mita to give a new organizational structure to the party, whereas the final collapse of the DC is the natural final point of our analysis.

In order to analyze the organizational evolution of the party, it is, however, necessary to start from a brief account of the original model that characterized the structure of the party in the late 1940s. The organizational reforms implemented by the party leader Amintore Fanfani in the second half of the 1950s represent a starting point to consider before studying the structure of the party in the 1980s: although they did not succeed in transforming the overall organization into a mass party, they surely represented the major efforts ever attempted in that direction during all the history of the party. The limited success of the Fanfani's reforms can be partly associated with the birth and prosperity of several factions, whose consistency hindered the emergence of strong party organizational structures. The weak institutionalization (Panebianco, 1988: 128) is therefore the fundamental factor that characterized the organization of the DC since its foundation. A brief account of the main organizational developments can help to set the basic framework for a better understanding of the period 1982–1993, attempting to investigate the emergence of possible new trends compared to the previous phases. This analysis will be pursued through a twofold strategy: on one side, the description of the "formal rules" as they can be drawn from the text of the most recent party statute (1984); on the other, the "actual" relations between the different party organs. The key reference for determining the different relevance of the organs is represented by the control over the "zones of uncertainty."[1] To this scope, the study of the formal party organization and of the internal "power games" represents an important point to stress for the determination of the most vital "zones" for the control of the organizational resources.

The territorial structure, that has sometimes been brought as an evidence of the weak peripheral organization of the party, will be described as an evidence of the effective poor structuration of the DC at the local level. Another important aspect to consider is the almost unlimited use of the state resources from which the party started to benefit since the early 1950s. Indeed, the uninterrupted permanence in office at the national level, along with the control of the majority of the local administrations, has clearly favored this practice of unrestrained exploitation of the state goods, as well as the progressive loosening of the ties with the flanking organizations, that had hitherto represented one of the major linkages with the civil society. In fact, it will be argued that some aspects of the "cartelization" of the party (Katz and Mair, 1995) were already evident in the DC case in the early 1960s, as they represented the main means through which the party could "emancipate" from the external dependence, both in legitimacy and in financial terms. While the two secretaryships of De Mita (1982–1989) and Forlani (1989–1992) are not so radically different as to need to be treated separately, the changes that occurred in 1992—the electoral crisis and, most of all, the judicial investigations—broke up the internal structure of the party: Martinazzoli's desperate attempts to reform the collapsing DC deserve a special emphasis, although they somehow recalled previous reformist efforts. Finally, the picture that will come out of this analysis will be compared to the dominant assumptions of the literature on party organization in order to verify the actual adaptability of the DC to the main models proposed.

POLITICAL FOUNDATIONS AND ORGANIZATIONAL STRUCTURE OF THE PARTY

The DC was founded in 1942 on the remnants of the old *Partito Popolare* (Italian Popular Party-PPI). Along with the leaders of the former party (*Popolari*), several components contributed to the birth of the DC. Among these, we could include: the *Movimento Guelfo*[2] (Guelf Movement), the leaders of the Catholic Workers Movement, the university organizations of the FUCI (Italian Federation of the Catholic Universities) and *Movimento Laureati* (Movement of Catholic University Graduates) as well as several local catholic organizations directly mobilized by the church (Galli, 1978; Baget Bozzo, 1974; Giovagnoli, 1996). All these components were bounded by the catholic inspiration, and they can be perceived as the very "source of the legitimation" of the party. The core organizational characteristic of the party consisted in its "external legitimation": the support of the church—both directly and through the catholic associations—constituted the root of the DC, and represented the major factor of influence over its organizational structure (Panebianco, 1988: 123). The church's legitimation and sponsorship resulted therefore in a low level of institutionalization of the party: the dominant coalition[3] was, since the foundation, very weak and divided, because none of the different founding components were dominant over the others, and as they were all linked—to a greater or lesser extent—to the catholic world (Leonardi and Wertman, 1989: 21–46).

The phase of organizational institutionalization of the party was dominated on one side by the church through the catholic associations (that provided also the recruitment of the political personnel), on the other by the emergence of the "situational charisma" (Panebianco, 1988: 52) of Alcide De Gasperi, former leader of the PPI, DC party secretary from 1944 to 1946 and prime minister in the eight first Republican governments from 1945 to 1953. The weak institutionalization was also enhanced by the peripheral development of the party, which was mainly characterized by "territorial diffusion," with the Center playing a very limited role, often supplanted by the catholic organizations both in the mobilization of voters during the electoral campaigns and of the membership for the local activities of the party (Poggi, 1968).

Hence, in the first ten years, the DC was clearly characterized by a weak organizational structure: the main concern of the leaders was directed to the emergence and consolidation of different factions, rather than on the penetration of the party at the local level or at the achievement of a numerous and active membership. In this sense the 1953 electoral defeat represented a first challenge to the organization of the party, stressing the need for stronger territorial structures to counterbalance the success of the highly organized PCI (Giovagnoli, 1996: 62). The key turning point for the evolution of the party organization is represented by the election of Fanfani as party secretary in 1954, as it influenced both the internal structure of the party and the external relations with the state and the civil society. To overcome the organizational problems that characterized the first years (Poggi, 1968: 205–216) and in order to build a party structure more independent vis-à-vis the external organizations, Fanfani made strenuous efforts in the direction of a stronger organization, pointing to the recruitment of more membership, the creation of new sections, with the distribution of incentives to the most active members and a more direct control on the internal discipline of the party (Poggi, 1968: 216–220). Maintaining the majoritarian rule[4], Fanfani *de facto* postponed the consolidation of the factions as main determinants of the distribution of competencies inside the party.

On the other side, the lack of a strong organization was counterbalanced, in the south, by the establishment of clientelistic ties and by the development of a network of notables, who managed to become the most important "brokers" for the recruitment of the party membership and activists (Bardi and Morlino, 1994: 246). Furthermore, since Fanfani's secretaryship, the DC started the "colonization of the state," achieved through the expansion of the public sector. The control of the party over the state holding companies (IRI, ENI, EFIM) and over the ministry of state holdings,[5] and the creation of the *Cassa per il Mezzogiorno* (Fund for Southern Development) during the 1950s, represented the beginning of a process which would have brought to the drain from the economic state sector substantial financial resources to the party.

However, in order to understand the process of occupation of the state, it is first necessary to focus on the fundamental actors that have dominated, at least since the 1960s, the control and the distribution of all the fundamental resources inside the party, the factions.

A DIVIDED PARTY: THE ROLE OF FACTIONS IN THE ORGANIZATION OF THE DC

The DC has never been a united party: democratic centralism, which characterized for a long time the organization of the PCI (Chapter 7, this volume), "never had the chance of becoming an accepted principle for the conduct of internal affairs" (Leonardi and Wertman, 1989: 90). The divisions that shaped the party since its foundation represented one of the most debated issues of the first congresses, during which the discussion over the legitimacy of the factions often dominated the organizational debate, after the formal acknowledgment of their existence in 1949 (Poggi, 1968). The adoption of proportional rules in the election of the party organs in 1964 represented the formalization of the power of the factions that, according to some scholars (Sartori, 1971; D'Amato, 1965), were even "created" by this new system. However, their previous existence supports the idea that proportionalism was simply the best way to institutionalize their role inside the party organization.[6] Their success was possible because they managed to establish their own organizations, that sometimes were stronger than the overall party structure.[7] In evaluating the character and the aims of the factions, we could conclude that both the *ideological* and *power-oriented* criteria (Hine, 1982) are causes of the affirmation of factional divisions in the DC case. In fact, while in the phase of institutionalization of the party of the 1940s and early 1950s major issues seemed to be at the root of the internal divisions (ideology more than power), their institutionalization in 1960 coincided with the emergence of a different pattern. Although the factions continued to be divided according to the different attitudes on the cabinet coalitions (both in the period of the center-left coalition with the PSI [1963–1974] and with the experiment of the "national solidarity" with the PCI [1976–1979]) the allocation of the organizational resources became in this period a more decisive factor than the decreased ideological divisions. What has happened then since 1982, after the new organizational renewal attempted by the party secretary Benigno Zaccagnini[8] (1975–1980), and just after the DC lost for the first time since 1945 the prime ministership in the new *pentapartito* coalition?

De Mita's election was not an exception compared to the past, if it is true that it was "the result of agreement among three top factional leaders" (Giulio Andreotti, Amintore Fanfani, and Flaminio Piccoli) (Leonardi and Wertman, 1989: 134). When he was elected, his first goal was the opposition to the consolidated power of the factions, but his efforts did not bring about relevant changes. In fact, De Mita's opposition to the factions was not inspired by an attempt to give a more unitary image to the party: the main aim, instead, was to achieve the greatest benefits possible for his own faction (*Base*) and, more in general, for the Left of the party, which had been marginalized in the previous years. De Mita's efforts against the other factions, as well as his leadership over the newest of the national bodies, the Political Office (which was originally created in 1979 because of the discontent of some factions that had hitherto been underrepresented in the major DC organs) can therefore be explained by his willingness to foster the Left of the party against the center-right of Andreotti and Forlani. Although the importance of this body was very limited, De Mita kept the offices of the Political Office "frozen" from 1986 to 1988, in order to avoid the representation of the hostile factions and, once he was forced to reconstitute it, he managed to have on the seats allocation a fundamental influence. Leaving aside this case—indeed very marginal for the overall determination of the power structure—De Mita did not succeed in reforming the overall structure of the party. In other words, he failed to build a centralized organization, more dependent on the power of the secretary than on the leaders of the factions.

THE FORMAL PARTY ORGANIZATION AND THE INTERNAL "POWER GAMES"

In order to determine the extent to which factions continued to be the channel of representation of all the internal groups between 1982 and 1993, as well as the major determinant of the relations inside the party machine, three indicators are particularly useful:

1. the criteria of selection and recruitment in the most important national bodies;
2. the relations between parliamentary group and the party;
3. the control over the process of candidate selection.

(1) According to the latest party statute (1984), the main organs of the party are the National Party Congress, the National Council, the National Executive (*Direzione*), the Party Secretary, and the Political Office, which has replaced the parliamentary group as official body of the party. The factional membership has been the most important criterion of selection for their composition. After 1964, when the adoption of a proportional system for the election of the National Council formalized the existence of the factions and institutionalized their role as primary channel of selection, their strengthening has been very clear.[9] The composition of the organs has almost always perfectly mirrored the distribution of the seats in the National Congresses, whose delegates were directly elected by the territorial assemblies, hence emanating from the rank-and-file (see Table 6.1).

In order to establish a "vertical" line of command among these organs it is necessary to use a twofold source: on one side the formal rules expressed by the party statute, on the other the actual functions played by each of them as far as the control of the most important organizational resources is concerned. Given the absence of a small executive organ (like a National Secretariat, which exists in most of the other Italian parties), and the limited relevance of the Political Office, the most important internal organ seems to have been the National Executive.[10] A detailed report of all the functions it is entitled to fulfill (Bardi and Morlino, 1992; DC, 1984) reveals how the National Executive has controlled the most important areas of internal relations, such as the process of selection and recruitment, communication with the peripheral organs and party financing.

In this respect, De Mita appears to have been much more successful in gaining more power in the National Executive (Manconi, 1988, 1989) than in all the other internal reforms he called for.[11] In this way he extended his control over the decision-making process, especially by selecting members of his faction (*Base*) or from his region (*Campania*), in order to break the traditional asset of the proportional representation of all the factions in the party organs. However, De Mita's control was always exercised under the

Table 6.1
DC Composition and Functions of the National Party Organs

Organ	Composition/ Selection	Functions
National Congress (since 1982)	--About 1,000 delegates, most of whom elected, every two years, by the local assemblies.	--Election of the National Council. --Debate on the general policies of the party. --In 1976, and since 1982, election of the secretary.
National Council (NC) (since 1989)	--220 members: 180 elected by proportional representation at the National Congress (80 Mps, 80 non-Mps, plus 20 seats reserved for women), 40 ex officio members.	--Election of the National Executive. --Debate on changes in party statutes. --Debate on the general policies of the party.
National Executive (since 1982)	--44-46 members (1982-89); 26 members (1993). 30 elected by (and within) the NC, plus the ex officio members (see appendix to Table 6.2).	--It is the leading executive body: all the most important decisions are taken here.
Political Office (since 1984)	--7-11 members chosen among those of the National Executive, also under the proposal of the Party Secretary, but to be finally ratified by the same National Executive.	--It should "cooperate with the Secretary in the implementation of the political lines as expressed by the party bodies." Practically, its importance is very limited.
Party Secretary (since 1980)	--Elected by the National Congress, normally every two years.	--Responsible of the party policies.

supervision of the other leading factions (*in primis* those led by Andreotti and Forlani) that, especially after De Mita's appointment as Prime Minister in 1988, were already fighting in order to regain the secretaryship.[12]

However, the rule of the incompatibility between ministerial positions and membership of the internal bodies plays a decisive role: even if the National Executive was the most important national organ, this did not imply that all the crucial decisions were simply taken by its members without external constraints. Hence, the uninterrupted permanence of the DC in the national governments has clearly influenced the composition and the power of the National Executive: the positions held by the members of the *Direzione* have indeed been, most of the times, means through which the leaders of the factions played their respective cards inside the party power games.[13]

(2) As far as the second indicator is concerned, according to Panebianco (1988: 126–127), the role of the DC parliamentarians was dominant vis-à-vis the rest of the party, even if the statute (art. 87) determined that the parliamentary group "should follow the general political lines established by the National Congress, and the guidelines expressed by the national organs" (DC, 1984: 90). The superiority of the parliamentary group over the party offices is not very easy to assess. What is more important, however, is to

Table 6.2
Turnover of the DC National Executive from 1982 to 1993

Congress	Elective			Ex officio	Total
	Old members	members New members	Total members	members (*)	members
XV 1982	18	15	33	13	46
XVI 1984	13	19	32	14	46
XVII 1986	21	9	30	14	44
XVIII 1989	17	13	30	14	44
(**) 1993	7	8	15	11	26

*The ex officio members are: the Party Secretaries (both the current and the former), the President of the NC, the Administrative Secretary, the Prime Minister; the presidents of the parliamentary groups. DC ministers and undersecretaries can participate, under the proposal of the National Executive or of the Party Secretary. Other members have often been the delegates of the young, women and elderly movements, even if their presence has not been formalized in the statute.

**The members of the National Executive in 1993 have been elected by the National Council.

Sources: data calculated by the author on information provided by the DC newspaper *Il Popolo*, various issues.

ascertain the degree to which the parliamentary career has been a means of selection for the party organs. Confirming the trend of the first 30 years (1946–76), when almost half of the members of the National Executive had a previous parliamentary career (Cotta, 1979: 119), the DC has maintained a pattern of recruitment quite different from that of the PCI, where the party career has often been a preliminary requisite for the entry into Parliament (Chapter 7, this volume). This, however, should not lead us to infer a supremacy of the parliamentary group over the rest of the party. In fact, the control of the factions over the process of candidate selection cuts across these relations, establishing a common dominance over both the processes: the key role is played once again by the leaders of the factions inside the dominant coalition, who were able to secure the seats for their respective deputies and ministers in office.

The low degree of renewal inside the National Executive is, on this respect, very significant, as it reflects the trade-off between the power of the factions and the external constraints. As the figures of Table 6.2 show, the greater turnover that occurred in 1984 and 1993 is associated to the electoral defeats of the previous years. Hence the higher exclusion of incumbents has often been an instrumental means to give an image of internal renewal of the party.

(3) The process of candidate selection (Wertman, 1988) is therefore one of fundamental importance: albeit it was formally decentralized, the National

Executive has always had the final decision about the "safe seats" and the recandidation of the incumbents as well as over the allocations of the heads of the lists (*capolista*) (Wertman, 1988). However, the factions' control over the candidatures was, paradoxically, related to a higher turnover in the DC in comparison to the other parties. As Katz and Bardi stress, the distribution of the candidatures among the different factions was an obstacle against the almost automatic election of the incumbents (Katz and Bardi, 1979). Each faction has sponsored the renomination of its own candidates, to such an extent that "about half of (the parliamentary) turnover has been due to losses in intraparty electoral battles for preference votes" (Wertman, 1988: 151). Among the three last general elections, there has been a higher percentage of new members in 1983 and 1992 compared to 1987 (Verzichelli, 1995: 303–304). While in 1983 these data were the result of an attempt to renew the parliamentary group, also by including some independent candidates on the DC ticket (Wertman, 1988: 152), in 1992 the highest exclusion of incumbents was probably due to the need to give a renewed image to the party.

To sum up, the 1980s can be seen as the period during which the national leaders of the main factions (Andreotti, Forlani, De Mita, Gava, Scotti and their respective local *capicorrente*) consolidated their control over the "zones of uncertainty" by means of dominance over all the important channels of selection and distribution of internal powers. The factions could therefore hold the trump cards because their power cut across the relations between the executive party bodies and the parliamentary group, determining the internal dynamics. The factional membership has been the key factor in the distribution of the organizational resources: the struggle for the leadership of the party has often been linked (as both De Mita and Forlani's cases show) to the privileges associated to this position in the allocation of the seats in the party bodies, and in the achievement of particular economic and "status" privileges.

Yet central organization of the party and power relations at the national level are not enough for ultimately assessing the overall distribution of power inside the DC. Local party structures, characteristics and size of membership and the role of clientelism will help to test the extent of the relevance of factions at the subnational level.

THE WEAK ORGANIZATION: TERRITORIAL STRUCTURE, CLIENTELISM AND THE MEMBERSHIP

All along the DC's history the various attempts of organizational reform have been characterized by a particular concern toward the establishment of a strong structure based on a national network of local sections, *sezioni*. Since Fanfani first perceived that the party needed more autonomy from the traditional sources of support like the catholic associations and the clergy, all the efforts have been concentrated in the strengthening of the weak peripheral structure. Nonetheless, as it happened for the national bodies, these reforms brought about only very limited changes, and the situation during the 1980s was, once again, not very different from the previous years.

Concerning the local organization of the party, De Mita reformed the position of the regional organs, giving more relevance to the regional secretaries (Manconi, 1988), being all the local assemblies structured in a very similar way to the national organs (Leonardi and Wertman, 1989: 142). Also in the reform of the regional organs, however, the aim of De Mita was more directed to obtain some privileges for his own part than toward a greater influence of the periphery.[14]

Some regions have clearly been more influential than others in the functioning of the party organization, both in terms of membership and of electoral consent. In particular, the South (*Mezzogiorno*), together with the areas of catholic subculture of Veneto and the eastern part of Lombardia (Caciagli, 1982: 267–268), represented the zones of the highest concentration of the DC vote (Caciagli, 1990) and membership[15] (Anderlini, 1989). As we have already mentioned, it was during the 1950s that the first important developments occurred. The party established a network of clientelistic relationships: as Fanfani's reforms encountered only a limited success,[16] the control over the local activities—namely, membership, recruitment and grassroots participation—was managed by some southern notables, who soon became the main linkage between the party and the members and voters. The importance of the agricultural sector in the economy of the underdeveloped areas of the *Mezzogiorno* is fundamental, and it provided a rich source of financing for the party, as well as a privileged channel of membership recruitment (Tarrow, 1967; Graziano, 1980). More in detail, the clientelistic use of the institutions was in the hands of the local leaders of the factions (the *capicorrente*), who controlled the organization of the party through the artificial expansion of the membership.[17] This was an easy task as the factions continued to enjoy the protection at the national level of their respective leaders up to the 1990s, and because the latter needed to maintain the linkage with their constituencies through the distribution of financial benefits, easily managed via the firm control of the DC on all the main institutes regulating the flux of economic aids to the south (*Cassa per il Mezzogiorno*). Researches on cities like Naples (Allum, 1973) and Catania (Caciagli, 1977) have shown how the "clientelism of notables has been replaced in the *Mezzogiorno* by the clientelism of the political party" (Caciagli, 1982: 274). The notables of the 1960s were hence "replaced" by a more direct control of the leaders of the factions, with the same De Mita controlling the distribution of economic resources in his area, especially after the 1981 earthquake of Irpinia legitimized the claim for special economic measures to help the reconstruction of the devastated zones (Becchi, 1992).

At first glance the figures of the national membership are quite impressive (Table 6.3). However, as various researches have demonstrated (Rossi, 1979,

Table 6.3
DC Membership, 1982–1993

Year	members
1982	1,361,066
1983	1,384,058
1984	1,382,278
1985	1,444,565
1986	1,395,784
1987	1,812,201
1988	1,693,346
1989	1,862,426
1990	2,109,670
1991	1,390,918
1992	*
1993	813,753

*1992 data are not available.

Sources: For years 1982–1986, see Anderlini (1989: 289); from 1987 on, see Ignazi and Katz (1995: 291).

1987; Anderlini, 1989; Scalisi, 1996), there has constanly been an inflation of the data, which are then clearly unreliable.

Moreover, if one looks at the effective participation[18] (Wertman, 1979), and sociodemographic characteristic of the DC members (Anderlini, 1989), the influence of the clientelistic links is again very clear.[19] All along the 1980s this trend continued without significant changes and it was only after 1991 that the need for a reform of the criteria of adhesion to the party appeared as very urgent.

The party National Conference, held in Assago from 28 to 30 November 1991 approved, among other reforms,[20] new rules for the membership, changing parts of the 1984 statute. The political significance of the Conference was, however, not as high as the leaders of the party claimed. Important reforms were implemented, starting with a new electoral system for local assemblies, the incompatibility between membership of party offices and public offices, the "limit" of four parliamentary mandates (see Il Popolo, 11 January 1992). The limit of these new provisions was that they were often very easy to overcome and proved to be of a very limited extent for the overall aim of reforming the party organization. A peculiar concern that emerges from the reading of the Conference is the need to give a new "identity" to the party, as the fall of the Berlin Wall was questioning the traditional validity of its anti-Communist appeal.

THE PARTY BETWEEN STATE AND CIVIL SOCIETY

As we have already stressed, the predominant position of the DC in the Italian political system had a clear influence over the distribution of power inside the party bodies. In a similar perspective, the consolidation and strengthening of this dominance must be viewed as strictly linked with the party colonization of the state, which was paralleled by a progressive loosening of the ties with the civil society (Katz and Mair, 1995). In this paragraph we will try to see whether the DC has been, in the period considered, a party significantly different from the one that had established its dominance through the patronage system and had benefited, up to the 1980s, from the direct support of the catholic organizations as sources of recruitment and electoral mobilization.

Starting with the links with the civil society, the DC enjoyed the direct sponsorship of the church and its position vis-à-vis the catholic world has been, already before the 1970s, of clear superiority, to the extent that some scholars have defined it as a relation of "dominance" (Morlino, 1995: 156). As Panebianco argues, one of the indicators of the degree of institutionalization of a party is represented by its relations with the "external collateral organizations" (Panebianco, 1988: 58–59). Among all the flanking organizations that sustained the party since its very foundation, we can find only one association that maintained a close relationship with the DC until the late 1980s: the *Coldiretti* (Small Farmers' Organisations). By contrast, other organizations, including *Associazione Cattolica Lavoratori Italiani*—ACLI (Association of Catholic Workers), *Azione Cattolica* (Catholic Action) and *Confederazione Italiana Sindacato Lavoratori*—CISL (Italian Confederation of Labor Unions), withdrew their direct support to the party during the 1960s.[21] On the other side, a new organization provided, since the mid-1970s, strong bases of support for the DC: the *Movimento Popolare*—MP (Popular Movement), the political arm of *Comunione e Liberazione*—CL (Communion and Liberation) (Leonardi and Wertman, 1989: 209–222). Both the *Coldiretti* and Popular Movement have been relevant for the internal life of the party: while the first continued to provide for candidates to be elected on the DC ticket—maintaining, furthermore, the party's relationships with the agricultural sector—the MP, founded in 1975, has achieved greater influence during the 1980s. Through a broad array of activities and a strong network of mass media (local radio stations, monthly and weekly periodicals), and above all during the annual CL "Meeting" of Rimini,[22] the MP has played a major role in DC policies up to the 1990s, in strong opposition to De Mita's leadership and openly supporting the alliance formed by Forlani and Andreotti in the second part of the 1980s.[23] Since these two cases are isolated inside a general pattern of a loosening of the ties with the flanking organizations, we can conclude that the relations with the external environment during the 1980s have seen the reinforcement of the trend already emerged in the previous decade toward a detachment of the party from its traditional ties with the catholic world, and from a civil society which was undertaking a slow, but progressive, process of secularization (Cartocci, 1994). From 1982 to 1992, the DC became less dependent on the support provided by the flanking organizations; however, the greater autonomy from the catholic associations did not always correspond to a similar decrease of the support of the church. During most of the electoral campaigns the Vatican continued to express the desirability of the permanence of the Catholics under the DC flag, and the catholic political unity remained a major issue all along the 1980s, with only some exceptions in the south.[24]

Concerning the relations with the state, following the scheme proposed by Leonardi and Wertman (1989: 236–241), we can focus our attention over three main sectors where the party concentrated its efforts for pursuing the hegemony over the national economic and political system:

1. the control over the public broadcasting sector (RAI);
2. the direction of the state holding companies (IRI, ENI, ENEL);
3. the direction of the banks.

1. The control of the mass media has been exercised by the DC since the foundation of the public television and without any contrast until the 1970s, when the Italian Constitutional Court ruled that a reform should have been implemented inside RAI (Marletti, 1988; Leonardi and Wertman, 1989: 240). Since the beginning of the 1980s, the "political direction" of the three public channels was divided among the three main Italian parties: RAI 1 to DC, RAI 2 to PSI and RAI 3 to PCI. The DC, nonetheless, kept a dominant position. De Mita succeeded in putting a man very close to him in the most important RAI office[25] and the party could well leave some positions to its allies without risking any sort of political opposition. The *lottizzazione* of the RAI represented a major factor of controversy until 1993 and, indeed, it still seemed to be unsolved, as the parties, with the DC still in the lead, were refusing to let go of the hold over such an important channel of communication.[26]

2. While the control of the television can be perceived as a channel of public support and propaganda for the party, the direction of the state holding companies and of the public banks is perhaps even more important, as they represent a primary source for the finances of the party. During the 1980s, as a consequence of its loss of the prime ministership in 1981, and in general as the minor parties of the *pentapartito* coalition gained more influence, the DC was forced to share its privileges with them, losing part of its hegemony. The extent of this share was, however, not enough to challenge the dominant position of the party until 1992. During this year the privatization of IRI, ENI, ENEL and INA[27] was started as a first measure to achieve the economic recovery of the state agencies and against the practices of the

lottizzazione in this sector. However, even after the reform—that abolished all the administrative councils, but distributed the seats among the governmental parties—the DC was still holding the grips on the key positions of all the firms.[28]

3. Until the referendum of 18 April 1993—when this rule was abolished—the appointment of the president and deputy president of all the Italian saving banks has been in the hands of the Ministry of the Treasury and of the CICR (Interministerial Committee for Credit and Saving). The DC kept a strict control over the offices until the early 1990s. A comparison between data of the mid-1970s (*Il Corriere della Sera*, 15 September 1976) and (the latest available figures of) 1992 (*Il Mondo*, 24–31 August 1992), shows how the DC has been able to maintain the direction over the majority of the banks. However, while in 1976 as many as 90 percent of the presidents (whose mandates had to be renewed) belonged to the DC area, in 1992 the party still controlled nearly 70 percent of the banks. This decline was caused by the increasing influence of the PSI and the other minor parties of the coalition.

Related to the control of the DC over the public resources is the financial funding of the party. The 1974 law on the public funding of political parties resulted in a substantial failure of its original aims. While it provided for the first time some data concerning the official finances of the Italian parties, the law "by establishing strict and cumbersome regulations and procedures, . . . also made it very difficult to provide for *legal* contributions" (Bardi and Morlino, 1994: 258). Since the starting of the inquiries of *Mani Pulite* in 1992, it appeared clear that most of the official figures provided by the parties were meaningless, and that the majority of the finances were composed of "black funds" obtained through the *tangenti* system. Four years after the beginning of the inquiries, a precise estimate of the funds seems still impossible to draw, but it clearly emerged that the initial "unofficial" financial sources (including various U.S. agencies, the business association [*Confindustria*] and the Vatican) have progressively been replaced by the colonization of the state sector and the exploiting of its economic resources.

To wit, the DC during the 1980s maintained the hegemonic position over the political system acquired during the previous years, though the general picture seems one of a decline of the traditional role. One could also argue that the aforementioned relations with the state industries and public economy are the natural consequences of the uninterrupted permanence in office of the DC at the national level. Be that as it may, it is undeniable that the party has, compared to the 1950s, further moved in the direction of the occupation of the state, even if it had to share its privileges with the minor parties of the governmental coalition and sometimes—as the RAI case illustrates—also with the opposition (PCI). What is less easy to determine is the exact time when the "occupation of the state" started. The colonization of the state resources started approximately in the same period when the factions were institutionalized as the main element of the internal power relations in the 1960s. The management of the state funds seems to have represented not only a partial replacement for the decreasing role of the initial sources of legitimation and financing, but also a founding component of the "party-state." On the other side, the links with the civil society have always been, including the phase of foundation of the party, instrumental to the functioning of the organization of the party: the DC has been able to "exploit" the support of the church and of the flanking organizations, which have provided strong means for the mobilization of the electorate and for the electoral success of the party.

TOO LATE TO CHANGE: MARTINAZZOLI AND THE COLLAPSE OF THE PARTY

In 1992, the *Mani Pulite* inquiries and the defeat in the general election, which pushed the party for the first time to under 30 percent of the votes, represented two major external threats which reaffirmed the need of a new, and this time "radical," organizational reform. The electoral crisis of the party was further deepened, after Forlani's resignation, by the local elections held in September in Mantua, a small city of Lombardia, where the Northern League became the first party.[29]

The election of Martinazzoli as Party Secretary gave rise to a new reform: for the first time the question of the inflation of the membership figures was dealt with seriously, after the starting of a new campaign with an "erasure" of the old membership records, with the proposal of new and more "transparent" rules.[30] Another important result obtained by Martinazzoli was the partial subtraction from the factions of their control over the process of candidate selection. In this respect the renewal clearly emerges in the administrative election of 6 June 1993, when only 23.5 percent of the incumbents were recandidated, with a scrupulous application of the three-mandate limit (Wertman, 1995: 141). However , the limited success of the reforms supports the view that "Martinazzoli's project was simply the latest attempt by a DC secretary to 're-establish,' 'revitalise' or 'reorganize' the party" (Bardi and Morlino 1994: 255) confirming that the "organizational inadequacy pre-dated the crisis of the 1990s by at least two decades" (ibid.). The commitment to change and reforms was not, indeed, as successful. The composition of the new National Executive elected in March 1993 confirmed the permanence of the traditional pattern: although all the members under investigation were excluded, the distribution of the seats was still regulated by the factional membership (*Corriere della Sera*, 24 March 1993). In 1993 the party was therefore different from the previous years, mainly because most of the leaders had been involved in the *Tangentopoli* inquiries: this made a major turnover inevitable, but did not correspond to a complete decline of the factions that these personalities had hitherto led.

The major threat to the existence of the party came from its "loss of centrality" since the beginning of 1993. In particular, the marginalization of the party in the administrative elections of June exposed it to major internal conflicts, aimed to preserve the different "souls" of the DC. After the split of Mario Segni (to form the Referendarian Movement in 1991) and the mentioned exit of the Mayor of Palermo Leoluca Orlando (to create the new party *La Rete*), the DC could not face any more splinters, at the risk of its own survival. But, the same June elections showed that Martinazzoli was not speaking on behalf of the all party, as yet another division (and this time quantitatively massive) was cutting the party in two different, big factions. It was not a question of a predominance of one faction over the other: the very existence of the party was under threat. Two main aggregations of factions, representing the Right and the Left—the first mainly concentrated in De Mita's region, Campania, in the south, the second led by the regional secretary of Veneto—started indeed to behave as two separate parties from 1993. It was the prologue of further future splits, which would have eventually led in 1995, to the existence of a multitude of small parties led by former Christian Democratic leaders, divided in the two major coalitions of center-left (Olive Tree, *Ulivo*) and center-right (Freedom Pole, *Polo delle Libertà*).

The National Constituent Assembly held in Rome (23–26 July 1993) approved the change of the name of the party into PPI (Italian Popular Party), readopting the old name of the party of Sturzo and De Gasperi. The diverse policies of the two components—which, indeed, organized separate conventions in September—made any further attempt of organizational reform impossible. The Assembly left to the future Congress[31] the task to rebuild the party structure, along with the final adoption of the new name and statute. The desperate attempts to save a party that by 1993 had seen the majority of its parliamentary group under investigation, were all the more utopistic as the popular discredit of the traditional parties of the "first republic" was reaching its zenith, to give boost to the anti-party campaign of the newcomers like the Northern League, *Forza Italia* and the old MSI (renamed AN), that formed in 1994 the heterogeneous and effimerous alliance that brought the DC system to a definitive end.

CONCLUSION: WHICH PARTY MODEL FOR THE LATE DC?

To summarize the core organizational dynamics of the party during the period considered, the first character to note is that the overall structure has maintained the basic features it had developed since Fanfani's reforms. Although he remained Party Secretary for seven years (in the last one he was also Prime Minister), De Mita did not represent the kind of "situational charismatic leadership" the DC had experienced with De Gasperi. The success of his reforms was limited to some marginal questions, even if the control he managed to obtain over the National Executive was not one to overlook.

However, all the most significant changes and reforms did not challenge the role of the factions, which were able to maintain the control over the "zones of uncertainty" even after the latest reformist efforts of Martinazzoli. The twelve years from 1982 to 1993 could therefore be seen as dominated by the power of the factions: while in the 1980s the Left regained positions compared to the past, the election of Forlani and the successive prime ministership of Andreotti represented a substantial recovery for the center-right of the party, which could already base its power on consolidated positions inside the bureaucracy, as well as in the financial and economic system. Moreover, the contrasts among the different factions during all the 1980s had not been policy-oriented as during the period of their consolidation. Indeed, as well as by the patronage connections, the divisions among the factions mainly originated from the different attitudes toward the PSI, the major coalition partner.[32] In other words, the failure of renewal of the party until 1992 was caused by the prevalence of the interfactional battles over the issue of organizational reform.

In order to sum up the main points so far analyzed, we can take four elements of the organizational structure of the party and see if their characteristics have changed significantly during the period 1982–1993, always bearing in mind the distinction between the "formal" rules as expressed by the party statute and official documents, and the "real" situation that emerged.

Authority of the party secretary. De Mita clearly had, both in formal and in real terms, a higher importance than the other two secretaries. Forlani's years (1989–1992) were not significant for his own powers, but for the alliance with Andreotti, which allowed them the control over the majority of the party and the new emargination of the leftist factions. Martinazzoli was given special competencies by the assemblies of the party to face the emergency: in fact, in practical terms, he could only exercise a very limited power on a party that was falling apart.

Power of the factions. Factions have almost always been irrelevant in formal terms, while in reality they have dominated, especially until 1992,[33] being still determinant in the composition of the renewed National Executive in March 1993. This is probably the key point for the overall understanding of the dynamics of the party organization: after their consolidation during the 1960s, the factions had been able to adapt to the different challenges they had to face, especially because almost all the party leaders, whether the secretary or simply members of the dominant coalition, have given priority to the success of their own part before looking at the unity and prosperity of the overall party.

Linkage with the flanking organizations. Apart from the *Coldiretti* and the *Movimento Popolare*, which have maintained a close relationship with the party during both De Mita's and Forlani's secretaryships, the vast array of ancillary organizations (ACLI, CISL, AC) had all loosened their ties with the party by the 1970s. One exception is to be found in the early 1990s, when the Left/Right factional division has been paralleled by a similar confrontation between the right-wing Popular Movement and the reformist attempts sponsored by FUCI and ACLI (Giovagnoli, 1996: 247). The crisis of the party during Martinazzoli's secretaryship saw a further detachment of the organizations from the DC: FUCI and ACLI sponsored the referendarian campaign launched by the ex-DC Mario Segni, while the splinter group of *La Rete* attracted parts of the left-wing associations, especially in the south.

Consistency of the membership. This has always been a "black hole" in the party organization: in front of high "formal" figures provided until 1992 by the official party sources, Martinazzoli's reforms have shown how the real data were different. An example of the substantial "continuity" in the organizational patterns of the party is indeed provided by the data on the renewal of the membership in 1993. According to a report of the weekly magazine *Panorama* (18 April 1993), in some provinces of the north the decrease after the erasure has been massive (−68 percent in Padua and Massa Carrara, −65 percent in Belluno, −64 percent in Venice and Vercelli) while in the south the hemorrhage was limited (−18 percent in Naples, −10 percent in Bari). A plausible explanation of this trend may be related to the different characteristics of the membership, more participant—and therefore "responsive" to the corruption investigations—in the north, dormant, "factionalized," and more dependent in the south (Cartocci, 1994). The mass-clientelistic model (Caciagli, 1982) seems therefore to fit the situation of the south, and therefore of the majority of the local activities,[34] still during the last few months of life of the DC.

On the other side, the party continued to benefit, for all the period considered, from its position as the catholic party. The need for a strong organization has therefore been always secondary as, during all the postwar period, the organization has acted "more as an instrument of the stabilization of the power than as means of electoral mobilization" (Anderlini, 1989: 287). The occupation of the state agencies has, in this sense, provided the necessary financial resources for the economic survival of the party, while the catholic inspiration has acted, along with the clientelistic system established in the south, as the most relevant source of mass support. The organization of the factions has counterbalanced the lack of a strong party structure, creating a multitude of "internal parties," often kept together more by the common will of the occupation of power than by a real unity of intents. How could we summarize the main characteristics of the organization of the DC in the period 1982–1993? Given the substantial continuity in the structures and the lack of important novelties since early 1960, the party from De Mita to Martinazzoli has been basically characterized by the same dynamics of state occupation, with a decreasing role of the catholic associations and a constant low structuration of the territorial organizations (Scalisi, 1996). The "cartelization" of the DC (Katz and Mair, 1995) is therefore not subsequent to the catch-all phase (Kirchheimer, 1966) but rather complementary to that, being a necessary step that the party had to undertake in the early 1960s in order to become completely independent from the external sources of legitimation and financing. Hence, the DC assumed some characters of the "cartel party" at the same time when it was lowering its ideological baggage, introducing more centralized internal relationships, loosening the ties with the flanking organizations, in other words, when it was becoming "the Italian party that most closely approached the catch-all-party model" (Farneti, 1983: 202). The coexistence of the two models of party organization shows that their chronological sequence is not confirmed by the evidence of the DC case. The study of the party organization from 1982 to 1993 has shown how the first signs of crisis of the late 1980s (higher secularization, erosion of the significance of the Communist/antiCommunist cleavage after 1989) could not substantially threaten the practices of factional dominance in the internal decision-making process. Hence none of the models traditionally proposed by the literature seems to approximate, by itself, the characteristics of the DC in the 1980s, a highly factionalized party where each faction has often been pursuing its own scopes independently from the rest of the party. This situation has paradoxically strenghtened the resistence of the party to the major external threats, like the growing secularization associated with the crisis of the catholic subculture and the first electoral defeats of 1992. Indeed, the discovery of the corrupted system, through the direct involvment of almost all the leaders of the factions (and therefore of the dominant coalition), was probably the only way to break apart the system of patronage that the party had established during its uninterrupted permanence in power.

NOTES

1. Panebianco, largely drawing from the work of Crozier and Friedberg (1977), describes them as the areas of "organizational unpredictability" (1988: 33). They are: competency, environmental relations management, internal communication, formal rules, organizational financing and recruitment.

2. This movement was created in 1928 by Piero Malvestiti and Gioacchino Malavasi, in strong opposition to the fascist regime. Already in 1942 the movement presented the first program of the DC, Il Programma di Milano della Democrazia Cristiana.

3. The dominant coalition is the group "composed of those—whether inside or, strictly speaking, outside of the organization itself—organizational actors who control the most vital zones of uncertainty" (Panebianco, 1988: 38)

4. Until 1964, the election of all the internal bodies was regulated by a majoritarian electoral law, then abolished to guarantee the representation of the minority factions.

5. This Ministry, created in 1956 for the control of the public sector and the state agencies, was held by the DC in all but three governments until 1980, when its control passed to the PSI until 1983, to switch back to the DC until 1992 (Leonardi and Wertman, 1989: 223–36).

6. This has been effectively summarized by Leonardi and Wertman: "factions rep-

resent the mechanism through which the dialectic of power operates within the DC and makes possible shifts from one political strategy to another, shifts between ruling elites, generational changes within the party, and the servicing of diverse group interests" (1989: 91).

7. In Poggi (1968), in this respect, the DC is referred to as a "federal party," where the internal groups can establish their own relations with the external environment, often acting independently from the rest of the party.

8. Zaccagnini's reforms included new rules for the election of the Party Secretary (in 1976 he was directly elected by the Congress, but, already in 1980, the old rules of election by the National Council were reestablished) as well as a strong emphasis on more direct rank-and-file participation and the organization, following the model of the Communist *Festival dell'Unità*, of the *Feste dell'Amicizia* (Friendship Festival) (Leonardi and Wertman, 1989: 131–3).

9. Although a definitive judgment on the contribution of the factions to the internal organization of the party seems difficult to reach, it also stands as hazardous, especially if we look at the factions as associated to clientelism, to claim that "factional structure makes, in effect, a positive contribution to the internal workings of the party . . . , the positive contribution made by the factions inside the party outweigh the negative elements" (Leonardi and Wertman, 1989: 91). Panebianco provided a clear picture of the significance of the 1964 reform, saying that the adoption of the new rules was the "ex post ratification of the dominant coalition's conformation" (1988: 128).

10. The literature seems to agree on this: Sani (1967), describing the leading organs of the decision-making process in the Italian party, lists the National Executive as the prevalent one. The National Executive has also been described as the organ "entitled for the essential role in the mechanisms of implementation of the decision making" (Manconi, 1989: 89), the "prominent political and decision-making organ" (Sebastiani, 1982).

11. In September 1986, De Mita reformed the structure of the central party offices, reducing their number from 93 to 31 (28 regular and 3 special ones; see *Il Popolo*, 23 September 1986). However, this reform did not bring about significant changes.

12. As Caciagli notes: "De Mita's long reign is all the more remarkable for the DC never tolerated the holding of excessive power by its party secretary and always preferred collegial, if hierarchical, leadership. De Mita's tenure can be explained by the weakness and disorientation that the DC found itself in during the early 1980s" (Caciagli, 1991: 10)

13. Giulio Andreotti, who had been member of all the national governments until 1992, either as premier or as minister, has never been Party Secretary, but his faction has been one of the most powerful, as it controlled two regions which provided the largest sources of votes and members, Lazio and Sicily.

14. In September 1986, De Mita instituted the Conference of the Regional Secretaries: among the 30 members of the National Executive, 7 were regional secretaries, 6 of whom were De Mita's allies.

15. Anderlini (1989) distinguished between the two zones according to the different characterization of the membership, which was far more active (and also less numerous compared to the votes obtained by the party) in the northeast than in the south.

16. The number of sections increased from 10,287 in 1953 to 12,672 in 1959 (this

latter figure is very close to the data reported by the Central Organization Office for the late 1980s; see Leonardi and Wertman, 1989: 129)

17. This process was of fundamental importance, since the votes in the local organs determined the selection in the offices of the party at the upper levels.

18. The level of participation and activism is totally incomparable to that of the PCI, so far that "the *quality* of the DC membership has always been lower than in the PCI" (Hine, 1993: 118)

19. Anderlini defines the membership "familiar and forced" (1989: 296), meaning that, considering the far lower level of female emancipation in the south compared to the north, these figures do not express a higher female activism, but a clear influence of the factions in recruiting all the components of the families, no matter how these could have been interested in being members of the party. This clientelistic method included cases where the local leaders of the factions were dealing with the heads of the families, the *capifamiglia*, and the members—women in particular—sometimes were not aware of this procedure, not to mention cases where names of dead people have been found in the registers of the party recorded as "active" members.

20. The political significance of the Assago Conference is not as high as the leaders of the party claimed. The reforms it approved (new electoral system for local assemblies, incompatibility between membership of party offices and public offices, "limit" of four parliamentary mandates [in fact very easy to overcome]; see *Il Popolo*, 11 January 1992) are of very limited extent, as the party was still perceived as quite "safe" in its positions. A peculiar concern that emerges from the reading of the Conference is the need to give a new "identity" to the party, as the fall of the Berlin Wall had questioned the traditional validity of its anti-Communist appeal.

21. The relation with the CISL became less direct, especially after 1969, when the rule of incompatibility between party and union offices was approved (Feltrin, 1991).

22. The Meeting of Rimini has reached greater popularity than the DC's Festival dell'Amicizia, and, according to Leonardi and Wertman, could be compared, at least as far as press coverage and public interest are concerned, to the PCI's Festival dell'Unità (Leonardi and Wertman, 1989: 220).

23. This alliance eventually proved to be decisive for the election of Forlani as Party Secretary in 1989, which was celebrated by the MP's weekly magazine *Il Sabato*, with a straightforward title: "Back To Freedom" (*Il Sabato*, 25 February 1989).

24. *La Rete* (the Network), the new movement founded by the Mayor of Palermo Leoluca Orlando, former DC leader and strong opponent of the Andreotti's faction, traditionally dominant in Sicily, has been supported by influential religious personalities such as Padri Gesuiti Pintacuda and Sorge.

25. De Mita's friend Biagio Agnes was elected RAI's Director-General. According to Marletti, this helped the achievement of De Mita's project of "control of the broadcasting sector through the concentration of powers in the hands of the director-general and the emptying of the office of the president controlled by the Socialists" (1988: 173).

26. After the 1993 reform and the nomination of a new administration council the DC was still blamed for the passage from a regime of *lottizzazione* to a regime of one-party (DC) dominance (Mazzoleni, 1995).

27. *Istituto per la Ricostruzione Industriale*—IRI (Institute for Industrial Reconstruction) is the largest Institute, controlling over two-thirds of the state holdings; ENI,

Ente Nazionale Idrocarburi (National Hydrocarbons Trust) controls over 400 firms in the sector of energy; ENEL, *Ente Nazionale Energia Elettrica* (National Energy Trust) is the State Trust which controls the sector of energy. All these institutes were part of the Ministry of State Holdings, held in 80 percent of the Italian governments by the DC and finally abolished after the referendum of 18 April 1993. INA (*Istituto Nazionale Assicurazioni*) is the largest Italian insurance institute.

28. As examples we could cite the president of IRI, Franco Nobili, and of ENEL, Franco Viezzoli, the General Director of INA, Mario Fornari, and the ENI's adviser, Giuseppe Ammassari (see *Il Sole*, 24 Ore, 8 August 1992).

29. The great impact of the party defeat in Mantua was probably decisive in the election of Martinazzoli (Galli, 1993: 301)

30. Both new and old members had to file new applications and sign a programmatic manifesto "A Quanti hanno Passione Civile" (for its content, see De Rosa, 1993: 596–598).

31. The Congress of the Popular Party was held in January 1994, after the right-wing factions had splintered away to form the CCD, *Centro Crisitiano Democratico* (Christian Democratic Center).

32. The Left had been, all through the 1980s, more suspicious toward the PSI and the Caesaristic leadership of Craxi, who was Prime Minister from 1983 to 1987. The center-right, on the contrary, had based its power on a strong alliance with Craxi: in a journalistic language the 1980s have been described as the years of the CAF (Craxi, Andreotti and Forlani) dominance. Although simplistic, this view is very close to the real situation until 1992.

33. Still in the 1992 election the power of the faction to mobilize the vote and channel the (single) preference is evident in the case analyzed by Feltrin and Pellicani (1993), who emphasize the survival of the faction of Dorotei in one of the traditional DC bulwarks in Veneto.

34. According to the latest available figures, in 1986, over half of the members of the party came from the south (Anderlini, 1989: 289)

REFERENCES

Allum, Percy (1973). *Politics and Society in Postwar Naples.* Cambridge: Cambridge Univeristy Press.

Anderlini, Fausto (1989). "La DC: Iscritti e Modello di Partito." *Polis* 3: 277–304.

Baget-Bozzo, Gianni (1974). *Il Partito Cristiano al Potere.* 2 vols. Florence: Vallecchi.

Bardi, Luciano and Leonardo Morlino (1992). "Italy." In Richard S. Katz and Peter Mair (eds.), *Party Organizations: A Data Handbook on Party Organizations In Western Democracies, 1960–1990*, pp. 458–518. London: Sage.

Bardi, Luciano and Leonardo Morlino (1994). "Italy: Tracing the Roots of the Great Transformation." In Richard S. Katz and Peter Mair (eds.), *How Parties Organize*, pp. 242–277. London: Sage.

Becchi, Ada (1992). "The Difficult Reconstruction In Irpinia." In Stephen Hellman and Gianfranco Pasquino (eds.), *Italian Politics, A Review* 7, pp. 110–128. Boulder, CO: Westview Press.

Caciagli, Mario (1977). *Democrazia Cristiana e Potere nel Mezzogiorno.* Florence: Guaraldi Editore.

Caciagli, Mario (1982). "The Mass Clientelism Party and Conservative Politics: Christian Democracy In Southern Italy." In Henry Z Layton (ed.), *Conservative Politics In Western Europe*, pp. 264–291. London: Macmillan.

Caciagli, Mario (1990). "Erosioni e Mutamenti nell'Elettorato Democristiano." In Mario Caciagli and Alberto Spreafico (eds.), *Vent'anni di Elezioni In Italia 1968–1987*, pp. 3–30. Padova: Liviana Editrice.

Caciagli, Mario (1991). "The 18th Congress: from De Mita to Forlani and the Victory of 'Neodoroteism.' " In Filippo Sabetti and Raimondo Catanzaro (eds.), *Italian Politics, A Review* 5, pp. 8–22. Boulder, CO: Westview Press.

Cartocci, Roberto (1994). *Fra Lega e Chiesa*. Bologna: Il Mulino.

Cotta, Maurizio (1979). *Classe Politica e Parlamento In Italia*. Bologna: Il Mulino.

Crozier, Michel and Erhard Friedberg (1977). *L'Acteur et le Système*. Paris: Ed. du Seuil.

D'Amato, Luigi (1965). *Correnti di Partito e Partito di Correnti*. Milano: Giuffrè.

DC (1984). *Statuto del Partito*. Roma.

De Rosa, Giuseppe (1993). "Per una Dc Veramente Nuova. La Sfida di Martinazzoli." *Civiltà Cattolica* 3426: 593–603.

Farneti, Paolo (1983). *Il Sistema dei Partiti In Italia 1946–1979*. Bologna: Il Mulino.

Feltrin, Paolo (1991). "L' Arena delle Relazioni Industriali e il Rapporto tra Sindacati e Partiti?" *Economia e Lavoro* 25: 39–53.

Feltrin, Paolo and Nicola Pellicani (1993). "L'Incredibile Tenuta dei Dorotei: la Circoscrizione Verona-Padova-Rovigo. In Gianfranco Pasquino (ed.)., *Votare un Solo Candidato*, pp. 133–175. Bologna: Il Mulino.

Galli, Giorgio (1978). *Storia della DC*. Bari: Laterza.

Galli, Giorgio (1993). *Mezzo Secolo di DC*. Milano: Rizzoli.

Giovagnoli, Agostino (1996). *Il Partito Italiano. La Democrazia Cristiana dal 1942 al 1994*. Bari: Laterza.

Graziano, Luigi (1980). *Clientelismo e Sistema Politico: Il caso dell'Italia*. Milano: Franco Angeli.

Hine, David (1982). "Factionalism in West European Parties: A Framework for Analysis." *West European Politics* 5: 36–53.

Hine, David (1993). *Governing Italy: The Politics of Bargained Pluralism*. Oxford: Clarendon Press.

Katz, Richard S. and Luciano Bardi (1979). "Voto di Preferenza e Ricambio del Personale Parlamentare In Italia (1963–1976)." *Rivista Italiana di Scienza Politica* 9: 221–244.

Katz, Richard S. and Peter Mair (1995). "Changing Models of Party Organization and Party Democracy: The Emergence of the Cartel Party." *Party Politics* 1: 5–28.

Kirchheimer, Otto (1966). "The Transformation of the Western European Party System." In Joseph La Palombara and Myron Weiner (eds.), *Political Parties and Political Development*. Princeton: Princeton University Press.

Leonardi, Robert and Douglas Wertman (1989). *Italian Christian Democracy: The Politics of Dominance*. New York: Macmillan.

Manconi, Luigi (1988). "Chi Comanda nella DC. La Leadership Democristiana: un Modello di Poliarchia Imperfetta." *Il Mulino* 37: 113–137.

Manconi, Luigi (1989). "Due tempi, due Ritmi. La Direzione Democristiana." *Polis* 3: 85–109.

Marletti, Carlo (1988). "Parties and Mass Comunications." In Raffaella Y. Nanetti, Robert Leonardi, and Piergiorgio Corbetta (eds.), *Italian Politics, A Review*, pp. 167–78. Boulder, CO: Westview Press.

Mazzoleni, Giuseppe (1995). "The RAI: Restructuring and Reform." In Carol Mershon and Gianfranco Pasquino (eds.), *Italian Politics, Ending the First Republic*, pp. 151–64. N.P.

Morlino, Leonardo (1995). "Consolidation and Party Government In Southern Europe." *International Political Science Review* 16: 145–167.

Panebianco, Angelo (1988*). Political Parties: Organization and Power.* Cambridge: Cambridge University Press. English translation of *Modelli di Partito.* Bologna: Il Mulino, 1982.

Poggi, Gianfranco (ed.) (1968). *L'Organizzazione Partitica del Pci e della DC.* Bologna: Il Mulino.

Rossi, Maurizio (1979). "Un Partito di 'anime morte'? Il Tesseramento Democristiano tra Mito e Realtà." In Arturo M. L. Parisi (ed.), *Democristiani*, pp. 13–59. Bologna: Il Mulino.

Rossi, Maurizio (1987). "Sezioni di Partito e Partecipazione Politica." *Polis* 1: 67–99.

Sani, Giacomo (1967). "Alcuni dati sul ricambio della dirigenza partitica nazionale In Italia." *Rassegna Italiana di Sociologia* 8: 126–141.

Sartori, Giovanni (1971). "Proporzionalismo, Frazionismo e Crisi dei Partiti." *Rivista Italiana di Scienza Politica* 1: 629–656.

Scalisi, Pietro (1996). "La Dissoluzione delle Strutture Organizzative di base dei Partiti." *Polis* 10: 221–244.

Sebastiani, Chiara (1982). "Organi Dirigenti Nazionali: Composizione, Meccanismi di Formazione e di Evoluzione 1945–1979." In Massimo Ilardi and Aris Accornero (eds.), *Il Partito Comunista Italiano. Struttura e storia dell'organizzazione 1921–1979*, pp. 387–444. Milano: Feltrinelli.

Tarrow, Sidney (1967). *Peasant Communism in Southern Italy.* New Haven: Yale University Press.

Verzichelli, Luca (1995). "Gli Eletti." In Stefano Bartolini and Roberto D'Alimonte (eds.), *Maggioritario ma non troppo*, pp. 401–425. Bologna: Il Mulino.

Wertman, Douglas (1979). "La Partecipazione Intermittente. Gli Iscritti e la Vita di Partito." In Arturo M.L. Parisi (ed.), *Democristiani*, pp. 61–84. Bologna: Il Mulino.

Wertman, Douglas (1988). "Italy: Local Involvement, Central Control." In Michael Gallagher and Michael Marsh (eds.), *Candidate Selection in Comparative Perspective: The Secret Garden of Politics*, pp. 145–168. London: Sage.

Wertman, Douglas (1995). "The Last Year of the DC." In Carol Mershon and Gianfranco Pasquino (eds.), *Italian Politics, Ending the First Republic*, pp. 135–150. N.P.

7

From Militants to Voters: From the PCI to the PDS

——————————————————— *Maria Pamini*

In its history, the *Partito Comunista Italiano* (Italian Communist Party—PCI) has faced various critical situations and subsequent organizational changes. Nevertheless, it has retained its own basic features: the Marxist ideology and the principle of democratic centralism. What prevented radical changes was, above all, its strong institutionalization. However, the organizational crisis which has occurred in the last decade has been so intense and so extensive as to force those innovations which produced, at the XXth National Congress (1991), the formation of a radically renovated party: the *Partito Democratico della Sinistra* (Democratic Party of the Left—PDS) (Ignazi, 1992).

In the period considered here, spanning from Alessandro Natta's appointment as General Secretary of the PCI in 1984 to the end of Occhetto's mandate in 1994,[1] the party underwent a process of renewal which moved it away from the model of the mass integration party. The best-fitted model for the late PCI and the PDS is the "professional-electoral party," in accordance with a revision in organizational terms of Otto Kirchheimer's catch-all party[2] (Panebianco, 1988: 264). This model is characterized by two parallel processes: the de-ideologization and the de-institutionalization of the party organization. Their effects can be summarized as follows: (a) loss of influence on the part of members and militants: the party turns mainly to the electorate at large and the electoral appeals emphasize specific topics rather than universal principles; (b) growing importance of professionals with technical abilities instead of bureaucrats, and of "careerists" instead of "believers" (selective incentives prevail over collective incentives); (c) increasing importance of the party leadership; (d) weakening of vertical organizational relationships and, in general, of the organizational party machine; (e) preeminence of public officeholders.

The change from the PCI to the PDS in 1991 not only implied a new leadership and ideological innovations, but above all, a new organizational order. Such a radical transformation was due to the pressure of structural societal changes (the modifications in the system of social stratification, which no longer follows the lines of class division; the cultural changes resulting from the diffusion of the secularization and of a high level of education, which have led to a heterogeneous and unstable electorate; and finally, the technological transformation of the means of communication) and party conjunctural ones (environmental challenges such as a series of electoral failures and the breakdown of the Communist countries in Eastern Europe).

This study aims to identify the new party organizational identity after the turning point in 1991, taking into account the process of change since the mid-1980s. The analysis will focus on three main aspects: ideological change, loosening of the integrative function and party embeddment and composition and turnover in the executive bodies.

1. The first area deals with the ideological changes established by the new dominant coalition in order to fully legitimate the party in the liberal-democratic system. The replacement of the final objectives corresponds to a resolute detachment from the Marxist-Leninist orthodoxy. The gradual de-ideologization of the PCI was simultaneous with "the process transferring authority from the external institution [the PCUS] to the party" (Panebianco, 1988: 164). It began with the "de-Stalinization" at the VIIIth National Congress (1956) and continued with the "break" (*strappo*) led by Enrico Berlinguer in 1981 after the Communist *coup d'etàt* in Poland by General Jaruzelski. Despite the fact that the legitimating reference to the myth of the Soviet society was losing "its propulsive strength" and displaying "illiberal features," Berlinguer's judgment of Social Democracy remained negative and Communism continued to be his ultimate aim. Therefore, even if international and domestic political factors urged for the party's complete integration into the Italian political system, the political militants were tied to their traditional ideological-cultural identity, and for these activists the collective incentives of identity were still the main factor of adhesion to the PCI. During the early 1980s, the Communist leadership promoted a process of articulation of aims. The party took steps toward increasing internal pluralism, giving voice to the reformist covert tendency in the National Congress of 1986 "healing the schism, having existed . . . for decades, between Communism and Social Democracy" (Urban, 1987: 131.)[3] This tendency was to be further developed during Occhetto's leadership.

In the first paragraph of this chapter the formal-institutional changes and the redefinition of aims that occurred in the period considered will be illustrated, analyzing the various changes in the party statutes.

2. The redefinition of the dominant coalition will be examined through the analysis of the composition, turnover and relationship among executive

party bodies: the *Comitato Centrale* (Central Committee), since 1991 *Consiglio Nazionale* (National Council), the *Direzione* (Executive Committee) and the *Segreteria* (Secretariat). The analysis of the new dominant coalition will include an examination of the power relationships among the different organizational units of the party. The de-institutionalization operating in the party in the last decade was revealed by a new relationship between center and periphery, and also between the party and its local and national representatives. There was an attempt to transform the old bureaucratic apparatus, with its monolithic and centralistic character, into a more flexible, open and decentralized organizational structure: "[the party's] level of institutionalization being reduced, new and completely original areas for manoeuvres open for its parliamentaries and in general for the representatives elected at all the levels" (Panebianco, 1988: 164). Our analysis will be concentrated on the horizontal exchanges between the national leadership and the parliamentary group, in order to verify whether there is still a subordination of the latter to the former.

3. The decrease in the integrative function implies a weakening of the party's relationship with the flanking organizations. The following analysis will try to assess how much the vertical linkages have loosened between the party and some of its traditional flanking organizations which were agents of mobilization of party's support in the civil society (FGCI/Sinistra Giovanile, ARCI, UDI, CGIL).

The main external factor which influenced the beginning of the renewal of the leadership was the negative electoral trend. After almost a decade of a continuous increase both in the number of votes and of party members, in the late 1970s the trend was inverted (see Table 7.1). Since 1979, the PCI has suffered remarkable electoral defeats in all contexts, except for the 1984 European Parliament elections in which the PCI gained 3.7 percent of the votes, coming in ahead of all other Italian parties. This outcome was mainly due to the emotional impact of the sudden death of the party leader, Berlinguer, during the electoral campaign. The following year, however, the PCI confirmed the negative electoral trend in the local elections, losing the control of some large cities and regional councils. The number of mayors elected on the PCI's list fell from 20 to 13 in the provincial capitals, and from 1,341 to 470 in the communes with populations of over 5,000.[4] In addition to this the PCI suffered another defeat in 1985 over the referendum concerning the *scala mobile* (wage cost of living indexation), which they themselves promoted.[5]

INSTITUTIONAL AND IDEOLOGICAL CHANGES

The renewal of the party elite always corresponds to specific innovations concerning the formal rules, the ideology and the political strategy. In the period considered here, the PCI/PDS drew up three new versions of the party

Table 7.1
PCI/PDS Membership, 1976–1992

Year	Members	New members	Rate of recruitment	Membership's decrease	
				No.	%
1976	1,814,317	75,948	9.69	---	---
1977	1,814,154	130,166	7.17	163	---
1978	1,790,450	103,310	5.77	23,704	1.30
1979	1,759,295	95,619	5.43	31,155	1.74
1980	1,751,323	91,149	5.20	7,972	0.45
1981	1,714,052	82,317	4.80	37,271	2.12
1982	1,673,751	67,905	4.05	40,301	2.35
1983	1,635,262	63,719	3.89	38,487	2.29
1984	1,619,940	65,157	4.02	15,324	0.93
1985	1,595,668	61,939	3.88	25,272	1.49
1986	1,551,576	51,442	3.31	44,092	2.76
1987	1,508,140	49,501	3.28	43,436	2.79
1988	1,462,281	42,574	2.91	45,859	3.04
1989	1,421,230	47,722	3.35	38,246	2.61
1990	1,319,905	57,828	4.38	101,325	7.12
1991*	989,708	52,280	5.28	330,197	25.01
1992	769,944	27,793	3.61	219,764	22.20

*Since 1991, PDS.
Sources: 1976–1989: Ignazi (1992: 101), Table 1; 1990–1992: official data provided by the PDS headquarters.

statute. While the statute approved at the XVIIth Congress (1986) was bound to the cultural and organizational identity of the past, the two statutes of 1989 (XVIIIth Congress), and especially the 1991 statute (XXth Congress) showed a clear-cut detachment from party traditions, in connection with the beginning of the political and generational turnover in the executive bodies. The statute's changes had two specific objectives: (1) to guarantee easier access to the party at top levels for the new political generation (i.e., the innovations regarding the internal democracy as the introduction of secret ballot for the election of the executive bodies in 1989 or the quota system for women); (2) to gain legitimacy from the external environment. In fact, the only way to obtain the green light to become a government party was the removal of those features peculiar to a Leninist Party, such as democratic centralism and the revolutionary character. However, on the contrary, in the statute of 1986, the PCI still stressed its own diversity compared to the other political forces, confirming democratic centralism as the rule governing the inner life of the party. At the same time, some exogeneous cultural elements following liberal-democratic values, such as the free representation of diverse internal political opinions, were introduced, increasingly exacerbating the contradiction between a unitary and centralistic party structure where discipline prevailed over participation. For example, although an explicit condemnation of the factions remained, the statute of 1986 recognized every member's right to "maintain and support, also in public, different positions from those of the majority arising each time" (Art. 6a). The not entirely predictable result of the innovations,[6] however marginal, was to influence the attitudes toward party organization by the apparatus, especially those members recruited in the years of the historical compromise. In sum, the distinction between written norms and customary practice became increasingly more evident.

In the 1989 statute, democratic centralism was no longer overtly spelled out, even if its logics persisted. But the introduction of a new rule legitimated the possibility of internal dissent: the Executive Committee and the Secretariat were elected with a secret vote (Art. 35, par. 6). In 1989, the question of female representation appeared for the first time: the statute established that the minimum quota of women within the ruling bodies had to be 40 percent (Art. 7). Finally, another Leninist vestige was removed: the basic party structure was no longer the "*cellula*" (cell) but the "*sezione*" (section), which had already predominated for many years.

In the PCI XXth National Congress (29 January–2 February 1991), having accepted internal democracy and pluralism, the PCI gave up once and for all the principle of democratic centralism on a normative level. Thus, the party adopted "the majority rule in the political decision," based "on the full recognition of pluralism, also autonomous forms and tools, of the different political-cultural positions." Among the members' rights appeared the right "to promote *also collectively* proposals and programmatic platforms" (Art. 6, italics mine). Moreover, the whole text was characterized by the principle of equality between males and females, at each organizational level. They could benefit from their new status on a local and national level, in order to define women party policies and initiatives (Arts. 2, 34 and 69).

Another meaningful formal change concerned the relationship between party headquarters and periphery. The basic structures were given greater autonomy in 1991, and the statute placed the regional dimension as the keystone of the whole party structure (Art. 10, par. 2). The political weight of regional secretaries grew: they were also allowed to take part in the activities of the Executive Committee with right of speech and proposal, even as non-members (Art. 35). The statute also acknowledged a greater autonomy to both regional and local council groups (Art. 57), and parliamentary groups, defined as "exclusive holders of the initiatives of direction and control, and of legislative initiatives" (Art. 60, par. 3). In these ways, the relationship between elected and voters changed: the party public officeholders were no longer restricted by party decisions, but became more responsive to the electorate. The new accountability did not concern the party as much as it did the voters. Furthermore, while permanent delegations of parliamentaries at the Central Committee (renominated National Council in 1991) had previously only had right of speech and proposal, they now were granted the right to vote on both the program and on institutional questions (Art. 32, par. 9).

The 1989 statute reflected a definitive departure from Marxist-Leninist culture. The language in the statute demonstrated the party's revised perceptions of class character: the party no longer addressed itself to the working class but "to women and men," adopting an individualistic viewpoint. Although the statute appealed "to the experience and traditions of the labor movement" and restated that the party's aim was "the pursuing of Socialist values," it also stated that the party was conceived "as a non-ideological organization" and that Democracy was not only the best means in order to reach a Socialist society, but was "the way to Socialism." The break-up from the old Communist political culture was momentous. On the economic level, the PCI statute attenuated the importance of state intervention and asserted that the "new economic democracy" is based on "a planning function of a state *which directs less* and exercises a more suitable directing function" (italics mine).

In the last statute (1991), there was a further detachment from the old ideological objectives. Its introduction included the invitation "to gather and go beyond traditions" as a consequence of the acknowledgement of the "failure of the despotic regimes constituted in the name of Communism." While Marx was mentioned only once in the preamble to the 1989 statute, in 1991 he was completely omitted, as were the fathers of Italian Communism, Gramsci and Togliatti. Instead, a reference was made to the "heritages of liberal and democratic revolutions, taking them beyond their historical class bounds."

THE EXECUTIVE BODIES

The analysis of the dominant coalition's renewal will be developed on two different levels: its new composition (the size of political and generational turnover) and its new conformation (internal and external power relationships) (Panebianco, 1988: 38–39). The latter aspect includes three indicators: the leadership's cohesion (the degree of power concentration); its stability (the capacity to reach agreements in the party elite); and the power relationships with the local and parliamentary elite and with the flanking organizations. The low or high degree of cohesion depends on the presence in the party of weakly or strongly organized groups, or in other words, tendencies or factions. In the last decade there has been a radical transformation of the internal groups. In the past, the rule of democratic centralism, although it guaranteed a high degree of the dominant coalition's cohesion, did not prevent competition among party tendencies. Since the 1960s, at least three such tendencies had been easily recognizable, in spite of their fluidity: Pietro Ingrao's Left tendency, Giorgio Amendola's right tendency (then led by Giorgio Napolitano from 1980), and the so-called "large Center" a group with less definite boundaries than the others that has always represented the position of General Secretaries. But since the early 1980s, internal divisions have increased.[7] The more visible new tendencies placed themselves at the extremes beyond the "historical" Left and Right. One is the "orthodox" tendency of Armando Cossutta that criticized the move toward the social democratization imposed by the leadership and the subsequent denial of the party's Marxist roots; and the other, at the opposite extreme, is the less relevant tendency of Napoleone Colajanni, favoring an acceleration of the process of secularization. Only in the late 1980s, as a result of the removal of democratic centralism, did these tendencies become organized factions, particularly after the special National Congress held in Bologna from 7 March 1990, which for the first time was structured around three competing motions. These three motions benefited from the same space in the party press and from the same financial and organizational means. They spanned the whole party, from the top to the bottom (Belloni, 1991: 143–170). Given these organizational resources, the Cossutta faction could react in a categorical way to Occhetto's turning point at the XXth Congress (1991): it refused to adhere to the PDS and founded an autonomous party, *Rifondazione Comunista* (Communist Refoundation—RC) (Hellman, 1992: 127; Daniels, 1992: 129–135).

In the late 1980s, a low degree of party stability corresponded also to a decrease in party cohesion. A clear sign of this was the end of the unanimity which had previously characterized the approval of political documents at the conclusion of National Congresses. In any case, the new dominant coalition was able to confront sensitive issues without deep divisions, thanks to certain tactical devices. For example, the final document of the XVIIIth Congress (1989), which did not satisfy Napolitano's faction, was passed because of Occhetto's proposal to vote for it only on its "general lines"[8] (Amyot, 1989: 121–122). Party policy negotiations and division of spoils (appointments) based on the power of the different internal factions thus became increasingly predominant.

The factionalization of the executive bodies, and the corresponding low degree of cohesion of the dominant coalition modified the profile of the leadership favoring its bargaining role. Until 1986, the designation of the highest degree of the Communist hierarchy had had the character of a consensual investiture: the elected secretary seemed the natural successor and became "tendentially a secretary for life" (Carrieri, 1987: 296). The lack of precise procedures for the election of the secretary (until 1989 the statute prescribed only which bodies were delegated to carry out this task—that is, the Central Committee and the Central Control Commission [*Commissione Centrale di Controllo*] in common session—without stating the modalities) allowed the leadership to pursue unanimity. Natta, unlike his predecessors Longo and Berlinguer (elected not only unanimously but also by acclamation), gained twelve abstentions even though elections were carried out with open vote. This novelty can also be explained by a different conception of the role of the secretary, no longer representing "an absolute leader" but rather "a leader guaranteeing internal pluralism" (Carrieri, 1987: 303). Natta's election as General Secretary was a first step in this direction. In 1991, when the secret vote was set up, Occhetto was not even confirmed as General Secretary in the first election as he was ten votes short of reaching the absolute majority, equivalent to 274 votes, a target which he would have exceeded if all the members of the majority had voted for him (Hellman, 1992: 122–123).[9]

In 1994, for the first time, the contest invested various candidates. However, the open competition between Massimo D'Alema and Walter Veltroni to fill in Occhetto's resignation was carried out in an *ad hoc* way. First, a consultative referendum was organized among all the members (which gave a slight majority in favor of Veltroni); then the National Assembly voted effectively for the two candidates, and contrary to the member's referendum outcome, D'Alema came first and became General Secretary (Bull, 1995).

A direct consequence of the party's factionalization was the continuous enlargement of executive bodies, and therefore the multiplication of available material incentives for every faction. This happened particularly to the Central Committee/National Council. Even though in the statute of 1989 the Central Committee was still defined as "the most important organ of political direction and of party resolution," its huge growth over time (a process in action before the 1980s) increasingly penalized its executive function in favor of the representative one, and has favored the two narrow organs, the Executive Committee and the Secretariat. The membership of the Central Committee/National Council was 179 in 1983, 219 in 1986, 300 in 1989, 357 in 1990, and reached a total of 544 after the XXth Congress (1991) (see Table 7.2). An important feature of the party, as far as the inner stability was concerned, was that the turnover occurred through a "marginal rotation" which did not remove *in toto* the old guard, but flanked to it a large intake of new members. In fact, in 1989 and in 1991, the years with the highest turnover, the number of new members (139 in 1989 and 268 in 1991) was almost equal to the number of members confirmed (161 in 1989 and 276 in 1991). So, the body's enlargement became a "modality of resolution of conflicts"; in this way renewal was less traumatic, and stability was safeguarded (Ignazi, 1992: 112). In the Congress of 1990 the old guard tried to stop political renewal. The number of newcomers was reduced to 89 and over half of those who were not confirmed had entered in the previous Congress (1989). Their mandate lasted only one term. This turnover is mainly related to the access of many newcomers belonging to the so-called group of "outsiders" (*esterni*), a delegation of people not enrolled in the party. This intake of nonparty members fulfilled the function of "opening" the party to the civil society, instead of promoting the party functionaries (Bardi and Morlino: 1994). Fi-

Table 7.2
Turnover of the Central Committee/National Committee, 1979–1991

Congress	N. Members	N. Confirmed	%(*) Confirmed	N. New Members	%(**) New Members
XVth (1979)	169	---	---	---	---
XVIth (1983)	179	122	72.1	57	31.8
XVIIth (1986)	219	142	79.3	77	35.1
XVIIIth (1989)	300	161	73.5	139	46.3
XIXth (1990)	357	268	89.3	89	24.9
XXth (1991)	544	276	77.3	268	49.2

*The percentage is calculated on the total of members of the previous CC/NC.
**The percentage is calculated on the total of members of the corresponding CC/NC.
Sources: 1979–1990: Ignazi (1992); 1991: official data provided by the PDS headquarters.

nally, part of the membership renewal of the Central Committee/National Council in the last years is due to the "anti-discrimination quota." The number of women in the assembly has risen steadily. There were 25 in 1983, 40 in 1986, 93 in 1989, 113 in 1990 and 190 in 1991: in spite of this increase, the minimum quota decreed by the statute has not yet been reached.

The Executive Committee has been for long "the stable barycentre" of Communist leadership (Sebastiani, 1982a: 433; Carrieri, 1987: 286). In 1989, there was an increase in membership (from 39 to 52 members, with the number of the newcomers rising from 13 to 22—that is, from 33.3 percent to 42.3 percent) to the detriment of the executive function, and in favor of strengthening the vertical power structure. While, in 1986, it was still possible to state that the Executive Committee did not have the function of representing the different tendencies (Carrieri, 1987: 282) (a trait which had, until then, distinguished it from the Central Committee), at the XVIIIth Congress (1989) some space was allowed for all emerging internal political positions (*l'Unità*: 6.4. 1989). Consequently, since 1989, the cohesion of the body diminished and power became more diffused.[10] In 1990, the number of members fell and it was possible to perceive an attempt to restore an executive function to this body, and a more balanced relationship with the Secretariat. But at the following Congress (1991) its membership increased again to 117, also owing to the reentry of nearly all of those excluded the year before.[11] Even considering the sixteen members who had reentered, the turnover was the highest ever attained, with 53.8 percent. Only five members left the Executive Committee, three of them to adhere to the splinter party, *Rifondazione Comunista*. Also in this case, the statute's rule concerning the gender quota contributed to the large replacement of membership: the number of women rose from 11 in 1989 to 39 in 1991, that is, 33.3 percent.

If we examine this turnover from a generational point of view, we observe that the average age of new members from the mid-1980s to 1991 does not show any clear trend: it was 50 in 1986, 44 in 1989, 48 in 1990 and 46 in 1991. The renewal becomes significant if we take into consideration the political generation of the new members, referring to the year of party enrollment rather than the year of birth. Among the newcomers in the Congress of 1989, the majority was composed of those who joined the PCI in the 1960s and above all in the 1970s (seven and twelve, respectively). In the last Congress (although the presence of these generations was still remarkable) there was a considerable percentage (almost 25 percent) of "absolute freshmen" who, in 1991, not only joined the PDS, but even entered the National Council and the Executive Committee at the same time. For the most part they were that group of outsiders mobilized in 1989, and this might explain their high average age, although they belonged to a younger political generation. These data show that another constant in the political careers of party leaders is being suppressed: the slow turnover due to a long *cursus-honorum*. In the past, the presence in the Central Committee before joining the Executive Committee lasted an average of five years, whereas in 1991, 25.6 percent of the members of the executive body had entered the Central Committee only in 1990, or even in 1991. The main reason for the accelerated rate of access to the highest levels of the party's hierarchy can be explained by the new leadership's need to avail itself of, as soon as possible, its own political generation.

Since the mid to late 1970s, the dominant coalition in the Executive Committee has been characterized by that generation who "approached politics outside of the party's traditional channels, who became party functionaries as their first employment," joined the PCI in early life (around the age of 20) and reached peripheral leading appointments after a short time (Sebastiani, 1982: 223). Later, this trend highly increased (Ignazi, 1992: 115) and led more and more to the professional-electoral model. However, the career of the majority of the leaders was still "internal," with a prevalence of professional politicians, even though the party leadership theoretically admitted the positive "role of the 'non-professional politicians' at every level."[12]

Another feature distinguishing the Executive Committee's membership in these years is the strong presence of members holding executive positions on a local level. The experience in local and/or regional secretariats became crucial to the new leaders' careers: of the seven regional secretaries, who entered at the XVIIIth Congress (1989) and left in the following one, a good six of them returned in 1991, and another five regional secretaries were added (see Table 7.3).

The nature of the Secretariat "as an équipe working in support of the secretary," can be considered the basis of the party's change (Ignazi, 1992: 119). A limited generational turnover began in 1986 when the historical leaders of the pre-war generation were replaced (three members in 1986 and four in 1987), but the generational renewal became radical only in 1989.

Table 7.3
Turnover of the Executive Committee, 1979–1991

Congress	N. members	N. Confirmed	% (*) Confirmed	N. New Members	% (**) New Members
XVth (1979)	32				
XVIth (1983)	33	26	81.2	7	21.2
XVIIth (1986)	39	26	78.7	13	33.3
XVIIIth (1989)	52	30	76.9	22	42.3
XIXth (1990)	43	31	59.6	12	27.9
XXth (1991)	117	38	88.4	79	67.5

N.B. Also the ex officio members, that is the presidents of the CC/CN and of the CCC/NGC, are included. The members co-opted during the intercongressional period are counted as new entries in the following Congress.

*The percentage is calculated on the total of members of the previous Executive Committee.

**The percentage is calculated on the total of members of the corresponding Executive Committee.

Sources: 1979–1990: Ignazi (1992); 1991: official data provided by the PDS headquarters.

During this time, the average age of its members noticeably lowered, from approximately 60 years old in 1983 to 52 in 1986 and to 43 in 1989 (the Secretary himself was the oldest member), much lower than that of the Executive Committee (50 years old in 1989). In 1992, the degree of turnover was very high: there were five newcomers, almost 50 percent (in the first Occhetto's Secretariat there was only one newcomer), two of them had joined the party and entered the National Committee as well as the Executive Committee only in 1991. In the Secretariat of 1992, as well as in the Executive Committee, the Emilia Romagna region, which was the party stronghold with one-quarter of all the members, was strongly represented with three members out of eleven. Because of internal factions, in 1989 the inner cohesion of the Secretariat decreased. After the party change, the 1992 Secretariat dominant coalition comprised, beyond Occhetto's center, the two Left factions. (*l'Unità*, 20. 6. 1992) The right-wing was kept out, and it voiced its dissent toward the Secretary by abstaining from voting in the new Secretariat. Nevertheless, this more ample support to the secretary guaranteed the high stability of the executive body.

A new organ replaced temporarily the Secretariat in 1991, the *Coordinamento politico* (Political Coordination). The institution of this "experimental" executive body was a sign of a centrifugal drive between old and new leaders. Its purpose consisted of a clearinghouse for inner conflicts, to reestablish a balance among the different political tendencies, and to carry out the transition to a new arrangement of the dominant coalition. The 24 members represented the different generations (including historical leaders) and the various internal factions (*l'Unità*, 26. 2. 1991; *Corriere della Sera*, 26. 2. 1991). Its collective character made it hard for it to fulfill a full executive function because of the high inner dispersion of power (*l'Unità*, 7. 3. 1991). Just after one year the Secretariat was reinstated, as a result of the need to consolidate the new party leadership.

THE PARLIAMENTARY GROUPS

In the past the PCI's national leadership have always prevailed over its parliamentary representatives. This relationship of dependence was due above all to the extra-parliamentary origin of the PCI and its centralized structure (Baldassarre, 1982: 449),[13] providing that the position within the party was the condition for entering them (Sebastiani, 1982a: 417; Carrieri, 1987: 289). In the period between 1946 and the mid-1970s, a high percentage of PCI's political personnel served in the Executive Committee before entering the Chamber of Deputies. This trend shows the unidirectionality of the sequence between party and parliamentary posts (Cotta, 1979: 120). During the 1980s, the party *iter* was still preferential in the political training of the MPs. In fact, in the period from 1983 to 1991, the average number of the Executive Committee members elected in Parliament before this appointment was 13; on the contrary, the average number of those who had been nominated members of the Executive Committee before becoming deputies or senators was 43. It must be noted, however, that in the XXth National Congress (1991), the number of members of the Executive Committee with experience in the representative institution doubled compared to the previous Congress (from 11 to 22). Although this result cannot be interpreted unequivocally on account of the recent disproportionate enlargement of the party organ, it neverthless demonstrates a growing importance of the elective-representative career in the early 1990s. This feature was reinforced by the "parliamentarization" rate of the main PCI's organs (see Table 7.4). The overlap between deputies and senators and Central Committee members had always been considerably lower than the overlap in the Executive Committee and the Secretariat. The parliamentary seat was acquired only after having accumulated important party offices; hence the percentage of members of the Central Committee/National Council who also hold a seat in Parliament remained very low. The same does not hold for the executive bodies where the rate of MPs was much higher. In 1991 there was a decreasing parliamentarization rate of the Executive Committee (only 30 percent), but this is related to the growth of the executive organs, and the simultaneous reduction in the number of seats gained by the PDS in the elections of 1987, on one side, and to the renewal of the national leadership, on the other side. These data suggest that the changes of the dominant coalition are experienced first in the party bodies and then they are transferred to the parliamentary groups. In fact, the low parliamentarization rate of the Secratariat in 1989 (55.5 per-

Table 7.4
Parliamentarization Rate of the Executive Committee, Secretariat and CC/NC

Congress	CC/NC N.	CC/NC %	Executive Committee N.	Executive Committee %	Secretariat N.	Secretariat %
XVIth (1979*)	43	24.0	19	59.5	8	88.8
XVIIth (1983*)	46	21.0	21	55.0	6	66.6
XVIIIth (1987*)	57	19.0	26	50.0	5	62.5
XIXth (1987*)	63	18.0	25	59.0	5	55.5
XXth (1987*)	67	12.0	35	30.0	-	-

*The date in parenthesis refers to the year of the general elections considered. The parliamentarization rate has been calculated considering how many politicians were present in Parliament when they undertook the party appointment. As far as the Political Coordination replacing the Secretariat after the XXth Congress is concerned, the percentage of its members elected at the general elections of 1987 is 64.0 percent, that is, 16 out of 25 (treasurer included). In the Secretariat of 1992 there are 7 members out of 11 (or 63.6 percent) elected in Parliament in the elections of the same year.

Source: official data provided by the PDS headquarters.

cent) shows that the renewal of the national leadership was still in progress, while the higher rate of the Secretariat in 1992 (63.6 percent) shows that the party's leadership was being consolidated. Therefore, the new leadership was ready to occupy the positions of power which were traditionally considered outside the party's central bodies.

A further point which demonstrates the subordinate position of the parliamentary party was that in the past the parliamentary activity was led by a narrow group of deputies and senators, and in particular by the head of the group, which was usually a highly authoritative party personality with a privileged relationship with the party leadership (Baldassarre, 1982: 462). These "frontbenchers" had high seniority in the Parliament. They dominated the "backbenchers," who had low seniority since their turnover was particularly high. This high turnover of the backbenchers is confirmed also after the general elections of 1983, 1987 and 1992. During that period, more than half of the parliamentary group was renewed at every election: 51 percent in 1983, 50 percent in 1987 and 59 percent in 1992. Moreover, the PDS statute itself established that "the mandate of each member of Parliament does not exceed, as a rule, two legislatures, except the case of a different decision by the Executive Committee, in agreement with the presidencies of the parliamentary groups" (Art. 58, par. 6). In 1992, 83.2 percent of both deputies and senators were absolute newcomers or had one legislature experience in Parliament. In the 1994 landslide election the PDS selected 61.5 percent freshmen in the Chamber of Deputy. These data further demonstrate the general renewal of the party's leadership.

THE FLANKING ORGANIZATIONS

For many years the PCI extended its social encroachment as a result of the support of several flanking organizations which, taking care of various non-political problems (sport and cultural activities are only a few examples), contributed to the widening of its political influence. However, already in the late 1960s it could be said that those associations which found "in their own aims, in their own particular purposes an opportunity and a reason of autonomy because these aims were more easily proposable than the party's general aims" (Manoukian, 1968: 181) were being developed and consolidated from an organizational point of view, thus freeing themselves (although in a discontinuous and irregular way) from the dependence upon resources granted by the party.

In order to verify the changes in the relationship between the still-functioning flanking organizations and the party, the cases of the *Unione Donne Italiane* (Union of Italian Women—UDI), of the *Associazione Ricreativa Culturale Italiana* (Italian Recreative Cultural Association—ARCI) and of the *Confederazione Generale Italiana del Lavoro* (Italian General Confederation of Labor—CGIL) will be considered. In addition to these organizations the *Federazione Giovanile Comunista Italiana* (Italian Communist Young Federation/Young Left—FGCI) should be included because, while it cannot be considered an external organization outside the PCI/PDS, it has always tried to obtain greater autonomy.

The UDI was founded in 1944 by Communist and Socialist leaders. Although the statute declared the UDI's independence from any political party, "both for the political alignment of its promoters and for the type of members already gained by socialist influence in a broader sense . . . it took shape as a flanking movement of the Marxist Left and above all of the PCI." (Manoukian, 1968: 214). This strong connection with the Communist Party existed both for the members (a high percentage of the UDI members also had the membership card of the PCI and the recruitment came overwhelmingly from "the Red belt," Emilia Romagna and Tuscany) and for the leaders (despite frequent organizational changes, executive bodies have always been made up mainly of Communist leaders) (Manoukian, 1968: 220–223, 227–228). During the early 1980s, the UDI sought more autonomy. At the XIth National Congress (1982) the UDI settled that the self-funding was "the only form of economic support of the organization" (Art. 6). Thus the UDI refused financial aid from the PCI and underwent an organizational revolution by dissolving the whole National structure including the apparatus of full-time functionaries. The elimination of the National Secretariat implied a removal of the privileged channel of communication with the party, and therefore a loosening of the ties joining them[14] Because a real form of enrollment no longer existed, correct information about the number of associates is not available. It is difficult to say exactly how many members identify themselves with the PDS, and to what extent, even though a strong intertwining persists (in spite of the decrease suffered by the local groups after 1982) in the traditional Communist areas.[15]

The ARCI was established in 1957 with the purpose of offering legal assistance to the various Communist associations, but from the 1960s the organization extended its field of operation.[16] In 1976, it joined with the *Unione Italiana Sport Per Tutti* (Italian Union for Sports For All—UISP), and later split into various autonomous associations such as the *Lega Ambiente*, *Arci Pesca*, *Arci Caccia*, *Arci Ragazzi*, *Arci Gay*, *Arci Gola*, *Arci Nova* and so on, which gave the ARCI a confederal form. This brought about an increase in financial resources, in permanent staff, and an overall increase in membership. The increase in membership has been as follows: 430,000 in 1962, 451,000 in 1968, 650,000 in 1973, about 700,000 in 1976 and about 1,200,000 in 1986.[17] Although the association stressed its origins within the labor movement and the ideals of the Resistance, the statute left out the strictly political features that had been present after the congress of 1962, when the ARCI had been committed to contributing also to "the struggle of workers for the increase of spare time and for its autonomous and democratic utilization" (Art. 1). Then, the ARCI took on, as a general objective, the task of fighting "against every form of exploitation, ignorance, injustice, discrimination, solitude and marginalization" (Art. 2). The concentration of forces in civil society and the resulting increase in associative and political strength enabled the ARCI to benefit from stronger contractual power and greater political autonomy.[18] Even though the ARCI acknowledged its adherence to the Left, its leaders defined the Left as a widespread concept, that it was "impossible to reduce simply to the dynamic of the party form and of the trade-union form."[19]

The most important PCI/PDS flanking organization was by far the trade union CGIL. In this organization Communist and Socialist workers coexisted even though the Communists by far outnumbered the Socialists. The relationship between PCI/PDS and CGIL changed throughout the years. From the early 1950s to the mid-1970s, the union was strongly dependent on the PCI even though part of its membership were PSI members. While the end of the so-called system of the *cinghia di trasmissione* (driving belt), and the 1969 decision of the incompatibility of party's and union's executive positions were above all symbolic (the CGIL's leaders attended meetings of party's executive bodies as "guests"), the CGIL became increasingly autonomous during the 1970s.[20] After the PCI's electoral success in the mid-1970s and the enforcement of the politics "Historic Compromise" the CGIL gave its own support to this strategy which strengthened the relationship between the party and the union. The PCI imposed political moderation on the CGIL, and used the political legitimation achieved by the presence of the union in order to strengthen the Left's position (Carrieri and Donolo, 1986; Carrieri, 1988: 333–335). But the defeat of the historical compromise strategy and the unions' growing importance in the corporatist negotiations (with government and entrepreneurs) somewhat marginalized the PCI in the industrial relations (Feltrin, 1991: 39–53). In the late 1970s, because of the growing politicization of the trade union action, the CGIL had a relationship of pseudo-equality with the PCI.

During the 1980s the relationship between the PCI and the CGIL became differentiated. Changes in the labor market gave rise on one side to new autonomous unions (Bordogna, 1988: 257–276) which eroded the CGIL's membership, and on the other side reduced the total membership of the labor force so that the CGIL was predominantly made up of pensioners.[21] The CGIL's crisis was also due to the violent political conflict between Bettino Craxi's PSI and the PCI. This conflict involved the Socialist and Communist components of the CGIL, and produced a growing internal division (Turone, 1992: 540). The most problematic issue was the "wage cost of living indexation" referendum of 1985, which caused a real split between the two components. The defeat in the referendum was important also for the union's relationship with the PCI (Lange, 1986: 127–150; Locke, 1994: 233–245).

The changes inside the PCI in the late 1980s had repercussions also on the CGIL. Its internal division increased, above all in the wake of the PDS birth, and the same Communist component split on Occhetto's proposal of renewal (but also about the union's strategy and other topics such as the Gulf War). The CGIL's General Secretary supported the PCI's transformation, while the Confederal Secretary opposed it, siding with Ingrao's opposition (Mershon, 1992: 137–166).

In 1991, at the end of this highly conflictual phase, the CGIL dissolved its Communist and Socialist components. This was above all a symbolic action because the election of its leaders continued to be conditioned by the criteria of distribution of the appointments between the two political parties (Turone, 1992: 550–551).

The foundation of the FGCI dates back to 1949 but the organization began its slow decline after only a few years. Since its founding, the decrease in membership has been almost continuous. There were 285,216 members in the year it was founded, reaching a peak of 463,954 in 1950. In the following years membership steadily decreased, and after the student revolt of 1968, it fell to 68,648 in 1969. In spite of a recovery during the 1970s (142,884 in 1976) due to the electoral success of the PCI, the crisis did not stop and in the early 1980s, the number of members fell to about 50,000.[22] The crisis of the FGCI is connected with its relationship with the PCI, that is, the ambivalent and unsolved question of the youth organization's autonomy from the party. The FGCI had always tried to promote the solving of the younger generations' problems (often in conflict with the Communist policies) without endangering the unity or subordinating the organization of the party. The FGCI often attempted to renovate itself by changing its organizational structure: from the so-called "reconstruction," in the XIXth National Congress

(1971), after the 1968 breakdown, to the several political and organizational changes of the last years.[23] The "re-foundation" in 1985 gave the FGCI a federal form, where the single federate organizations were independent with their own structure.[24] This organizational setting coincided with a high degree of political-ideological independence of the young Communists whose political stands were often in opposition to the political lines of the PCI. A few of these issues were: the fight against nuclear power, the concern for the environment, the reflections about Red terrorism, the proposal of legalization of soft drugs, and above all, the criticism of the Communist ideology confirmed by the adhesion to the International Union of Socialist Youth (IUSY) as advisory partner (Anastasia, 1991: 233–251). The XXVth National Congress (1990) enforced more radical organizational change, which led to a confederation of different associations.[25] This change did not imply a detachment from the PDS but rather FGCI endorsement of the process of renewal in the party (Anastasia, 1991: 244). But the formation of the PDS and a further decline in the number of members led the FGCI to change its organizational form again. At the National Assembly held in December 1991, the *Sinistra Giovanile nel PDS* (the Young Left in the PDS) was founded, allowing the various associations to choose their alignment to the party and the promoting committee aimed not "at giving birth to a young organization strictly linked to the PDS but at foreseeing and guaranteeing an autonomous center in the PDS."[26] In this way the young association was again somewhat subordinated to the party. At any rate, the new organization rising from the FGCI accelerated its decline by becoming too dependent on the PDS (and this is a sign of the party's difficulties in relating itself to the young generations), while the associations originated from the area of the young Left, but more independent from the party, have managed to gain their own space.

In sum, the PCI/PDS relationship with its more relevant flanking organizations demonstrated a growing weakening of the traditional linkages. Societal process of secularization and differentiation and the party's abandoning of the old "total integration" aproach can explain this loss of control on the external environment.

CONCLUSIONS

The organizational framework of the PDS is rather different from that of the PCI. The PDS acquired many features of the professional-electoral model but it did not completely give up some features typical of the mass-integration party. With regard to party's identity and basic aims, the PDS brought the process of "secularization" of the Marxist-Leninist ideology to a conclusion, a process that was accelerated after the collapse of the Soviet system. The reference to "Democracy" instead of "Communism" in the new party's label showed clearly the choice of different cultural and political principles. The party's leadership together with the progressive articulation of ends led to an overall change in political and electoral strategy. In fact, while the PCI was traditionally an "anti-system" party, it increasingly became a more pragmatic opposition party running for government (which it finally accomplished in 1996). The long-term dilemma between the "principle of identity" and the "principle of legitimization" (i.e., acceptance of and by the liberal-democratic system) (Pellicani, 1983: 292) finally led the PCI to extend party boundaries by including social components which did not belong to the traditional *classe gardée* (Panebianco, 1988: 311). At this point, the concern that every voter had to became a member and that every member be a militant was no longer of importance because the electorate in and of itself had became of utmost importance. According to the professional-electoral party model, the PCI and above all the PDS put the policy-making function ahead of the integrative-expressive one and thus chose a cross-class electoral strategy. This change required the integration of the electors loyal to the old identity with the new electors who were less ideologically aligned.

With regard to the new dominant coalition, the high turnover (political and generational) caused a high level of "amalgamation" of the party's elite (Panebianco, 1988). The new political generation which founded the PDS was composed of 40-year-old politicians, of middle-upper-class origin, with a high level of education. The remarkable percentage of members of the party's bodies with loose links with the party's bureaucratic structure contributed to the party de-institutionalization. This higher permeability of leadership, together with lower inner cohesion was due, above all, to the strengthening of the internal factions which gave rise to a more widespread and fragmented distribution of power.

Even if the PDS's bureaucracy was undermined, it remains, however, a basic party feature today. Two observations support this statement. First, the share of full-time party's functionaries among the new leaders was the greatest in the Executive Committee in 1991, and in the Secretariat in 1990 and 1992. Second, the influence of the federations, mainly run by the party's functionaries, remains crucial. In fact, the success of Occhetto's policies was also due to the support of the strong federations of Emilia Romagna (where in 1990 Occhetto's motion obtained the greatest number of votes).[27]

Another important point emerging from the present analysis was the new party's "map of power" that emphasized the pre-existing tendency to strengthen the power of the executive bodies to the detriment of the representative ones. The role and the power of the Secretariat and, in particular, of the General Secretary became greater: a development that was partly due to the increasingly personalized character of the electoral campaigns. In 1994 the internal electoral competition for the Secretary between D'Alema and Veltroni clearly shows the increased distance from the previous standard.

Also, as far as the relationship between the party and the external organizations is concerned, during the last decade the flanking organizations achieved (or attempted to achieve) a greater autonomy while maintaining strong cultural, and sometimes political links with the party. This loosening of the political and organizational links was promoted by both the party and the organizations. Some flanking associations wanted more autonomy because the changing forms of political participation induced the younger generation to prefer organizations which were detached from parties, or which had specific issue-oriented goals (see, for instance, the ARCI). But at the same time, even though the PDS wanted to keep links with those associations because the majority of its membership belonged to the party's traditional constituency, the party itself demanded a greater freedom of action in order to achieve an interclass political program. This especially applied to the relationship with the CGIL. The PDS found it difficult to restore a dominant relationship with the union. In fact, the increasing functional differentiation of the industrial relations made it difficult for the PDS to control the CGIL as a contractual actor, since the main direct form of organizational link (the interchange of the careers) was very limited in the last years (Feltrin, 1991).

As far as the relationship between the PDS and its parliamentary representatives is concerned, there were signs of the growth of power of the latter, even if at the same time the internal and centralized character of the leadership still existed. The increasing political importance of the public representatives was unquestionable and it was the consequence of political and institutional developments. The most important of these concerns was the expansion since the 1970s of the PCI's governmental responsibilities at the local level (Hellman, 1988). Communists elected in local administrations have increasead their internal power as a result of the legitimation springing directly from the electorate, and of the autonomous capacity to allot material incentives due to the control of patronage resources. Moreover, the electoral reform in 1994, for both general and local elections, emphasized the personalization of the electoral campaigning, and therefore placed a higher importance on the candidate. In contrast, the continuing strength of the party's apparatus restrained the development of the PDS as a professional-electoral party.

In conclusion, the difficult cohabitation between these two different party models of the electoral-professional and the traditional mass-party and the continuing inner tension, together with the transformation of the external political and institutional environment, shows that the new organizational order is precarious. In fact, since the main input of the political and organizational changes was the party's negative electoral trend, the further defeat at the general elections in 1994 (that marked the end of Occhetto's leadership) proves that the transition was not sufficient. The strategy adopted by the new leadership of D'Alema, setting up a broader electoral coalition (L'Ulivo—The Olive Tree), and the further internal renewal seems to lead the PDS more and more toward the electoral-professional model.

NOTES

1. The period under consideration takes as *terminus a quo* the initial move to a different organizational order timidly initiated by the Natta secretary and as *terminus ad quem* the transformation to the PDS and the change of leadership in 1994.

2. According to Farneti (1983: 192), already in 1975 "the reference to the model of the 'catch-all party' . . . prevails with an unequivocal evidence," as "the PCI has taken a series of initiatives which, being aimed at enhancing or keeping its votes, according to a viewpoint ascribing a decisive value to the electoral victory or defeat, [which] led it to take on some essential features . . . belonging to the catch-all party."

3. For the political strategy of Natta, see Hellman (1986: 49–77) and Sassoon (1988: 155–172).

4. For 1980 and 1985, see *Organizzazione, Dati, Statistiche*, PCI Department.

5. The referendum for the reintroduction of some quite minor economic benefits for the workers was called by the PCI which mobilized all its organizations. The defeat (54.3 percent) produced a deepening of the cleavage with the trade unions, in particular the Communist-led CGIL, and the first wave of criticism to the party politics.

6. Concerning this ambivalence typical of rules, see Panebianco (1979: 511–536). The first leak in the normative body of the party was represented by the Secretariat's rule (in view of the National Congress of 1979) concerning the relationship between delegates and congressional assemblies of the sections. That document stressed the "absolute autonomy of judgement" of delegates; moreover, a sort of fiduciary relation, alien to the Marxist tradition, replaced the former relation based on delegation (Lanchester, 1982: 621).

7. For the different tendencies see Amyot (1989: 131–152). In the past, the only internal organized minority was the group of the "*Manifesto*." Its members were expelled from the PCI in 1969.

8. See also Hellman (1992: 121–122). While on the crucial issues of the PDS foundation there were 807 votes in favor, 72 against and 49 abstentions, Occhetto's motion concerning the withdrawal of the troops from the Gulf War received only about 60 percent of the approvals, and the abstentions were counted among both the Left and the Reformist tendencies. As a term of comparison, one may observe that the final document of the XVIth Congress (1983) obtained only 7 votes against and 9 abstentions (*l'Unità*, 7. 3. 1983).

9. The results of the first poll were: 264 votes in favor, 102 against, 41 abstentions and 8 blank or spoiled voting-papers. Although more than 20 percent of the members of the new National Council were not present at the voting, the defeat was commonly attributed by the commentators to *franc-tireurs*, estimated between a minimum of 21 and a maximum of 50.

10. The members of the Executive Committee among the different political factions in 1991 are the following: 65 supporters of Occhetto (55.8 percent), 27 of Ingrao's left-wing tendency (22.9 percent), 17 of Napolitano's reformist (14.1 percent) and 9 of Bassolino's wing (7.6 percent) Cfr:. *l'Unità*, 17. 2. 1991.

11. *l'Unità*, 29. 3. 1990.

12. This point was emphasized by Article 39, paragraph 2 of the statute of 1991 stating that: "In the formation of the structures of direction and work, it is necessary to pursue the largest use of leaders who are not functionaries and who are taken up partially in party activity."

13. Regarding the relationship between parliamentary party and party leadership, see Bardi and Morlino (1994: 242–277).

14. See the opening report at the XIth National Congress of the UDI, in Michetti et al. (1984: 453)

15. This loosening of ties is revealed by political conflicts with the party. In 1988, the PCI women affairs department that was responsible, Livia Turco, "pointed out policies opposite to those of the UDI, even if they share a common ideal and personal root." *Noi Donne*, 1988: 28. In the same article Grazia Zuffa, ex-functionary of the UDI and member of the Central Committee of the PCI criticizes the separatist and independent choice of the association because "the right way is not a drastic separation . . . autonomy has to be built on the field. On the field of the relationship with the party."

16. For an outline of the ARCI's development until the late 1960s, see Manoukian (1968: 275).

17. For the data until 1973, see Barbagallo and Cazzola (1982: 815). The data of 1976 and 1986 are taken from *Materiali per la discussione all'VIII congresso nazionale*, supplement to *Notizie Arci* (1986: 6–7).

18. See the report of G. Rasimelli at the Xth National Congress held in Rome in 1992.

19. *Notizie Arci*, n° 1, 1992, p. 29.

20. For an outline of the interchange of leaders between PCI and CGIL until the late 1970s, see Ferrante (1982: 673–91). For the rule of incompatibility see Accornero, (1992: 175–176, 206)

21. In 1990, pensioners made up almost half the CGIL's membership. For the data about its membership, see Pirani et al. (1991: 52–56).

22. The data until 1976 are taken from Franchi (1982: 783–800). As regards the last decade, the number of members remains around 50,000. Today it is difficult to know the real number of the members of the PDS's young organization, but the negative trend is certainly continuing.

23. In the late 1960s, the FGCI tried to " 're-found' itself, turning from an organization . . . strongly subordinated to the party, into a movement open to the collaboration and also, in prospect, to the fusion with all the forces of the young people recognizing themselves in ideal anti-capitalistic and anti-imperialistic discriminants." (Franchi, 1982: 787).

24. The 1985 final document reads: "A phase is closed. The age of a FGCI like a spokesman or mediator of relations between the young people and the party, of a FGCI like a young organism of the PCI is concluded," *Documento finale approvato dal XXIII Congresso*, in *Una nuova Fgci per cambiare la politica e la società*, 1985.

25. These associations were: *Sinistra, Città Futura, Lavoro Nuovo, Università Futura*.

26. *Protagonisti del nostro futuro. Materiali preparatori all'Assemblea Nazionale del 20, 21 e 22 dicembre 1991.*

27. Regarding the vote of the motions, see Belloni, 1991: 151.

REFERENCES

Accornero, Aris (1992). *La Parabola del Sindacato*. Bologna: Il Mulino.

Accornero, Aris, Renato Mannheimer and Chiara Sebastiani (eds.) (1983). *L'Identità Comunista*. Milano: Feltrinelli.

Amyot, Grant (1989). "La Via Italiana al Riformismo. Il PCI e il Nuovo Corso di Occhetto." In Raimondo Catanzaro and Raffaella Y. Nanetti (eds.), *Politica In Italia*, pp. 131–152. Bologna: Il Mulino.

Anastasia, Stefano (1991). "Per una Storia della Fgci Rifondata." *Democrazia e Diritto* 1: 233–251.

Anderlini, Fausto (1990). *Terra Rossa, Comunismo Ideale, Socialismo Reale.* Bologna: Istituto Gramsci.

Baldassarre, Antonio (1982). "I Gruppi Parlamentari Comunisti." In Massimo Ilardi and Aris Accornero (eds.), *Il Partito Comunista Italiano. Struttura e Storia dell'Organizzazione, 1921/1979*, pp. 445–497. Milano: Feltrinelli.

Barbagallo, Roberta and Franco Cazzola (1982). "Le Organizzazioni di Massa." In Massimo Ilardi and Aris Accornero (eds.), *Il Partito Comunista Italiano, Struttura e Storia del'Organizzazione, 1921/1979*, pp. 801–823. Milano: Feltrinelli.

Bardi, Luciano and Leonardo Morlino (1994). "Italy: Tracing the Roots of the Great Transformation." In Richard S. Katz and Peter Mair (eds.), *How Parties Organize*, pp. 242–277. London: Sage.

Belloni, Franco (1991). "Il Partito Comunista Italiano In Bilico tra la Dissoluzione e l'Ignoto: Prime Valutazioni sulla Svolta." In Fausto Anderlini and Robert Leonardi (eds.), *Politica In Italia*, pp. 143–170. Bologna: Il Mulino.

Bordogna, Lorenzo (1988). "Arcipelago Cobas: Frammentazione della Rappresentanza e Conflitti di Lavoro," In Piergiorgio Corbetta and Robert Leonardi (eds.), *Politica In Italia*, pp. 257–276. Bologna: Il Mulino.

Bull, J. Martin (1995). "Il Fallimento del'Alleanza Progressista." In Piero Ignazi and Richard Katz (eds.), *Politica In Italia*, pp. 97–120. Bologna: Il Mulino.

Carrieri, Mimmo (1987). "Dopo la Stagione dei Leader una Leadership Negoziale?" *Democrazia e Diritto* XXVII: 269–314.

Carrieri, Mimmo (1988). *Sindacato: Cambiamenti e Crisi In Francia e In Italia.* Milano: Franco Angeli.

Carrieri, Mimmo and Carlo Donolo (1986). *Il Mestiere Politico del Sindacato.* Roma: Editori Riuniti.

Casagrande Pirani, Stefano, Patrizio Di Nicola, Carla Maria Ricci and Claudia Tagliavia (1991). "Gli anni 80 del Sindacato." *Nuova Rassegna Sindacale* 34: 52–56.

Cotta, Maurizio (1979). *Classe Politica e Parlamento In Italia. 1946–1976.* Bologna: Il Mulino.

Daniels, Philip (1992). "The Democratic Party of the Left and the 1992 Italian General Elections." *The Journal of Communist Studies* 3: 129–135.

Farneti, Paolo (1983). *Il Sistema dei Partiti In Italia. 1946–1979.* Bologna: Il Mulino.

Feltrin, Paolo (1991). "L'Arena delle Relazioni Industriali e Il Rapporto tra Sindacati e Partiti." *Economia & Lavoro* 2: 39–53.

Ferrante, Gianni (1982). "Interscambio di Dirigenti tra Partito e Sindacato." In Massimo Ilardi and Aris Accornero (eds.), *Il Partito Comunista Italiano. Struttura e Storia dell'Organizzazione 1921/1979*, pp. 673–691. Milano: Feltrinelli.

Franchi, Paolo (1982). " L'Organizzazione Giovanile 1968/1979." In Massimo Ilardi and Aris Accornero (eds.), *Il Partito Comunista Italiano. Struttura e Storia dell'Organizzazione 1921/1979*, pp. 783–800. Milano: Feltrinelli.

Hellman, Stephen (1986). "Il Partito Comunista fra Berlinguer e Natta." In Piergiorgio Corbetta and Robert Leonardi (eds.), *Politica In Italia*, pp. 49–77. Bologna: Il Mulino.

Hellman, Stephen (1988). *Italian Communism in Transition*. Oxford: Oxford University Press.

Hellman, Stephen (1992). "La Difficile Nascita del PDS." In Stephen Hellman and Gianfranco Pasquino (eds.), *Politica In Italia*, pp. 111–135. Bologna: Il Mulino.

Ignazi, Piero (1992). *Dal PCI al Pds*. Bologna: Il Mulino.

Lanchester, Fulco (1982). "I Delegati ai Congressi nazionali." In Massimo Ilardi and Aris Accornero (eds.), *Il Partito Comunista Italiano: Struttura e Storia dell'organizzazione 1921/1979*, pp. 619–672. Milano: Feltrinelli.

Lange, Peter (1986). "La Fine di un'Era: Il Referendum sulla Scala Mobile." In Piergiorgio Corbetta and Robert Leonardi (eds.), *Politica In Italia*, pp. 127–150. Bologna: Il Mulino.

Lazar, Marc (1992). *Maisons Rouges*. Paris: Aubier.

Locke, Robert M. (1994). "L'Abolizione della Scala Mobile." In Carol Mershon and Gianfranco Pasquino (eds.), *Politica In Italia*, pp. 233–245. Bologna: Il Mulino.

Manoukian, Agopik (1968). *La Presenza Sociale del PCI e della DC*. Bologna: Il Mulino.

Mershon, Carol A. (1992). "La Crisi della Cgil: Il XII Congresso Nazionale." In Stephen Hellman and Gianfranco Pasquino (eds.), *Politica In Italia*, pp. 137–166. Bologna: Il Mulino.

Michetti, Maria, Margherita Repetto and Luciana Viviani (1984). *Udi: Laboratorio di Politica delle Donna*. Roma: Roma Cooperativa libera stampa.

Panebianco, Angelo (1979). "Imperativi Organizzativi, Conflitti Interni e Ideologia nei Partiti Comunisti." *Rivista Italiana di Scienza Politica* 3: 511–536.

Panebianco, Angelo (1988). *Political Parties: Organizations and Power*. Cambridge: Cambridge University Press.

Pellicani, Luciano (1983). "La Strategia del Paguro." In Renato Mieli (ed.), *Il PCI allo Specchio*, pp. 251–317. Milano: Rizzoli.

Poggi, Gianfranco (1968). *L'Organizzazone Partitica del PCI e della DC*. Bologna: Il Mulino.

Sassoon, Donald (1988). "La Sconfitta Elettorale Comunista: un Ritorno agli anni Sessanta?" In Piergiorgio Corbetta and Robert Leonardi (eds.), *Politica In Italia*, pp. 155–172. Bologna: Il Mulino.

Sebastiani, Chiara (1982a). "Organi Dirigenti Nazionali: Composizione, Meccanismi di Formazione e di Evoluzione 1945/1979." In Massimo Ilardi and Aris Accornero (eds.), *Il Partito Comunista Italiano: Struttura e Storia dell'Organizzazione 1921/1979*, pp. 387–444. Milano: Feltrinelli.

Sebastiani, Chiara (1982b). "Il Ceto Politico del Compromesso Storico." *Laboratorio Politico* 2–3: 211–240.

Turone, Sergio (1992). *Storia del Sindacato In Italia. Dal 1943 al Crollo del Comunismo*. Bari: Laterza.

Urban, John Barth (1987). "Il XVII Congresso del PCI e il Nuovo Internazionalismo." In Piergiorgio Corbetta and Robert Leonardi (eds.), *Politica In Italia*, pp. 131–147. Bologna: Il Mulino.

8

MSI/AN: A Mass Party with the Temptation of the Führer-Prinzip

—————————————————————— *Piero Ignazi*

The right-wing pole of the Italian party system has been occupied since January 1995 by *Alleanza Nazionale*—National Alliance (AN). This party, which scored 15.7 percent at the 1996 elections gaining the third place in the Italian party system, is the direct offspring of the old, established neofascist party, *Movimento Sociale Italiano*—Italian Social Movement (MSI). This chapter will highlight the main features of the MSI in order to assess the degree of change and continuity of AN. A large part of the analysis will therefore be devoted to the originating party, the MSI, which was founded immediately after World War II. The focus will involve the MSI's genetic model and the heritage of the past regime, the establishment of a highly centralized and cohesive structure, the degree of internal factionalism and the ideological divide. Finally, the features of the originated party, AN, will be contrasted with the MSI organizational framework.

THE INNER CONTRADICTION: A NEOFASCIST PARTY IN A DEMOCRATIC SYSTEM

The MSI has represented since its foundation (December 1946) the extreme Right, neofascist constituency. This characteristic clearly emerges by analyzing its originary model (Panebianco 1982). The party was in fact founded by former fascist leaders and cadres and by veterans of the 1943–1945 fascist Army.

The ideological references of the party resided in the fascist tradition. As fascist ideology is a *mare magnum* where many different sources and streams have melted and lived together (Sternhell, 1989; Payne, 1995) the seminal distinction between fascism-as-movement and fascism-as-regime (De Felice, 1976) is extremely useful. The former type refers to a "Left" tendency—Republican, anti-bourgeois and anti-capitalist—which was particularly relevant in the years before the fascist seizure of power (1919–1922) and in the period of the *Repubblica Sociale Italiana*—Italian Social Republic (RSI), the regime founded by Mussolini in the north of Italy in 1943–1945. The latter type refers to the mainstream tendency—Conservative, petty-bourgeois, clerical—which prevailed after the stabilization of the fascist regime. Both tendencies were recuperated by the MSI and they formed the internal debate with minor variants throughout the party's history (Ignazi 1989a, 1989b).

The MSI's recruitment was addressed to all the ex-fascists, with particular emphasis, in the first years, to the veterans of the RSI and to the militants of the fascist Republican Party established in 1943–1945. The MSI's appeal was addressed primarily to the rank-and-file because the most visible former fascist leaders could not afford public scenes due to the after-war climate. In fact, the first General Secretary, Giorgio Almirante, was a young RSI government official and all the members of the first *Direzione* (executive body) kept a low profile. The continuity with the old fascist elite was, however, guaranteed by the backing of a group of "notables" which directed the party's activity behind the scene. Continuity with the past is confirmed by the characteristics of the seven MPs elected in the first Parliament (1948): only two MPs were extraneous to the fascist tradition and/or organizations, while the other five had been committed to the fascist party or the RSI, even if with low profile positions in the hierarchy.

Therefore, *in terms of political personnel and ideology the MSI was set up as a neofascist, nostalgic party.*

The MSI, like many anti-system parties, lived in a constant contradiction: it referred to and projected a different regime, according to its manifest ideology (which is clearly antagonistic and antithetical to the liberal-democratic one), but it adapted itself to the constraints of the democratic political environment. Therefore, first, it explicitly renounced (at least up to the end of the 1960s) the adoption of violent means in politics (the youth and students *bagarre* are of different kind); and second, it organized internally along a formally democratic structure. Contrary to the tradition of the fascist parties which were structured around the paramilitary unit of the "militia" (Duverger, 1951) the MSI adopted the mass-party model. With its first statute the local branch was depicted as the basic unit of the organization and the decision-making process. The party platform was defined through a bottom-up flow of decision-making through section (local), federation (provincial) and then National Congresses. The same goes for the election of the executive bodies and secretaries at each level of the party's echelon. Finally, the deep ideological divide within the party enforced a plausible degree of internal democracy.

Notwithstanding the MSI's anti-system imprinting, the party was able to operate overtly in the system. Its questionable legitimacy to operate in a democratic setting was basically in the hands of the dominant party in the first postwar years, the *Democrazia Cristiana*—Christian Democracy (DC). The DC adopted an ambivalent attitude, alternating between a friendly relationship and tough confrontation. In fact, even when the MSI reached a relevant success in the 1951/1952 administrative elections in the center-south, when it ran on a joint ticket together with the monarchists and collected more than 10 percent of the vote and the control of important cities such as Naples, Bari, Catania and others, its full legitimacy was undermined by the almost simultaneous approval of a DC-sponsored bill which banned all "parties wishing to rebuild the fascist party." This law, however, was never enforced.

THE GENETIC MODEL

The key factors which mould the organizational features of a party (Panebianco, 1982: 104–110) are: (a) the charismatic character of the leadership; (b) the derivation from pre-existing organizations which sponsor the party's formation; (c) the development by "diffusion"—a process of aggregation of various autonomously born associations—or by "penetration"—a process of conquest led by a group of political entrepreneurs who "colonize" the rest of the country.

The first two modes in the MSI's formation[1] should be immediately excluded: one concerns the birth by a charismatic personality, the other through a pre-existing organization. The first mode was impossible "by definition" because no one could even think of substituting the charismatic figure of Mussolini. The founder and head of fascism was such a mythical reference that no one could present himself with the aura of the revolutionary and innovative leader. On the other hand, the destruction of all the organizational networks of the fascist party and regime forced the MSI to build up its own organization autonomously and independently from any other pre-existing structure. Even if in the first months after the war many nostalgic groups and associations flourished, they never acted as a sponsor for the MSI: their dimension did not overcome a threshold of significance. Analogously, the MSI development was not affected by the *Uomo Qualunque*—Common Man Party, a protest, flash party which appeared and gained a certain momentum in 1946 but soon disappeared.

Regarding the third mode of party formation—diffusion or penetration—the MSI followed a somewhat mixed path. In the immediate postwar years there was a spontaneous diffusion of tiny (and sometimes covert) "nostalgic" organizations in many different towns without any kind of linkages. The founding group of the MSI was not the direct expression of this network: it rather emerged as a group of former fascists and veterans (mainly concentrated in Rome) who joined to "keep the idea of fascism alive." As soon as they officially established themselves as a "central" neofascist organization they aggregated and unified all the various groups under the new party's heading. This means that a mixed process was underway: a process of penetration led by a cohesive group of experienced political entrepreneurs intertwined with a process of aggregation of external and autonomous organizations. However, the lack of relevant external groups and/or of competing leaders led to an emphasis more on the aspect of penetration. On the other hand, the new party had its own very clear and identifiable constituency all over the country, the nostalgic fascists. Once the MSI acquired the status of the neo-fascist party *par excellence* (thanks to the support of all the former surviving fascist elite), all the other groups merged or disappeared (or, in a few cases, carried on terrorist actions).

Finally, it can be assessed that the MSI's genetic model is characterized by the absence of a charismatic figure, the absence of a sponsor from a pre-existing organization, and the development more by penetration than by diffusion. These traits, in particular autonomous legitimacy and penetration, point to a strong institutionalization assessed by control over its own domain and the functional and territorial articulation of the party itself (Panebianco, 1982).

THE ORGANIZATIONAL MATURITY: A CENTRALIZED, VERTICALLY ALIGNED AND COHERENT ORGANIZATION

For almost 50 years the MSI's organizational structure remained basically unchanged. The following analysis will focus on the major shifts which occurred throughout the MSI's history with some reference to the (somewhat) new organizational features that have been purported with the recent transformation into *Alleanza Nazionale* in January 1995.

The MSI's genetic model is codified quite clearly by the statute approved at the first National Congresss held in 1948. The party's institutionalization was quite rapid. After having passed successfully the challenge of the first legislative elections (1948), electing seven MPs and one senator, the first National Congress (1948) codified an already existing, articulated structure by providing formal rules which gave way to a *complex, centralized and closed organization*.

A Controlled Membership Recruitment

The *closeness* of the organization is related to the party's particular origin and location in the party system. As already specified, the party was born in contradiction with the postwar democratic, anti-fascist regime. The anti-systemicness of the MSI was overt and declared but, in spite of constitutional provisions and specific laws banning "whatever neofascist party," it never suffered from any kind of constraints. However, for a long period, at least until the late 1980s, the party was a "world apart" with its symbols, references and myths, which did not communicate with the external world. This is because the external world, the democratic anti-fascist system, was, by definition, hostile (on this point, see Tarchi, 1995a; Chiarini, 1995). This mutual denial of legitimacy implied a very attentive strategy of recruitment. For example, to become a member one had to exhibit an application signed by two party members. The application was then scrutinized by the section secretariat and sent to the federation for final approval. This attentive and cautious strategy of recruitment never underwent relevant changes, and exists in the present AN statute (Art 4: 1995). In addition, some special conditions of "indignity" and "incompatibility" made the recruitment even more scrutinized. These conditions varied over time but some aspects remained constant.

As far as the indignity is concerned, two criteria were adopted. The first one reflects the status of "besieged fortress" and marginalization of the first decades of the party up to 1980; it refers to "political indignity": a vague formulation which enabled the party to keep out radical fringes or *agents provocateur*. On the other level, it was also a means in the hands of the local or national leadership to control the dissident factions with the threat of expulsion which could have been employed *ad libitum* against whomever, by the leadership. After 1980 this vague formulation was abandoned referring only to "those condemned for highly censurable crimes."

The second criterion of disqualification on the basis of indignity refers to "those who betrayed the country failing to fulfill their duties as citizens and *soldiers* (my emphasis) (Art. 4b: 1948). This disqualification was meant to stigmatize those who had accepted the armistice in 1943 and had not followed Mussolini in the 1943–1945 Salò Republic. In 1948, when this provision was established, the internal cleavage between the true believers— those who where loyal to Mussolini and fascism *jusq'au bout*—and the "opportunist" fascists—those who managed to survive in the center-south waiting for the end of the war—was very deep: the former RSI veterans who dominated the party at the time wanted to underline the difference, to trace a borderline.

While this statutory provision had a particular salience in those years, *it was not formally abandoned afterwards*, even when the moderate faction took over in 1950, and it was maintained until the transformation into AN. The reason for this long-lasting prescription is that it was never really enforced systematically; rather, it was selectively employed to marginalize or ban internal opponents. And, even more, the maintenance of such a backward provision acquired a different meaning, that of an *identity symbol*: a purely symbolic reference to a crucial element of the party's identity.

The second obstacle to becoming a party member regards the "incompatibility," especially in reference to affiliation to "covert associations." This wording had a double purpose. On one hand, it meant to prevent the entrance of radical Right fringes which might have endangered the attempt of legitimacy which the party tried to achieve. On the other hand, it meant to reinforce the traditional fascist hostility against the Masonry, as it was clearly specified in the 1952 statute. The latter element became a very sensitive point in the internal debate. In fact, in 1973, when the party attempted to renew its image by presenting itself as a more mainstream "National Right," such reference was suddenly abandoned. This timely coincidence raised the doubt that some of the newcomers were Freemasons and therefore that disqualification needed to be abandoned. This conjecture is reinforced by the fact that when the project of "National Right" failed in 1979 the anti-Masonic exclusionism was restated, even more rigorously. This disqualification while it does not mention the Masonry, is still in the AN statute (Art.2: 1995)

These elements of indignity and incompatibility remained until the early 1990s and were largely integrated into the AN statute: *this reveals a lasting attachment to elements, attitudes and symbols of the formative years of the party and of the endurance of the fascist subculture.*

In sum, the closeness of the party was, and still is, very tight. There is no easy access and no easy life for opponents, given the unaccountability of certain rules. However, this is only the "official story," because the party leadership *has always promoted* mass membership.

Data about membership and local branches are scarcely reliable (to say the least). The party has never declared less than 100,000 members and according to official internal sources it reached a maximum of 451,897 in 1972 (Ignazi 1989a: 293ff). This is in contrast to less triumphant and more realistic estimates (see Bardi and Morlino, 1992: 485) which retrench the membership to less than half.[2]After a period of stagnation the success in the local election of December 1993 and in the legislative elections of 1994 can justify an increase that has been stated in the wake of the foundation of AN (January 1995) to 324,124 members.[3] While the official numbers may be exaggerated, it is unquestionable that the party has always availed itself of a substantial degree of militantism and it is active beyond the electoral arena. Many branches (the official numbers range between more than three and less than two thousand), especially in the south, are effective centers of political activity. Also in the case of the local branches their numbers have rapidly increased (see Table 8.1) in the recent years, even if the official members—more than 8,000—are totally unrealistic.

The Overall Organizational Framework: Complexity and Centralization

The degree of *complexity of the formal structure* is quite high. The MSI was articulated along four hierarchical territorial levels—*sezione* (section), *federazione* (federation), *organi regionali* (regional bodies), *organi centrali* (national bodies)[4]; it has a clearly statutory relationship with the flanking organizations; it has an elective procedure for all offices, with a few excep-

Table 8.1
Turnover in the MSI National Executive (*Direzione Nazionale*)

Year	% new members	% first time members	old members (n.)	% old members	total members (n.)
1948	100	100	-	-	15
1950	46.7	46.7	8	53.3	15
1952	53.3	53.3	7	46.7	15
1954	66.7	60.0	10	66.6	30
1956	64.5	58.1	11	36.6	31
1963	59.5	43.2	15	48.3	37
1965	53.3	40.0	21	56.7	45
1970	52.5	35.6	28	62.2	59
1973	39.3	31.5	54	21.5	89
1977	42.9	39.3	48	53.9	84
1979	32.9	30.6	57	67.8	85
1982	30.4	21.6	71	83.5	102
1984	23.8	19.8	96	94.1	126
1987	29.6	23.9	83	65.9	117
1990	33.0	25.0	67	67.0	100
1995*	69.6	46.0	31	30.4	102

First Column (New Members) refers to all those who had not served in the immediately preceding NEC. The second column includes members with no previous experience in NEC.

*AN National Executive.

Sources: 1948–87: Ignazi 1989: 325; 1990–1995: official data provided by the MSI/AN headquarters.

tions, in particular for the election of the party's delegates at the various levels from the section up to the federation, the region and the National Congress; it has very strict regulations for recruitment and similar prescriptions for members, sanctioned with disciplinary rules.

The "Party on the Ground"

Consequently to these formal rules, which never changed in their basic features and have largely been adopted by the AN statute, "the party on the ground" (Mair 1994) is structured along the traditional mass-party format. The local section is the center for political activity. At least once a year a plenary meeting should be held. The section's assembly elects the Secretary and, when a National Congress is called, it selects delegates for the hierarchical superior structure, the Federation Congress.

The federation, which more or less reflects the administrative division of the provinces, is the real core of the MSI's network in the periphery. Since the mid-1950s the figure of the federation's secretary has acquired a special status. The federation's secretary is not bounded by the deliberation of the federation's executive but only by the National Executive (Art. 24: 1954). In this way the federation's secretary acquires a high degree of autonomy vis-à-vis the federation bodies; and, on the other hand, the Center has a direct link with the secretary, bypassing the collective body (the federation executive). It goes without saying that a single person is more "accountable" (i.e., controlled) than a collective body. And finally, the procedure for the election of the secretary provides an opportunity for the National Executive to exert a heavy influence. In fact, the Federation Assembly designated to elect the secretary is dominated by ex-officio members (members of the Central Committee, elected officials, etc.) which usually are more loyal to the Center. In sum, the federation secretary is highly *authoritative* because he is legitimated by the vote of the assembly, and *autonomous* because he is independent by the federation bodies, but *tied* to the Center because it is the local *terminus* of the National Executive.

The control of federation offices is therefore a crucial position to acquire. In fact, it has traditionally been a harsh battlefield in the struggle among internal factions. One of the most powerful and controversial means of controlling the federation was the power to authoritatively remove the federation's secretary, directly or indirectly, by the national secretary. Such regulations were introduced and cancelled various times in party statutes, but when in operation they were quite often implemented. The AN statute confers to the national leader, "in accordance with the National Executive" (Art. 23: 1995) the right to remove the federation's chief.

The regional level is not very important as it performs a role of advice and coordination. Only after the reform which introduced the regional level all over Italy (1970) the MSI, similar to the other parties, institutionalized a regional structure while deprived of a real political life. The regional secretary was nominated (until 1988) by the Center, the National Executive first and the national secretary later: he was a mere *longa manus* of the Center. Only in 1988 did the regional body acquire the power to nominate the regional secretary. The 1995 AN statute eliminated the elective procedure and reinstated the nomination from the national secretary (president in the AN terminology) directly. This strict control of the national leadership is linked to the allocation of more power to the regional secretary which includes the shutdown of local units.

The Central Offices

Complexity and centralization emerge even more clearly in analyzing the central offices. First of all, following the standard model of the mass party, the National Congresses is the most important body as it "defines the party policy," elects the Central Committee and, after 1977, the National Secretary too. The Central Committee elects the National Executive which, in turn (at least until 1972), elected the National Secretary. The peculiar feature of the MSI National Congresses is provided by the high number of ex-officio members. In 1982 a specific statutory provision (Art. 58: 1980) stated that they could not exceed 50 percent of the members. The inflation of ex officio members demonstrated the attempt by the central bodies to exercise strict control on the decision-making process.

The Central Committee was, in principle, the *locus* of crucial political decisions. Actually, it has always performed this function as important decisions were debated in that body and the secretary's policy was always under scrutiny. Further, the secretary's position can be contested and reversed leading to his resignation (as was the case of Almirante in 1950, Fini in 1989 and Rauti in 1991). Therefore, the control of the Central Committee is a crucial resource on a double level. First, because its control assures stability for the dominant coalition (in this body, in fact, the number of ex-officio members has grown over time). Second, because access to the Central Committee is one of the most important and rewarding incentives that could be distributed to the party's middle-level elites. As the MSI could provide almost no external resources in terms of patronage—therefore no selective incentives were available for the party on the external market—the only available incentives were concentrated in the party and public offices.[5] Precisely because membership in the Central Committee was such a relevant reward, its size enlarged over time, overcoming the threshold of 300 members after 1988.

The National Executive (nominated by the Central Committee) has progressively lost its centrality, first when the secretary was no longer responsible to it (after 1970) and then when it did not elect the secretary itself any longer (after 1977). The final strike to its power has been provided by the AN formal rules as the executive is no longer elected by the Central Committee but *nominated* by the party's president: nothing but a tool in the hands of the leader. Notwithstanding this decline the executive has maintained one of the classical features of the traditional mass party: the control over the members of Parliament. It is specified in the statute that the party "states the guidelines for the parliamentary groups" (MSI: Art. 65: 1988; AN: Art. 30: 1995).

The national secretary was the central figure in the MSI power structure. Even if it has always exercised a *de facto* strong influence in the party's decision-making only, the 1970 statute (Art. 57) asserts *de jure* its autonomy vis-à-vis the National Executive. In the following years its powers greatly increased: it appoints a Secretariat without any approval by the executive; it appoints the secretary of the youth organization; it personally collects the state funds; it appoints the regional secretaries; it presents and endorses the president of the party; it sets the agenda of the collective bodies; and it can initiate a disciplinary scrutiny of any member. In sum, after the 1970s the secretary acquired more autonomy and more power of policy direction and appointment.

Absolute autonomy, control of the financial resources, distribution of selective incentives, sanctionary power; all these means produced a very powerful secretary. This concentration of power led to the secretary's election directly by the Congress: more power needed a more direct legitimation. That was especially true given the particular political contingency of the

Congress which moved to the direct election of the secretary (1977). In that occasion the party had to face the split by the more moderate and accommodating wing which eroded a large part of the parliamentary group and quite a few members of the various national bodies. Therefore, the secretary was elected directly by the Congress in order to enforce more legitimacy for the leadership of a challenged party.

A further, highly relevant resource in the hands of the dominant coalition is the candidature to public offices. It is apparent that controlling the parliamentary turnover was far from absolute power. The dominant coalition always had to bargain with its own internal tendencies and also with the opposing factions. In terms of circulation of the parliamentary elite the turning point in recent MSI history is represented by the split in 1976 which affected more than half of the parliamentary groups which represented the bulk of the traditional party's elite. As a consequence of that split, Almirante led a new dominant coalition which was deeply restructured with new entries of former opponents and younger members: more than one third (37.2 percent) entered the Parliament for the first time in the 1979 elections and were then confirmed in the 1983 and the 1987 elections. These MPs were selected according to the model of the party of apparatus (Cotta, 1979) where the candidates display an "internal" *cursus honorum*: membership and/or leadership in the youth organizations—which is almost a necessary requirement—party offices at local level, membership in the national bodies, membership and/or leadership in the flanking organizations. The only exception concerns the group of notables which had access in two peculiar phases: former fascist leaders in the early 1950s entered without passing through the party, thanks to their belonging to the same ideological world; and in 1972 non-MSI notables were welcomed in order to strengthen its (unsuccessful) ideological-political modification. On the other hand, the control of the party over the parliamentary group has always been formally instituzionalized and is maintained in the AN statute as well.

Summarizing, the MSI could be defined in terms of a highly centralized and vertically aligned party (Janda, 1993). The degree of intraparty coherence is demonstrated by the clear and detailed statutory rules which define the relation between the various bodies, the spheres of competence, the modes of election and nomination. The decision-making process is aligned along a progressively more accentuated top-bottom chain of decision-making where the national bodies control the periphery either via the National Executive or, more and more, via the national secretary. This process reaches the fullest expression in the new AN organizational articulation.

The Corporatist Structures

The traditional organizational features that have been highlighted up to now, which fit the MSI into the classical mass-party model, have been, however, internally questioned. For a long time, in fact, the MSI attempted to build a completely different kind of organization along corporatist guidelines according to the ideological imprint of the party; that is, the ideal of corporatist state which overcomes the conflicts between labor and capital and offers a well-defined niche for every kind of economic-professional activity. Starting from the early 1970s the party implemented the "corporatist structures" of the organization: sort of parallel structures along functional lines. At first, they were limited to a *Consulta Corporativa*—Corporatist Assembly, both at provincial and national levels whose presidents (elected by the respective local Consulte) had the right to participate (without voting) in the National and Provincial executives. Afterward, in the 1980s, the party tried to go further by promoting the idea (no more than an idea) that each member should be part of a professional "nucleus": in this way the standard territorial articulation of the party was doubled by the functional-professional one. This attempt of modelling the party along its "ideological" reference, however, remained merely proclaimed rather than effectively implemented. On the other hand, it represents somewhat of a novelty in the party's organizational philosophy. At any rate, as these structures were deprived of any kind of power or influence they were a mere homage to ideological guidelines.

The Flanking Organizations

The further element which incorporates the MSI into the mass-party model, and strengthens the complexity and (partially) the centralization of its organization, concerns the establishment of, and the relationship with, flanking organizations.

The MSI's traditional and most established flanking organizations are: the set of youth organizations (see infra); the trade union (CISNAL); the veterans of the RSI (UNCRSI and FNCR); the Italians abroad association (CTIM); the sport and leisure association (Fiamma) and, more recently, the women's association and the ecologist one (GRE). The youth and women organizations have a statute-defined relationship with the party and nominate their representatives in the executive bodies, while the others have looser links.

The youth organizations have acquired quite a special status thanks to their high membership and degree of militantism since the foundation of the party. The MSI, up to 1972, had three separate youth organizations: high school students, *Giovane Italia*—Young Italy; young people under 21 years of age, *Raggruppamento giovanile studenti e lavoratori*—Youth grouping of students and workers; university students, *Fronte Universitario di Azione Nazionale*—University Front of National Action (FUAN). The first two melted into the *Fronte della Gioventù*—Youth Front (FdG) in 1973. These groups provided a crucial reservoir of militantism that could be calculated in thousands of regular members (official figures declared even more than 100,000 members for the FdG in 1975 but these data are not very reliable).

The degree of autonomy of the youth organizations vis-à-vis the party (these groups have an autonomous membership but they are linked to the party in a formal way) has been an endless source of internal quarrels. Along with the restructuring of the youth movements in the 1970s the party imposed a stricter control: for example, it is the Party Secretary who had the right to choose the FdG secretary among the seven who collected more votes in the FdG National Congress. However, this control was not so effective as to avoid the presence of radical Right members and even the protection/acquaintance of right-wing terrorists in local youth branches during the "lead years" of the seventies. On the other hand, within the youth organization a critical tendency grew, mainly inspired by the French *Nouvelle Droite*, which led many young MSI members to leave the party in the early 1980s and to devote themselves to cultural activities only. In the late 1980s new, semi-autonomous organizational structures were "stimulated" by the FdG, such as *Fare Fronte*—Making Front and *Fare Verde*—Making Green, in order to capture the attention of young people without binding them directly to the party.

The only relevant flanking organization which had an autonomous life was the trade union CISNAL. Founded in 1950, it wanted to offer an alternative to the traditionally leftist and catholic trade-unionism in the name of "socialization and corporatism." CISNAL inherited the long-dated ideological debate, almost entirely mirroring the fascist one of the 1930s,[6] on the labor-capital relation, where a Left, revolutionary, anti-capitalist tendency confronted a more moderate, "corporatist" tendency. This latter group prevailed while the more radical group was quite active only until the late 1960s. The relationship between party and CISNAL was almost symbiotic as its historical leader was one of the founders of the MSI. This linkage broke when the CISNAL leader left the party in 1976. After a couple of years of turmoil the party recaptured control over the trade union.

In sum, the MSI attempted since the first years a strong "organizational encapsulation" (Wellhofer 1979: 206) *via* an extended network of flanking organizations. The increase in party centralization brought about by the foundation of AN has modified the role of these organizations: most of them were in fact too ideologically denotated (i.e., identified with fascism) to fit the mainstream image the party wanted to project; and therefore new associations, especially in the various occupational categories, have been fostered, with limited success up to now.

IDEOLOGY AND FACTIONALISM

The MSI enforced, as did all the other parties, its own network of publications, research centers, political-ideological stages, summer camps for youth, and so on. This aspect of the party is amazingly rich in terms of quantity, while so poor in terms of quality. The party promoted, more or less directly, many cultural and editorial activities but, with a couple of exceptions, it had an extremely poor intellectual profile. All these activities were circumscribed to an internal audience without any circulation beyond the neofascist constituency and presented, over and over, a reaffirmation of the validity of fascism with stainless faith and nostalgia. No new interpretation, analysis of the contemporary reality or critical assessment of the past are traceable in the dozens of journals edited directly or sponsored by the party, nor in the thousands of debates and meetings promoted by the various national and local party-related cultural centers. This quite intense cultural activity, largely promoted by the youth component, was totally self-referential. Even when a topic such as neocorporatism emerged in the general cultural-political debate, the specific MSI-sponsored institute devoted to this topic, the *Istituto di Studi Corporativi*—Institute of Corporatist Studies, and its journal *Rivista di Studi Corporativi*, were unable to offer an effective response. The political marginalization of an anti-system party such as the MSI was reflected in the marginalization of its cultural activity too (and not because of an external censorship attitude but, again, for lack of content).

Instead of forwarding ideas in the electorate at large, such cultural and editorial effervescence provided a reinforcement of the ideological references within the party. Therefore, the means by which to promote the internal debate became an important internal resource to control. On one hand, availing itself of the daily newspaper—*Il Secolo d'Italia*, founded in 1953 and still the official newspaper of *Alleanza nazionale*—and of the various cultural centers and editorial productions, implied the possibility of providing some selective incentives, to the most committed militants. On the other hand, these means offered the capacity to control the ideological debate by the dominant coalition. In an anti-system party which lives mainly on symbolic incentives, the control of the cultural-ideological sphere is of utmost importance for the leadership.

The party's internal ideological debate had always been very vivid and had produced a neat divide. In fact, the party had been highly factionalized since the beginning. Even if fascism was never put under the minimum scrutiny, the debate around *which kind of fascism* should be followed was very intense and produced conflicts and tensions all through the party life. The same fascist history with its various tendencies and streams provided the legitimation for a divisive ideological debate and therefore organized factions. Contrary to the absolute banning of faction in the PCI, where the doctrinaire system was totally rigid, inside the MSI factions were legitimated by the multifaceted fascist ideology on one hand, and, at the same time, by their absolute identification with the basic aims and the manifest ideology of the party. By keeping alive the fascist nostalgia but also enforcing a confrontation on its *nuances*, the party offered a highly mobilizing symbolic incentive.

As mentioned above, the traditional MSI ideological divide regarded the moderate bargaining-oriented faction led by Michelini, Almirante (after its election to the secretary in 1969) and then Fini, grossly recalling the fascism-as-regime tradition, and the Left, revolutionary, anti-capitalist one led by Almirante in the 1950s and the 1960s, and later by Rauti, recalling the fascism-as-movement tradition.

Table 8.2
Membership of MSI/AN, 1960–1995

year	members	year	members
1960	191,397	1978	152,234
1961	200,348	1979	174,157
1962	198,995	1980	165,810
1963	240,063	1981	176,417
1964	227,214	1982	159,169
1965	191,029	1983	165,308
1966	161,890	1984	180,688
1967	160,043	1985	141,623
1968	199,950	1986	156,520
1969	175,709	1987	165,427
1970	188,878	1988	151,444
1971	205,794	1989	160,960
1972	239,075	1990	142,344
1973	225,030	1991	150,157
1974	210,018	1992	181,243
1975	212,120	1993	202,715
1976	217,110	1994	324,344
1977	160,339	1995*	467,539

Data for 1994 refers to AN.
Source: official data provided by MSI/AN headquarters.

With the exception of a few years, the former tendency ruled the party. However, the dominant coalition was neither completely stable nor cohesive. Changes in its composition alternated with longer periods of stability. Major modifications in the dominant coalition occurred in the late 1980s (Table 8.2). The turnover in the National Executive (*Direzione nazionale*) dropped almost constantly during the 1950s, reaching the minimum of 19.8 percent in 1984.

This quite limited turnover is even more reduced if we take into consideration the persistence of the members. In fact, as the executives were substantially enlarged year after year, almost all the previous members kept their positions. For example, when in 1973 the executive almost doubled its size, *more than 90 percent* of the previous members maintained their seats. With the exception of 1977, because of the above-mentioned split and the obvious higher turnover, this trend was confirmed until 1987. In that circumstance a new phase started with a decrease in the presence of former members.

As the membership in the executive (as well as in the Central Committee) represented a resource in the hands of the dominant coalition which could in this way distribute (internal) selective incentives, the progressive enlargement of its size reflected the necessity of availing more resources to co-opt new members in the dominant coalition and/or to satisfy the needs and quarrels of the opposition.

LEGITIMATION AND TRANSFORMATION

In 1987 an older and ailing Almirante "imposed" on the XVth MSI Congress his successor, the 34-year-old Gianfranco Fini, former leader of the FdG. This proposal reopened an intense internal struggle which recollected once more the juxtaposition between the Left, represented by Rauti, and the Right, represented by Almirante and the old ruling class. However, part of the traditional supporters of Almirante failed to support Fini who was elected by a strict majority. This enfeeblement of the traditional moderate right-wing dominant coalition became critical when Almirante and a couple of other historical party leaders died. The young Fini proved unable to control the party, adopting very extreme and provocative initiatives against the internal opposition such as the shutdown of some local federations. Moreover, Fini was not able to end the marginalization of the party more or less overtly proclaimed by the anti-fascist parties. He rigidly kept a fierce anti-system profile and proclaimed more and more loyalty to fascism (one of the party manifestos he promoted was significantly called "fascism for the year 2000"). In the absence of other kinds of incentives or rewards, in order to keep his coalition bounded, Fini stressed a collective symbolic incentive: identification with fascism. Unfortunately, it was not enough, as Fini was overthrown by the internal alignments in the dominant coalition in December 1989 and was forced to resign just in the wake of his Congress. In that highly dramatic Congress, held in January 1990, Fini was defeated by Rauti, thanks to a novel agreement among the various factions (eight different factions presented their own candidates for the election of the Central Committee in that occasion).

Rauti's election represented a watershed in the MSI's history. Rauti was in fact the first leader of the leftist faction elected by a (somewhat) congruent majority. The most dramatic change introduced by this change of leadership concerned the ideological frame rather than the party's organization or the central office. No significant alteration of the party structure was introduced and the National Executive was just slightly renovated but not so dramatically compared to other circumstances. On the other hand, while fascism remained the key reference with a strong emphasis on the "fascism-as-movement" tendency, a more heterogeneous political culture surfaced. The anti-capitalist, anti-bourgeois (*and also anti-racist*)[7] positions that Rauti promoted were intended to appeal to the left-wing electorate in order to capture its anti-system and anti-capitalist sentiments "betrayed" by an adaptive and no longer militant PCI. This very innovative politics, while it did not endanger the collective identity of the neofascist constituency, disoriented, however, the traditional MSI electorate and provided dramatic defeats to the party up to the point which led Rauti to resign. In this occasion no Congress was called and the Central Committee renominated Fini as Party Secretary in July 1991.

The very short Rauti secretaryship had no lasting impact, as Fini could continue to pursue the previous "traditional" MSI politics. However, such politics was devoid of any success. The MSI remained very isolated and incapable of political initiative. Only the external circumstances, that is, the Clean Hands investigation on political corruption and the collapse of the old party system with the erruption of new forces such as the Northern League and, above all, Berlusconi's *Forza Italia*, helped the MSI to get out of its ghetto. In a few weeks—similar to what happened to the French Front National in 1983–1984—from the local election in December 1993 to the general election in March 1994, the MSI, and Fini leadership, took off.

This sudden and amazing success—the party passed in the 1994 general election from 5.4 percent to 13.5 percent and above all entered the Berlusconi government—produced a series of effects on the party's organizational order. First of all, Fini's leadership became uncontested and he filled in all of the party's positions with his loyal followers, achieving the double effect of a generational and political turnover. Second, thanks to the absolute control of the party, Fini could move toward a (very limited) "articulation of ends," especially in order to cool down the international concern that the first neofascist presence in a Western government had produced. Fini attempted to relegate fascism to the "evaluation of history" but he could not restrain himself in a very famous interview to consider Mussolini the "greatest Italian statesman of the XX century" (Ignazi, 1994a). Third, the MSI, for the first time, had an amazing quantity of resources to distribute. The access to government and the identification of the MSI as the pro–state-economy party of Berlusconi's government produced a virtual circle between state-owned industries' managers and executives on one side, and the party on the other side: the former needed a "political reference" for their career and the party needed professionally skillful personnel. In other terms, the party benefited from contacts and liaisons with sectors of the ruling class who had always disregarded the minor, anti-system and powerless. Finally, last but not the least, the access to the media—from practically nil in the pre-1993 years to an almost daily presence afterwards—was almost monopolized (and efficaciously run) by Fini himself.

Thanks to the control of all these crucial resources, Fini gained full control of the party and could lead the transformation from MSI to AN.

THE NEW PARTY: AN

Such transformation did not imply any dramatic trauma (contrary to what happened to the PCI four years earlier). In particular, the trauma was prevented by a dexterous management of the party's identity features. The new party founded in January 1995, *Alleanza Nazionale*—which adopted the name of the electoral label added to the MSI in the 1994 electoral campaign—did not imply a "substitution of ends" (Panebianco 1988). The manifest ideology was skilfully articulated and fascism was diluted into the mainstream of the Right; the "illiberal traits" of fascism were condemned and freedom and democracy were exalted, but fascism was not rejected once and for all (on this point see Ignazi, 1994, 1996; Sznajder, 1995; Tarchi, 1995b).

On the other hand, thanks to the political and electoral success, except for the very few true believers who left the party together with Rauti,[8] no one could even think of opposing whatever project, proposal or idea the General Secretary had suggested. Moreover, full control of ideology, of formal rules, of information, of turnover, and, for the first time, of selective incentives other than the internal party's offices, was almost all concentrated in Fini's hands. Therefore, the new party was born easily and smoothly.

The organizational features changed to a limited extent. The most emphasized novelty would concern the introduction of a new local structure called "circles." Actually, the AN statute indicates two types of circles: a territorial one and a functional one (literally spelled out "of the environment"). As one can see the territorial one recalls the former branch and the functional one the former corporatist structure. The innovation in organization regards the equivalence in the roles played by both kinds of local structures, as both contribute to the nomination process of the federation/provincial bodies (while this was previously reserved to the traditional sections only).

Beyond these (and other) semantic novelties, AN's formal rules implemented those Caesarist-centrist traits that were more and more emerging in the later years of the MSI. One of these traits is revealed by the transformation of the former Central Committee into an *Assemblea Nazionale*—National Assembly. This body grew up to 500 members, 120 more than the previous Central Committee. This oversized feature is self-explanatory of its loss of power. The National Assembly is totally controlled by the leadership thanks to an election system where 200 are elected in a blocked list (in practice, controlled by the majority), 200 proposed by the leadership who can only be cancelled by the leadership, 50 directly nominated by the secretary and finally, 50 elected by the Congress.

Even more relevant is the loss of any real power by the National Executive: as it is "*designated by the party leader*" (Art. 29: 1995) and ratified by the National Assembly, it is a docile instrument in the hands of the president (the new definition of the Party Secretary).

The power is concentrated in the hands of the president. He does not only keep the previous prerogatives (shutting down of provincial bodies, disciplinary indictment for any member, nomination of the regional secretary—renominated "coordinator"—nomination of the party press responsible); his control is greatly increased in the distribution of the posts in the national bodies (National Assembly and Executive). Moreover, he controls, via the National Executive, the elected representatives in Parliament (Art. 30: 1995); and, finally, he is "not responsible" to Central Committee because it cannot dismiss him (as did happen to Fini himself in December 1989 and to Rauti in July 1991); only the Congress has that power.

The turnover in the 1995 AN National Executive was very high compared to the 1990 MSI National Executive elected in the previous National Congress; 71.2 percent are freshmen. The split of the Rauti faction from one side and the entrance into the party of previously nonpartisan "notables" who needed to be rewarded with a position in the National Executive partially explains this very high turnover. Moreover, it should be noted that the comparison is made with the 1990 National Executive when Rauti was elected secretary while a change of secretary—with a change in the composition of the National Executive—had occurred in 1991. Whatever is the explanation, the leader has in this way filled the executive body with "his own men." And finally less than 10 percent had no previous MSI affiliation. This implies that AN did not attract so many "external" middle-level elites.

The AN dominant coalition appears highly stable and cohesive. It comprises almost the entire party even if some differentiation still exists (and emerged after the unsatisfactory results of the 1996 elections) along the classical, historical lines of cleavage in the MSI, as more than one list competed for the elective posts in the National Assembly (*Area vasta*, Fini's hyperloyalists and *Cantiere Italia*, the "socially minded").

The new map of the organizational power reflects a strengthening of the authority lines of command. The AN president is a sort of absolute king. Such a transfer of so much power to the leader by a party which has been so highly factionalized, and which had a rather decent democratic functioning, could be explained by the sentiment that the president, Gianfranco Fini, was the best person in the party to control and seize the external environment. Its leadership was indeed a relevant part of the party's amazing success. Therefore, the entire party (with the exception of the true believers who left) agreed to delegate power to him. Statutory provisions, and the uncontested dominance and charismatic-like aura of the leadership introduced traits of "führer-prinzip" in AN.

The last point would concern the crucial resource represented by the party's identity. In a transformation like this the control over the ideological reference is a key factor. The debatable question on how much AN is different from the MSI as far as ideological references are concerned (see Griffin, 1996; Ignazi, 1996; Tarchi, 1995b) is not so relevant in this context. Whatever the similarities or differences, what is crucial here is the smooth acceptance by the party of the denunciation of the undemocratic character of fascism. This smoothness is confirmed by the fact that, of the same delegates who almost unanimously voted for Fini's document, 68.6 percent then considered fascism "a good regime" (Baldini and Vignati 1996). Even if these data confirm the presence of contradictory political attitudes, no acute tension has arisen. The explanation for that is basically provided by the role acquired by the party's leader. Fini could play freely on this very sensitive field because he was perceived as a authoritative and legitimate representative of the party's (fascist) tradition and, above all, he guaranteed everybody with his success. Therefore, to oppose Fini when the party attained such unbelievable electoral and political results would have been considered either a suicidal drive or an irrational antagonism (as demonstrated by Rauti's small fringe).

Summing up, the transformation of the MSI into AN does not imply that AN could be considered a *new* party. The conformation of the dominant coalition is somewhat modified: in particular, changes implied a generational turnover in the national bodies, an articulation of ends in the party manifest ideology, a strengthening of the centralization (vertical linkages) thanks to a higher concentration of power in the hands of the party leader. The political personnel in the national bodies and in Parliament has passed through an impressive turnover indeed, but such renewal did not introduce novel political personnel, extraneous to the MSI "subculture." Rather, it promoted a generational change with an internal upward mobility of the middle-level elites socialized within the MSI.

The articulation of the party's manifest ideology is still in the making; the organizational features recall the traditional ones with nominalistic changes rather substantial ones and the political personnel, notwithstanding the massive generational turnover, has been politically socialized within the MSI. Therefore, the party's image has radically changed, but the identity still shares many traits of the past.

NOTES

1. On the MSI genetic model, see Ignazi (1989a: 257ff)

2. To add confusion to confusion the 1977 statute prescribed that "renewal of membership is automatic" (Art. 3: 1977). Even if this rule was cancelled in the following statute the praxis to register former members remained.

3. Courtesy of AN Department of Organization.

4. The *sezione* (branch) corresponds to the municipal level but in the larger cities more·sections are set up; federation corresponds very closely, but with a few exceptions, to the 95 provincial administrative levels; region corresponds to the 20 Italian regions.

5. Such limited availability of resources is *part* of the explanation of the high level of competition on the allocation of party offices.

6. The continuity with fascism is exemplified by the first presidency of the CISNAL

held by the former General Secretary of the *Confederazione fascista dei lavoratori dell'Industria*—Fascist Confederation of Industrial Workers, in the fascist regime.

7. Rauti was the promoter of a completely different approach to the question of immigration. Contrary to the xenophobic extreme Right movements such as the French Front National, Rauti developed an anti-racist attitude relying upon anti-capitalist standings: the exploitation of the Third World forces people to migrate and therefore immigrants are the victims of the "financial-capitalist world domination."

8. At the 1995 Congress, Rauti left the party and founded the *Movimento Sociale-Fiamma Tricolore*—Social Movement-Tricolour Flame. This splinter group aimed at maintaining certain features of the traditional party ideology and it contested the 1996 elections with some success, inhibiting the election of AN (or AN-sponsored) candidates in some constituencies (Sani, 1996).

REFERENCES

Baldini, Gianfranco and Rinaldo Vignati (1996). "Dal MSI ad AN: Una Nuova Cultura Politica?" *Polis* 10: 1, 81–101.

Bardi, Luciano and Morlino Leonardo (1992). "Italy." In Richard Katz and Peter Mair (eds.), *Party Organization 1960–1990*, pp. 418–468. London: Sage.

Carioti, Antonio (1996). "From the Ghetto to Palazzo Chigi: The Ascent of National Alliance." In Richard Katz and Piero Ignazi (eds.), *Italian Politics. The Year of the Tycoon*, pp. 57–78. Boulder, CO: Westview Press.

Chiarini, Roberto (1995). *La Destra Italiana*. Venezia: Marsilio.

Cotta, Maurizio (1979). *Classe Politica e Parlamento in Italia 1946–1976*. Bologna: Il Mulino.

De Felice, Renzo (1976). *Intervista sul Fascismo*. Bari: Laterza.

Duverger, Maurice (1951). *Les Partis Politiques*. Paris: Colin.

Griffin, Roger (1996). "The 'Post-fascism' of Alleanza Nazionale: A Case Study in Ideological Morphology." *Journal of Political Ideology* 1:123–145.

Ignazi, Piero (1989a). *Il Polo Escluso. Profilo del Movimento Sociale Italiano*. Bologna: Il Mulino.

Ignazi, Piero (1989b). "La Cultura Politica del MSI-DN." *Rivista Italiana di Scienza Politica* 19: 431–465.

Ignazi, Piero (1994). *Postfascisti? La trasformazione del Movimento sociale in Alleanza nazionale*. Bologna: Il Mulino.

Ignazi, Piero (1996). "From Neo-Fascists to Post-Fascists? The Transformation of the MSI into the AN." *West European Politics* 19, 4: 693–714.

Janda, Kenneth (1993). "Comparative Political Research and Theory." In Ada W. Finifter (ed.), *Political Science: The State of the Discipline, II*, pp. 163–192. Washington, DC: American Political Science Association.

Mair, Peter (1994). "Party Organization: From Civil Society to the State." In Richard Katz and Peter Mair (eds.), *How Parties Organize*, pp. 1–22. London: Sage.

Panebianco, Angelo (1982). *Modelli di partito*. Bolgna: Il Mulino.

Payne, Stanley (1995). *A History of Fascism 1914–1945*. Madison: University of Wisconsin Press.

Sternhell, Zeev (1989). *L'Ideologie Fasciste*. Paris: Fayard.

Sznajder, Mario (1995). "Has Neofascism Disappeared in Italy?" Paper presented at the Conference on "Extremism and Nationalism in Europe Fifty Years after World War II," Jerusalem.

Wellhofer, Spencer (1979). "Effectiveness of Party Organization: A Cross-National Time Series Analysis." *European Journal of Political Research*. 18: 515–533.

Tarchi, Marco (1995a). *Esuli in Patria*. Parma: Guanda.

Tarchi, Marco (1995b). *Cinquant'anni di Nostalgia. La Destra Italiana dopo il Fascismo* (Intervista di Antonio Carioti). Milano: Rizzoli.

Part III

Greece

9

The Political System in Postauthoritarian Greece (1974–1996): Outline and Interpretations

—————————— P. Nikoforos Diamandouros

This chapter has two major goals: first, to provide a factual, narrative account of the construction and development of Greece's postauthoritarian (1974) political system, with special emphasis on political parties and elections; and, second, to offer an analysis and interpretation of that system's nature and dynamics and to render more readily intelligible both its increasingly fewer exceptionalist characteristics as well as those which bring it closer to its counterparts in the more established democracies of advanced industrial societies.

ELECTIONS, PARTIES, TRENDS

The current Greek political system was born in July 1974, in the wake of the collapse of the authoritarian, military regime installed in 1967. The regime's demise was brought about by its inability to respond to the Turkish invasion of Cyprus, following the Greek regime's unsuccessful attempt violently to overthrow the constitutional government of Cyprus and to unite that island state with Greece. The return to civilian rule in that country was led by the longtime conservative leader, Constantine Karamanlis, who returned from an eleven-year-long, self-imposed exile in France to head a national unity government, which held office between 24 July and 17 November 1974.[1]

The national elections held on that latter date—the first since February 1964—were contested by many parties, chief among which were the following: (a) *Nea demokratia* (New Democracy—ND), a new conservative party founded by Karamanlis, which inherited some of the political personnel of the preauthoritarian right-wing party, the *Ethnike Rizospastike Enosis* (National Radical Union—ERE); (b) the *Panhellinio Sosialistiko Kinema* (Pan-hellenic Socialist Movement—PASOK), another new party established by Andreas Papandreou, an American-trained, former academic and leader of the reformist wing of the preauthoritarian *Enosis Kentrou* (Center Union—EK) headed by his father, George Papandreou; (c) the *Enosis Kentrou-Nees Dynameis* (Center Union-New Forces—EK-ND), a political formation based overwhelmingly on the pre-authoritarian Center Union, whose novelty lay in its alliance with new aspirants for political power, who had distinguished themselves in the resistance against the colonels' authoritarian regime; (d) the Communist left, legal for the first time since 1947 and united in a single electoral alliance, the *Enomene Aristera* (United Left), which sought to paper over the sharp split that, as of 1968, had separated the orthodox *Kommon-ounistiko Komma Hellados* (Communist Party of Greece—KKE), which had remained loyal to the Soviet Union from the *Kommonounistiko Komma Hel-lados Esoterikou* (Communist Party of Greece-Interior—KKE-Interior), which represented a reformist, Euro-Communist tendency. Included in the alliance was the tiny *Eniaia Demokratike Aristera* (United Democratic Left Party—EDA), which, in the post–civil war years had served as the surrogate for the outlawed Communist left and had occupied the extreme Left position on the political spectrum; and (e) the *Ethniko Demokratike Enosis* (National Dem-ocratic Union), which sought overtly to appeal to erstwhile supporters of the authoritarian regime.

The elections were handily won by the ND, which received 54.4 percent of the vote (see Table 9.1). Thanks to the complex electoral system of rein-forced proportional representation, which discriminates in favor of the larger parties in an electoral competition, the ND won an overwhelming 216 out of 300 seats in the Greek Parliament. ND's victory, one of the largest in Greek parliamentary history, should be read in two ways: positively, it represented a clear preference for the "safe and reassuring" option concerning the future, which Karamanlis and his New Democracy held out during the tense and uncertain initial moments of the postauthoritarian period; negatively, it con-stituted evidence of that same electorate's unwillingness to entertain bold new alternatives such as the ones envisaged by PASOK's calls for a radical break with the past, including the rejection of Greece's traditional alliances, the adoption of a Third World orientation, and the search for a new, third road to Socialist transformation, capable of eschewing the perceived perils of extant Socialism and of Social Democracy.

The EK-ND came in second with 20.5 percent of the vote, won 61 deputies, and emerged as the official opposition party in Parliament. This success, however, was meager compensation for the sharp decline in its electoral fortunes relative to its performance in the last elections in the pre-authoritarian period (February 1964), when it had won a resounding 52.7 percent of the vote. In fact, it was a painful indication of its waning fortunes, which were to lead to its disappearance after the 1977 elections. PASOK came in third, with 13.6 percent of the vote and fourteen seats, much to the disappointment of its charismatic leader, Andreas Papandreou. Finally, the United Left obtained just under 10 percent of the vote and eight seats in Parliament, while the extreme right-wing EDE received just over 1 percent of the votes and secured no parliamentary seats.[2]

The Greek party system underwent further change in the 20 November 1977 elections, which the ND won again handily (41.8 percent of the vote and 171 deputies), albeit with a significantly reduced majority, largely as a result of the emergence of a far-Right party, the National Front, which won 6.82 percent of the votes and 5 seats. The major loser of these elections was the EK, which saw its share of the vote reduced by almost half to 11.9 percent and its parliamentary representation from 61 to 16 seats.

Conversely, the major winner of the 1977 elections was PASOK, which, having adopted a highly successful, populist electoral strategy that won it the solid support of what its leader called the "nonprivileged" strata of Greek society, almost doubled its share of the vote, gaining 25.3 percent of all valid ballots cast; increased its parliamentary representation almost sixfold to 93, and emerged as the uncontested major opposition party in Parliament.

Finally, an important dimension of this election was the clear victory of the orthodox Communist Party of Greece (9.4 percent of the vote and eleven seats) over its Euro-Communist rival, the KKE-Interior (2.7 percent of the vote in alliance with four other small parties and a total of two seats).[3]

The consolidation of the new Greek party system can be said to have occurred in the context of the 1981 elections, which ended the ND's seven-year rule, triumphantly brought PASOK to power, and confirmed the complete dominance of these two parties over postauthoritarian Greek politics. Although formally present in this contest, the EK was entirely annihilated, receiving a mere 1 percent of the vote. Its demise signaled the definitive capture of that part of Greek political space by PASOK.

Weakened by the absence of Karamanlis, who, as of 1980, had been elevated to the position of president of the Greek Republic, and led by the head of its liberal wing, George Rallis, a veteran conservative political figure, the ND proved unable to react to what appeared to be the irresistible rise of PASOK to power under the vague but powerful slogan of "Allaghi" or "Change." With 35.8 percent of the popular vote and 115 seats in Parliament, it emerged as the major party of opposition, a position in which it was to remain for the ensuing eight years.

Rather ironically, the ND's loss at the polls came just a few months after Greece had become the tenth member of the European Communities, fulfilling one of Karamanlis's most fundamental political goals and securing the country's entry into the charmed circle of advanced industrial economies and societies in Europe. Although not sufficiently appreciated at the time, this was a development which was to have the profoundest of implications for Greece's politics, society and economy.

Table 9.1
Results of National Elections, 1974–1996

PARTIES	1974	1977	1981	1985	1989 (June)	1989 (Nov.)	1990	1993	1996
New Democracy (ND)	2,669,133	2,146,365	2,034,496	2,599,681	2,887,488	3,093,479	3,088,137	2,711,737	2,586,089
% votes	54.37	41.84	35.87	40.84	44.28	46.19	46.89	39.30	38.12
N. seats	216(a)	171	115	126	145	148	150(f)	111	108
National Democratic Union (EDE)	52,768	349,988	95,799	37,965	--	--	--	--	--
% votes	1.08	6.82	1.68	0.60					
N. seats	--	5	--	--					
Neoliberal Party (KN)	--	55,494	--	--	--	--	--	--	--
% votes		1.08							
N. seats		2							
Center Union-New Forces (EK-ND)	1,002,559	612,786	83,534	--	--	--	--	--	--
% votes	20.42	11.95	1.46(d)						
N. seats	61(a)	16	--						
Democratic Renewal (DIANA)	--	--	--	--	65,614	--	44,077	--	--
% votes					1.01		0.67		
N. seats					1		1		

Political Spring (POL:A.)									
% votes	2.94	4.88	--	--	--	--	--	--	--
N. seats	--	10							
199,686	336,460	--	--	--	--	--	--	--	
Panhellenic Socialist Party (PASOK)									
votes	2,814,779	3,235,017	2,543,042	2,724,334	2,551,518	2,916,735	2,726,309	1,300,025	666,413
% votes	41.50	46.88	38.61	40.67	39.13	45.82	48.07	25.34	13.58
N. seats	162	170	123	128	125	161	172	93	15(a)
Communist Party (KKE)									
votes	380,046	313,001	677,059	734,611	855,944	629,525	620,302	480,272	464,787
% votes	5.60	4.54	10.28	10.97	13.12	9.89	10.93	9.36	9.47
N. seats	11	9	19	21	28	12	12	11	8(b)
Communist Party Interior (KKE Interior)									
votes	--	--	--	--	--	117,135	76,404	139,356	--
% votes						1.84	1.34	2.72(c)	
N. seats						1	--	2	
Democratic Social Movement (DIKKI)									
votes	300,954	--	--	--	--	--	--	--	--
% votes	4.43								
N. seats	9								

185

Table 9.1 (continued)

Coalition of the Left and Progress (SYN)							
% votes	--	--	--	--	--	2.94	5.12
N. seats	--	--	--	--	--	--	10
PASOK-SYN							
% votes	--	--	--	0.16	1.02	--	--
N. seats	--	--	--	1	4(g)	--	--
(votes)	--	--	--	10,972	66,861	--	--
Greens							
% votes	--	--	--	0.58	0.77	--	--
N. seats	--	--	--	1	1	--	--
(votes)	--	--	--	39,158	50,868	--	--
Others							
% votes	1.08	0.81	2.45	1.41	1.76	--	--
N. seats	--	1(e)	1(e)	1(e)	2(h)	--	--
(votes)	53,314	53,502	160,647	95,014	115,996	--	--
(SYN votes)	--	--	--	--	--	202,887	347,236

[a]Distribution of seats was finalized following the decisions of the Electoral Court and the bielections of April 20, 1975, held to replace deceased deputies or to fill seats vacated because the original election in that district had been invalidated.

[b]United Left: 5 seats for KKE, 2 for KKE interior, 1 for EDA (United Democratic Left).

[c]KKE interior in coalition with four other small parties (Coalition of Left and Progressive Forces). 1 seat for KKE interior, 1 seat for EDA (United Democratic Left).

[d]Small Center Parties (Kodiso 0.70, Edik 0.40, Liberal Party 0.36).

[e]One of the two independent Muslin deputies, who received a total of 34,145 votes in June 1989 and 36,353 votes in November 1989.

[f]Following a decision of the Supreme High Court at the end of 1990, ND finally won 151 seats and PASOK 124. Thus, following the decision of the DIANA deputies to join ND, the latter had a total of 152.

[g]Of which 2 seats for PASOK and 2 seats for SYN. If one adds to the votes received by PASOK and SYN the share of the vote issuing from the five joint candidacies in single-member districts, the percentage of PAS OK becomes 39.3, and for SYN 10.6.

[h]Two independent Muslims who received a total of 45,981 votes.

Loss of power served as a catalyst for a host of important readjustments within the party. Deprived of its historical leader and founder, the ND went through a crisis of identity which had three concrete results: first, it produced three changes in leadership within the short span of four years. The last of these brought to the party's helm Constantine Mitsotakis, a veteran liberal politician, whose profound antipathy, if not enmity, for Mr. Papandreou and his capacity to serve as a pole of attraction for those opposed to PASOK's charismatic leader were deemed to constitute significant assets in the party's search for the road back to power; second, it brought about a considerable reorientation of the party away from the more moderate, center-right position captured during the Karamanlis and Rallis years to a more right-wing orientation and, over time, to ideas associated with neoliberalism; and, third, it contributed to the adoption of a more confrontational, almost ideological style of politics, which, at the level of discourse, imparted a polarizing, populist and somewhat strident note to Greek politics that matched and, in many ways mirrored, similar practices on PASOK's side.

With 48.1 percent of the vote and 172 seats in Parliament, PASOK, on the other hand, consolidated its position as the dominant party in Greek politics. The party's meteoric rise to power within just seven years of its founding served as the ultimate proof of the major realignment of the traditional Greek party system and, more generally, of Greek politics, which the postauthoritarian period had brought about.[4]

The elections of 2 June 1985 confirmed the pattern established in 1981 and further expanded its scope. Despite a significant, five percentage point increase in the ND's performance relative to the 1981 results (40.8 percent versus 35.8 percent in 1981), PASOK won a second four-year term, witnessing only a minor, 2.3 percent reduction in its share of the popular vote (45.8 percent as opposed to 48.1 percent in 1981) and, thanks to the built-in advantages of the electoral system, securing a comfortable majority of 161 seats in Parliament.

The 1985 election was remarkable for another reason: it confirmed PASOK's final abandonment of its erstwhile radical profile and signaled the start of a long and tortuous road that was eventually to lead it to positions closer to those of European Social Democracy. More specifically, the elections marked PASOK's final accommodation with Greece's traditional foreign policy orientations and underscored its reconciliation with membership in the European Communities and NATO as well as the improvement of its relationship with the United States. At the same time, they ushered in the first economic austerity program in the postauthoritarian period. Although brief in duration and reversed in 1987, this shift in policy, which contrasted sharply with the major increases in social spending that had been characteristic of the previous decade and, especially, of the first four years of PASOK's rule (1981–1985), signaled initial recognition of the problems arising from

Greece's integration in the international economy and of the pressing need to engage in substantive restructuring of its economy.[5]

Increased evidence of inability to confront Greece's mounting political and economic problems, and the resulting popular disillusionment and dissatisfaction, combined with a series of economic and political scandals reaching the highest levels of PASOK's government and the serious illness of Andreas Papandreou in 1988 to produce a major political crisis which severely undermined PASOK's political fortunes and served to deprive it of its broad support. Dominated by mounting calls for "catharsis" (purging) from the financial scandals and allegations concerning Papandreou's involvement in them, the elections of 18 June 1989 resulted in a significant decline of PASOK's share of the popular vote (39.1 percent) and in its defeat.

The major consequence of this election, however, was that it ushered in a one-year period of political uncertainty, due to the inability of any one party to secure a parliamentary majority on its own and, hence, led to the formation of coalition governments, a rare phenomenon in postwar Greek politics. Contributing to this development was a PASOK-inspired change in the electoral law that was designed to strengthen proportionality in such a way as to make it more difficult for the first party to gain on its own a majority of the seats in Parliament. With 44.3 percent of the vote, the ND came in first but won only 145 out of 300 seats. PASOK obtained 125 seats, and the Alliance of the Left and Progress 28 seats with 13.1 percent of the vote.

Given these constraints, the most spectacular outcome of the June 1989 elections was the unlikely collaboration of the ND and the Left (Alliance for the Left and Progress) in forming a government. The political raison d'être of this coalition was to ensure that those allegedly responsible for the scandals could be brought to justice. Its long-term significance, however, lay in the fact that, in bringing together in a government the two direct descendants of the opposing forces in the civil war, it signaled the symbolic end of that conflict, 40 years after the cessation of military hostilities. A novelty of the Parliament issuing from these elections and a direct byproduct of the new electoral law was the election of an independent deputy representing the Muslim minorities in Thrace.

The elections of 5 November 1989 confirmed the continuing ascendancy of the ND which obtained 46.2 percent of the vote but, with 148 seats, once again fell short of the required majority in Parliament. Thanks to the peculiarities of the electoral law, PASOK, with 40.7 percent, was able to gain 128 seats, while the Left won 11 percent of the vote and 21 seats. Also represented in this Parliament were the Muslim minorities in Thrace and one newly emergent ecological movement in Greece. Each held one seat.

Given the inability of any one party to form a government, the November 1989 elections gave rise to a three-party government consisting of the ND, PASOK, and the Left. Its most salient features were three: first, the continuing presence of the Left in government; second, PASOK's return to power, a mere five months after its defeat in the midst of the scandals that had rocked its very foundations; and third, the patent inability of the three parties effectively to collaborate within the context of a coalition government.

The impasse thus produced was mercifully solved by the elections of 8 April 1990, albeit with the slightest of margins. With 46.9 percent of the vote, the ND obtained the absolute minimum (150) number of seats needed to form a government. Given the very high degree of discipline observable in the Greek party system, the ND was able to rule for the ensuing three and a half years. It fell only when Andonis Samaras, a former Foreign Minister seeking to exploit the negative public sentiment generated by the party's policies concerning the vexed Macedonian Question, resigned his parliamentary seat in October 1992, founded a new party, Political Spring, in June 1993, and eventually brought down the government in September of the same year, by causing ND deputies loyal to him to leave the government party and deprive it of its majority.

The ND's three years in power were distinguished by two developments: first, the attempt to steer Greece in the direction of neoliberal politics and to embark upon policies of deregulation and of privatization; and, second, the adoption of an austerity policy designed, however belatedly, to bring Greece's enormous public spending and, especially, debt under control and to place the country's economy on a sounder footing that would render more feasible its convergence with (rather than divergence from) trends observable among its European Union partners.

In the elections of April 1990, PASOK obtained 38.6 percent of the vote and 123 seats, the Alliance for the Left got 10.3 percent of the vote and 19 seats, the ecologists one seat, and the candidates of the Muslim minorities two. PASOK's capacity to survive a series of electoral contests under extremely unfavorable conditions (scandals, corruption, etc.) pointed to its impressive organizational strengths. At the same time, its performance served as strong confirmation of the fact that its hard-core support hovered around 38–40 percent of the electorate.[6]

The elections of 10 October 1993 were held under a slight variant of the reinforced proportional representation system that, with rare exceptions, has been consistently used in Greece throughout the postwar period. They produced an alternation in governmental incumbency, bringing PASOK back to power and returning the ND to the opposition. It is worth noting that, while obtaining the exact same percentage of votes as the ND had won in 1990 (46.9 percent), PASOK, under the new law, which was expressly designed to penalize the second party, obtained a comfortable majority of seats in Parliament (170) and has been spared the kinds of problems which the barest of majorities posed for its rival while in office.[7]

PASOK's latest term in power has been marked by three major developments: the first concerns the adoption of an austerity policy, which has effectively continued, but has also substantively built upon, the one adopted by its predecessor. Most notable in this area have been the concerted efforts of the government's financial team to expand the tax base, to apply existing legislation more equitably, to combat tax evasion, and, more generally, to improve the health of the Greek economy.

The second development which profoundly influenced PASOK's latest administration was a major deterioration of Andreas Papandreou's health, which became especially noticeable from 1994 onward and eventually led to his collapse and hospitalization in late November 1995. With the single and important exception of the economic ministries, the capacity of the government to conduct its business was adversely affected by the Prime Minister's failing health and it came virtually to a halt during the period of his hospitalization.

Issuing directly out of Mr. Papandreou's illness, the third salient feature of PASOK's latest term in office was the decision, in January 1996, to appoint Constantine Simitis to replace the party's ailing founder, who, however, retained the powerful post of party president. The choice of Mr. Simitis was notable for two major reasons: first, because it represented a victory, however narrow and precarious, for the so-called modernizing wing of the party—whose standard-bearer Mr. Simitis has long been considered—which is closely identified with the call for substantive and far-reaching reforms in Greek society and politics; and, second, because the Simitis election was the outcome of a process in which the rules of internal party democracy, so glaringly ignored during the years of Mr. Papandreou's rule, were scrupulously observed.

On the other hand, Mr. Simitis's election poses a number of novel, interesting and potentially troublesome issues for the Greek political system. To begin with, this is the first time in Greece's experience with modern, mass parties in which the leader of the government is not also the head of his party. How this state of dyarchy will be resolved remains unclear. PASOK's fourth Congress, scheduled for July 1996, will undoubtedly have to address these and other issues. In so doing, it will also be testing its capacity for renewal and for steering Greece in the direction of much-needed reform and of its further integration in the world of advanced industrial societies which it belatedly, but with much hope, joined in 1974.

THE BROADER CONTEXT

To be properly understood and evaluated, the political system established in Greece in 1974 should be conceptualized as the successful outcome of a long quest for a fully democratic regime in that country, which had its roots in the interwar period and which, during the four decades preceding the establishment of Democracy, had twice (1936–1941 and 1967–1974) led to authoritarian involutions and once (1946–1949) into an internecine civil war.[8]

The central dilemma over which all three abortive attempts at democratization ultimately collapsed was whether to incorporate (or, conversely, to continue to exclude) the rural masses, at the time by far the largest social class, and the urban working classes from the liberal political system, established in 1909 and dominated ever since by the Greek middle classes. In all previous occasions, the resolution of the dilemma had been in favor of exclusion or, at best, marginalization.

The fundamental challenge facing the architects of Greece's post-1974, democratic political system was how to extricate the country from the legacy of the latest exclusivist system, constructed by the victors in the civil war with an eye to perpetuating in peacetime the advantages gained over the vanquished side in the battlefield. Simply put, this was a system steeped in the culture of the Cold War, which, whether in its parliamentary (1950–1967) or authoritarian (1967–1974) phase, had privileged its nondemocratically accountable institutional actors, the crown and, especially, the armed forces, over its democratically accountable one, Parliament. The result had been a sharply discriminatory political system, which, formal constitutional guarantees notwithstanding, effectively distinguished between first- and second-class citizens on the basis of political beliefs, favoring those deemed to hold "healthy," that is, anti-Communist, views and penalizing those suspected of the opposite.[9]

The country's extrication from its exclusivist political heritage was greatly assisted by three developments, which, taken together, can be said to have constituted the negative preconditions for the establishment of a democratic political system in Greece: first, the sharp split which the imposition of the colonels' authoritarian regime in April 1967 brought about within the ranks of the conservative political elite, in the process helping to distinguish its democratic from its anti-democratic component. The quasi-unanimous refusal of this elite to collaborate with or otherwise support the authoritarian regime effectively isolated the country's anti-democratic Right from its democratic counterpart and paved the way for the latter's integration in, and critical support for, the democratic political system erected after 1974.

The second negative precondition for democratization was the removal of the armed forces from active and direct involvement in Greek politics. This was attained as a result of the devastating blow to the Greek armed forces' prestige and legitimacy, which the attempt to topple Cypriot President Makarios in the summer of 1974 and, especially, the armed forces' patent inability successfully to cope with the ensuing Turkish invasion of Cyprus, brought about. Chastized by the experience of their involvement in what had proved to be a most unpopular regime, and humiliated by the Cyprus crisis, the Greek military withdrew to the barracks and, for the first time in its history, unequivocally accepted the principle of civilian control. In so doing, it opened the way for the establishment of a democratic political system in that country.

The elimination of the monarchy from the Greek political landscape constituted the third, and final, precondition for the establishment of a democratic political system in postauthoritarian Greece. The monarchy, an institution with a long and controversial history of deep involvement in twentieth-century Greek politics, served as a central pillar of the exclusivist, anti-Communist system of the post–civil war period. The pivotal role which it played in fiercely opposing demands for the liberalization of that system during the mid-1960s, its deep involvement in the events which led to the imposition of military rule in 1967 and its initial accommodation with the colonels' regime greatly damaged its legitimacy and rendered possible its elimination from the Greek political landscape, following an impeccable plebiscite in December 1974, in which almost 70 percent of the Greek electorate voted in favor of a republic.

In conjunction with the collapse of the colonels' regime, the elimination of these structural constraints opened the way for the establishment, in 1974, of the first, fully democratic political system in modern Greek history. The basic institutions of the new system and the fundamental rules of the democratic game were set in place during the critical but brief period of the transition to Democracy, which lasted from the transfer of power to the civilians, on 24 July 1974, to the plebiscite on the monarchy, on 8 December 1974. In the ensuing seven years, these institutions and the behavioral practices and attitudinal stances associated with the new system became gradually crystallized. In short, the system as a whole became consolidated.

The salient features of the new system were the following: (a) the abolition of discriminatory legislation dating back to the post–civil war state and, more generally, the establishment of substantive, as opposed to formal, political equality for all citizens; (b) the effective integration of heretofore excluded or marginalized masses into the political system; (c) the modernization of the Greek Right, the abandonment of its erstwhile, fanatically anti-Communist positions, and its transformation into a moderate, center-right political force fully supportive of Democracy; (d) the founding of a new political party, PASOK, which occupied the critical left-of-center space in the Greek political spectrum that the polarizing logic of the post–civil war exclusivist system had caused to remain vacant; (e) the modernization of the Greek party system and the transformation of the non-Communist Greek parties, which constituted the overwhelming majority of the electorate, from parties of notables to mass parties; (f) the centripetal rather than centrifugal logic governing partisan competition in the new system; and, as a cumulative result of the above: (g) the modernization of Greek politics, in the sense of its closer approximation of the structure and dynamics of politics observable in established democracies.

The abolition of the discriminatory legal and administrative practices of the post-civil war system constituted a major step forward in the direction of establishing and securing the rule of law in Greece. Put otherwise, it contributed decisively to national reconciliation and greatly promoted national integration. The most visible beneficiaries of this change were the Communists, who had been unable to operate legally in the country, since the outlawing of the Communist Party of Greece in 1947, at the height of the civil war. The end of the state of anomaly dating back to that event, however, greatly transcended the Communist left and encompassed a much larger part of Greek society extending to its political center and center-left, which had suffered great political disabilities in the quarter century following the end of the civil war. The political rehabilitation of the Left, moderate and radical alike, greatly enhanced the legitimacy of the state, substantively improved the quality of state-society relations, and commensurately benefited the new political system, endowing it with significant dynamism and, above all, legitimacy.[10]

The modernization of the Greek Right proved equally critical for the consolidation of the new system. Under the confident and far-sighted leadership of Constantine Karamanlis, the veteran conservative leader who had dominated Greek parliamentary politics in the 1950s and early 1960s and who triumphantly returned to Greece from self-imposed exile on 24 July 1974 to assume power, the conservative political forces managed successfully to break with its profoundly anti-Communist past and anti-democratic heritage that reached back to the mid-1930s. In founding a new political party, appropriately but also astutely named "New Democracy"—a term strongly associated with a leftist discourse calling for the construction of a "new democracy" in Greece—Karamanlis helped situate the major conservative political formation in that country away from its traditional position at the far Right of the political spectrum and close to the Center. As the party in government, from the founding elections of 17 November 1974 to the coming of PASOK to power, on 18 October 1981, New Democracy convincingly exhibited the traits of a modern, conservative party, occupying the center-right space on the political spectrum. In so doing, it imparted democratic legitimacy to the Greek conservative world and served as a critical constituent element in the consolidation of Greece's new, democratic political system.[11]

The birth of the Panhellenic Socialist Movement, PASOK, in September 1974, within a month and a half of the collapse of the colonels' regime, constituted a major milestone in the process leading to the emergence and crystallization of the new political system. Shorn to their essentials, PASOK's distinctive characteristics were three: first, it was a brand new political formation, the triple product of (a) radicalized preauthoritarian centrist elites, (b) cadres issuing from the resistance to the authoritarian regime, especially the Panhellenic Liberation Movement created and led by Andreas Papandreou, the new leader of PASOK, and (c) a technocratic component which sought to promote substantive reform in Greek society. Proclaiming its determination to bring about a complete break with practices of the past, PASOK quickly and successfully occupied the center-left space of the Greek political spectrum, which the logic of the post–civil war state had kept vacant in an attempt to insulate the holding "healthy" political views from ideological contamination from the Left.[12]

Taken together, the emergence of the ND as a modern, conservative party occupying the center-right of the political spectrum, and of PASOK (its initial radical leftist rhetoric notwithstanding) covering the center-left, effectively brought about the profound restructuring of partisan competition in Greece. The result was a decisive move away from the extreme polarization inherent in the centrifugal logic of the preauthoritarian system and the adherence to a more moderate and centripetal logic which, despite the persistence of a polarizing political discourse, has remained a distinctive feature of the new political system to date.

The transformation of political parties, from parties of notables to mass parties, undoubtedly constitutes a distinguishing and enduring feature of postauthoritarian politics in Greece. Until 1974, only the Communist Party of Greece, outlawed between 1947 and the fall of the colonels, had been organized as a modern, mass party. With the emergence of PASOK, however, mass parties became dominant in the political space occupied by non-Communist political parties. PASOK's spectacular growth and rise to power within a mere seven years of its founding served as tangible proof of the benefits of organization for Greek political elites. More specifically, it had two major spillover effects: first, it forced PASOK's principal rival, the ND, to follow suit, if only in order to survive politically and to be able to compete on an equal footing in the new rules of the game created by the emergence of mass politics in Greece; second, and perhaps most important, it greatly strengthened the organizational basis of Greek politics and commensurately benefited Greek democracy. Put otherwise, the long-term effect of these changes was the fundamental transformation of the Greek political landscape, the structural modernization of its political and party systems, and the significant approximation of patterns of politics observable in more established democracies.[13]

The reference to the more established democracies is not accidental. It is meant, rather, to serve as a reminder of the problems generally associated with politics in contemporary advanced industrial societies. Having belatedly entered the world of modernity, Greek politics and political parties soon encountered some of modernity's most salient discontents. To understand these better and to assess their implications more accurately, it is best to think of the evolution of the postauthoritarian system as involving two distinct phases. The first extends from its inception in 1974 to 1985 and the second from that latter date to the present.

The principal characteristic of the first period was its integrative dynamic. This was a dimension which profoundly affected Greek culture, economy, society and politics at both the domestic and the international levels. At the domestic level, the modernization of Greek politics entailed the integration into the new democratic system of the extensive social strata (primarily the rural masses and the urban working class), which the pre-authoritarian system had systematically excluded or, at best, marginalized, denying them the opportunity for autonomous organization. The role of the new, mass parties in all these developments was pivotal. In acting as the central institutional mechanisms facilitating the integration of these strata in modern Greek politics, the parties also decisively contributed to the consolidation of Democracy in Greece. This can be safely said to have occurred by 1981, when with the coming of PASOK to power, the erstwhile excluded strata, which this party disproportionately represented, became politically ascendant.[14]

At the international level, 1981 marks Greece's integration in the European Community (now Union) and through it in the open economies of advanced European industrial societies. This development has had profound long-term effects for Greek society and politics. Through a variety of policies, most of which bore the marks of decidedly particularistic logics, a major part of the very large funds transferred from Brussels to Greece found its way into the hands of newly integrated strata and groups, in the process further empowering them, cementing their allegiance to the new political system and contributing to the deepening of Democracy in that country.[15]

The political parties were also major beneficiaries of these developments. Their central role in channeling these funds in the direction of particular constituencies and, more general, their deep involvement in the redistribution of wealth that this whole process entailed, greatly enhanced their power, added to their organizational strength and commensurately augmented their legitimacy. As a result, political parties emerged, during the initial postauthoritarian period, as the undisputedly dominant institution in the new political system, quickly penetrating the trade union, student and feminine movements and playing a central role in an ever-widening circle of activities.

In sharp contrast to this first, euphoric period in the life of the new political system, the second, symbolically identified with the institution, in October 1985, of the first austerity policy since 1974, has been characterized by retrenchment, uncertainty and anxiety about the future. The deeper source of these feelings is the belated recognition by the quasi-totality of elites and masses alike that the strategy of political integration adopted by the Greek political class in the first postauthoritarian period, with an eye to ensuring the speedy consolidation of the new democratic regime, entailed a conscious and systematic downplaying of the pressing need for structural adjustments in the Greek economy, if it were to operate competitively within the open market environment of the European Union.

Although temporarily abandoned between 1987 and 1990 because of the strong resistance and downright hostility which the beneficiaries of new entitlements exhibited toward any notion of belt-tightening, austerity has, in fact, been the order of the day for most of the second postauthoritarian period and, especially, since 1990. It has been applied by both PASOK and the ND, with little actual difference as to content, although the scope of adjustment has increased somewhat under PASOK since 1993.[16]

This abrupt about-face has had an important adverse effect on the political system and the parties. To the extent that the latter are regarded as increasingly unable to solve economic problems, to contain (let alone reduce) unemployment and to generate growth, they inevitably become the object of disapproval and disaffection. The political system seems no longer to be able to provide solutions for the problems confronting Greek society. Talk about the "end of a cycle" or of an era has become commonplace in the mass media, among intellectuals or within the political class. In a short period of time, Greece has joined the host of other European countries facing similar challenges to their political systems.

Somewhat inevitably, political parties have borne the brunt of these changes. Recent polls measuring voters' intentions suggest both a sharply declining rate of approval for the parties at the level of the public at large and a steep increase in the expressed preference for a blank vote or for abstention, despite the legally mandatory nature of voting in Greece. This is not to argue that Greece is moving in the direction of Italy. These trends notwithstanding, the two largest parties have received an average of 85.5 percent of the votes cast in the last four elections. This figure rises to an impressive average of 95.3 percent for the top three parties in the same elections, with the important qualification that the emergence of Political Spring, the political party founded by Mr. Samaras following his departure from the ND, reduced the total share of the votes gained by the top three parties in the 1993 election to 91.2 percent, down 4.6 percentage points since the last electoral consultation.

What the declining approval ratings do suggest, however, is a growing recognition that Greek political parties are becoming increasingly less able to perform according to expectations in ever-growing areas affecting public policy. Put otherwise, Greece's first generation of mass parties (of the catchall if not the cartel variety) seems to be caught in an intriguing structural paradox of its own making. On the one hand, having, in the initial postauthoritarian period, successfully penetrated not merely the state but also a very large number of institutions in civil society and having directly or indirectly occupied a very extensive part of Greek political space, they contributed mightily to the speedy consolidation of the new and democratic political system. The darker side of this success story, however, has been threefold: (a) the foundation upon which Greek Democracy was consolidated turned out to be very narrow, virtually excluding other institutions of civil society from autonomously contributing to the development of the new system; (b) thus empowered, political parties have developed increasingly unaccountable organizational structures, the most glaring negative aspects of which have been the virtual, if not complete, absence of internal party democracy, the prevalence of authoritarian practices, especially observable in PASOK, and the adoption of a powerful populist discourse reinforcing authoritarian practices and adversely affecting the quality of the political system; and (c) overreliance on the parties for finding solutions to all problems has inevitably resulted in their becoming overextended and unable to satisfy the wave of rising expectations which they were instrumental in bringing about. The result has been a significant delegitimation of political parties and a democracy of fairly low quality.

This assessment notwithstanding, recent trends in Greek society allow for some cautious degree of optimism concerning the system's capacity for self-reform. The visible decline in the parties' control of the trade unions in the past four to five years, similar and more pronounced developments in the student movement, the more assertive and creative role played by both the General Confederation of Greek Workers (GSEE) and the Federation of Greek Industries (SEB) in expanding and redefining the scope of industrial relations in the country, and the emergence of a number of citizens' movements constitute hopeful signs of invigoration in Greek civil society. Time will show whether these trends, combined with the presence of reformist groups in the current government, will constitute harbingers of a better future for what, despite its many and glaring drawbacks, is by far the most modern and most democratic political system in modern Greek history or just a missed opportunity for its further modernization and qualitative improvement.

NOTES

1. On the founding of Greece's new political system in the 1970s, see Psomiades (1982: 251–273); Verney and Couloumbis (1991: 103–124); Arvanitopoulos (1989); and Diamandouros (1986: 138–165). On the consolidation of the Democratic political system, very few works have appeared, to date. For three works dealing with this, see Alivizatos (1990: 131–153); Diamandouros (1984: 50–71); and the more comparative, collective work Gunther, Diamandouros and Puhle (1995).

2. On the 1974 election, see Penniman, (1981) and, for the nature of the postauthoritarian party system, Mavrogordatos (1983a: 70–94). See also, Featherstone (1987: 34–63); Clogg (1987); and Alivizatos (1990: 131–153).

3. On the 1977 elections, see especially the various contributions concerning each of the major parties in Penniman (1981) and Mavrogordatos (1983a: 70–94) as well as the other sources cited in note 2 above.

4. On the landmark 1981 elections, see Mavrogordatos (1983b); Lyrintzis (1983a: 99–118); Limberes (1986); as well as the works by Featherstone (1987: 34–63); Clogg (1987); and Alivizatos (1990: 131–153). For the electoral aspects of the decade of the 1980s, as a whole, the best work in Greek is Lyrintzis and Nicolacopoulos (1990).

5. On the 1985 elections, see the works by Featherstone (1987: 34–63); Clogg (1987); and Alivizatos (1990: 131–153).

6. Very little has, so far, been written in English concerning the three consecutive elections of 1989–1990. For a brief but informative analysis, see Pridham and Verney (1991: 42–49). Reference in the text to Muslim "minorities" (as opposed to the more

standard "minority") is meant to point to the existence of three ethnically distinct but, politically, increasingly homogeneous populations in Thrace: the ethnically Turkish Muslims, the Bulgarian-speaking Muslims, known as Pomaks, and the Muslim Roma (gypsies).

7. To date, no systematic studies focusing exclusively on the 1993 elections have appeared in English. For an excellent comparative analysis, which includes these elections within a broader context, see Morlino (1995: 315–388).

8. The latest work in English on the Greek civil war is Iatrides and Wrigley (1995). On the Greek authoritarian regime of 1967–1974, see Clogg and Yannopoulos (1972); Mouzelis (1978); Alivizatos (1979).

9. On the exclusivist nature of the post–civil war system, see, among others, Alivizatos (1979); Diamandouros (1986: 138–165); and Meynaud (1965).

10. On the circumstances favoring, and the strategies promoting, the consolidation of a democratic political system in postauthoritarian Greece, see Ioakimidis (1984: 33–60); Diamandouros (1984: 50–71); and Alivizatos (1990: 131–53).

11. On the modernization of the Greek Right, see, in addition to Chapter 11 by Takis Pappas in this volume, the same author's unpublished doctoral dissertation (1995); John C. Loulis (1981: 49–83); and Katsoudas (1987: 85–111).

12. Of all the parties of the postauthoritarian Greek political system, PASOK has received the greatest attention. For a thorough listing of pertinent sources, see note 1, in the contribution by Michalis Spourdalakis, Chapter 10 in this volume. The major unpublished works on the subject in English include Lyrintzis (1983); and Sotiropoulos (1991).

13. For initial assessments of the new political system, of its structure and dynamics, and of its impact on state-society relations, see Mavrogordatos (1983a: 70–94); Lyrintzis (1984); and Diamandouros (1991: 15–35).

14. For the most recent assessment of political developments in Greece during the 1980s, see the various contributions in Richard Clogg (1993). For a study employing a different analytical perspective on the same period but dealing directly with the integration dynamic of the new system, see Diamandouros (1994).

15. On the links between the European Community/Union and Greek politics, see Verney (1990: 203–223; 1987: 253–270); and Tsingos (1994).

16. On the daunting challenges associated with the need for structural adjustments in the Greek economy, society and politics, see the various contributions in Allison and Kalypso (1996, forthcoming), as well as Kasakos (1991: 94–114). For an interpretative analysis of the political conflicts during the retrenchment period, centering on the threat to new entitlements acquired in the course of the euphoric phase of integration, see Diamandouros (1994: 34–54).

REFERENCES

Alivizatos, Nicos (1979). *Les Institutions Politiques de la Grece a Travers les Crises 1922–1974*. Paris: Librairie Generale de Droit et de Jurisprudence.

Alivizatos, Nicos C. (1990). "The Difficulties of Rationalization in a Polarized Political System: The Greek Chamber of Deputies." In Ulrike Liebert and Maurizio Cotta (eds.), *Parliament and Democratic Consolidation in Southern Europe*, pp. 131–153. London: Pinter Publishers.

Allison, Graham and Nicolaidis Kalypso (eds.) (1996). *The Greek Paradox: Promise vs. Performance*. Cambridge, MA: Center for Sciences and International Affairs, Harvard University.

Arvanitopoulos, Constantine (1989). *The Political Economy of Regime Transition: The Case of Greece*. Unpublished Ph.D. dissertation. The American University.

Clogg, Richard (1987). *Parties and Election in Greece. The Search for Legitimacy*. London: C. Hurst.

Clogg, Richard (1993). *Greece 1981–1989. The Populist Decade*. London: Macmillian.

Clogg, Richard and George Yannopoulos (eds.) (1972). *Greece Under Military Rule*. New York: Basic Books.

Diamandouros, P. Nikiforos (1984). "Transition to, and Consolidation of, Democratic Politics in Greece, 1974–1983: A Tentative Assessment." In Geoffrey Pridham (ed.), *The New Mediterranean Democracies. Regime Transition in Spain, Greece and Portugal*, pp. 50–71. London: Frank Cass.

Diamandouros, P. Nikiforos (1986). "Regime Change and the Prospects for Democracy in Greece: 1974–1983." In Guillermo O'Donnel, Philippe C. Schmitter and Laurence Whitehead (eds.), *Transition from Authoritarian Rule. Prospects for Democracy*, pp. 138–165. Baltimore: Johns Hopkins University Press.

Diamandouros, P. Nikiforos (1991). "PASOK and State-Society Relations in Post-Authoritarian Greece (1974–1988)." In Speros Vryonis Jr. (ed.), *Greece on the Road to Democracy: From the Junta to PASOK 1974–1986*, pp. 15–35. New Rochelle, NY: Caratzas Publishers.

Diamandouros, P. Nikiforos (1994). *Cultural Dualism and Political Change in Post-authoritarian Greece*. Madrid: Centro Juan March de Estudios Avanzados en Ciencias Sociales.

Featherstone, Kevin (1987). "Elections and Voting Behaviour." In Kevin Featherstone and Dimitrios K. Katsoudas (eds.), *Political Change in Greece: Before and After the Colonels*, pp. 34–63. London: Croom Helm.

Gunther, Richard, Nikiforos P. Diamandouros and Hans-Jorgen Puhle (eds.) (1985). *The Politics of Democratic Consolidation. Southern Europe in Comparative Perspective*. Baltimore: Johns Hopkins University Press.

Iatrides, John O. and Linda Wrigley (eds.) (1995). *Greece at the Crossroads. The Civil War and Its Legacy*. University Park: Pennsylvania State University Press.

Ioakimidis, P.C. (1984). "Greece from Military Dictatorship to Socialism." In Allan Williams (ed.), *Southern Europe Transformed. Political and Economic Change in Greece, Italy, Portugal and Spain*, pp. 33–60. London: Harper & Row.

Kasakos, Panos (1991). "De Integrationspolitischen Initiativen der 80er Jahre und die Griechische Europa-Politik." *Sudosteuropa Mitteilungen* 31: 94–114.

Katsoudas, Dimitrios K. (1987). "The Conservative Movement and New Democracy: From Past to Present." In Kevin Featherstone and Dimitrios Katsoudas (eds.), *Political Change in Greece: Before and After the Colonels*, pp. 85–111. London: Croom Helm.

Limberes, Nickolas M. (1986). "Mass Voting Behaviour: the Factors that Influenced the Conservative Vote during the Greek General Elections (of 1981)." *European Journal of Political Research* 14: 113–137.

Loulis, John C. (1981). "New Democracy: The New Face of Conservatism." In Howard R. Penniman, (ed.), *Greece at the Polls. The National Election of 1974 and 1977*, pp. 49–83. Washington, DC: American Enterprise Institute.

Lyrintzis, Christos (1983a). "The Rise of PASOK: The Greek Election of 1981." *West European Politics* 5: 99–118.

Lyrintzis, Christos (1983b). *Between Socialism and Populism: The Rise of the Panhellenic Socialist Movement.* Unpublished Ph.D. dissertation. London School of Economics and Political Science.

Lyrintzis, Christos and Nicolacopoulos Ilias (eds.) (1990). *Ekloges kai Kommata ste Dekaetia tou '80. Exelixeis kai Prooptikes tou Politikou Systematos* (Elections and Parties in the Decade of the 1980s. Evolution and Perspectives of the Political System). Athens: Themelio.

Mavrogordatos, George Th. (1983a). "The Emerging Party System." In Richard Clogg (ed.), *Greece in the 1980s*, pp. 70–94. London: Macmillian .

Mavrogordatos, George Th. (1983b). *The Rise of the Greek Sun. The Greek Election of 1981.* London: King's College, Center for Comtemporary Greek Studies.

Meynaud, Jean (1965). *Les Forces Politiques en Grece.* Lausanne: Etudes de Science Politique.

Morlino, Leonardo (1995). "Political Parties and Democratic Consolidation in Southern Europe." In Richard Gunther, P. Nikiforos Diamandouros and Hans-Jurgen Puhle (eds.), *The Politics of Democratic Consolidation. Southern Europe in Comparative Perspective*, pp. 315–388. Baltimore: Johns Hopkins University Press.

Mouzelis, Nicos P. (1978). "Capitalism and Dictatorship in Post-War Greece." In Nicos P. Mouzelis (ed.), *Modern Greece. Facets of Underdevelopment*, pp. 115–133. London: Macmillian.

Pappas, Takis (1995). *The Making of Party Democracy in Greece. 1974–1981.* Unpublished Ph.D dissertation. Yale University.

Penniman, R. Howard (ed.) (1981). *Greece at the Polls. The National Election of 1974 and 1977.* Washington, DC: American Enterprise Institute.

Pridham, Geoffrey and Susannah Verney (1991). "The Coalition of 1989–1990 in Greece." *West European Politics* 14: 42–49.

Psomiades, Harry J. (1982). "Greece: From the Colonels' Rule to Democracy in John H. Herz (ed.), *From Dictatorship to Democracy: Coping with the Legacy of Authoritarianism and Totalitarianism*, pp. 251–273. Westport, CT: Greenwood Press.

Sotiropoulos, Dimitrios A. (1991). *State and Party: The Greek State of Bureaucracy and the Panhellenic Socialist Movement (PASOK), 1981–1989.* Unpublished Ph.D. dissertation. Yale University.

Tsingos, Basilios Evangelos (1994). *Underwriting Democracy, Not Exporting It: The European Community and Greece.* Unpublished dissertation. Magdalen College, Oxford.

Verney, Susannah (1987). "Greece and the European Community." In Kevin Featherstone and Dimitrios K. Katsoudas (eds.), *Political Change in Greece: Before and After the Colonels*, pp. 253–270. London: Croom Helm.

Verney, Susannah (1990). "To Be or Not to Be Within the European Community: The Party Debate and Democratic Consolidation in Greece." In Geoffrey Pridham (ed.), *Securing Democracy: Political Parties and Democratic Consolidation in Southern Europe*, pp.203–223. London: Routledge.

Verney, Susannah and Theodore Couloumbis (1991). "State-International System Interaction and the Greek Transition to Democracy in the Mid-1970s." In Geof-frey Pridham (ed.), *Encouraging Democracy: The International Context of Regime Transition in Southern Europe*, pp. 103–124. Leicester, UK: Leicester University Press.

to the commitment of a democratic organization based on a decentralized concept of membership participation. Thus, in its founding document ("Declaration of the 3rd of September 1974") its fourfold strategic goals included the promise for "democratic procedure."[5] It was clear that PASOK from the beginning, as in so many other aspects, tried to respond to the demands for new forms of political mobilization.[6] The exclusionist political practices of Greek politics in the 1950s, as a result of the civil war, the delayed "entrance of the masses" into Greek politics in the 1960s and the experience of the dictatorship contributed to a widespread questioning of the party system of the country and the existing patterns of political mobilization. Not rarely, in the mid-1960s, this questioning took the form of intraparty dissent, giving rise to a number of organized factions and tendencies in almost all the parties across the political spectrum. This "dissent" was expressed either as a problematic within the dominant right-wing governmental party (ERE), intended to revise the inner workings of the political system itself (to redefine the relationship between the legislature and the executive), or as concrete organized efforts of leading political figures of the opposition (both the Left-EDA and the Union Center) to democratize political mobilization and recruitment (Spourdalakis, 1988: 18–33). The fall of the Junta in the summer of 1974 signalled among other things the end of the old party system.

PASOK proved to be the party that most effectively articulated this demand. The new party's organization was clearly an effort to go beyond both the traditional Left's centralized structures and the clientelism of the old Center. Thus, PASOK became the first party in Greek political history to resemble a mass party with nationwide mass membership,[7] an example soon to be followed by its conservative counterpart: New Democracy.

The decisive push in the construction and articulation of PASOK's genetic organizational model was the early call for the first post-Junta election.[8] Indeed, the fact that PASOK was confronted with its first electoral campaign only two months after its inaugural address set the logic of the movement's structure on a certain course and left an imprint on its genetic organizational model and on its unfolding political and organizational practices. Under the circumstances, the task of organizing and running an electoral campaign appeared a gargantuan undertaking and the new-born party dealt with it in a rather innovative fashion. It made an open appeal to the "Greek people" for self-organization. The appeal was remarkably successful and almost overnight the movement acquired a nationwide network of local organizations. These "initiative committees" became the backbone of its organizational structure and living proof that its mobilizing premise was different from that of its counterparts. It was an organizational development which, to use Panebianco's terms, was conceived and performed as "territorial diffusion" since local elites spontaneously and in effect autonomously, from the Center, established a plethora of local associations throughout the country, but soon evolved as "territorial penetration" (Panebianco, 1988: 50–51) since the Center took initiatives toward the nationwide integration of the party structure by creating regional and peripheral collective bodies. While this organizational development nicely fits the description as "mixed type" genetic model, the case of PASOK is not so simple.

Indeed, the inevitable "emergency" nature of its initial organizational construction along the lines of "territorial diffusion," the political and social diversity of its membership, as we will display directly below, in combination with the lack of experience in mass collective procedures, brought to the fore some backward organizational traits putting at the same time an important twist in the logic of PASOK's genetic ("mixed type") organizational model. This twist has to do with the party's leader A. Papandreou, whose strong leadership, under the pressure of certain impulses and thrusts, was transformed into a charismatic one. The charismatic twist in PASOK's genetic organizational development has, of course, to do with the inertia of traditional patterns of political mobilization characterized by personalized and clientelistic politics, permeated by a widespread mistrust toward mass participation, which preserved a special role for strong leadership, but the most important factor has been the diversity of its membership. Thus, the unquestionable charisma of Papandreou has been a "situational" and not a "pure" one,[9] as it was the outcome of a number of circumstantial pressures and not a founding component of the party. Key in understanding the logic of PASOK's genetic organizational model, and especially its charismatic dimension is, as I already said, the pluralistic nature of its political composition and the tacit development of the three tendencies within the party.

Papandreou has repeatedly said in his rhetorical, although admittedly often insightful fashion, that PASOK is the creation and the ultimate expression of the desires and the agonies of three different generations: " the generation of the resistance" (i.e., the 1940s anti-fascist movement); "the generation of the Unrelenting Struggle" (i.e., the 1960s generation which fought against the crown's unconstitutional initiatives and generally sought the termination of exclusionist post–civil war political practices); and the "generation of the Polytechnic School" (i.e., the generation of the resistance against the regime of the Junta). In spite of its simplistic nature, the statement amply identifies the political pools from which PASOK draws its support and underscores the extent to which the diversity of such support determines the party's organizational genetic model. Indeed the accumulated demands of these "generations" gave rise to different political currents which, in turn, marked the creation and the subsequent evolution of the young movement. Within the social and political clientele of PASOK we can distinguish, from the very beginning, three different political currents or tendencies which had to be accommodated by its organizational structure. The identity (strengths and weaknesses) and the dynamic of these tendencies is the key for analyzing PASOK's organizational structure and for understanding the ("situational") charisma of A. Papandreou. Although the borders of these currents of the movement were unclear and still remain so, and despite their extensive overlap, we can at least schematically speak of a *Left*, a *Conformist* and a *Technocratic* tendency.

The *Left* or *Socialist tendency* appeared in the beginning to be the dominant group in the new movement. Most of its "membership" had been active in radical (anti-Junta) resistance organizations. However, this section of the organization was not quite unified, since, among the membership with clearly Left leanings, one could distinguish two more groups. The first was composed of the disillusioned activists of the traditional Left of the generation of the 1940s and 1950s, whose major political concern and priority, though still Socialist, was the democratization of the chronically undemocratic Greek political system. The other part of the Left tendency of PASOK was composed of the generation which had become politicized during the resistance against the Junta both within the country and especially abroad. This younger generation had been exposed to the ideas of the "New Left," which were fairly popular at the time. This distinction is rather important since it was primarily the former group within the movement and not the latter, which faded away along with their ideas—a development which provided PASOK, once in government, with an alibi toward the Communist left, as the movement reversed its initially radical social program. On the whole, for the Left Socialist current, the main points of political attraction to the new movement were (a) the emphasis of the Declaration of the 3rd of September on "National Liberation" and the ability to link the latter with domestic policies and, thus, to allow for class analysis and (b) the document's reference and commitment to themes and areas of political activity derived from the political mobilization of the 1960s (i.e., women's liberation, environment).

Although it was at first not particularly outspoken, the *conformist tendency*[10] in PASOK was composed primarily of the old politicians (*palaiokommatikoi*) of the 1960s' Center Union. The widespread postdictatorship demand for new political expression and new mode of political mobilization led this group with its sharp political instincts to join the new movement simply as this was its best bet for political survival. In addition, PASOK's founding document contained something for the electoral constituents of this group, who were none other than the farmers of the countryside and the traditional petty bourgeoisie of the cities. This was the programmatic promise for the reorganization of the primary sector and the anthropomorphic rejection of monopoly capital—both of which constituted main poles of attraction to the movement for this current and its constituents.

Finally, PASOK was also composed of a third, and initially weak, *technocratic tendency*. At first, this group was of little significance. After 1977, however, when PASOK, as leading opposition party, found itself at the threshold of power, the political weight of the technocratic tendency increased geometrically. Composed primarily of highly educated, relatively young members of the movement, this tendency represented, at least indirectly, and in addition to its members' interests, the demands of all those parts of capital, which, in the early 1960s, were interested in restructuring and modernizing the country's economic structures. PASOK's promises for "administrative decentralization," for rationalization of various sectors of the economy, for the strengthening of the state's role and, finally, its expressed commitment to the modernization of the archaic role and structure of various state institutions (i.e., army, church, school system) served, for obvious reasons, as this group's attraction to the movement.

To the extent to which these tendencies corresponded to the political trends unfolding in the postdictatorship to keep them in a functional unity meant political efficiency and success. PASOK was really effective in that department. Instrumental to this performance has been, as I already have mentioned, both the founding promise of the party for "democratic procedures" and Papandreou's charisma. Indeed, the promise stated in the party's founding Declaration that its organizational construction would follow democratic paths, functioned as a linchpin for all the tendencies. This is because everyone could hope to have a fair chance in determining the organizational and political development of the young movement, while at the same time, a failure to do so could not mean exclusion from its political future. In addition, the constant reassurance that PASOK was not a party with a specific and fixed program and orientation but a "movement" in which almost every issue is open to amendment, increased the tolerance level of the three tendencies and reduced the centrifugal dangers. Of course this initial organizational conception, in spite of its overall success, was not free of contradictions or turbulence. A series of internal party frictions and crises developed which resulted in a gradual concentration of power in the top leadership, since internal dissent was dealt with a plebiscitary and a high-and-mighty style which also became the modus operandi of the movement.[11]

If the promise for internal party democracy functioned as the initial organizational cement on an abstract and long-term level, the charisma of A. Papandreou served as the most important unifying factor for the movement in its actual day-to-day life. This charisma, however, as we already mentioned, is not a pure one nor is the result of Papandreou's unquestionable intellectual capacities, as both admirers and critics seem to suggest. It is rather based on the fact that his personality happens to simultaneously capture and express the concerns of his entire organization and the political orientation of all three tendencies. The Left tendency could identify with Papandreou's recent radical background, demonstrated by his involvement in the resistance and the revival of radical economics in the 1960s. Papandreou's political origin in his father's Center Union and his criticisms of it were seen by the *palaiokommatikoi*, the conformist current of the movement, as the basis for his leadership. In this context he represented both a break and yet a continuity with traditional political practices. Furthermore, Papandreou was not only a member, though by proxy, of the international Left intellectual community but also an academic with highly specialized expertise, which made him the spokesman *par excellence* of the technocrats.

In other words, in a fashion similar to the founding Declaration of PASOK, A. Papandreou managed to become the political adhesive necessary to keep the diversity of his movement's membership together. For these reasons, and given that no tendency had enough organizational or political support to assume leadership, Papandreou has been of irreplaceable value to his movement. PASOK's life and development has been so much associated with Andreas's[12] charisma that it has led many erroneously to argue that PASOK equals Papandreou. This, however, is a superficial claim since his charisma has been anything but pure, as was vividly displayed when his withdrawal from active politics did not result in the party's dismantling but rather in its strengthening.

In sum, the (unfulfilled) political demands of Greek society which the fall of the Junta brought forward stood at the base of PASOK's organizational "genetic model." PASOK's structure was marked by the need to articulate all three unintegrated and rather incompatible tendencies, which surfaced during the transition-consolidation to Democracy period and represented both the break from, and the continuation with, the country's political past. It was the inchoate and not-fully developed nature of these political tendencies, in combination with their foggy social base and the dictates of the 1974 election that made Papandreou's role irreplaceable, creating a party structure which was institutionalized only in form. Indeed, PASOK became a mass membership party of a rather rare variety, as its institutionalization was not only slow in coming but it was carved singlehandedly by its unaccountable leader and the small party elite he chose to have around him.

THE LOGIC OF A FEEBLE INSTITUTIONALIZATION

The genetic organizational model of a party and even the analysis of its logic does not predestine the organizational development of parties or the level and the pace of its institutionalization. Parties are voluntaristic political institutions *par excellence*. Thus, although they cannot easily escape from the logic of their genetic organizational structure, their ultimate development is to a great extent the direct result of how the leadership decides to seek and/or stay in power, to capitalize on a number of set political patterns, or to respond to a historical conjuncture. Consequently, the logic of party organization is neither self-evident nor shaped overnight. On the contrary, the organizational development of a party is the outcome of its long, strategic initiatives, its day-to-day practices and of its overall relationship with the sociopolitical environment. PASOK has not been an exception to this rule.

In the case of PASOK, the logic of its organizational development started to be shaped after the first post-Junta elections (November 1974). It was then that the movement's electoral performance was judged to be rather poor and the leadership, especially A. Papandreou himself,[13] seems to have decided that the party had to seek power at a much faster pace. In retrospect, this meant a gradual but steady undermining of its promise to develop along the lines of a mass democratic and institutionalized party, capable of breaking away from the traditional patterns of political mobilization. This decision to expedite the pursuit of power regardless of the cost to the party's own institutionalization was accompanied—probably in contrast with the historical development of most Western European Socialist parties—with a watering down of its radicalism. And it is this development that has made reasonable the claim that PASOK's own Bad Godesberg came as a result of its successful "short march to power" (Spourdalakis, 1988: 180–189).

A key factor in this strategic shift of PASOK away from its original organizational postulates was the objective challenge to (if not pressure upon) the young movement to deal with and even exploit the unusual capacities of its leader. The charismatic qualities of A. Papandreou in a society unfamiliar with collective democratic practices did not, and probably could not, act as a stepping-stone for a complete rupture with the traditional modes of political mobilization of the pre-1967 era. Indeed Papandreou was proven to be very much in tune with the tradition of some dominant figures in postwar Greek politics: Papagos, Karamanlis and G. Papandreou. It has been a leadership which, if it did not display a contempt for collective procedures, it stayed systematically outside institutional constraints or accountability, looked at party politics as an extension of personal politics and often resorted to plebiscitarian ones. This in the case of PASOK does not mean a complete absence of any form of institutionalization, nor a freezing of the functioning of its formal collective bodies. Rather, it means that the process of organizational solidification was put, often with the employment of arbitrary if not authoritarian methods, under the control of A. Papandreou himself and a small circle of "yes men," who were guaranteed a free hand to decide on strategy and tactics. Under the circumstances, the "institutionalization" of Papandreou's charisma was not only slow in coming but also feeble. This is because, despite the formal statements regulating party life, in effect that was left to the discretion of arbitrary initiatives by the leadership and its chosen camarilla. Consequently, the official form of party structure became a dead letter to be resurrected selectively every time it was needed to neutralize internal party dissent or to legitimize some controversial decision.[14]

Political and social structures as well as relations and institutions with long histories develop a tremendously strong immunity system and a subsequently admirable inertia to environmental changes and challenges. Structures, relations and institutions that are related to the clientelism of Greek society are cases in point. And it is this clientelism that acted as another negative factor in, or at least as a destabilizing contributor to, the institutionalization of PASOK's structure. More concretely, the strong demand, as we mentioned, to do away with past modes of political mobilization in the post-

Junta period did not effectively cancel out clientelistic practices. The ill-functioning of both the labor and the capital markets led in practice to a hesitation to fully transcend old forms of clientelistic structures and relationships, proving once again that old habits die hard. This of course does not mean that the post-Junta clientelist relations and structures have remained the same as in the 1950s and 1960s.

Indeed, neither at the level of its organizational articulation nor at the level of its effectiveness and content does clientelism in post-1974 Greek politics display significant differences from the past (Charalambis, 1989: 264–283). To begin with, clientelistic relations have lost their personalized character. The citizens' relationship to the government and in general to the resource structures is no longer based on their personal connection to the local MP or the local political notables. It was through the party structure and activity that clientelism resurfaced. Political parties having assumed, as we said, almost all responsibilities for the transition to and consolidation of Democracy became the sole structure of political mobilization and thus integrated clientelism into their mass organizational structures. PASOK, as in so many other facets of party development, was a true vanguard in this process. Party membership meant special attention to individual demands by the various "committees of solidarity" the party had established at local, regional and national levels. Of course, these patterns not only resulted in depersonalizing traditional clientelistic structures but also lay at the base of and consolidated the functional role of party structure, which, however, could not develop into anything more than an apparatus for distributing favors. It is obvious that such an organizational configuration was not conducive to the institutionalization of any party and that PASOK could not be an exemption. Clientelism, which meant in effect serving noninstitutionalized interests and demands, greatly influenced the logic of the movement's organizational development.[15] It was mainly the (by definition) noninstitutional nature of clientelist behavioral and organizational habits that made PASOK's institutionalization feeble. Thus, PASOK's party structure became, on the one hand, a mere machine for distributing favors (especially in the 1980s when it moved to power) and on the other, an apparatus for running elections.

Last but not least, the logic of PASOK's organizational development was influenced by the organizational structures and practices of the other Greek parties, especially those on the Left. The Democratic party practices of the existing parties and even more the lack of any tradition of mass parties in the country seem to have had a rather negative effect upon PASOK's development, as they could not constitute a "standard" or a prototype, a model upon which the movement could carve its organizational strategy and more importantly be judged by its social base. In fact, if one makes the reasonable assumption that the left-wing parties have historically set the limits and the pace of political and party modernization (after all, mass parties are an invention of the Socialist and workers' movements), then it would also be reasonable to argue that the absence of any Socialist tradition on the one hand and particularly the impact of KKE's (Communist Party of Greece) political and organizational discourse on post-Junta Greek politics contributed decisively to PASOK's controversial organizational development.[16]

All these factors led to the logic of the movement's organization, which was none other than its quick electoral effectiveness and success, and which in turn was bound to make its institutionalization both slow in coming and feeble. More concretely, PASOK's organizational strategy has evolved around the quantitative expansion (Pantazopoulos, 1987) of its membership at any cost. This initially meant mass recruitment on the basis of technocratic, accountant-like planning from above,[17] but soon the membership of the movement started to follow its electoral ups and downs, a pattern observed to this date. The underlying strategy of this hyperorganizational activity was the unconditional expansion of electoral support for the movement. This was a strategy which came constantly to a head-on collision with the movement's original promise for democratic and participatory party structure. This is because democratic ethics and especially intraparty democracy in a historical setting, marked by an absence of strong traditions or training processes, need time. Consequently, the efforts to push for electoral effectiveness were bound to undermine membership participation and party democracy, and led naturally to friction, though not always open and clear or consistent, between: (a) all those who hoped for a democratic party freed from both the experience of the traditional Left as well as the personalized clientelistic organizational practices of the mainstream parties of the past, who in fact were closer to the movement's original promise for "democratic procedure"; and (b) those who had uncritically pursued an exclusively traditional electoralist strategy.

The end result of the frictions deriving from the latter was that the story of PASOK became a series of internal crises and splits.[18] As no sense of collective decision-making was ever allowed to develop and both party finances and resources (e.g. local and peripheral appointments) were at the disposal of A. Papandreou and the Executive Bureau, which in effect he had appointed, the realization of the party's organizational promise was becoming even more distant. To put it differently, the overdetermination of the movement's institutionalization by the leadership's electoralist strategy made it feeble. The end result of such a development was multifold: (a) entering the electoral competition with an institutionally weak organization resulted inevitably in its conformism and eventual conservatism; (b) failure to produce new leadership capable of standing up to the standards its charismatic leader had set[19] and (c) the weakening of the undemocratic political culture among its membership.

At this point I must say that PASOK's peculiar institutionalization, or lack thereof, was not expressed and articulated through a mere absence of internal party democracy. On the contrary, PASOK adopted a peculiar type of pluralism (Spourdalakis, 1988: 182–184), which acted as a safety valve for the membership's recurrent and divergent discontent regarding the lack of intraparty democracy. More concretely, this pluralism, which was established by the movement's day-to-day political practice, was articulated in a twofold political discourse—one internal and one public. In its public functions the party appeared more "realistic," more thoughtful and in essence more conservative, while within the party structure, a clearly radical and not rarely Marxist discourse was promoted by the radical party functionaries. There is no doubt that the former was, by definition, more important since it was promoted by the parliamentary caucus and the party officials who were perceived by the general public to carry more political weight.[20] In practice this meant that members of the movement could believe in and advocate just about anything as long as they did not challenge the leadership's (namely, A. Papandreou's) decisions. Given the social and political diversity of PASOK, this peculiar pluralism, needless to say, was of vital importance if the party were to continue to successfully articulate the concerns of its political currents.

PASOK's structure and organizational practice meant that no political current felt itself outside of the movement's development. If our hypothesis is correct, that the political tendencies of PASOK were, to a great extent, conditioned by the social interests formed within the Greek social formation, then it is not difficult to conclude that this intraparty pluralism has in turn been instrumental to its organizational strategy. Without it, PASOK's political range of appeal would have been significantly curtailed, and in effect it would have been impossible to serve the logic of its organizational development.

To be sure, as the "short march to power" was reaching its goal, not all three tendencies of the movement carried the same political weight. Soon after the 1977 election, when PASOK became the leading opposition party, it was clear that a controversial "alliance" between the technocrats and the *palaiokommatikoi* had been formed and was calling the shots. The composition of the cabinets in all the PASOK governments, both in the 1980s and the 1990s, is a case in point. This alliance, however, has proven to be rather delicate, and every time that one of the two tendencies seemed to get the upper hand it was seriously challenged by the other—a development which somehow undermines the gains deriving from the alliance. A prime example of this pattern is the crisis of 1987, when the conformist tendency's reaction to the technocrats led to an extensive cabinet reshuffling and the canceling of a comprehensive austerity program adopted only eighteen months before. In any case, what must be underlined here is that the control of the party by these two tendencies has led to the marginalization of the Left tendency, which in effect functions as an alibi with regard to the left-wing clientele of the movement: political personnel associated with the ideas of this tendency are used only at governmental agencies of secondary importance. However, and despite the latter development, PASOK's organizational power and political appeal are still three-dimensional. A serious disturbance of this delicate balance would mean, ceteris paribus, its demise.

As we have already mentioned, the distinction between the logic of party structure and the logic of party organizational development helps in the periodization of PASOK's overall development. Periodization should not be seen, as is often the case, simply as the identification of some key dates in the party's development. Periodization should be based upon the changes within each period, which appear as a result of internal contradictions, frictions and crises and which are the force behind the entire process of transformation. Using this perspective we can identify four main periods in PASOK's organizational development, which also outline its timid steps toward its institutionalization:

(a) The period from September 1974 up until the summer of 1975, which could be described as the phase of spontaneous organization and radical promises. It is the period in which the logic of PASOK's structure is revealed and articulated by the call for self-organization. The period ends when this strategy is considered electorally ineffective and the leadership decides to bypass the slow process of institutionalizing the party by putting forward an electoralist strategy, which would serve as the logic of the party's organizational development.

(b) The period that can be described as the "short march to power," which started with the organizational crisis of the summer of 1975, with the expulsion from the party ranks of a significant number of the party members and functionaries who objected to the dominance of electoralist strategy over the logic of the party's organizational development and which ended with the triumphant rise to power in 1981. This period was marked by a number of internal crises which in effect consolidated the victory of all those (foremost the leadership) who did not want to take any serious steps toward the movement's institutionalization. It was during this period that the practices (e.g., two-tiered internal-external political discourse) of peculiar pluralism, we mentioned above, were established as the way of articulating the movement's political and social diversity.

(c) The period which starts with PASOK's 1981 rise to power until its Second Congress in 1990. This is the period in which the movement is confronted for the first time with the shortcomings of its controversial organizational development. It is the period in which PASOK's government faced the hard realities of power and at the same time tried to tame the hyperactivity and reconcile the controversial demands and expectations of its membership.[21] The party's lack of institutionalization had resulted in a number of problems, which in combination with the inertia of societal and political traits of the Greek social formation proved to be the reasons behind the party's signs of decay in the late 1980s: first, the profound lack of regular patterns of political recruitment led the government to rely on the ad hoc recruits the leadership had made with clientelist criteria which in turn resulted in flooding of the state echelons with incompetent individuals of questionable intention. Second, the government's initiatives to establish welfare policies as well as its efforts toward administrative reforms not only lacked genuine popular support but also deepened the democratic deficit of the Greek state and resulted in extensive corruption and corrupt practices. The movement's first Congress in 1984, which was supposed to deal with some of these problems, not only failed to address them in any effective way but reconfirmed the established logic of the organizational development of the party.[22]

(d) Finally, the current period of the party which can be described as a "rush toward organizational maturity." The first signs of this period appeared in the aftermath of the June 1989 election, when the party experienced its first electoral setback since its establishment. It is the period which is characterized by PASOK's efforts, though not necessarily smooth, to advance itself toward a party of principle. Here, the extensive intraparty debates on the reasons behind electoral defeats as well as the unusual appeals to the constitution and collective procedures are cases in point. The problematic of the movement to speed up the integration of its collective, democratic institutionalization became clear at the party's Second Congress (September 1990) and it was reconfirmed at the Third Congress (April 1994). It is a period in which the shock of electoral defeat, the illness of A. Papandreou and his eventual resignation from the Prime-Ministership (January 1996) forced the party to reevaluate the status of its organization, to prepare itself for the "post-Papandreou" era as well as to revise its political and ideological orientation. Thus, its newly adopted constitution aims to strengthen the party collective processes and at the same time to keep it separate from the government. The establishment of the position of the Secretary General of the party, who cannot be a member of the cabinet, the abolition of the Disciplinary Council and the unprecedented tolerance of membership criticisms of the government are cases in point. At the same time, PASOK seems to be abandoning its controversial, vague, radical, often rather third-worldly discourse, as it gradually coordinates its programmatic orientation with the problematic of other European Socialists, who are trying to come to terms with the crises of the post-Communist era. Signs as well as contributors to this development are: PASOK's official membership in the Socialist International (1990); its participation in the funding of the European Socialist Party (1992), its active presence in the Socialist Group of the European Parliament; and especially the election of K. Simites, a "modernizer" and mainstream Social Democrat and an opponent of the leadership's organizational choices for Prime Minister by the party's parliamentary caucus. This development has already been articulated in the moderate tones of the movement's new Declaration published on its nineteenth anniversary (September 1993).

To conclude, there is no doubt that the Panhellenic Socialist movement has put itself on a course of organizational and (subsequently) programmatic maturation. However, one has to be cautious as to the final outcome of this restructuring organizational activity of the party. The fact that the three founding tendencies of the movement still determine the logic of its structure, while their (social) constituencies are often engaged in zero-sum relations, makes the prospect of PASOK's institutionalization unsure. In fact, we could argue that certain conjunctural events are not particularly conducive to this process. The movement's recent easy return to power, as a result of the right-wing New Democracy's disastrous record, so far seems to have slowed it down. The under-the-table dealings and the personalized criteria that dominated the election of the Executive Bureau that followed the party's Third Congress are strong indications that PASOK's organizational culture is far from having purged its old habits. At the same time, the fact that the charismatic leadership of Papandreou seems to have come to an end, in combination with the inability of any of the party's tendencies to impose their will on the movement's strategy and organization, will have to lead to some constitutional and organizational arrangements, if, of course, the party is to stay together after its leader's departure.

NOTES

The author would like to express his gratitude to P.N. Diamandouros for his constructive comments, and to R. Gillespie, whose editorial comments and encouragement were crucial.

1. Although by international standards PASOK has not been studied extensively, it remains the best-studied political party of the Greek party system. See: Mavrogordatos (1983); Lyrintzis (1983, 1987, 1989); Diamandouros (1991, 1994); Spourdalakis (1988, 1991, 1992); Elephantis (1981); Clogg (1987); Paschos (1986); Pantazopoulos (1987); Papasarandopoulos (1980). Also for analyses of PASOK's governmental policies, see Spourdalakis (1996); Clogg (1993); Kariotis (1992); Stavrou (1988); Tzannatos (1986); Papasarandopoulos (1980); Kotzias (1985). Also for analyses of PASOK's governmental policies, see Spourdalakis (1996); Clogg (1993); Kariotis (1992); Stavrou (1988); Tzannatos (1986); Featherstone (1990); Spourdalakis (1988); Catephores (1983); Kalogeropoulou (1989); Tsakalotos (1991); Kazakos (1990: 129–164); Karabelias (1989); Featherstone (1990); Spourdalakis (1987); Catephores (1983); Kalogeropoulou (1989); Tsakalotos (1991); Kazakos (1990: 129–164); Karabelias (1989).

2. The term is borrowed from H. Kitschelt (1983: 57–85), who uses it to describe conjunctural and institutional factors affecting the development and the dynamic of social movements: see also Rootes (1990: 5–17). However, I believe that the term can be employed in the study of parties' genesis and development; see Spourdalakis (forthcoming).

3. For a theoretical analysis of the relationship between parties' organizational genetic model and their institutionalization as two dimensions of parties' concrete organizational development, see Panebianco (1988: 47–68).

4. Of course this does not mean that there is a clear-cut distinction between objective and subjective factors affecting party structure and statutes. In fact, there is a

constant interplay between factors such as traditional and developing patterns of political mobilization, conjunctural events (objective) and a leadership's own choices (subjective), which hardly make this distinction a simple task.

5. The others being "National Independence," "Popular Sovereignty" and "Social Liberation."

6. See Clogg (1987, Appendix I: 217–224); and also Spourdalakis (1988, Appendix I: 288–296). For a detailed analysis of the Declaration (Spourdalakis, 1988: 61–71).

7. The significance of PASOK's unprecedented organizational development has been recognized even by its bitter critics. See for example, Andrianopoulos (1980: 190).

8. On the significance of the first (early) post-Junta elections, see Diamandouros (1984, 1986); and Alivizatos (1990).

9. The distinction has been made by Tucker and adopted by Panebianco (1988: 51).

10. The "populist logic" which characterizes this tendency has led many students to call it populist and to classify PASOK as a populist phenomenon [see note 1].

11. Indeed, PASOK experienced severe internal crises during which it lost thousands of members (1975, 1976, 1977, 1986–1987). Most of them were centered around procedural disputes and were always resolved with the further strengthening of the Papandreou position. See Spourdalakis (1988: 99–130, 143–153).

12. Needless to say Papandreou's popularity and appeal extends far beyond the internal politics of his party. The fact that Greek people refer to him by his first name is very indicative. One has to note that the latter derived from the need of the party's membership to rationalize their (subjective) affiliation with the movement by regarding it as an extension and natural evolution of their association with the country's older parties. Mavrogordatos (1993: 146), refers to a revealing statement of a delegate to PASOK's 1977 conference: "I was for Venizelos, then for Plastiras, afterwards for Georgios Papandreou, now for his son."

13. Many observers who have been following PASOK very closely have witnessed Papandreou's own great disappointment after the electoral results were announced, as he expected to become the leader of the opposition and his party had come third with less than 14 percent of the popular vote. See among others the recent Paraskevopoulos (1995: 74–76). The evidence has been corroborated in a recent book published by his youngest son, according to whom, on the night of the election, A. Papandreou even considered leaving Greece and politics and flying back to Canada. See Papandreou (1995: 209–13).

14. This was an organizational behavior PASOK developed early on when the first attempt of A. Papandreou to control the party was initiated by an arbitrary organization of a "Pre-congress" which not only legitimized itself but gave a perfect excuse to the leadership to control the members of the newly elected Central Committee (Spourdalakis, 1988: 99–114).

15. At this point I have to say that there are some new trends in the demands that impeached on the institutionalization of party structure and on PASOK in particular. These trends have to do with the noted changes both in the content and the range of the demands seeking to find arrangement through extra-institutional arrangements. More often before, these demands were not only small, individual and fragmentized, but more recently had to do with major individual favors (i.e., business arrangements) or the distribution of collective privileges (i.e., support for community projects, special

arrangements for certain social collectivities). This qualitative change in the content of social demands further consolidated the institutionalization of clientelist structures, which in turn undermined the permanence of party organization as a structure for citizen participation in the party and in the political developments of the post-Junta period.

16. The influence of the traditional Left on PASOK has been more extensive and more clearly discernible in the party's political stands, especially during the first years of its development. Thus, in its 1974 Declaration, the movement defined its political goal as an effort to supersede capitalism and to "cease the exploitation of man by man" [for a detailed analysis of the Declaration, see Spourdalakis, 1988: 61–71]; while Papandreou demarcated Social Democracy as being merely "capitalism with a human face" (A. Papandreou, interview in *Ta Nea*, November 3, 1975) and even the subservient agent of U.S. foreign policy (*Exormise*, January 30, 1976). Furthermore, and much closer to the Communist discourse, he conceived of the state as an instrument of the ruling class which meant that the anticipated "socialist society . . . [would have to be] a state to express the hegemony of workers, peasant, salary earners" (Papandreou, 1981: 17), and it accepted Marxism as "the historical method of analysis . . . of class struggles, structures of power, and of developing dialectic" [Papandreou, 1979: 37].

17. See for example PASOK's organizational directives in the *Isigisi gia ti Mellontiki Organotiki Poria tou Kinimatos* (Proposal for the Future Organizational March of the Movement), Athens: December 7, 1977, where the whole concept of the movement's organizational development is based on achieving a certain ratio between electoral support and membership. It is a document full of numerical examples and a complete absence of any statements concerning the principles governing these recruitments.

18. For a detailed analysis of the significance of these crises, see Spourdalakis (1988: 114–62).

19. This became particularly clear after 1993, when the party was confronted with the task of replacing A. Papandreou, who, due to his illness, no longer could perform his functions.

20. Of course this is a trait of mass parties in general; the intensity of the debates within the British Labor Party in the early 1980s is a case in point. However, in the case of PASOK the friction between parliamentary and nonparliamentary wings of the party went far beyond the usual phenomena of this kind.

21. I have argued elsewhere that PASOK's major problems once in power were not the accumulated problems of the country, which were exacerbated by the recession, but rather the controversies of its program, which "had been promising too many things . . . to almost every possible constituency" (Spourdalakis, 1988 : 212–213).

22. Although it took PASOK almost ten years to organize its First Congress, which is probably a negative world record for a Socialist Party, the Congress left the organizational patterns of the party untouched since it did not advance its institutionalization, and it became simply a process for mobilizing support for the upcoming election.

REFERENCES

Alivizatos, Nicos (1990). "The Difficulties of Rationalization in a Polarized Political System: The Greek Chamber of Deputies." In Ulrike Liebert and Maurizio Cotta (eds.), *Parliament and Democratic Consolidation in Southern Europe: Greece, Italy, Portugal, Spain and Turkey.* London: Pinter Publishers.

Andrianopoulos, Andreas (1980). "I Politiki Phisiognomia tou PASOK" (The Political Physiognomy of PASOK). In P. Papasarandopoulos (ed.), *PASOK kai Exousia* (PASOK and Power). Thessaloniki: Parateretes.

Catephores, George (1983). "Greece: The Empiricist Socialism of PASOK." *The Socialist Economic Review.* London: The Merlin Press.

Charalambis, Dimitris (1985). *Stratos kai Politiki Exousia: I Domi tis Exousias stin Metemfiliaki Ellada* (Army and Political Power; The Structure of Power in Post–Civil War Greece). Athens: Exantas.

Charalambis, Dimitris (1989). *Pelateiakes Scheseis kai Laikismos: I Exothesmiki Sinainesi sto Elliniko Politiko Systima* (Clientelistic Relations and Populism: The Extra-Institutional Consensus in the Greek Political System). Athens: Exantas.

Clogg, Richard (1987). *Parties and Elections in Greece.* London: C. Hurst & Co. Ltd.

Clogg, Richard (ed.) (1993). *Greece 1981–89. The Populist Decade.* London: Macmillan.

Diamandouros, P. Nikiforos (1984). "Transition to, and Consolidation of Democratic Politics in Greece, 1974–1983." *West European Politics* 7: 50–71.

Diamandouros, P. Nikiforos (1986). "Regime Change and the Prospects for Democracy in Greece: 1974–83." In Guillermo O' Donnel, P.C. Schmitter and L. Whitehead (eds.), *Transitions from Authoritarian Rule.* Baltimore: Johns Hopkins University Press.

Diamandouros, P. Nikiforos (1991). "PASOK and State Relations in Post-Authoritarian Greece 1974–1988." In Spyros Vryonis, Jr. (ed.), *Greece on the Road to Democracy from the Junta to PASOK 1974–1986,* pp. 15–35. New Rochelle, NY: Caratzas.

Diamandouros, P. Nikiforos (1994). *Cultural Dualism and Political Change in Post-Authoritarian Greece.* Madrid: Juan March Center for Advanced Study in the Social Sciences.

Elephantis, Angelos (1981). "PASOK and the Elections of 1977: The Rise of the Populist Movement." In H.R. Penniman, *Greece at the Polls: The National Elections of 1974 and 1977.* Washington, DC: American Enterprise Institute.

Featherstone, Kevin (1990). "The 'Party-State' In Greece and the Fall of Papandreou." *West European Politics* 13: 101–115.

Kalogeropoulou, Efthalia (1989). "Election Promises and Government Performance In Greece: PASOK's Fulfillment of Its 1981 Election Pledges." *European Journal of Political Research* 17: 289–311.

Karabelias, Giorgios (1982). *Mikromesea Demokratia* (Lower-Middle Democracy). Athens: Kommouna.

Karabelias, Giorgios (1989). *Kratos kai Koinonia sti Metapolitefsi (1974–1988)* (State and Society In the Metapolitefsi [1974–1988]). Athens: Exantas.

Kariotis, C. Theodore (ed.) (1992). *The Greek Socialist Experiment: Papandreou's Greece 1981–1989.* New York: Pella Publishing Co., Inc.

Kazakos, Panos (1990). "Economiki Politiki kai Ekloges O Politikos Elenchos tis Economias stin Ellada: 1979–1989" (Economic Policies and Election, the Political Control of the Economy in Greece: 1979–1989). In Christos Lyrintzis and E. Nicolakopoulos (eds.), *Elliniki Etairia Politikis Epistimis* (Hellenic Society of

Political Science). *Ekloges kai Kommata sti Dekaetia tou '80* (Elections and Parties in 1980s), pp. 129–164. Athens: Themelio.

Kitschelt, Herbert (1983). "Political Opportunity Structures and Political Protest." *British Journal of Political Science* 16: 57–85.

Kotzias, Nicos (1985). *O "Tritos Dromos" tou PASOK* (PASOK's "Third Road"). Athens: Sygchrone Epochi.

Kouloglou, Stelios (1986). *Sta Ichni tou Tritou Dromou: PASOK 1974–1986* (In the Traces of the Third Road). Athens: Odisseas.

Lyrintzis, Christos (1983). *Between Socialism and Populism: The Rise of the Panhellenic Socialist Movement.* Ph.D. dissertation. London School of Economics.

Lyrintzis, Christos (1982). "The Rise of PASOK: The Greek Election of 1981." *West European Politics* 5: 308–313.

Lyrintzis, Christos (1989). "PASOK In Power: The Loss of the 'Third Road to Socialism.' " In T. Gallagher and A. Williams (eds.), *Southern European Socialism.* Manchester: Manchester University Press.

Lyrintzis, Christos (1987). "The Power of Populism: The Greek Case." *European Journal of Social Research* 15: 667–686.

Mavrogordatos, Th. George (1983). *The Rise of the Green Sun.* London: Center of Contemporary Greek Studies (Occasional Paper 1).

Mavrogordatos, Th. George (1988). *Metaxy Pityokampti kai Prokrousti: oi Epagelamtikes Organoseis sti Simerini Ellada* (Between Pityokamptis and Prokroustis: Professional Organizations in Greece Today). Athens: Odysseas.

Mavrogordatos, Th. George (1993). "Civil Society under Populism." In Richard Clogg (ed.), *Greece 1981–89. The Populist Decade*, pp. 47–64. London: Macmillan.

Merkel, Wolfgang (1992). "After the Golden Age: Is Social Democracy Doomed to Decline?" In C. Lemke and G. Marks (eds.), *The Crisis of Socialism In Europe.* Durham, NC and London: Duke University Press.

Panebianco, Angelo (1988). *Political Parties: Organization and Power.* Cambridge: Cambridge University Press.

Pantazopoulos, Andreas (1987). "I Koinoniki Synthesi tou Stelechiakou Dynamikou tou PASOK 1974–81" (The Social Background of PASOK's Functionaries 1974–1981). *Politis* No. 83, September.

Papandreou, Andeas. 1975. Interview in *Ta Nea*, November 3.

Papandreou, Andreas. 1976. Interview in *Exormise*, January 30.

Papandreou, Andreas. (1979). *Gia mia Sosialistiki Koinonia* (On a Socialist Society). Athens: Aechmi.

Papandreou, Andreas (1981). *Metavasi sto Socialismo. Provlimata kai Stratigiki gia to Elliniko Kinima* (Transition to Socialism, Problems and Strategy for the Greek Movement). Athens: Aechmi.

Papandreou, Nicos (1995). *Deka Mythi kai mia Historia* (Ten Myths and a History). Athens: Kastaniotes.

Papasarandopoulos, Petros (ed.) (1980). *PASOK kai Exousia* (PASOK and Power). Thessaloniki: Parateretes.

Paraskevopoulos, Petros (1995). *Andreas Papandreou.* Athens: Sygchrone Hellenike Historia.

Paschos, Giorgios (1986). "Ethniki Laiki Enotita kai Eklogiko Systima" (National Popular Unity and the Electoral System). *Politis* No. 71, January–March.

Petras, James (1983). "Class Formation and Politics In Greece." *Journal of Political and Military Sociology* 11 (Fall).

Petras, James (1987). "The Contradictions of Greek Socialism." *New Left Review*, No. 163 (May–June).

Rootes, A. Chris (1990). "Theory of Social Movements: Theory for Social Movements?" *Philosophy and Social Action* 16: 5–17.

Schumpeter, Joseph (1962). *Capitalism, Socialism and Democracy*. New York: Harper Torchbook.

Spourdalakis, Michalis (1988). *The Rise of the Greek Socialist Party*. London: Routledge.

Spourdalakis, Michalis (1991). "PASOK In the 1990s: Structure, Ideology, Political Strategy." In J.M. Maravall et al., *Socialist Parties in Europe*. Barcelona: Institut de Ciences Politiques in Socials, pp. 157–186.

Spourdalakis, Michalis (1992). "A Petty Bourgeois Party with a Populist Ideology and Catch-all Party Structure: PASOK." In Wolfgang Merkel et al., *Socialist Parties In Europe II: of Class, Populars, Catch-all?* Barcelona: Institut de Ciences Politiques i Socials, pp. 97–123.

Spourdalakis, Michalis (1996). "PASOK's Second Chance." *Mediterranean Politics* 1: 320–336.

Spourdalakis, Michalis (forthcoming) *On the Theory and the Study of Political Parties*. Boulder, CO: Lynne Rienner.

Spourdalakis, Michalis, Ralph Miliband, John Saville, M. Liebman, and Leo Panitch (eds.) (1986). "The Greek Experience." In *Socialist Register*, pp. 247–268. London: Merlin Press.

Stavrou, Nicos (ed.) (1988). *Greece under Socialism*. New York: Orpheus Publishing Inc.

Tsakalotos, Euclides (1991). *Alternative Economic Strategies: The Case of Greece*. Aldershot: Gower.

Tsoukalas, Constantine (1983). "Kinonikes Proektasis tis Dimosias Ergodosias stin Metapolemiki Ellada" (Social Implications of Public Employment in Post-War Greece). *The Greek Review of Social Research* 1: 1–50.

Tzannatos, Zaphires (ed.) (1986). *Socialism in Greece: The first four years*. Aldershot: Gower.

11

Nea Demokratia: Party Development and Organizational Logics

Takis S. Pappas

Party organization is too multiform a concept to be employed carelessly; it permeates most studies on political parties and yet its usage is hardly an equivocal one. In fact, each party model—from Duverger's (1954) "mass party" to Kirchheimer's (1966) "catch-all party" to Panebianco's (1988) "electoral-professional party" to, more recently, Katz and Mair's (1995) "cartel party"—seems to suggest different types of organization. This is a rich area of research. But, surprisingly, we continue to know precious little about party organizations and their development (Katz and Mair, 1992; Mair, 1994).

This chapter sets out to provide a long-term empirical inquiry of the intraorganizational developments of the Greek *Nea Demokratia* (New Democracy—ND). Seeking to identify patterns of change and adaptation, emphasis will be placed on the concrete (internal and external) political circumstances that conditioned both party creation and party growth, as well as the main actors (individual and collective) who determined its organizational development over time. To this purpose, I will focus on the ND party structures having two concerns in mind. The first is to narrate the "official story" (Katz and Mair, 1992: 6) of the ND organization by examining formal party records, statutes, rules, procedures and the party verbiage. My second concern is to survey the continuous struggles for power and authority within ND in order to obtain a less formalized and yet more "real-life" comprehension of the party's inner life. Internal struggles may be due to endogenous (e.g., changes in the party rules) as well as to exogenous (e.g., defeat at the polls) factors. The point, however, remains that party internal conflicts do create new balances of intraorganizational power and generate new logics of organizational development.

In what follows, I am going to identify three distinct logics of organizational development in the process whereby the conservative ND sought to metamorphose itself from the assembly of notables it was at the time of its creation in 1974 to the organized party it has become today. ND provides a particularly interesting case to see how party organizations work, how they change and how they adapt. It also appears to be a paradoxical case since, against all odds, it managed not only to survive after its initial phase of development, but it also succeeded in becoming a modern and competent mass party. I shall come back to this theme in the last section of this chapter, where some theoretical remarks on party organization are also included.

THE KARAMANLIS LEADERSHIP, 1974–1980: THE LOGIC OF PARTY ORGANIZATIONS AS INSTITUTIONAL REQUIREMENT

When, in July 1974, the Greek military dictatorship collapsed under the weight of its own grave failures, Constantine Karamanlis was recalled to the country from his long, self-imposed exile to "rescue the situation." More than that, Karamanlis actually set out to build what became the present Third Greek Republic. Of key importance to the democratic program he sought to apply, and which I have described elsewhere in detail (Pappas, 1995), was the existence of new, principled and well-organized political parties.[1]

Organization thus became one of the main priorities of ND top leadership for their party. Considering the fact that the cardinal political objectives of Karamanlis were the building up of an institutionalized democratic regime and the entry of Greece into the European Community (EC), it is apparent that the existence of fully developed parties became a quite necessary (but, of course, not sufficient) condition for meeting both ends.[2] Thus, in the first place, according to the political design for Democracy applied by Karamanlis, parties were meant to be bodies for incorporating the hitherto politically excluded masses in both an orderly and enduring way. To be in a position to do so, it was understood that "a political party cannot exist for any reasonable time unless it is democratically organized so as not to identify its own fate with that of its leader" (Karamanlis, 1977). In the second case, Greece, a formal applicant for full membership in the EC as of June 1975, had to convince its would-be partners of its main political forces' determination to adopt democratic practices and, ultimately, facilitate the consolidation of the newly established democratic regime.

Intentions aside, however, ND, at least during its initial development phase, was confronted with three enormous obstacles to its organizational buildup. First, it was a party personally created and ruled by a charismatic leader. Practically exercising a tight grip over his party and not really tolerating dissent, Karamanlis nevertheless encouraged the early organizational efforts of ND, thus offering the party an opportunity to develop an inner life of its own. Second, ND was a typical ruling party, which is to say that distinguishing governmental activities from the need to attract a mass membership, as well as develop an autonomous party organizational structure outside the state structures, was not to be an easy task for it. Finally, ND was a deeply conservative party. Many of its elites belonged to the traditional oligarchic type of politician, who had acquired and enjoyed political prominence mainly because of family pedigrees. To those party notables, party organization would be a nuisance, not to mention the threat presented to them by the party cadres to spring from within it.[3] In general, the supremacy of the leader, a tendency toward limiting the elected elites' power, and the concomitant attempt to upgrade the party organization, are reflected clearly in the early endeavors of ND to articulate a party structure at a formal level. Let us briefly follow those attempts.

In the earlier years of ND development, it was exclusively the party leader who appointed the party organs, prescribed their roles, and controlled their functions. The first ND organs to exist were two small committees, one administrative and the other executive, composed of extra-parliamentary personalities who were faithful to Karamanlis and steadfast to the political principles he represented.[4] Theoretically, those committees' task was the designation of a strategy for the organization of ND. Practically, however, lacking both institutional autonomy and real scope of action, they failed to do more than merely rubber-stamp the decisions taken by the party leader and his closest aides.

Things showed some signs of change as early as April 1977, when ND convened its first preliminary Congress. To be sure, the overwhelming majority of party delegates participating in the proceedings were appointed by higher party officials rather than elected by the ND base. Yet, as the study of the official party documents suggests, there was in that Congress a quite evident effort to give the occasion an air of due political animation and organizational enthusiasm. That attempt of ND to copy its leftist adversaries' largely administrative organizational structures looked somewhat odd at that time and certainly, given the high degree of power concentration at the summit of the party, self-contradictory and incongruous with reality.

The preliminary Congress of ND produced a sufficiently elaborate and well-articulated formal charter to regulate the party's inner life. Yet there were still serious problems. While the leader's supreme authority over the party remained securely beyond any dispute,[5] the most important issue underlining procedural formalities were the attempts of both the top leadership and the growing extra-parliamentary party to restrict the influence of the parliamentary group in ND's internal affairs. As a result, the sitting deputies of the party failed to gain access to either the administrative or the executive committees in both central and regional levels of party organization. They were also unsuccessful in their intention of being the sole organ responsible for selecting the party leader. They managed, however, to remain in possession of the field vis-à-vis the party base, since they succeeded in reducing the power of the regional and local organizations in the selection of candidates for the party lists (New Democracy, 1977, 1: 85–87).

The ND parliamentary group was thus able to seriously undermine any attempts the party was making toward the training and creation of professional party cadres,[6] let alone the building of a mass membership cleansed of clientelistic marks.[7] At the same time, however, a different spirit grew steadily, if to a lesser degree, within the party. Its most visible manifestation was the so-called Volvi movement, which emerged from within the party's grass roots and demanded the invigoration of the ND internal organization. That movement became particularly vocal when, as early as 1976, it convened its own shadow congress in a resort near the spa of the Volvi lake in northern Greece, after which the movement was named. Its participants stood against the traditional party notables as well as their practices of familism, nepotism, favoritism and political patronage. Instead of such old-fashioned politicking, they demanded that the top party leadership (which, significantly, they never put under dispute) promote the organizational strengthening of the party base and the fostering of democratic procedures within ND.

Two years later, with the completion of Greece's accession into the EC already in full sight but also with Karamanlis's rumored departure from the party leadership looming large in the political future of ND, the latter hastened to convene, in May 1979, its First Congress. For, obviously, after its founder and leader would be gone, the party had to survive in order to defend and further reinforce the policies already implemented by Karamanlis. This time all Congress delegates were directly elected by the party base, which had in the meantime experienced a significant growth in numbers.[8] The old configurations of power within ND remained, nevertheless, approximately the same and conflicts broke out along lines that were already familiar from the past.

Perhaps most crucially, in the 1979 ND Congress a deliberate yet cautious attempt was made for the first time to set the limit of the leader's extensive authority over the party. Accordingly, at a symbolic level first, the term "president" replaced, at least in the official party parlance, the label "leader" hitherto used to refer to the head of the party. The leader's personality cult was further impaired by other symbolic acts. Most important was the abandonment of the portrait of Karamanlis, which so far had served as the party's symbol, and its replacement with an ordinary emblem—a hand gripping a lit torch, all placed in a circle. Concerning the actual powers of the party leader, the major novelty of the 1979 charter was the introduction of indirect controls on those aspiring to the ND leadership after the departure of Karamanlis. In point of fact, the party parliamentary elites acquired the right to elect (and dismiss) the future leaders of their party.

Thus, the parliamentary group of ND emerged from the first Party Congress with its role upgraded and its intraparty power position formally reinforced.

That the prerogative for the election of party leaders passed from the ND Congress (this meaning to embody the supremacy of the extra-parliamentary party) to the party parliamentary elites was but one of the latter's relative gains in the struggle for intraparty power. Besides managing to become king-makers, the sitting deputies of ND also won the right to participate in their party's governing body, the administrative committee.[9] In that already enlarged organ of seventy active party members, eighteen would now be incumbent deputies appointed by the parliamentary group. Finally, in contrast to previous ND charters, the 1979 charter recognized the parliamentary group as one of the party's central organs, together with the president, the Party Congress, the administrative and the executive committees.

THE RALLIS AND AVEROFF LEADERSHIPS, 1980–1984: THE LOGIC OF PARTY ORGANIZATION AS VEHICLE FOR VOTER MOBILIZATION

By and large, under Karamanlis's leadership the development of internal party structures was essentially prompted as a matter of form and with a view to lending ND a valid institutional voucher for claiming its (severely disputed) democratic qualities. Hence the fact that most initiatives toward organization-building came from the top leadership of the party. It is not surprising, therefore, that its architects shared a conception that "in the main, intraparty procedures are not intended as 'organizational weaponry' [toward competing parties] but as an essential component of [ND's] philosophy, that is to say, a basic ingredient of the party's political credo" (New Democracy, 1979: 11).[10]

By the end of the 1970s, ND seemed to be losing, one after the other, the relative advantages it had so far enjoyed and which had enabled it to remain firmly in power. In May 1980, Karamanlis withdrew from the leadership of the party and had himself elected to the presidency of the Greek Republic. In the bitter contest for the ND leadership that followed he was succeeded by the liberal yet uninspiring George Rallis. Although the party managed to survive its founder's departure, the void left by Karamanlis's charismatic (let alone unifying) presence starkly exposed the weakness of the ND organization as an adequate substitute for him. Furthermore, ND was now facing the growing challenge of PASOK, which, by dropping its extreme ideological overtones and thus presenting a more moderate political discourse, offered assurances that it was not a party good only in opposition but a credible alternative for government, as well. Driven by a spectacular (both in numbers and volume of activity) party organization finely tuned to the maximization of its electoral influence through the "massification" of its organization base (Spourdalakis, 1988: 193–199), PASOK had become a potent rival for ND and a real threat to the latter's remaining in office.

In this new and unfavorable political environment for ND, the theoretical justification for the need for a rigid organizational party structure started to gradually change. The initial quest for legitimacy did not seem enough any longer. So, as party organization started developing on grounds of political expediency, ND became a typical case of "contagion from the left" (Duverger, 1954: xxvii). Significantly, the ranks of ND had in the meanwhile been thickened with the valuable addition of centrist politicians and cadres, who, despite their failure to eradicate the traditional party elites' oligarchic mentality, introduced and encouraged a new conception of organization for the party. Thus, faced for the first time since the transition to Democracy with the gloomy prospect of losing office and under the mounting pressure of competition from PASOK, emphasis on ND organization was now shifting from intraparty affairs to interparty conflict and from institutional formalism to electoral effectiveness.

Despite his typically conservative leanings, it was Rallis, the new party leader, who emerged as the main champion of the new organizational logic. Determined to fight the forthcoming crucial election on equal terms with his leftist political opponents, he called for intense activation of his party's grassroots organizations. Trying, in consequence, to establish a two-way communication between the top leadership and the rank-and-file, Rallis convened a series of regional party congresses, the most important of which was the one held in Athens in June 1981, only a few months before that year's national elections. At the same time, ND made a last-ditch effort to contribute to the development of its district organizations by having the party's administrative committee adopt ad hoc regional statutes. It all turned out to be of no avail.[11] ND lost the elections to PASOK, for, as one author has put it, "it was too late for ND to change either the popular desire for change or its own image. . . . The general election of 1981 was fought with the same dated and unsophisticated methods, albeit with more mobilisation of a now more conscious and active party base" (Katsoudas, 1987: 100).

Still shocked by their defeat and unprepared to pass into the opposition, most of the old party strongmen grew impatient with their leader's political moderation and refused to entrust him with a fresh vote of confidence. Instead, duly observing the statutory provisions, ND's parliamentary group opted for a staunch right-winger, Evangelos Averoff, to combat PASOK and lead their party back into office. The most visible consequence for the party of Averoff's rise to its leadership was a shift of ND's hitherto ideological orientation from the center-right to more ultra-conservative positions. Embracing the far Right and employing scaremongering as key tactics in his political confrontation with PASOK, the new leader alienated many a liberal politician of the party, thus causing considerable discord at the top echelons of ND.[12]

Perhaps ironically, defeat at the polls also seemed to give the party a new life. While, after 1981, PASOK was busy pulling its party organization into pieces to staff the state mechanism, ND launched a new effort to increase its own organized base. During Averoff's leadership, the party experienced its most spectacular growth in terms of numbers. By the end of 1983, ND local committees, already rising to 2,000, could be found in the remotest corners of the Greek countryside and 70,000 new members had thickened the party's ranks (Averoff, 1983). Besides those developments, ND set up its women's organization department and elaborated a new regulation for its district committees.

To settle preliminaries for the final phase of ND's organizational development, a further note of analysis seems to me necessary at this point. For, behind the façade of a formal party structure, one may already detect most of the clues leading to the subsequent logic for ND's organization. Under the leaderships of Rallis and Averoff, there was an effort to establish a mass-party organization that was, however, constrained by the growing independence of the parliamentary party. As the political system grew extremely polarized (Mavrogordatos, 1983; Papadopoulos, 1989), and party competition in Greece was essentially restricted to only two power contenders (i.e., PASOK and ND), the role of party organizations was also upgraded since they became the chief mechanisms for contesting elections.[13] Only now, the mass organization was not supposed to support the parliamentary party but instead the party leader who acted as an agent of the party organization. The major consequence of that development was to render the ND parliamentary group (as a collective body but also on a more individual basis) relatively powerless vis-à-vis the leader and the active party cadres. Contrary to what had been a common practice in the past, deputies would find it increasingly difficult in the future to hold semi-autonomous positions within the party merely on account of their own clientelistic networks.[14] For, according to the new logic, besides the ability to mobilize its membership the party should also be able to maintain its solidarity in order to face successfully Andreas Papandreou—its main (and, indeed, only) political adversary.

THE MITSOTAKIS LEADERSHIP, 1984–1993: THE LOGIC OF PARTY ORGANIZATION AS THE LEADER'S (IRON?) MAINSTAY

ND fought the 1984 Euro-elections under Averoff's hard-line leadership without significantly managing to improve its political fortunes. In the wake of that defeat Averoff resigned from his post and a new contest for the party leadership was promptly arranged. The reason that led the convention of ND's sitting deputies to pick Constantine Mitsotakis as their new leader was as plain as it could be. By sustaining an animosity that dated from the pre-dictatorship years, he was a declared archenemy of Papandreou; that he also was a shrewd and experienced politician only added to his other credentials. Mitsotakis was meant to be the anti-Papandreou. But here there is a snag. The new leader was not a right-wing Conservative born and bred. Drawing his political lineage from the traditional (and already extinct) Center, he had transferred his allegiances to ND only as late as 1978. Bearing in mind that Mitsotakis was now assigned the task of beating the still quite formidable PASOK, but also the low degree of toleration to his person by the party strongmen—who never ceased considering him a foreign body, not to say an intruder, in their party—one can easily understand the new ND leader's predicament.

The first opportunity both to test the leadership capacities of Mitsotakis and assess the current dynamics of real power distribution within ND appeared as early as June 1985. In that year's general elections, ND, some electoral gains notwithstanding, lost again to PASOK. Crucially, however, in the aftermath of that election Mitsotakis remained firmly in power within the party. What is more, a group of dissenting ND deputies, mostly expressing personal grievances rather than substantial political disagreement, and led by Costis Stefanopoulos, a prominent party figure and main rival of Mitsotakis in the last contest for ND's leadership, split away from ND and founded the party of Democratic Renewal (DIANA).[15] Failing for the time being to beat PASOK, Mitsotakis was nonetheless able to use his celebrated political shrewdness in outmaneuvering his opponents within ND. Immediately after Stefanopoulos had abandoned the party, Mitsotakis resigned, at the same time asking his party's parliamentary group for a fresh vote of confidence. With his mandate renewed, he then called the second party Congress (February 1986) in order to finally have all accounts settled.

The main aim of that Congress was to circumscribe the extensive powers of ND's parliamentary group and the other collective organs of party administration. For, as it was argued, those had developed "corporate structures," thus enjoying "an excessive degree of autonomy in decision-making, which blurs areas of responsibility in district organizations and this causes, in turn, a great deal of parallel action" (New Democracy, 1986: 141). As remedies to such an organizational malady, the Party Congress proposed (a) the balancing of responsibility within ND between the party organization and the parliamentary party; (b) the thickening of the party's vertical structures by the addition of medium-rank organs, to establish better communication between the party base and the summit of ND; and (c) the upgrading of ND's grass roots, by giving them greater say in decisions made at the party top level.

On the whole, the 1986 ND statutes provided for greater participation of the rank-and-file in the higher party organs primarily at the expense of the party's parliamentary group. This became particularly evident with the innovations introduced by the new party statutes concerning the role of the party organizations in any future election of a party president as well as the nomination of the party's parliamentary candidates. Thus, contrary to what had been the case under the previous ND statutes, the election of the leader was not to be entrusted anymore solely to the parliamentary party. Instead, so the new charter ruled, future party presidents would be elected by a special electoral body convened ad hoc and consisting, besides sitting ND deputies, of representatives of the party's district organizations (Art. 14, par. 2). Equally, if not more important, and to the open resentment of the sitting deputies, was the participation of the ND mass organization in the nomination of the party's candidates for a parliamentary seat. The formation of the party's electoral lists now involved a process that was initiated at the district-level organizations, those proposing their own lists to the central Executive Committee. After an initial screening, the Executive Committee submits the lists to the president who "finally selects the candidates and draws up the party electoral lists, which, in the main, include those proposed by the district assemblies" (Art. 20, par. 2).

No less noteworthy than the upgrading of the party's mass organization vis-à-vis its parliamentary elites, in terms of decision-influencing, was the creation, shortly after the 1986 Congress, of a thick administrative network of central party services to supervise and coordinate the party organization across the country. According to the new charter, it was the party president who made the selection and appointed the top personnel to the newly established secretariats and special offices that became responsible for such vital issues as political planning and party programming, education and training of party cadres, press briefing, electoral mobilization and so on. The point that needs to be made here is that, during his presidency, Mitsotakis succeeded in practically colonizing the party mechanism with young, nonparliamentary, professional cadres who were (and gave assurances of remaining) loyal to him.[16]

At all events, soon after the 1986 Congress, ND's base grew both to an impressive size and dynamism—especially if one judges from the performance of the party's youth organization, ONNED, and its women's departments, which became the two social categories that spearheaded all electoral battles ND was to give in the future.[17]

With PASOK floundering about in a scandal concerning money embezzlement and bribery by some of its most prominent members, ND emerged victoriously in the June 1989 general elections. However, due to the complexities of the electoral law, it was unable to form a government since it failed to win a majority of the parliamentary seats. Although the party performed somewhat better in the repeat elections of November of the same year, it still did not manage to form a one-party government. Finally, in April 1990, in the third election that took place within only ten months, ND, under the leadership of Mitsotakis, was able to take office with a narrow parliamentary majority.

As the recent statutory provisions were in force in the first of the aforementioned series of elections, ND's district assemblies did actually forward their chosen candidates for the available parliamentary seats.[18] Given, however, the fact that the party mechanism has come under the control of the party leader, it can be fairly securely assumed that most future deputies would hereafter owe their allegiances to him. The matter is not insignificant, especially if one considers that, in June 1989, ND renewed its political elites by an unprecedented 46.9 percent of its total parliamentary presence since 1974 (Drettakis, 1993: 83).

Back in office, and once again taking advantage of the state and state resources, ND left its organization to atrophy. On the other hand, Mitsotakis made all efforts possible to enhance his domination over the party and its functions. By assigning key party posts to trusted associates and his family members, he managed to maintain a strong grip on the party's inner affairs. More than that, with his control over the majority of ND's parliamentarians sufficiently secured, Mitsotakis was also successful in effectively silencing most internal dissent (e.g., the cases of Evert, Dimas, and Kanellopoulos) or forcing his party opponents to resign (e.g., the case of Samaras).

Should any doubts remain about the authority Mitsotakis exercized upon the ND organization, it will suffice to note that, for the most part, it was his own approved candidates that were actively promoted by the party organization and eventually won parliamentary seats in the national elections held in October 1993.[19] Be that as it may, ND lost at the polls to a reemergent PASOK. Sensing that he could not hold onto the ND leadership anymore, Mitsotakis resigned immediately after that defeat, to the benefit of his main internal opponent, Miltiades Evert, who was elected new party leader by an overwhelming vote of both the ND parliamentary group and the party base. Thus, to quote Michels (1935; cited in Camavitto 1936: 798), "it was not the organization that overthrew the leader but rather a new leader who took advantage of the organization to bring this about." But, I would add, not before conditions had become ripe and the time seemed opportune.

FROM PARTY ORGANIZATIONAL LOGICS TO INTRAPARTY POWER LOGISTICS

Like most other parties, ND is not a unitary actor; it must rather be seen as the sum of subunits struggling for power within it, indeed an "arena" of internal party politics itself. After the foregoing survey of the ND party development for almost 20 years, we are now in a position to map more systematically the changing balance of intraparty power. As already seen, ND's internal powerhouse is inhabited by three bedfellows, who, antagonistic as they normally are, vie with one another for more room and, ultimately, party dominance: the party leader, the party parliamentary group, and the extra-parliamentary party. Of course, all this happens under the pressure of external constraints, overlapping demands, random political developments and, not unusually, in crisis situations. Above all, however, it depends upon internal party processes, most notable of which is the prevailing configuration of power among the main party subunits at particular points of time. Given that all incumbent ND leaders were instrumental in devising and then

Table 11.1
Intraparty Power Possessed by Each of ND's Subunits

a. The Party leader

	1974-1980	1980-1984	1984-1993
Charismatic qualities	Y	N/N	N
Domination over parliamentary group	Y	N/N	Y
Control of formal party organization	Y	N/S	Y
General power assessment	STRONG	FEEBLE	STRONG

b. The Parliamentary group

	1974-1980	1980-1984	1984-1993
Non-dependence on leader for candidacy nomination	N	N	S
Influence in leader's election	N[a]	Y	Y[b]
Potential for fractional autonomy within the party	N	Y	N
General power assessment	FEEBLE	STRONG	FEEBLE

c. The rank-and-file

	1974-1980	1980-1984	1984-1993
Numerical strength	N	N/Y	Y
Existence of substantive intra-party vertical structures	N	N	Y
Influence in party decision-making	N	S	Y
General power assessment	FEEBLE	FEEBLE	STRONG

Key to Table 11.1, a–c: Mark "Y" stands for yes (or, according to the case, large); "N" stands for no or little; "S" denotes some. In the party leadership column for 1980–1984 there are two marks, one for Rallis's and the other for Averoff's leadership.

[a]Despite the 1979 party statutory provision that gave ND sitting deputies the right to elect their party leader; under Karamanlis's authority such a potential remained practically out of range.

[b]Only partially, given the role played by the special electoral body introduced by the 1986 statutes; *supra*, p. 14.

bringing the party organizational logics into effect, I will start with this party subunit first.

If leaders play a vital role in formulating party interests and setting organizational priorities, the question becomes, what are the means available to them for realizing such aims? Without obvious exceptions, in order to succeed, party leaders have to rely either on charisma or bureaucratic authority. In Table 11.1a, I have employed three corresponding criteria (i.e., variables) to assess strength (or feebleness) during the successive ND party leaderships. Karamanlis was certainly able to exercize both a high degree of authority over the party parliamentary elite and enjoy the privileges of charisma relative to the party organization. In contrast, none of his successors to the party leadership managed to score high on either of those grounds. Reluctantly and sometimes painfully, Rallis accepted the role of primus inter pares inside the party, while Averoff agonized in vain over bridging the gap between the ultra-conservative and the liberal forces that had meanwhile developed within ND. Mitsotakis, finally, despite his lack of charismatic qualities, succeeded in imposing himself over ND, partly by tight controls over its organization and partly by systematic manipulation of internal dissent. There can be no doubt that Mitsotakis's leadership was a strong one, hence its relative longevity.

Turning now to the party parliamentary group, it has already been stated that, when Karamanlis formally instituted ND in 1974, they were little more than a gathering of local strongmen motivated by political opportunism rather than ideological principle. Under the long shadow of their first leader, but also thanks to the prolonged tenure of the party in office during the earliest period of the young republic, ND's parliamentary party remained collectively feeble and largely unified (Table 11.1b); hardly was it, however, permanently tamed. A danger for ND to disintegrate—as has been a common practice for nonleftist parties in postwar Greek politics—appeared after the 1981 electoral defeat, when the party passed into the opposition, and charisma, together with authority, vanished into the vacuum left behind by the departure of Karamanlis. ND's parliamentary group was thus able to make strong claims on party power and, for all practical purposes, become partners in leadership, first with moderate Rallis and then with wavering Averoff. In those circumstances, it was in essence only the fear of PASOK that helped ND maintain a fragile unity. Once on the party top himself, Mitsotakis already knew that the symbiosis of a strong leader with an equally strong parliamentary party was not possible, unless charisma complemented authority. He engaged, therefore, in a great effort to railroad ND's elites into submission. Striking numerous deals, offering concessions, and sometimes machining, Mitsotakis managed to gain, and indeed maintain for a long time, control over ND's parliamentary party.

Similarly to the other party components, let us also employ three distinct criteria, the first quantitative and the other two qualitative, for assessing degrees of strength (or feebleness) for ND's mass organization. As shown in Table 11.1c, the extra-parliamentary party was, under Karamanlis's leadership, extremely weak both in numbers and voice. As ominous echoes started coming from the rise of PASOK, ND felt the need to increase its own party membership. Yet, no similar pressure was exercized to give the newly organized rank-and-file of ND real political responsibilities in the party life. This came about only when Mitsotakis took over the ND leadership and for reasons that already have been explained. The fact, however, remains that, despite ND's thin parliamentary majority while in government from 1990 to 1993, Mitsotakis, almost certain that the fear of a possible electoral loss would prevent his intraparty opponents from deserting ND, was able to enjoy the cynical pleasures derived from manipulating the party organization. When

Table 11.2
Overall Assessment of Relative Distribution of Power within ND

	1974-1980	1980-1984	1984-1993
Party leader	STRONG	FEEBLE	STRONG
Parliamentary party	FEEBLE	STRONG	FEEBLE
Mass organization	FEEBLE	FEEBLE	STRONG

the effects of such manipulations became evident, it was already too late for ND to avoid a new electoral defeat and for Mitsotakis himself to retain the party leadership.

All said and done at the micro-level of intraparty competition, let us now turn our attention to the macro-dynamics associated with it. Table 11.2 presents a simple compilation of the individual power evaluations for each of ND's components, as they were assessed in Table 11.1. Some final remarks are in order. There is an apparent paradox. Our empirical evidence refutes rather than validates the often-stated thesis on the mass-party demise (e.g., Lawson and Merkl, 1988). During the period under examination ND experienced a spectacular, and indeed linear, growth in terms of organized members, volume of party activity, and size of party bureaucracy. Moreover, as appears in Table 11.2, the balance of power among the party components during the whole period 1974–1993 moved from the party leader to the parliamentary party to, finally, the extra-parliamentrary party. How did this happen? And how can we account for the strong leadership under Mitsotakis despite his lack of charisma?

There seem to be two answers to the first question. ND displays a tendency to develop bureaucratic structures relative to its remoteness from office. In other words, when disapproved at the polls, the party encouraged, and indeed promoted, internal organizational growth. Conversely, when in office, its organized structure either slackened or decayed. A second reason also seems important and more theoretically promising at that. Other things being equal, ND gained in organizational vigor proportionally to the exhaustion of charismatic qualities at the summit of the party leadership. For, it needs little explanation, a leader bereft of charisma has to control the party organization if he wants to remain in power and to ensure that his party will not revert to an assemblage of conflicting individuals or individual factions. Evident as it is, the foregoing thesis nevertheless needs some further qualification. Otherwise, we are confined in the plain territory governed by the iron (hence, inflexible) law of oligarchy, according to which "the increase in the power of leaders is directly proportional with the extension of the [party] organization" (Michels, 1962: 71).

Karamanlis's departure from the ND was promptly followed by what Weber called the "routinization of charisma" which involved the veneration of the leader and the preservation of all symbolic and ideological apparatus associated with him. The party organization became progressively a vessel for the diverse interests of the intraparty components who tried to mould it to their needs. In the second phase of ND organization, in the absence of strong leadership selfishly motivated elites tried to oppose the development of organized structures for fear of losing their time-honored privileges. (In fact, the power of the party leader—whether it stems from charisma, bureaucratic authority or a combination of both—is inversely proportional to the power of the parliamentary party.) Nonetheless, the party organization continued to grow and amass resources. When Mitsotakis became the party leader, he was capable of capitalizing upon them and centralizing his control over the party organization. Given, however, that the latter had already become a complex structure of interests, Mitsotakis could certainly plunder the organization, but was incapable of tearing it down.

NOTES

Many thanks to Chic Perrow for comments in an earlier version of this chapter.

1. In the postwar period and until the establishment of the military Junta in 1967, all bourgeois parties in Greece were no more than opportunistic assemblies of individual notables (see, for instance, Meynaud, 1965).

2. Accession of Greece into the EC was an end in itself as far as the prospects of the national economy were concerned. Perhaps more crucially, however, it also was a means toward the further strengthening and permanent consolidation of Greek Democracy. For a discussion about the importance of political versus economic gains for Greece from the country's accession into the EC, see Verney (1987).

3. Contrary to the early PASOK, which, by advocating the "democratic road to Socialism" was bound to construct a detailed party organization and maintain a permanently active membership at least as long as it remained in the opposition, ND emphasized a relaxed liberalism in the polity, whose application would be mainly guaranteed by the new 1975 Constitution. In such a climate of "aristocratic republicanism" (Kioukias, 1993: 57) and with the formal functioning of representative Democracy sufficiently secure, political parties were thought of by the ND top leadership as being the most legitimate means of containing the masses.

4. According to George Missaïlides who, at the time, served as general director of the party, by 1977 ND had set up 50 district committees and 40 local ones throughout the country. A first, albeit shy, attempt was also made toward forming professional party organizations (New Democracy, 1977: 31).

5. Characteristic in this respect was the absence from this early ND charter of any provisions (a) regarding the election (or reelection) of the party leader; (b) regulating the latter's relation to the General Assembly on one hand and the parliamentary group on the other; (c) restating the clause of an earlier ND party charter, which explicitly declared the General Assembly to be "the dominant organ of the party." Last, but not least, Article 24 of the 1977 charter, under the title "Ultimate Provisions," summarily entrusted all party-related powers to Karamanlis until the convention of ND's first Congress, which was to definitively ratify the provisions of the preliminary one.

6. Quite typical were, for instance, the recommendations to the party by George Dalakouras, a congress delegate, concerning the importance of cadres for ND (*New Democracy*, 1977, 1: 65–67). That the creation of a bureaucratic organization remained a desideratum for the ND is reflected in the speech at the preliminary Congress made by the party General Director, who declared that "the most obvious aim of our organizational endeavor will be the establishment of democracy within the party, that is, the functioning of internal democratic institutions so as to create equal opportunities for all of our cadres" (*New Democracy*, 1977).

7. By and large, especially during the initial phase of party development, ND supporters continued "to be linked with the party not through its organization but— exactly as in the past—through the local M.P., who continued to distribute personal favors strengthening his patron-client ties" (Loulis, 1981:73).

8. According to official party estimates, in the course of the two years that elapsed between the preliminary and the first party Congresses, ND had increased the number of its members from 20,000 to 150,000; of its local committees from 233 to 380; and of professional party committees from 8 to 25 (*New Democracy*, 1979: 36).

9. According to Article 8 of the 1979 ND statutes, the administrative committee became the organ responsible for organizing the party, carrying out its program, and implementing any decisions taken at party congresses (*New Democracy*, 1979: 285).

10. Similarly, Article 1, paragraph 2, of the 1979 party charter states that "[T]he democratic organization and functioning of the party . . . is for ND a *fundamental principle*" (emphasis mine).

11. Rallis's bitter imputations during the electoral period will suffice to depict the underdevelopment, let alone inefficiency, that plagued ND's organization in the years 1980–1981. In his political memoirs, he admitted that ND suffered from its "endemic illness, that is the lack of eagerness for organization, which continues to be feeble. . . . There is organization on paper, but it is not enough. What is badly needed is the intense activation of our supporters, which is missing from our party altogether, whereas it abounds in PASOK and the Communist Party" (Rallis, 1983: 117). He also complained about the fact that the party cadres "could not realize that it is not enough for the electoral struggle to be conducted solely by myself and a few ministers through interviews in the press, barnstorming, and speeches in the parliament and the countryside; that, if they fail to contribute to [the leaders'] efforts, as our opponents' party organizations do, we will not be able to win the elections" (Rallis, 1983: 105).

12. Most noteworthy are the cases of Yannis Boutos, a prominent party deputy and contender for the party leadership, who was referred to ND's disciplinary committee for daring to express his criticism of the leader, and that of Themistocles Sofoulis, who was summarily expelled from the party by Averoff for urging a party conference to address the leadership issue.

13. It suffices to mention that, whereas the two major parties among those contesting the 1974 general elections received *in common* 74.8 percent of the national vote, and, in 1977, their respective percentage dropped to 67.2 percent, sharp bipolarity in the elections of 1981 pushed that figure to an astonishing 84.0 percent of the total vote. Thereafter, the polarization between ND and PASOK was to take the form of a confrontation *not* simply between two parties, but, as Averoff once put it, "between two ways of life."

14. In this regard, the warning that "the sheep breaking out of the fold are eaten

by wolves," as the saying goes, was Averoff's favorite, if one considers that he missed no opportunity of reciting it.

15. That party, squeezed between the two monoliths of PASOK and ND and never succeeding in having more than an anemic presence in domestic political affairs, remained stillborn until it finally disappeared altogether in 1994.

16. In this sense, ND came to resemble Panebianco's "electoral-professional party," which is mainly staffed, not by devoted party bureaucrats, but rather by well-paid publicists, consultants and media experts.

17. By 1987, ND could claim 3,500 local committees, 70 district committees, and almost 400,000 party members. Those figures, formidable as they are in themselves, become even more impressive if we consider that ND's ratio between members and voters was 1:7.7—not significantly different from that of the Communist Party, which, for the same time period, presented a ratio of 1:6 (Kafetzis, 1987: 33).

18. The November 1989 and April 1990 elections were too close to that of June 1989, as well as to each other, so no political party had enough time for preparing new electoral lists. Instead, all parties used the June 1989 lists with only minor changes.

19. Most notable cases of those failing to win reelection were those of Vassilis Kontoyiannopoulos, a prominent yet dissenting party figure, and Krinio Kanellopoulos, the daughter of Athanasios Kanellopoulos, a ND strongman and overt opponent to Mitsotakis. No less impressive was the loss of the first place among ND candidates in Athens by Miltiades Evert, who had held it continuously since 1977, to Stephanos Manos, a declared favorite of Mitsotakis.

REFERENCES

Averoff, Evangelos (1983). Address to ND's Administrative Committee, 16 December.
Camavitto, Dino (1936). "Roberto Michels—In Memoriam." *American Sociological Review* 1: 797–799.
Drettakis, Manolis G. (1993). *The Anatomy of the Parliament. 1974–1990* (in Greek). Athens: Gutenberg.
Duverger, Maurice (1954). *Political Parties: Their Organization and Activity in the Modern State* (translated by Barbara and Robert North). London: Methuen & Co. Ltd.
Kafetzis, Takis (1987). "ND, 1974–1987: The Embryo That Became a Giant and the 'Challenge of Politics' " (in Greek). *Anti*, No. 357, 9 October.
Karamanlis, Constantine (1977). Speech at ND's Preliminary Congress, 2 April.
Katsoudas, Dimitrios K. (1987). "The Conservative Movement and 'New Democracy:' From Past to Present." In Kevin Featherstone and Dimitrios K. Katsoudas (eds.), *Political Change in Greece: Before and After the Colonels*. London and Sydney: Croom Helm.
Katz, Richard S. and Peter Mair (1992). "Introduction: The Cross-National Study of Party Organizations." In Richard S. Katz and Peter Mair (eds.), *Party Organizations: A Data Handbook on Party Organizations in Western Democracies. 1960-90*, pp. 1–20. London: Sage.
Katz, Richard and Peter Mair (1995). "Changing Models of Party Organization and Party Democracy: The Emergence of the Cartel Party." *Party Politics* 1: 5–28.

Kioukias, Dimitris (1993). "Political Ideology in Post-Dictatorial Greece: The Experience of Socialist Dominance." *Journal of Modern Greek Studies* 11: 51–73.

Kirchheimer, Otto (1966). "The Transformation of West European Party Systems." In Joseph LaPalombara and Myron Weiner (eds.), *Political Parties and Political Development*. Princeton: Princeton University Press.

Lawson, Kay and Peter Merkl (eds.) (1988). *When Parties Fail: Emerging Alternative Organizations*. Princeton: Princeton University Press.

Loulis, John C. (1981). "New Democracy: The New Face of Conservatism." In Howard R. Penniman (ed.), *Greece at the Polls: The National Elections of 1974 and 1977*, pp. 49–83. Washington and London: American Enterprise Institute for Public Policy Research.

Mair, Peter (1994). "Party Organizations: From Civil Society to the State." In Richard S. Katz and Peter Mair (eds.), *How Parties Organize: Change and Adaptation in Party Organizations in Western Democracies*, pp. 1–22. London: Sage.

Mavrogordatos, George Th. (1983). *Rise of the Greek Sun: The Greek Election of 1981*. London: Center of Contemporary Greek Studies, King's College. Occasional Paper no. 1.

Meynaud, Jean (1965). *Les Forces Politiques en Grèce*. Paris: Etudes de Science Politique.

Michels, Robert (1935). "Social Mobility in General with Special Reference to the Post-War Mobility." Communication to the XII International Congress of Sociology, Brussels.

Michels, Robert (1962). *Political Parties: A Sociological Study of the Oligarchical Tendencies of Modern Democracy*. New York: Free Press.

New Democracy (1977). *First Preliminary Party Congress, Minutes* (in Greek), 2 vols.

New Democracy (1979). *First Congress, Minutes* (in Greek).

New Democracy (1986). *Second Congress, Minutes* (in Greek).

Panebianco, Angelo (1988). *Political Parties: Organization and Power*. Cambridge: Cambridge University Press.

Papadopoulos, Yannis (1989). "Parties, the State and Society in Greece: Continuity within Change." *West European Politics* 12: 54–71.

Pappas, Takis S. (1995). *The Making of Party Democracy in Greece*. Ph.D. dissertation. Yale University.

Rallis, George I. (1983). *Hours of Responsibility* (in Greek). Athens: Euroekdotiki.

Spourdalakis, Michalis (1988). *The Rise of the Greek Socialist Party*. London and New York: Routledge.

Verney, Susannah (1987). "Greece and the European Community." In Kevin Featherstone and Dimitrios K. Katsoudas (eds.), *Political Change in Greece: Before and After the Colonels*. London and Sydney: Croom Helm.

Part IV

Spain

12

The Spanish Political Parties from Fragmentation to Bipolar Concentration

—————————————— *Gabriel Colomé and*
Lourdes Lòpez-Nieto

THE SPANISH POLITICAL SYSTEM

The beginning of the Spanish transition to a democratic political party system is sometimes dated from July 1976 when Adolfo Suárez became the new prime minister (Caciagli, 1986) and sometimes from June 1977, the time of the first election (O'Donnell and Schmitter, 1986). For our purposes, we will begin with the approval of the new Constitution in December 1978.

The Spanish democratic system and its consolidation are conditioned by a series of features differentiating it in some aspects from other Western European systems. First, the authoritarian political history emphasizes the tradition of personalized and reduced political participation; in this sense, the debate about the nation's political culture is still alive. Although the population supported a democratic political system, the lack of experience has translated into a passive, nondemocratic behavior; with power concentrated among political elites (Cotarelo, 1992).

Second, the process of political transition makes political parties—both the new ones and those emerging from clandestinity—act as agents more of political and social control than of mobilization, to be integrated in the democratic process through collaboration and agreement. Their essential role in this phase will be rewarded with great protection in the new system for the winners, as clearly seen in the approval of significant public funding, and in electoral legislation reinforcing the role of the two major statewide parties (UCD-PSOE and since 1982, PSOE-AP/PP) and the two nationalist parties (PNV in the Basque Country and the CiU coalition in Catalonia).

This legislative engineering provided the political elite with a number of mechanisms designed for the parties: a system of financial subsidies and privileges for parliamentary groups and an electoral system of numerous representative bodies producing a proliferation of public posts, in addition to those based on the spoils system. These measures favored the success of the parties as the almost exclusive actors within the political system. This process, initiated at the start of the transition in response to the previous weakness of the parties, was maintained and reinforced during the period of democratic consolidation. It may indeed have contributed to the development of a new type of party, similar to the so-called "cartel-party" (Katz and Mair, 1992).

This new party model, able to construct alliances and to conciliate, played an important role in the consensual transition to Democracy and in the development of Spanish parties during the consolidation process.

Third, the political action of these "young" but strengthened actors is taking place in a moment when the mass media, particularly television, have acquired a remarkable influence on the dynamics of politics.

These three features have allowed Spain to carry out the transition consensually and have had a profound impact on the development of the new political system. The tendency to a compromise was reflected in the decision to maintain Democracy. Under the new constitution, Spain is now a parliamentary monarchy, with two asymmetric legislative chambers: the lower house is powerful with 350 seats elected by a proportional system; the members of the Senate are elected partly directly and partly by the regional chambers, through a majoritarian system. The Constitution established also a decentralized state, with seventeen regions (Autonomous Communities) with different degrees of autonomy; in addition, the prerogatives of the Prime Minister (as they have been exercised both by Manuel Fraga and Felipe González) are very great, so great that some authors call this system semi-presidential.

These factors explain the reason of the leadership selection pattern, to which we will return after explaining the leadership selection patterns of the two major parties, the *Partido Socialista Obrero Español* (PSOE)—Spanish Workers' Socialist Party—and *Alianza Popular*—Popular Alliance—today *Partido Popular*, Popular Party (AP/PP).

ORIGINS OF THE NEW PARTY SYSTEM

Today we must add to the traditional studies on "power personalization" in the liberal democracies those that grant a relevant role to the party leaders when media are the channel that centralizes the communicative action of parties during the electoral campaign. In the case of the modern democratic political systems (Linz, 1986) innovative leaderships, besides considering the silent and non-activist majority, adopting decisions which may be risky and unpopular, and being flexible in negotiations, must also have authority in the party and the ability to obtain votes among the potential electorate (Linz,

1990). At the same time, the new generation rejects autocratic rule (Botana and Mustapic, 1988). Under such conditions, party leaders are significantly weaker in traditional systems than in consolidated systems (Lòpez-Nieto, 1992), and have short tenure in office. The net result is a great weakening of the party and consecutive crisis. Candidates change constantly, whole parties disappear, party volatility is higher in Spain than in other nations in Europe (Montero, 1992). These conditions, rather than electoral volatility (Barnes, 1986) have produced a highly unstable party system. The parties themselves have responded in a variety of ways.

Disappearance of the Party

The most significant example is that of *Unión de Centro Democrático* (UCD)—Democratic Center Union—the electoral coalition winner of the first democratic elections created around the President of Government using the institutional mechanisms of the Old Regime. The party disappeared from the political scene when its founder resigned. Adolfo Suárez left the government presidency and that of UCD in January 1981. Some days later A. Rodríguez Sahagún was elected president of the party in the Second and final Conference of the coalition and the candidate for the government presidency was Calvo Sotelo. Several months after his election a group of the party elite left and moved to other parties. Landelino Lavilla assumed the presidency in February 1982, but the party was already collapsing and the following elections sanctioned its death (Caciagli, 1986).

Adolfo Suárez created a new party, the *Centro Democrático y Social* (CDS)—Democratic and Social Center—but it appears to be following the same process. Again, the former president and party leader resigned after the electoral defeat in the local and regional elections of 1991 and today the party is in full decline.

Party Split

Two of the parties solved their crises by breaking apart. The crisis in the *Partido Nacionalista Vasco* (PNV)—Basque Nationalist Party—came with the confrontation between the party leader and the President of the Basque Government. Because no solution to the inner conflicts among the power elite seemed to exist, the party broke down and the dissenting section created a new party, *Eusko Alkartasuna* (EA). This division has created problems in regional government, as the decisions adopted by the PNV leader have not always coincided with those of the EA President of the Basque Government.

A second case is that of the *Partido Comunista de España* (PCE)—Spanish Communist Party—which failed in its hope to become the first party of the Left opposition. Party leader Santiago Carrillo managed to control the two tendencies, Leninist and Euro Communist, until the 1979 Party Conference, when the issue of ideological revision and inner democratization contributed to the radicalization of adversarial factions. That was the origin of crises and breaks that continue even today. Several crises that started in 1979 are still in process. After the 1979 Conference the party split into two Communist parties. Before the 1986 general elections the PCE created a coalition, *Izquierda Unida* (IU)—United Left—seeking to reestablish a unitary party (Gunther et al.,1986) and in 1992 this electoral coalition became a federation of parties in which PCE is still the hegemonic party, despite attemps made by the rest of the associates to reduce its dominance.

Processes of Unstable Coalition

Another party, the *Alianza Popular* (AP) aimed at organizing the highly fragmented Right in the new Spanish political system (Lòpez-Nieto, 1988). This party and its leader Manuel Fraga tried to organize a strong right-wing alternative by integrating prominent politicians and making coalitions with small parties, especially during pre-electoral periods. The breakdown of the Right had a negative effect: it meant the nonconsolidation, and thus the instability, of many coalition processes.

AP was born as a coalition of seven Francoist politicians in September 1976; it broke apart two years later during the discussions regarding the new Constitution. Since then Fraga has led the party into a series of coalitions with small right- and center-right-wing parties (*Coalición Democrática* (CD)—Democratic Coalition—just before the 1979 elections; *Coalición Popular* (CP)—Popular Coalition—before the 1982 elections). But the intensity of negative sentiments in the electorate makes it difficult to form coalitions with other parties which the AP continues to consider allies (Linz and Montero, 1986: 645–662). In 1989 AP changed its name to *Partido Popular* (PP) and incorporated some UCD ex-leaders and some Christian Democratic politicians into the party. The definition of the party as Conservative and Christian-Democratic in the 1989 Party Conference—after twelve years spent in search for allies—may be a sign of party consolidation. The AP's integration in international Conservative and Christian-Democratic organizations has also contributed to stabilizing its position.

Party Integration

Several Socialist parties participated in the first general elections of the new regime: the PSOE, as a coalition of small regional Socialist parties; the *Partido Socialista Popular* (PSP)—Popular Socialist Party—whose leader was Tierno Galván and which obtained six seats (this party merged into the PSOE in 1978), and the *Alianza Socialista Democrática* (ASD)—Socialist Democratic Alliance—created in 1974, when one wing of the Socialist movement rejected González's leadership at the party conference held in France

(Gunther et al., 1986). The PSOE was able to bring together all these different Socialist options and thus made itself into a true alternative to the government. This is the only example of a party reform process carried out satisfactorily in the new political system.

Since the elections, the unstable coalition has differed from an integration model in a number of ways. In the first place, the PSOE has achieved the union of the Socialist political area by the integration of all the other Socialist parties in itself, whereas the AP cannot integrate the Right in one political force and thus finds itself in a state of permanent instability.

Second, both hierarchy and inner cohesion are imposed in the PSOE due perhaps to the abilities of the leader. The party had to face a complex internal situation, with the coexistence of historical leaders, severe critics and many young people joining the party because of its possibility of becoming an alternative to the government. The crucial moments of this process were the 28th Party Conference in 1979 and the Extraordinary Conference later that year at which Felipe González obtained his reelection and succeeded in persuading his followers to abandon Marxist principles (Caciagli, 1986). No such process has taken place in the AP.

Third, as a result of the two factors already mentioned, Felipe González has remained the indisputable and hegemonic Socialist leader since his election in 1974. In contrast, the AP's leader Fraga's effort to unify all the Right around his party led to two temporary resignations and to an important renewal in the party's leadership, and the AP has only recently been able to determine its political identity.

Finally, although there is a strong leadership personality in both parties affecting the inner party as much as the outside, in the PSOE this role is positive, both internally and externally, whereas in the AP the leader's role is positive within, but negative outside the party.

In both parties the leader's influence imposes itself on the method of selection (Schonfeld, 1980; Blondel, 1987). Manuel Fraga kept his leadership in AP until 1989 despite the instability of the party, whereas Felipe González has a stable leadership in the PSOE. Jose Aznar, a young leader, has replaced Fraga, and the AP has thus undergone a generational change that the PSOE had already experienced before the transition process.

In the Spanish situation the parties' crises (1978–1979) and especially the change in their structure and dynamics since 1982, have strongly influenced the renewal of elites. The renewal and mobility rates of Spanish political elites contrast with those traditional in Spain and also with those in other current European democracies, as suggested by the theory of the "cartel party." Failures or unsuccessful leaderships are more frequent in these essentially leadership-oriented parties (Katz and Mair, 1992: 26–27), as are also the renewal of the successful leaderships weakened by time. The importance of mechanisms and formal procedures of selection is conditioned by the role each party plays in the political system.

The halting efforts of the AP to develop the organization and create successful coalitions provoked two provisional resignations of its leader and a high degree of renewal within the party elite, whereas the predominance of the PSOE in the government and public administration helped to decrease the inner tensions in the party and influenced the composition and renewal process of the party's elite (ministers, presidents of Autonomous Communities' Governments, etc.) in the Federal Committee Commission.

The personalization of power has also been a consequence of the influence of the media in the activities of all the parties, with a growing emphasis on the creation of images in the economy of the party campaign. The media, and particularly television, are the mediators between politicians and parties and society. In a country like Spain, with really low reading levels, citizens have moved from the radio to television broadcasting without the critical view given by the daily press. Although the television factor appeared after the settlement of the party system, it has modified the strategies of the electoral campaigns and propaganda and particularly the identification of the parties through their images.[1] In this sense, we might think that electors choose not on the basis of party manifestos, but rather through the comparison of leaders' images which symbolize the basic programmatic messages of the parties they represent.[2]

Although it does not necessarily follow that the audiovisual impact of party leaders' image, by itself, decides the outcome of elections, it has been, in any case, an extremely important factor, not only in specific campaigns, but in determining the nature of the new Spanish party system from its outset.

As for the parties, political transition brought about new leaders (Suárez, González) almost without previous political careers, together with a group of rather professional politicians, coming either from the underground opposition or from the authoritarian regime itself (Carrillo, Fraga). The latter ones had often to be more adaptive to the new situation and, generally speaking, have been less successful than the former ones. On the other hand, the relative young age of the leaders, along with a relative political "amateurism" and a significant parlimentary and party elite turnover clearly differentiate Spain from other European democracies

Leadership, as we noted, has particularly influenced both the PSOE and the *Convergencia i Uniò* (CiU)—Convergence and Unity. Although scarcely democratic leadership selection has been the rule, the stable and long-lasting leaderships (González and Pujol) which ruled for more than a decade favored a process of consolidation. In other cases, conflicts among leaders, especially for their selection, have generated intraparty divisions and a significant number of splinter factions, which, encouraged by the payoffs of electoral legislation and the significant public funding of electoral campaigns, can explain the continuous increase in the number of lists running at general elections through the years (Montero and Torcal, 1992).

THE NATURE OF THE SYSTEM

Is the Spanish system a unitary one with different subsystems corresponding to nationalities and regions or, on the contrary, is there a plurality of differentiated party systems each with its own characteristics? To answer this question, it is important to analyze three different periods in its development: the first one begins with the first elections (1977) and finishes with PSOE's victory in 1982, corresponding with the governments of *Unión del Centro Democrático* (UCD). The second period covers the Socialist governments with absolute majority, and the third, after the 1993 election, when the distance between the two major parties had been reduced and the government was forced to look for allies in the Parliament in order to achieve the majority

First Period: 1977–1982

The party system that emerges from the first democratic elections after the death of Franco in 1977 (Table 12.1), which remained unchanged until the 1982 elections, is a system first dominated by Adolfo Suarez's *Unión de Centro Democrático* (UCD) coalition of small parties covering a wide political spectrum from reformist Francoists, through Christian Democrats and Liberals to Social-Democrats. Overall, the party system consisted of twelve parties, but only six were significant: two major parties, one of center-right (UCD) and the other one in the center-left (PSOE); two minoritarian parties, one on the Right (AP) and the other on the Left (PCE); and, lastly the Basque and the Catalan nationalist parties (*Partido Nacionalista Vasco* and *Pacte Democràtic de Catalunya/Convergència i Unió*, respectively).

The UCD was the strongest party, although it did not obtain a majority in the *Cortes Generales* (Parliament and Senate), but won two general elections (1977 and 1979). Its fall began with the successive defeats in the 1979 local elections and continued through the four regional elections held in 1980–1981 (in the Basque Country—PNV, in Catalonia—CiU, Galicia—AP and Andalucía-PSOE) and, as noted earlier, the party disappeared in 1981.

The PSOE became the second electoral and parliamentary force, followed by the PCE and the AP. Two nationalist parties, the Basque PNV and the Catalan electoral coalition PDC, afterwards CiU, were also represented in Parliament, with respectively seven and eight seats.

This period is characterized by consensus politics with the participation of all the parliamentarian forces in the writing of the Constitution (1978) and the Statutes of Autonomy of the historical nationalities (Catalonia, the Basque Country and Galicia), which then broke down with the discussion of the Statute of Autonomous Region of Andalucía. Consensus politics resulted from the effort of the democratic forces to establish and consolidate Democracy. The party in government, UCD, ruled without forming a formal ruling coalition and with the parliamentary support of the Catalan and/or Basque nationalists, depending on the agreements, and of the conservative party AP

Table 12.1
Spanish Electoral Results, 1977–1996

Parties	1977		1979		1982		1986		1989		1993		1996	
	% votes	n. seats	% votes	n. seats	% votes	n. seats	% votes	n. seats	% votes	n. seats	% votes	n. seats	% votes	n. seats
UCD	34.6	166	35.0	168	6.8	11	--	--	--	--	--	--	--	--
PSOE	29.3	118	30.5	121	48.4	202	44.6	184	39.9	175	38.7	159	37.5	141
AP-PP	8.3	16	5.9	9	25.9	105	26.2	105	26.0	107	34.8	141	38.9	156
PCE	9.4	20	10.8	23	4.0	4	4.5	7	--	--	--	--	--	--
PSP-US	4.5	6	--	--	--	--	--	--	--	--	--	--	--	--
PDC	2.8	11	--	--	--	--	--	--	--	--	--	--	--	--
UC-DCC	0.9	2	--	--	--	--	--	--	--	--	--	--	--	--
PNV	1.7	8	1.5	7	1.9	8	1.5	6	1.2	5	1.2	5	1.3	5
IU-IC	--	--	--	--	--	--	--	--	9.1	17	9.6	18	10.6	21
CDS	--	--	--	--	2.9	2	9.2	19	7.9	14	1.8	0	--	--
CiU	--	--	2.7	8	3.7	12	5.0	18	5.1	18	4.9	17	4.6	16
CC	--	--	--	--	--	--	--	--	--	--	0.9	4	0.9	4
HB	--	--	1.0	3	1.0	2	1.1	5	1.1	4	0.9	2	0.7	2
Others	8.5	3	12.6	11	0.8	4	7.9	6	9.7	10	8.6	4	5.5	5
Total	100.0	350	100.0	350	100.0	350	100.0	350	100.0	350	100.0	350	100.0	350

and the PSA-PA's Andalucists. The UCD's split and following disappearance was a product of the disagreements among the "family" members of the ruling party.

The inner crises of the ruling party (UCD) and the PCE put an end to this period, with the complete disappearance of the first, broken into diverse parties which would join Fraga's rightist coalition or the PSOE, or would create a new party, as in the case of Adolfo Suárez (*Centro Democrático y Social*, CDS). The PCE attempted to discipline inner militant sections and split when those dissenters created a new party. These two crises had a notable electoral importance, as they liberated wide social sectors which had voted both political forces.

The 1982 elections, after the 1981 coup attempt, appeared polarized between two parties, PSOE and *Coalición Popular*, the AP's new name. The PSOE, with a slogan ("the change") that captured Spanish society's sensibility at the time, obtained the majority of seats at the new Cortes Generales.

Second Period: 1982–1993

The PSOE's victory in the 1982 general election came with a great plurality of votes (some ten milion) and a majority in the two legislative chambers, mostly due to Felipe González's charismatic personality, defined as the Socialist "electoral engine." Personification of leadership is one of the Spanish systemic characteristics, as elections have become an audiovisual confrontation of the leaders who personify the party and its ideals.[3] This victory had a continuing positive effect for the Socialists, who also obtained the majority of the thirteen regional governments in the 1983 elections, and gained votes also in the same year's local elections.

The UCD's electoral collapse and following disappearance, together with the PCE's crisis, contributed to the restructuring of the electorate. The newborn CDS, led by Adolfo Suárez, was not able to collect the old centrist vote, a failure that increased the vote of the *Coalición Popular* (AP) and the PSOE. The latter party also took advantage of the Communists' crisis, gaining part of the PCE votes.

The most decisive moment for the Socialists in their first mandate was undoubtedly the issue of the Spanish membership in NATO. The policy change of the party leadership, from its refusal to enter the Alliance when it was an opposition force, to (once in government) a determination to remain in NATO, caused a bitter campaign for the referendum called to solve the question. The government's position was successful and in the 1986 general election the PSOE obtained a new victory that confirmed its electoral support with majorities in both chambers. The coalition of rightist parties obtained similar results to the previous elections, the CDS experienced a strong increase—from two to nineteen deputies—and the PCE also gained seats, albeit remaining at lower levels than in the period previous to the crisis.

Although Socialists maintained their force at the 1987 local elections, they lost some regional governments to statewide Right and Regionalist parties.

The 1989 general election was influenced by the general strike of December 14, 1988—jointly summoned by the majoritarian trade unions, including the *Unión General de Trabajadores* (UGT)—Workers' Trade Union—and particularly by the erosion caused by seven years of government and management of the economic crisis. The PSOE obtained the largest number of votes, the majority at the Senate and a near majority, lacking one seat, at the Deputies' Chamber.

This party system can be defined as a dominant party system. A single party obtained majorities at successive general elections, and also obtained, regained and kept most of the principal cities at the three local elections (1979, 1983 and 1987) and most of the seventeen regional governments. From the 1991 local and regional elections we can begin to see a turning point as various coalitions formed around the *Partido Popular* (PP) to replace the PSOE in the control of the main cities (Madrid, Sevilla and Valencia are the maximum exponents), although in half of the regional governments the same relation of majorities stays in force, that is, the PSOE kept its primacy.

This period is characterized by the divisions within the Right, unable to create a homogeneous electoral space and plagued by internal crises.

The CDS turned out to be a "short life" party that sank after the 1993 elections; as partisanship "engineering" that was intended to build up a center-oriented party failed (1989); while the AP made its way through its own refoundation period, culminating in the emergence of Aznar as new leader.

Third Period: 1993–1996

These changes together with some others that occurred between both executive and legislative bodies, allow us to talk about a path toward a new era in the political system and the party system that clearly emerges after the 1993 political elections.

The 1993 and the 1996 legislative elections opened a new definition period in the Spanish party system, with the PSOE (1993–1996) and the PP (since 1996) ruling with a simple majority. One can wonder whether the 1982–1993 era was exceptional and if the party system turns again to the original design that was initiated by constitutional founding fathers. That framework was meant for not allowing any party to govern without the consensus of the rest of the House.

NOTES

1. In this respect, Puhle states that "it must be taken into account that post-Francoist Spain is one of the first cases (in the "first world," at least) where party system has established itself after TV has conquered hegemony in the mass media market, thus being able to model the new mechanisms of political advertising and electoral cam-

paigns. As far as we know, more traditional vehicles and instruments of political action have not had a relevant impact on electors' mobilization and choice, and have often been limited to distributive functions. The 1982 general election campaign, as previous ones, took place mainly on TV screens, where the leader incarns the party, be it alone or surrounded by some of his/her collaborators" (Puhle, 1986).

2. Sani, in this same line, states that "party leaders enjoy, in Spain and elsewhere, an enormous public visibility and, for many electors, they are the symbol of party and its policies. There are reasons to think that the images projected by parties' leaders and, even more, the comparative assessment made by voters, have become another dimensions of the political composition of the vote."

3. As Valles puts it, "the mentioned circumstances—lack of programmatic definition, scarce reciprocal criticism—together with the modern advertising requirements, also lead to a personification of the political options. The election becomes in fact 'presidential' instead of parliamentarian, and attention is focused mainly on the leaders' images."(Valles, 1981).

REFERENCES

Aguila, J. (1980). *El sistema de partits polítics al País Valencià*. Valencia (Almudín).

Aguila, R. and Juan R. Montero (1984). *El discurso político de la transición española*. Madrid: CIS, p. 221.

Barnes, Mc. (1986). "Volatile Parties and Stable Votes in Spain." *Government and Opposition* 21: 32–61.

Bartolini, Stefano (1982). "Gli iscriti ai partiti di massa: Analisi dell'esperienze socialista in Europa (1889–1978)." *Rivista Italiana di Scienza Politica*: 12: 241–278.

Blondel, Jean (1987). *Political Leadership*. London: Sage.

Botana, N. and A. Mustapic (1988)."La reforma constitucional frente al régimen político argentino." Doc.101, Centro de investigaciones sociales, Buenos Aires.

Botella, Juan (1984). "Elementos del sistema de partidos políticos de la Cataluña actual." *Papers* 21: 27–45.

Caciagli, Mario (1986). *Elecciones y Partidos en la Transición Española*. Madrid: CIS.

Caciagli, Mario and Piergiorgio Corbetta (1987). *Elezioni Regionali e Sistema Politico Nazionale*. Bologna: Il Mulino.

Cayrol, Roland and Colette Ysmal (1982). "Les Militants du PS, Originalité et Diversité." *Projet* 165: 572–586.

Colomé, Gabriel (1989). *El Partit dels Socialistes de Catalunya*. Barcelona: Ediciones 62.

Cotarelo, R. (1992). (ed.) *Transición política y consolidación democrática en España*. Madrid: CIS.

Cotarelo, R. and Lourdes Lòpez-Nieto(1988). "Spanish Conservatism, 1976–1987." *Revista de Estudios Políticos* 2: 80–95.

Corcuera, J. and A. Perez Calvo (1979). "En torno al referéndum del Estatuto de Autonomía del País Vasco. Notas sobre el subsistema de partidos vasco." *Revista de Estudios Políticos* 12: 179–196.

Corcuera, J. and M.A. Garcia Herrera (1980). "Sistema de partidos. instituciones y comunidades nacionalistas en Euskadi," *Revista de Política Comparada* 2: 155–190.

De Esteban, J. and L. Lopez Guerra (1982). *Los partidos políticos en la España actual.* Barcelona: Planeta.

Duverger, Maurice (1981). *Los partidos políticos.* México: FCE.

Gillespie, Richard (1992). *El Partido Socialista Obrero Español.* Madrid: Alianza.

Gunther, Richard, Giacomo Sani and Goldie Shabad (1986). *El sistema de partidos políticos en España. Génesis y evolución.* Madrid: CIS.

Justel, M. (1991). *El líder como factor de decisión y explicación de voto.* Working paper no. 51 (ICPS). Barcelona.

Katz, Richard and Peter Mair (eds.) (1992). *Party Organizatons: A Data Handbook. Party Organizations in Western Democracies.* London: Sage.

Linz, Juan (1990). "Democracia, presidencialismo, parlamentarismo. ¿Hace alguna diferencia?" In Oscar Godoy Arcaya (ed.), *Hacia una democracia moderna. La opinion parlamentaria.* Santiago: Universidad Catolica de Chile.

Linz, Juan et al. (1981). *Informe sociológico sobre el cambio político en España, 1975– 1981.* IV Informe FOESSA. Madrid: Euramérica.

Linz, Juan and Jose Montero (1986). *Crisis y cambio: Electores y partidos en la España de los años ochenta.* Madrid: CEC.

Lopez Guerra, L. (1976). "Sobre la evolución de las campañas electorales y la decadencia de los partidos de masas." *Revista Española Opinión Pública* 45: 91– 110.

Lòpez-Nieto, Lourdes (1988). *AP: estructura y organización de un partido conservador.* Madrid: CIS.

Lòpez-Nieto, Lourdes (1992). "Los sistemas representativos en las nuevas democracias." *Cuadernos de Capel* 35: 59–81.

Maravall, J.M. (1984). *La política de la transición.* Madrid: Taurus.

Marcet, J. (1984). *Convergència Democràtica de Catalunya.* Barcelona: Ediciones 62.

Martinez Cuadrado, M. (1980). *El sistema político español y el comportamiento electoral regional en el sur de Europa.* Madrid: ICI.

Molas, I. (1973). *Los partidos políticos.* Barcelona: Salvat.

Montero, Jose (1981). "Partidos y participación política: Algunas notas sobre la afiliación política en la etapa inicial de la transición política." *Revista de Estudios Políticos* 23: 33–73.

Montero, Jose (1992). "Las elecciones legislativas." In R. Cotarelo (ed.), In *Transición política y consolidación democrática en España.* Madrid: CIS.

Montero, Jose and J. R. Torcal (1992). "Autonomías y Comunidades autónomas en España." *Revista de Estudios Políticos* 70.

O'Donnell, Guillermo and Philippe Schmitter (1986). *Transitions from Authoritarian Rule. Tentative Conclusions about Uncertain Democracies.* Baltimore: Johns Hopkins University Press.

Pitarch, E. et al. (1980). *Partits i parlamentaris a la Catalunya d'avui, 1977–1979.* Barcelona: Ediciones 62.

Rae, Douglas (1977). *Leyes electorales y sistemas de partidos políticos.* Madrid: Cilep.

Santamaria, Juan (1977). "Sistemas electorales y sistemas de partidos." *Cuadernos Económicos de ICE* 1: 5–24.

Sartori, Giovanni (1980). *Partidos y sistemas de partidos.* Barcelona: Alianza.

Schonfeld, William (1980). "La stabilité des dirigeants des partis politiques." *Revue*

Française de Science Politique 3: 477–505, and *Revue Française de Science Politique* 4: 846–866.

Tezanos, J.F. (1980). "Radiografía de dos congresos. Una aportación al estudio sociológico de los cuadros políticos del socialismo español." *Sistema* 35: 79–99.

Tezanos, J.F. (1981). "Estructura y dinámica de la afiliación Socialista en España." *Revista Estudios Políticos* 23: 117–152.

Valles, J.M. (1981). "La vida electoral a Catalunya: Eleccions i referenda entre 1976 i 1980." In Equip de Sociologia Electoral de la Uab, *Atlas electoral de Catalunya (1976–1980)*. Barcelona: F. Bofill.

13

The Organizational Dynamics of AP/PP

—————————————————— *Lourdes Lòpez-Nieto*

Introduction

To examine the organization of a party that is only 20 years old would appear to be a fairly simple task. However, due to various factors, this is not so: first of all, the party was created at a time (1976) when major changes were taking place in European political systems, and these particularly affected political parties and political/electoral behavior. One well-known example of these changes was the impact of the mass media which, by altering the relationship between representatives and those they represented, gave political leadership a major role, affecting the leading role of party organizations.

Second, the history of the right wing in Spain is traditionally a "tale of disillusionment and disunity" (Cotarelo and Lòpez-Nieto, 1988: 1); a condition which has only recently and partially been overcome by democratic consolidation.[1] Disunity is largely explained by a continuing cleavage between the Center and the periphery: localism and regionalism are deeply rooted in the political classes and, consequently, there is a lack of articulation between the elite and the political center (Linz, 1985). This problem, moreover, affects the center-right wing more than the Left, and the result is a proliferation of regional political groups that are not very integrated into national politics. In addition, the former authoritarian regime encouraged an individualist approach amongst the political elite that made center—and right-wing politicians' traditional habitual independence yet more acute.

Third, the creation of the *Alianza Popular* (Popular Alliance—AP), took place at the beginning of a process of political change from an authoritarian regime (September 1976), when there was great deal of uncertainty. The seven founders of the party had all played important roles in the previous regime, each to a different extent. Although they agreed to take part in the new political system they could not agree on how to do so, and within two years only one of them, Manuel Fraga, was still an active member of the party, many of the others as well as of the party's first supporters having been expelled for voting against the new Constitution (November 1978).

Finally, the organizational uncertainty and the weakness of others parties (see Colomé and Lòpez-Nieto in this volume), was occurring at the same time that Fraga, the main leader of the party, was developing his project: providing the party with a strong organizational structure and, building alliances with politicians and groups from the center-right wing, an integrationist policy that was naturally accompanied by some tension within the party.[2] The party was found to respond to these two factors : internal divisions and the disappearance of key parties, particularly at the center-right. These factors help explain why the construction of the party was a combination of regional penetration and diffusion: there was a stable central organization that controlled the development of some of the nucleuses of the external structure, but the party also absorbed local groups that remained only basely coordinated with the central organization.[3]

As we shall see, these factors have been present throughout the party's short life. The party is, nevertheless, very tightly organized, due to the practice of two key ideas that the leader has maintained and that have necessarily affected each other. Analysis of the party clearly supports the hypothesis analyzed in this book: changes in official regulations and their interpretation and redefinition coincide with the movements of the party elite, including the rather special career of the main leader. The numerous organizational changes that have occurred in this party, open to "unstable coalitions" (Colomé and Lòpez-Nieto, 1988: 6), have enabled it to overcome the various divisions and disappearances that have occurred. But this open-party model, which is relatively autonomous and systematic, has not enabled it to achieve the political performance of the PSOE or of the Catalan coalition CiU, groups that have both, mostly thanks to their internal cohesion, remained long in power. The key characteristics of this model are: symbolic changes, institutional reforms and renewal of the elite.

Among the symbolic changes are the various different names of the party: *Alianza Popular*, an abbreviation for *Partido Unido de Alianza Popular* (PUAP), and the *Federación de Alianza Popular* (FAP); since 1989, it has been called *Partido Popular*, Popular Party (PP), although at various times it has used other names, launched during electoral processes and maintained during the subsequent legislative period (*Coalición Democrática*, CD [1979] or *Alianza Popular-Partido Demócrata Popular-Partido Liberal*, AP-PDP-PL [1982]).[4] The party logo has also changed several times, the latest one having been introduced at the 1993 Party Conference.

As regards institutional reforms, the party has held conferences almost annually (twelve in twenty years), in spite of the fact that the statutes cancelled their yearly basis in 1982.[5] This political practice is common among many European parties, demonstrating the strength, stability and vitality of such organizations, but it is almost unheard-of in Spanish parties. In the case of the PP, the constant holding of national conferences, in which the organizational structures have been modified, has had the purpose of gradually establishing the party and adapting it to its role in the political system. Like the UCD this party was originally created by exploiting its leaders' earlier positions of power, recruiting political staff from the political and administrative structures of the authoritarian regime. However, in spite of the political defeats suffered during the first three years of its life,[6] the party was able to set up an organization strong enough, both nationally and regionally, to avoid disappearing like UCD, and even to profit by that disappearance. Although it remained an opposition party nationally until 1996, it managed to become the governing party in more and more Autonomous Communities and city councils. In the period 1980–1983, the AP/PP controlled only one of the seventeen Autonomous Communities; it increased these figures to two in 1984–1987; five in 1989–1991 and eight in 1992–1995. In 1979, it gained only 2.5 percent of the 8,000 offices and its quota increased to 31 percent in 1980–1983, 27 percent in 1984–1991and 43 percent in 1992–1995.

Finally, one should mention the heavy renewal of party leaders that has taken place and affected almost all the party's internal and representative positions. This feature is shared with the other Spanish parties, and affects both public positions as well as internal leadership roles. Such constant turnover is consistent with the weakness of parties during periods of transition and democratic consolidation. The degree of political mobility, unheard of previously, may become a feature of new democracies or of this time in politics for various reasons, such as political corruption. In the case of the PP, the tendency is heightened by the effort to integrate similar parties (from the political Center and right wing), bringing a constant influx of politicians from other groups, as well as inspiring others to leave or to take, as did one politician, a temporary "rest period."[7]

The most significant exception to the principle of elite renewal is that of the main leader, Fraga, who has remained in the party since it was founded; yet his presence in representative positions is an example for the openness and uniqueness of the "careers" of most of the PP politicians. Fraga held, within the party, the positions of General Secretary (September 1976–April 1979), National Chairman (December 1979–November 1986 and February 1989–March 1990), Founding Chairman (March 1990, onward). His public positions were: National MP (1977–1987), MEP (1987–1989), member of Galician Autonomous Parliament and of the Galician regional government since 1989.[8] These are all examples of the organizational flexibility of the party, which has mirrored and also led to successive reforms in the statutes.

Table 13.1
AP/PP Members and Percentage of the Electorate*

Year	Members	% of Electorate
1979	5,000	0.47
1981	20,000	-----
1982	85,412	1.5
1984	163,062	------
1986	223,068	4.3
1988	246,678	------
1989	262,755	5.0
1991	300,988	-----
1993	326,960	4.0
1995	490,223	

*Index according to Katz and Mair (1992a: 329–345): membership by overall national electorate.
Source: membership data from the party's central office.

THE ORGANIZATION OF THE POPULAR PARTY

The Party on the Ground

The party's current organization is the result of its adaptation to its gradually increasing presence in representative bodies, particularly in regional areas, a presence which has corresponded to the main periods or cycles of the political system.[9] Membership developed on a parallel with these periods of party institutionalization (see Table 13.1), and grew steadily from the second half of the second period (around 1982). This was partly due to the central headquarters' greater control of membership and partly to the general environment of low political participation that occurs in democracies nowadays. The year 1982, which was the year of the collapse of UCD, and the latest period, when the party became established as an alternative power (1990–1992), are two periods which have seen a dramatic increase of new members. The party is fairly evenly established regionally, as can be seen from both the distribution of members' votes and deputies. The sole exceptions are the Basque Country and Catalonia, thanks to the presence of strong regional-nationalist parties close to PP (Table 13.2). In other regions internal difficulties of either personal or ideological nature led the middle-level elite to often found new parties or to back non-AP/PP candidacies, particularly in regional elections.[10] During the latest period, there has been a major renewal of middle-level positions which would appear, among other things, to be aimed at coping with the party's usual conflicts by creating new leaders, particularly in regional areas. In 1993 the party adopted a rule of "incom-

Table 13.2
Distribution of Party Votes, Members, Delegates and Offices by
Autonomous Communities, 1993

	Votes (N.)	Votes (%)	Party members	M/V(*)	Delegates (%)	Offices (N.)
Andalucía	1,193,389	29.9	57,133	4.8	17.5	166
Aragón	249,444	32.9	9,330	3.7	3.8	20
Asturias	256,857	37.6	8,727	3.4	2.4	19
Baleares	191,120	46.4	7,356	3.8	2.4	28
Canarias	274,311	34.0	12,746	4.6	3.8	40
Cantabria	121,610	37.0	7,061	5.7	2.2	11
C. Mancha	462,519	43.1	22,961	5.0	8.6	56
C. León	768,360	47.5	29,065	3.9	13.9	44
Cataluña	622,866	17.1	16,468	2.6	4.9	57
Extremadura	237,615	35.9	17,931	7.5	4.8	29
Galicia	734,203	47.4	42,978	5.8	12.0	60
Madrid	1,368,928	43.9	36,167	2.6	7.8	58
Murcia	310,237	47.4	15,757	5.1	3.8	39
Navarra(*)	111,519	36.1	-	-	-	-
Rioja	78,452	46.3	3,425	4.4	1.6	8
P.Vasco	175,145	14.7	2,240	1.3	1.7	13
C.Valenciana	985,996	40.6	35,282	3.6	9.0	131

*The PP had an agreement with the UPN (Regionalist Party): members and offices belonged to the UPN, but in national elections the list is PP.

patibility," declaring that no one could occupy both elected and internal party positions, a change intended to encourage exclusive dedication to party affairs by those in regional leadership roles, as well as to reduce tensions caused by double mandates.[11] It is difficult at the moment to assess the advantages of such a mechanism, because of the short amount of time that has elapsed, but one would have to examine, among other things, how the coordination mechanisms between the internal organization and elected candidates actually work.

The middle-level party elite is a faithful example of the sociological profile of present members, and of change in membership that has taken place over the last ten years.[12] From 1981 to 1993, the members tended to become older, and live in small rural towns and large cities. The professional profiles of both members and of the middle-level elite are composed of employees and professionals who "guarantee" greater professionalism in Parliament.

Moreover, the PP/AP seems to have softened its "ideology." In 1981, 50 percent of the delegates to the Party Conference put themselves on positions 8–10 of the ten-point Left-Right scale, while only 29 percent did so in 1993. *A contrario*, in 1981, 26 percent located themselves on the center-right (positions 6–7 of the scale) and they increased to 42 percent in 1993.

Organizational Chart and Regulations

At each of the twelve conferences the party held, statutes[13] were presented and discussed. Modifications were aimed at adapting the organization to the political requirements of each period. Changes have involved integration into party structures of: (a) individuals (when coalitions were being formed or distinguished politicians from other parties joined); (b) elected officials (mayors, members of Parliament and other autonomous officials, members of European Parliament) (as they began to occupy positions in new political structures); (c) members from other regions or those living abroad, and related organizations (such as the youth organizations, *Nuevas Generaciones* (NNGG)), when these grew significantly and became established. The integration process consisted of incorporating people or groups, ex officio, into the two national executive bodies (the National Management Committee (JDN), and the National Executive Committee (CEN)), both of which have existed throughout the party's history. The internal composition of these has changed, increasing the number of members or, at different times, creating new subpositions (vice-secretariats, deputy general secretariats, coordinators, etc.). In 1993, the CEN was composed of 53 members: 8 ex officio, 15 members of the Secretary staff, 30 elected in the party internal competition. Overall, 47 out of 53 are public officeholders. There has also been a heavy renewal of the leaders that held these positions: in 1993, 61 percent of the CEN members had been appointed to this body after the 1989 refoundation of the party. Other bodies appeared (the Founding Committee, the Political Committee), but, as they depended on the situation at the time, they were temporary. Finally, other posts and committees were created in order to improve internal efficiency (the Electoral Committee) to establish better control of the party's finance (Treasurer[14]), to improve internal party coordination (intermunicipal and party-parliamentary committees) and to improve relationships between the party and its local environment (area secretaries or coordinators).

In any case, the party is officially a presidential organization with a pyramidal structure, although it is also flexible. Besides two individual positions (the Leader and the General Secretary), there are three main organs: the Conferences, the Managing Committee and the Executive Committee, the authority of which are subject to that of the party leader either directly or via those in his immediate entourage.

The party's internal organization was thus in a process of constant modification. The statutes were substantially modified on four occasions (1976–

1979, 1979–1982, 1982–1989 and 1989–1993). These dates coincide with fundamental periods in the party's history: its original creation (until 1979) and its institutionalization, with subperiods due to the reappearances and departures of the charismatic leader. Moreover, the renewal of a large part of its executive elite and the changes resulting from factors outside the party (such as election results, and the disappearance or breaking up of center-right-wing parties, etc.) must also be considered. Yet despite this volatility, in each period elements can be found that demonstrate the party's continuity.

1976–79: the original period of creation of the "coalition party," which was founded in September 1976, two months after the political transition began. The new formations that competed in the first elections were complex and heterogeneous. In this period, *Alianza Popular* was a federation (FAP) of political parties and a party (*Partido Unido de Alianza Popular*), composed of six associations created under the authoritarian legislation by a trading association.[15] This peculiar group combined a collective and federal organization with a semi-presidential structure and two collective organisms (JDN and CEN). However, Fraga and the sectors around him (RD) soon began to take the lead in key national positions. This did not occur in many regional areas of the organization, however, which had a higher number of former Franco supporters. In any case, the external image of the group was one of neoauthoritarianism.[16] This public image lasted many years, in spite of the expulsion from the party in 1978 of the leaders and militants who were most closely identified with the authoritarian regime, probably because Fraga accepted his right-wing position in the political spectrum. It was only with the disappearance of UCD in 1982 that the party was able to pick up part of the central electorate (see Chapter 12, this volume).

The party's institutionalization process began at the end of 1979. Once the first legislative and local elections were called, Fraga sought reformist political figures to join the party and head some of the candidacies in its lists.[17] After the poor election results, he left the party for a few months, during which an effort was made to organize and reinforce the party's internal structure. The period of creation was over, although the changes that were made were so substantial that it could almost have been called a new party. This hypothesis must be dismissed, however, mainly because of the continuity of the leader and a small executive core, as well as some basic structures which, although materially weakened, remained in place.

1979–1982 was the first subperiod of the institutionalization process, beginning with the Third Conference in December 1979. The financial situation was very precarious and this undoubtedly restricted efforts to build the party. The chairmanship was permanently established in the person of Fraga, and the Foundation Committee, a collective organ composed of the founders of the party, was abolished. National headquarters were established and began to undertake substantial technical responsibilities. Regional organization was also handled from Madrid, via the General Secretary and various departments at headquarters. These departments were consolidated by the remains of the party core that had not been expelled, and new ones were created by central headquarters, with careful attention to their progress as the party prospered in the wake of the disappearance of the UCD.

1982–1989: the Socialist victory by absolute majority stimulated process of incorporation of, or coalition with, center- and right-wing groups and individuals, as the party sought to counter the Socialist lead in regional areas. The emergence of new "Autonomous Communities"[18] provided a further source of renewal. Members of Parliament and Autonomous Communities' Government officials were incorporated into the party's main bodies and the Political Council was created to coordinate regional elected officials with the party's central organization. By 1987 this strategy began to show results for the center-right and its nucleus around the PP, as electoral distances from the PSOE began to lessen and, in come cases, exceed them. On the other hand, the Socialists remained in the lead in all the national institutions[19] and this may be one of the factors that explained the PP's increased internal activity. Four conferences were held in which the headquarters and the two main collective organisms, JDN and CEN, were reinforced, although their tasks were successively readjusted for various reasons including a lack of stable definition in policy priorities, and rapid leadership turnover as Fraga departed and open lists were used for electing collective positions.[20] In any case, the central organization was strengthened and consolidated. It found a new headquarters and hired new staff, thanks to the better electoral results and the generous public funding that the parties approved for themselves at this point. The central headquarters centralized the membership files, and members received more attention in the organization, which in turn led to more frequent reference to rights, duties and discipline within the party. The party's regional organization was still handled from Madrid, and acquired new strength because of the party's public representation in some Autonomous Communities and town halls (Table 13.2).

THE PRESENT ORGANIZATION: 1989–1996

This period began with the so-called "re-foundation of the party" (Ninth Conference, January 1989), a reform basically intended to establish the party as a "governing party." In order to achieve this and to overcome the "Fraga ceiling," it was essential to develop a more centrist political image, since most of the electorate had moved to the Center since the beginning of the political transition. At this time the party held four national conferences in order to discuss the main alterations that were to establish the party's new image.

Changes were introduced in all the party's fields of activity: leadership, organization, program, symbols, external relations with national and foreign political groups, social sectors and, finally, electorate. The new name, *Par-*

tido Popular, with the inclusion of the term "party," was an attempt to standardize the name with that of the European parties, as well as to give more significance to the idea of "party" as opposed to that of "coalition" which had hitherto been the dominant conception associated to the *Alianza*. The new logo, along with the rest of the symbols, were the result of the greater attention associated with the party's new political activity. For the first time, relations with social groups became institutionalized via a specific section of the Executive Committee, set up to coordinate the party links with them (for example, regular information on the party parliamentary activity). A specific section for the contact with the media has also been created, as well as forms of external collaboration with experts for the party activities, training executives, also financed by new funds. These activities have revealed a greater sensitivity and openness of the party, although the degree of the change is still quite difficult to ascertain, since the old relations are still important.

Although AP belonged to the International Conservative group since 1982, its position was one of great isolation. During this period the party joined the European Popular Party and increased its presence in international center-right-wing organizations, both in Europe and in Latin America. European leaders have been invited to electoral campaigns and conferences, and the PP has been one of the first European parties to accept foreign members. As for the relations with other Spanish regional and center-right-wing parties, federate integration and "last-minute" electoral coalition have been dropped. On the other hand, government agreements are made on a regional basis from a stronger (or less subordinate) position. Meetings are also held more frequently with leaders of the two main regional nationalist parties (PNV and CiU). External relations are becoming more "normal," compared to the little attention they received before.

But the scope of these transformations, which was larger during this most recent period, was mixed (Panebianco, 1988): the change was only partly necessary, intentional and outwardly aimed, and this can be seen in all the points that were changed and in their thoroughness. The result of the 1993 election and moreover of the 1996 election which gave a majority of seats to the PP is only partly linked to its new professional approach, since the PSOE is worn out by ten years in power and frequent involvment in cases of corruption.

The organizational change has been horizontal, as well as vertical: practically since the beginning of this period, the PP has had a young new leader, José-Maria Aznar,[21] representing a generational change in the party. The executive bodies he has set up have greater stability and cohesion, since elected with a new formula: a closed list is presented along with the presidential candidacy, of approximately 30 people elected by majority vote. They are made up by UCD executives (25 percent) as well as by some of the older Fraga entourage, most of whom were co-opted or appointed ex officio.[22] However, Aznar promoted two other components: a young generation (35–

40 years old) who joined the party recently; an intermediate age group (of which the General Secretary is a member), who have held important positions in the party practically since it was refounded. This varied executive group occupies headquarters (which employs a staff of around 200), and is also the hub of the main collective organism between conferences, the CEN and its permanent committee. At the last two conferences, the leader made new appointments, many of whom are women, to public positions such as town councils, regional governments or parliaments; in the last two CENs, 90 percent were members in public offices.[23] This is clearly in tune with the party's higher government profile and the heavier influence of this "side" of the party (Katz and Mair, 1992b), which becomes decisive. The new leader also has advisors from outside the party who have a large influence on decision-making. This, of course, generates internal tension at times, but shows the increased "technicalization" of the political task.

This generational renewal has been even more acute in the party's regional organisms, where the rule of "incompatibility" has also been introduced. It is as yet too early to assess the political and electoral performance of these reforms, although the party did well in the regional and local elections of 1995 and the rule of incompatibility clearly gave militants new opportunities for party posts (and thus the advancement of their political careers). In addition, many of the technicians recently appointed to important posts in regional and local administrations have subsequently become active militants in the party.

Another demonstration of the generational renewal is to be found in the increased importance and independence of the party's most important flanking organization: the youth organization *Nuevas Generaciones* (NNGG). This organization, which was created at the time of the party's origins, has now taken a strong leadership role, not only because of the size of its membership, but also because of the growing influence of its members in the party's executive bodies and in various public positions, giving the party a new composition and image: for example, 577 members of the NNGG are local councillors, 15 are regional deputies and 5 members of the Parliament.

The party is now taking a more pragmatic and empirical approach to politics. The principle of legality defines responsibilities among the executive organisms and is combined with greater organizational flexibility, permitting the party to take into account Spain's "assortment" of regional peculiarities, while at the same time centralizing responsibilities. This process reinforces headquarters and the relationship between party organs and elected officials. One of the organizational novelties of this period has been the establishment of mechanisms for building stronger ties between the party and its newly elected representatives in the European Parliament, the national parliament, the parliaments of the Autonomous Republics and the town councils. As such officials have a strong influence on executive organisms at all levels of the party (see, for example, the percentage of members of Parliament in the

CEN), it is important, but not easy, for the party to find new ways to bring them into accord with party practices and policies.[24]

Furthermore, the donation to the party of a part of elected officials' salaries has for the first time been made compulsory, which is perhaps more symbolic than effective when it comes to achieving a greater degree of subordination or connection to the party.

In general, the statutory changes of this latest period are more precise in defining the responsibilities, authority and functions of the various organisms, adapting them to the party's wider public presence. They are instrumental ("framework statutes"), and contrast with the former statutes, which were more complex but less effective than those now in place.

CONCLUSION

The evolution of the AP/PP is a good example of political performers' skill in adapting to internal and external needs. Organizational changes have been carried out that respond to internal and external factors. They are both natural and rational and were necessary to permit the party to play a significant role in the political system. In the 1994 European elections, the 1995 regional and local elections, the PP became the first national party.

In the 1996 general elections, it overcame the PSOE both in terms of votes and seats and Aznar became Prime Minister. Change in party organization—as well as in political orientation—seems to have reached its main target: the PP is a governing party. However, PP's success has a great challenge. Balfour (1996) suggests that "it will not be easy for PP leaders to preserve the unity of the party whose different tendencies have been brought together mainly by the alluring prospect of power." But it seems that President Aznar assumed clearly this risky challenge, when he decided to select its first government (May 1996), according to the traditional AP-PP's integrative policy. Almost all the ministers (78 percent) belong to the National Executive Committee (they were elected in the National Congress [January 1996]); the rest of the ministers are independents. This percentage will go up if we sum up the president of the Chamber of Deputies and six state secretaries, which were members of the National Executive before the elections. Furthermore, between those ministers that belong to the National Executive, 54 percent entered the party before 1982; 36 percent became members in the second period of the party (1982–1989); the rest (10 percent) joined the PP after 1989. Almost all the main PP's ideological tendencies are equally represented in this first government (Liberals, Conservatives and Christian Democrats).

Finally, which kind of party is the PP? With reference to established typologies in the literature, the case of a new party, such as AP-PP, raises problems of clear-cut definition, partly because the internal changes have never been institutionalized: therefore, in a new party the traditions and interests are not solidly settled between the main leaders. In this context it is possible to define AP-PP as a party with elements of the cartel party, of the catch-all party and also of the mass party. There are some elements of a mass party: AP-PP has a significant and increasing number of militants; they play a significative role in the party electoral results: where it has party territorial organization, it used to have good electoral results; besides this fact, the militants are intensively involved in the electoral process (almost an election each year). The electoral campaigns are long and they combine traditional elements (i.e., numerous meetings) with modern instruments (i.e. mass media); the communication between different "faces" of the party combines also new channels, such as the mass media, and traditional ones such as party press and party meetings. Alongside the history of the party, the main leader, Fraga and his main successor Aznar have been building a solid organization which has an unusual size and relevance for a right-wing party.

The AP/PP shows traits of a catch-all party: it can be said so because its plural ideological definition (i.e., Liberal, Christian Democratic and Conservative); because of the the heterogeneous characteristics of both its members and electorate from a social, economic and territorial point of view. This heterogeneity can be explained by another solid idea firmly settled and developed by the two main leaders: the agreement policy with politicians and groups from the center-right wing. This traditional characteristic of the catch-all party is combined with a new one in the last cycle of the party life: a participative policy for nonmilitants in important activities (preparation of manifestos, positions in PP regional governments). This integrationist policy, which produced some tension within the party was, however, positive in modifiyng the AP/PP image. Finally, AP/PP has some elements of a cartel party: the organizational uncertainty and the weakness of the Spanish parties at the beginning of the transition process can explain the complex institutional framework built by these embryonic parties. As a consequence of this network, they became the main and nearly the sole actors of the political system; they "institutionalized" public financing, an extensive use of the public mass media and an important patronage system. The AP/PP has been enjoying all these instruments and, as a consequence, it is possible to say that this party has elements of the cartel model, in which the "party in public offices" is the main "face" of it; but it must be remembered here the role played by militants and by the headquarters; this last "face" is integrated by the central core of the party whose members also occupy the most important positions controlled by the party.

NOTES

1. The coalition of political groups, or rather, of political figures, that made up the *Union de centro Democratico* (UCD), around the central figure of President Suarez, lasted five years (1977–1982). Its members left to join other political parties ranging from the Socialist Party to *Alianza Popular* and other minority regionalist

parties. Another sector made up a new party, CDS (Democratic and Social Center) which is currently almost nonexistent, and many others have abandoned politics altogether, either temporarily or permanently.

2. For example, negotiations for incorporating center-right politicians guaranteed leading candidates in districts where seats were assured, to the detriment of members of the regional party organization.

3. Ever since the party was founded in September 1986, the group that acted as the core of the organization was the one led by Manuel Fraga, *Reforma Democratica*, later known as the *Partido Unido de Alianza Popular* (PUAP). The other groups joined through a federation of parties, known as the *Federacion de Alianza Popular* (FAP), which they left or were expelled from two years later. However, the federation was still the mechanism by which other small, weak and very personal groups joined up until the 7th Party Conference, in 1986.

4. From here onwards I shall use the initials PP (*Partido Popular*) rather than any previous name such as *Partido Unido de Alianza Popular*, PUAP or AP).

5. After the 5th Party Conference, the statutes established a two-yearly regularity for national conferences, and four years later, at the 7th Conference, this became three-yearly. However, it is only since the current leader, Aznar, became party chairman, that the Statutory Rule has been obeyed (10th Conference in 1990 and since then every three years).

6. At the first democratic election in 1977, it only obtained 16 seats out of a total of 350, and at the next election in 1979, only 9 seats.

7. Over the years, many leading politicians in the UCD and other similar parties that were subsequently created (CDS, Liberal Party, etc.) have joined the PP and are today part of the party's national organisms; others, such as the General Secretary who remained longest in the position (1979–1986), Verstringe, is currently a Socialist militant. Others have abandoned active politics, although in most cases these would seem to be temporary departures.

8. His resignations in 1979 and 1986 were due to electoral failures, although the second resignation appeared to be definitive because, when he resumed the chairmanship in 1989, it was only for a few months until he became President of the Galician Government. At the 10th Congress in 1990, he was nominated Founding Chairman of the party, which is an honorary position, although he still has a significant political influence (Colomé and Lòpez-Nieto, 1993).

9. The first two cycles were defined by Montero (1988b) and the last one by Delgado and Lòpez Nieto (1992). The transition period (1976–1982); the consolidation period, characterized by the hegemony of the Socialist majority (1982–1989); and a third cycle or readjustment which began with the 1989 elections has lasted until now. For PP, this has involved: being a minority opposition group during the first period, until 1982; a period of internal consolidation and the leading opposition party (until 1989); and since then, a possible government alternative.

10. During the first period of the history of the party (Lòpez-Nieto, 1988), I have pointed out that the building of the internal structure was conditioned, until 1978, by the ideological tension that existed between the groups that formed the AP. Many of the founders were also expelled from the party for their anti-constitutional attitude. Subsequently, various conservative and central positions have cohabited (Christian Democrats, Liberals, Regionalists), and this has caused some internal tension regarding the definition of the program of the party, particularly in regional areas. Contrasts

have also emerged as a result of the individualist attitude of a great number of politicians, a leftover from authoritarian politics, which encouraged individualism as opposed to organization.

11. Throughout the history of the AP, there have been very personal clashes among national members of the Parliament who, at the same time, presided on the regional party organizations (provincial presidents, etc.).

12. I obtained this information from a questionnaire that I distributed to the delegates at the 11th Party Conference, in February 1993. Data from another survey made at the 4th Conference in 1981 (Botella, 1985) showed a slightly different profile: members were older and had a higher professional level; there were fewer women and many provinces were not represented. The political self-location has also moved toward more centrist positions.

13. Papers on the statutes, on policy and programs are the only ones which have been discussed at every conference, and during the 9th Conference they represented the only matter of discussion. Other program proposals varied over the years, incorporating some issues (environmental or women issues, etc.), or excluding or reorganizing others (taxation policy/finance, regional autonomous organization, etc.). The interest in different policies has been the logical response to new social or political demands. These changes can also be attributed to the great distance from government tasks, which was also evident in the lack of a shadow cabinet until the last six years.

14. Spanish parties receive substantial public funds: electoral subsidies (almost every year) and annual subsidies. These items make up the bulk of their finance, although there has been some parallel income from financial operations that have brought about cases of political corruption (Castillo, 1985).

15. In order to demonstrate its openness, the authoritarian regime accepted some associations within the single party. These were joined mainly by civil servants and a large part of the unionist, regional and political organizations. Another sector of the Franco's political staff, who were in favor of a wider political reform, created officially trading associations. These were embryonic political groups, such as the one led by Fraga (*Reforma Democratica*), and those making up the UCD. Fraga, a former Franco minister, argued for the reform of the authoritarian regime in various of his writings from the end of the 1960s, although when the time came he included non-reformist sectors in his coalition party. Suarez, Prime Minister and leader of the future centrist coalition, the UCD, and who had belonged to one of the associations in the single party, occupied the political center, leaving Fraga to become the conservative force.

16. The leadership position of the Fraga nucleus was mainly seen in national organs: Fraga was elected General Secretary and Chairman, and other heads of the JDN and CEN were members of his entourage. This situation continued after the 2nd Conference (January 1978). Fraga also represented this party in the constitutional paper. This image, which was identified with the Franco regime, continued to survive later on, as shown by different surveys and analyses (Montero, 1986, 1988a).

17. At the local elections, candidatures were only presented at 12 percent of the town councils, due to a lack of party structure. This also happened to the other major parties.

18. In 1983 the process of autonomy was completed by calling the first elections for the Parliament of thirteen "non-historical" Autonomous Communities (CCAA). This regional political dimension had an internal effect on the party, which held its 6th Conference in Barcelona in 1984, just before the second autonomous elections in

Catalonia. At the autonomous and local elections in 1983, the PSOE was very successful and maintained its leadership position, while AP was the second party in these subnational elections (with very few exceptions, such as Catalonia and the Basque Country).

19. For example, Socialist authority hegemonically overruled almost all the parliamentary initiatives of the opposition, with what has become known as the Socialist "roller." At this time the basic political institutions were very weak, because the Socialist leadership was accompanied by a withdrawal of the opposition's public activity.

20. After the departure of Fraga in 1986, there was an interim leader, M. Herrero (former leader of UCD), who prepared an extraordinary Conference in February 1987 (the 8th), during which he ran as candidate for the presidency. However, he lost to Hernandez Mancha, a regional leader, in the only occasion when there have been two candidacies (Colomé and Lòpez-Nieto, 1993). Although both were traditional party candidatures, Hernandez Mancha's victory over an ex-leader of UCD is an example of the usual tension between those who had belonged to the internal organization for a long time and those who had joined from other parties. The losers, who remained to form an internal opposition, insisted that Fraga would run again at the following Conference (the Ninth, "refoundation" Conference, in 1989). This decision was taken when the Conference had already been called, and Hernandez Mancha had already presented his candidacy. In the end, Mancha did not run. The open lists that the party used in regional internal elections were used at three conferences during this period. This internal democratic procedure undoubtedly had its greatest impact at the Eighth Conference, the only competitive one.

21. In December 1989, Fraga decided to stand as candidate for the Galician autonomous elections and named the 38-year-old Aznar as chairman of the party. This position was then ratified by the Tenth Party Conference a few months later (March 1990). Several reasons justified this choice; first of all, the proposal came from the charismatic leader; then there is Aznar's skill at integration—he belonged to the party elite and had collaborated with the previous leader Hernandez Mancha, although he was part of the other camp; and finally there was his governing experience as president of the Autonomous Government.

22. The number of such officials in all the party bodies must be several times smaller than that of the elective ones: ex-officio members must be five times less numerous than those chosen by members.

23. The last CEN (January 1996) has increased its number to 58 members: 17 percent ex-officio as presidents of regional governments; 13 percent ex-officio as members of the Central Office; 8.6 percent named by the president of the party; 56 percent—including Aznar—elected by the delegates of the Twelfth Conference.

24. The problems which have arisen from local governments' financial models have brought about a number of agreements between mayors of different parties, which have at times crashed with the decisions made by the National Executive (Lòpez-Nieto, 1993).

REFERENCES

Alda, M. and Lourdes Lòpez-Nieto (1993). "The Parliament in the Transition and in the Consolidation Process, the Case of Spain." In L.D. Longley (ed.), *Working Papers on Comparative Legislative Studies*. N.P.: Appleton.

Balfour, Sebastian (1996). "Bitter Victory, Sweet Defeat: The March Election in Spain." *Government and Opposition* 31: 275–287.

Botella, Juan (1985). "Las Elites Intermedias de los Partidos Españoles: Resultados Preliminares." In *Problemas Actuales del Estado Social y Democrático de Derecho*, pp. 89–103. Alciante: Universidad Alicante.

Castillo, Pilar (1985). *La Financiación de Partidos y Candidatos en las Democracias Occidentales*. Madrid: CIS.

Castillo, Pilar (1988). "La Financiación Pública de los Partidos Políticos y su Impacto en las Instituciones Representativas." In Angel Garrorena (ed.), *El Parlamento y sus Transformaciones Actuales*, pp. 80–92. Murcia: Tecnos.

Colomé, Gabriel and Lourdes Lòpez-Nieto (1993). "The Selection of Party Leaders in Spain." *European Journal of Political Research* 24: 349–360.

Cotarelo, Roberto and Lourdes Lòpez-Nieto (1988). "Spanish Conservatism." In Klaus Van Beyme, *Right-Wing Extremism in Western Europe*, pp. 80–95. London: Frank Cass.

Delgado, Irene and Lourdes Lòpez-Nieto (1992). "Un Análisis de las Elecciones municipales." *Revista de Estudios Politicos* 76: 195–220.

Katz, Richard and Peter Mair (1992a). "The Membership of Political Parties in European Democracies, 1960–1990." *European Journal of Political Research* 22: 329–345.

Katz, Richard and Peter Mair (1992b). *Party Organizations: A Data Handbook*. London: Sage.

Lòpez-Nieto, Lourdes (1988). *Alianza Popular: Estructura y Evolución Electoral de un Partido Conservador (1976–1982)*. Madrid: CIS.

Montero, Juan (1986). "El Subtriunfo de la Derecha." In Juan Linz and Juan Montero (eds.), *Crisis y Cambio: Electores y Partidos en la España de los Años 80*, pp. 345–432. Madrid: CEC.

Montero, Juan (1988a). "More than Conservatism, Less than Neoconservatism." In Brian Girvin (ed.), *The Transformation of Contemporary Conservatism*, pp. 145–163. London: Sage.

Montero, Juan (1988b). "Elecciones y Ciclos Electorales en España." *Revista de Derecho Político* 25: 9–34.

Panebianco, Angelo (1988). *Political Parties: Organization and Power*. Cambridge: Cambridge University Press.

14

The PSOE: The Establishment of a Governmental Party

――――――――――――――――――― *Gabriel Colomé*

A HISTORICAL OVERVIEW

The *Partido Socialista Obrero Español* (Spanish Socialist Workers' Party—
PSOE) was founded in 1879 by Pablo Iglesias, and joined the Workers' International. The PSOE, among the Socialist family, is defined by its statism,
laicism, Republicanism and its tendency toward Jacobinism and centralization. It established its initial power in Madrid and in the Basque Country, but
was unable to attract members in Catalonia, one of the most industrialized
areas in nineteenth-century Spain. Although some of the PSOE members
founded the *Unión General de Trabajadores* (General Workers' Union—
UGT), in 1888 the party did develop a slight presence in Spanish politics
during its early years, and it was not until after the election of Pablo Iglesias
as Member of Parliament in 1910 that the party achieved some popularity.
In 1921 the party suffered a division as some members of the PSOE adhered
to the Third International and founded the *Partido Comunista de España*
(Communist Party of Spain—PCE). In 1930, the Socialist Party joined the
Pacto de San Sebastián (San Sebastian's Agreement), in which the democratic
forces agreed a compromise to establish a Republic after the collapse of the
monarchy. The PSOE was one of the winners in the 1931 local elections,
joining the government of the new Republic established on 14 April 1931.
In 1936, the Socialists joined the Popular Front, a coalition of Left and center-
left parties that won the February 1936 general elections, and formed a new
government. With the outbreak of the civil war in July 1936 the PSOE participated in successive Republican governments, and sometimes held the
premiership. After the collapse of the Republic in 1939, the party leaders
went into exile and the Socialist Party lost many of its members due to

Franco's repression. While the party's executive was being recomposed abroad, inside the country some Socialist groups were founded, mainly in Madrid, the Basque Country and Andalusia, and maintained few or no connection with the leaders in exile. In this period, the PSOE promoted anti-dictatorship activities but did not work with the Communist Party, owing to conflicts over the policies of the Soviet Union. In the 1974 Party Conference, held in Suresnes (France), Felipe González, leader of the party's "interior group," succeeded Rodolfo Llopis, General Secretary in exile, forming a new Executive Committee with interior members. At this point, the PSOE suffered a deep renovation that turned it into a completely new party. In 1976, it proposed the *ruptura democrática* (democratic break) with the regime and the establishment of the Republic. In 1977, in the first general elections, it became second party both in number of votes and seats and in 1978 it unified with the Popular Socialist Party of Enrique Tierno Galván (elected Mayor of Madrid in 1979). The homogenization process of the Spanish Left and center-left had begun.

The turning point of PSOE's recent history was the XXVIIIth Party Conference in 1979, in which González proposed dropping Marxism. Although this proposal was rejected and González resigned, at an extraordinary conference held later in the year, he was reelected and the party agreed not only to his unquestioned leadership as General Secretary, but also to the definitive abandonment of Marxism. In 1982, the Socialist Party won the general elections and formed a mono-color Socialist government under the presidency of González. The party's traditional pacifist and anti-NATO position changed: in the referendum held in 1986 to decide what Spain's role should be in the Atlantic Alliance, the party campaigned for staying in the organization. This caused its Left wing, led by Pablo Castellano, to leave and found the *Partido de Acción Socialista* (Socialist Action Party—PASOC) which joined in turn the Communist Party in the *Izquierda Unida* electoral coalition (United Left—IU). Under the Felipe González government Spain joined the European Economic Community. During these years, the Socialist-inspired Trade Union, UGT, led by Nicolás Redondo, loosened its ties with the Socialist Party. The PSOE gained control over local government, in particular in the biggest cities, as well as in most of the Autonomous Communities. At the same time, it increased membership dramatically (Table 14.1).

In the early 1990s, the party was shaken by incidents of corruption which provoked, in particular, the resignation of the party General Vice-Secretary (Alfonso Guerra) from his position of Vice-President of the Government in 1991. From then on a leftist and populist tendency emerged within the party, a sort of a "*guerrista*" wing opposing the *liberal* wing represented by the Ministers of Economy of the Government, such as Carlos Solchaga. The inner break was even more visible in the results of several elections that took place in the beginning of the 1990s (Gillespie, 1992), as the *Partido Popular* (Popular Party—PP) steadily gained electoral positions. Finally, in the general

Table 14.1
PSOE Members at Conference Year

Conference	Year	Membership
XXVI	1974	3,000
XXVII	1976	6,000
XXVIII	1979	150,000
XXIX	1981	99,408
XXX	1984	152,000
XXXI	1988	212,942
XXXII	1990	262,895
XXXIII	1994	350,000

Source: official data provided by the party headquarters.

elections of 1996 the PSOE took only 37.5 percent of the votes and was once again in opposition.

THE PARTY'S ORGANIZATIONAL STRUCTURE

On the ground, the first level of organization of the PSOE is the town. Alternative forms of organization—such as sections in the workplace—have been proposed, but rarely exist. Local sections can aggregate at the level of the provinces. The decisive local bodies, as links with the center of the party, are, however, the regional or, where they exist, the national federations. The PSOE is thus organized along the lines of the Spanish regions or nationalities. The regional federations and the national party organizations keep great autonomy, having their own congresses and programs (the latter naturally in accordance with the PSOE general orientation), as well as their own committees and Executive Commissions. In other words, the PSOE is "a political organization with a federal character" (Article 14 of the statutes). As Caciagli argues (1986: 218), " the choice of a federal structure by the Spanish Socialists goes back to 1917, at least on paper. It was made necessary after Franco's death when the question of the nationalities arose as an important issue for the new political system: the PSOE, accused of having been, in the past, too "centralist" and "statist," adapted its structures to the new requirements.

As pointed out by de Esteban and Guerra (1982: 74), "these are in any case regional groups whose activities are favored by the autonomy allowed by the party's federal structure; if they achieve control over the corresponding regional federations, they usually cooperate closely. Nevertheless, with the party leadership without any serious ideological problem, this cooperation is being favored by the Federal Committee's peculiar structure. One can add that, with the exception of Catalonia (Colomè, 1989), the various regional or national federations scarcely used this decentralization.

The division of power within the party follows a classical pattern: the Federal Executive Commission represents the executive power; the Federal Committee, the legislative; and the Federal Commission of Conflicts, the judicial. The Federal Conference, held every three years, is the top decision-making body in the party. Each body's powers are typical for those of Socialist mass parties (Duverger, 1981).

The leading bodies and their respective powers are the following:

1. *Federal Conference.* It is the party's sovereign body. Its inner working rules must be in accordance with the following principles (Article 22 of the statutes):

1.1. The Conference is made up by delegates elected by the provincial conferences.

1.2. The number of delegates is determined by the Federal Committee.

1.3. The Federal Conference defines the party's general principles, establishes its program and decides its political line and strategies.

1.4. The Federal Conference elects, by secret vote, the Federal Executive Commission, the Commission of Audits, the Federal Commission of Conflicts and a part of the Federal Committee. Candidatures must be ratified by a special commission.

2. *Federal Committee.* It is the PSOE's leading executive body, in the period between conferences (Article 27, statutes) and includes:

2.1. Ex officio members: members of the Federal Executive Commission; General Secretaries of regional parties, representatives of the Socialist Youths; the president of the parliamentary group at the *Cortes Generales* (Parliament).

2.2. Elected members are elected by the Conference, the rest by each regional party or provincial federation. The Federal Committee is, in particular, entitled to define the party's policy between conferences, to control the Federal Executive Commission's activities, to elaborate the national electoral platform and to ratify each federation's and nationality's electoral program (Art. 29, statutes).

3. *Federal Executive Commission.* It develops the nationwide policy defined by the legislative bodies (Conference and Federal Committee). In other words, the Federal Executive Commission carries out, under the leadership of its General Secretary, the party's general policy.

The party structure is complex, rigid and strong: complex because there are many levels, each part conforming to the level above it and none able to work without the rest; rigid and strong because both the party statutes and the different internal rules do regulate its inner life thoroughly and precisely.

This thoroughness is intended to guarantee participation of both the members and the diverse structural elements that form the party. It is an attempt to protect the fundamental principles of political democracy within the Socialist Party by the division of powers as well as by ensuring participation. Lower levels are represented at all higher levels. However, owing to the influence of the electoral law, the proportional d'Hondt system with closed and blocked lists, and to the party's own internal electoral system, this inner democracy is more apparent than real. The effect of the national electoral law is to force the party's local sections to establish strong contacts among themselves in order to be able to achieve agreement on the candidatures for elective offices (Duverger, 1981: 75; for the application of Duverger's definition of mass party to the PSOE, see Maravall et al., 1991; and Satrustegui, 1992). It also strenghtens the power of the Federal Committee in the final formulation of the candidatures. This need to reach agreement with other sections and to accept that the final decision will be made by the Federal Committee clearly limites the ability of each section's members to determine its candidates on its own.

Furthermore, the party's own electoral system works against internal democracy, inasmuch as the party does not permit the smallest groups any representation in its bodies. As Sartori states: "when political careers must advance through the party's career system, the key variable is the internal electoral system; and it is so because the electoral activity represents, from the leadership's point of view, the central element of their opportunities 'structure' " (Sartori, 1980: 136).

The federal structure of the party, its articulation in different levels and the vertical linkages are the three main aspects of the PSOE's organization. Puhle (1986: 578) states that "when we analyze the centralizing processes and the increase of decisions adopted at the top of the party, we must consider whether a democratic Socialist Party, relatively small and scarcely institutionalized and bureaucratic as is the PSOE, does not need perhaps in a period of democratic consolidation after decades of dictature, a higher level of centralization and centralism than mass organizations with a long life as the German SPD or the British Labor Party. But, on the other side, the increasing centralization implies some risks. It can strengthen the tendency within the party to develop a hierarchical mentality and easy obedience, reducing the potential participation and the process of decision-making from the bottom up, and do so moreover in a moment when precisely the contrary is needed: the strengthening of democratic procedures from below in order to face the increase of patronage, the pressures of the officialist sector and the *force des choses* that affect a ruling party." The crisis between Felipe González, Prime Minister and General Secretary of the party, and Alfonso Guerra, former Vice-President of the Government and General Vice-Secretary, and the internal confrontation between the so-called renewal and guerrista sectors give evidence of the dilemmas pointed out by Puhle. In any case, as the 1993 legislative campaign showed, Felipe González's leadership was the party's fundamental organizational asset. According to Mario Caciagli (1986: 221),

Table 14.2
PSOE Turnover within the Federal Executive Committee

	1981	1984	1988	1990	1994
N. of members	13	11	15	16	12
N. of new members	--	2	4	2	5
% of new members	--	18.2 %	26.6 %	12.5 %	41.7 %

"the leader's authority guarantees, finally, the loyalty of national parties and federations." Even in the 1996 national elections, the direct involvement and commitment of González has decisively contributed to the electoral recovery of the party, which lost fewer votes than forecasted.

THE SOCIALIST LEADERSHIP

The central core of the Socialist Party is formed by those members who have participated in all the Federal Committees. It concentrates around itself a numerous group of members active in the refoundation of the Socialist Party. "The inner circle of the inner circle" is, however, made up of those belonging to the Federal Executive Commission (FEC). From 1981 to 1994, only 24 people obtained seats in the main executive body of the PSOE. Among them, five were constantly members of the FEC. The rate of turnover was relatively low, with the exception of 1994 when five people who had never been on the FEC were elected (Table 14.2).

Members of the FEC thus represent the regular leadership core of the party. It cannot be said that they are a shadow power, out of the party's control, nor that power lies with a minimal core of the FEC or with new members who have acquired their own weight in the party. As Duverger (1981: 176) asserts, "people's love to imagine stories about secret powers and mysterious leaders [but this view] must be interpreted with a particular mistrust." There is evidence of an inner core of leadership, that the decision-making power goes through it. The duties and the importance of each of the members of this core may be suggestive, but do not take us further than that.

As described by the party's statutes, the General Secretary is directly elected by delegates to the Congress, as are all the members who make up the Federal Executive Committee. The Federal Congress, consisting of the delegates elected by the regional federations, chooses a part of the Federal Committee (the ruling body between conferences); the rest of it is formed by the Federations' General Secretaries as ex officio (Art. 23 of the statutes).

The vote of the leading bodies is done through the delegation's spokesman according to the represented mandates, i.e., through a weighted vote. Federations with more members play a major role in the internal decision-making process thanks to this "weight."

Cayrol and Ysmal (1982: 572) state that "political parties' Conferences constitute a particularly significant issue for those interested in militants' sociology. Indeed, they gather together, in a moment full of solemnity in the organization's political culture, all the party's animators, namely, the intermediate cadres and active representatives of the base, who participate in this "tempus fortis" of their political organization's life where the party's line during the next months and years is defined, where the new leadership is appointed, where the face of the party is designed for the exterior and the media."

The representativeness of the Socialist Conference delegates has changed through the years. They represent not the members, but rather the militants, the party's so-called "inner circle," or even party elites. Botella (1980: 164) explains the nonrepresentative quality of the delegates: "[only the] more respected, more acknowledged or more ancient members of the party are likely to be elected as delegates." A Party Conference, he points out, requires intense dedication for several days and persons who cannot make that kind of commitment (older members, housewives, etc.) naturally have less chance of being elected. The prevailing cultural and social values also influence the choice of delegates, working against women's presence or in favor of a major representation of those persons with a higher cultural level. Furthermore, political parties, with the aims of creating a certain "image" among the public opinion, promote and encourage a major presence of certain sections or groups. It can be said that the Socialist Party's leadership is of a monocratic kind. Schonfeld's model (1980) can be applied to the PSOE.

The power is in the hands of a sole person who controls the party but, cannot, however, appoint his collaborators. As Puhle (1986: 342–343) states, "if the PSOE has a problem, this is not that of democratic leadership but, in the worst case, that of extending inner democracy and political participation from below. The leader seems assured, strong and indisputable, in a way not known anywhere else in the European democracies. But it depends essentially on one person who cannot be replaced even by his closest collaborators." In all the time Felipe González has been the General Secretary of the party there has never been any internal confrontation about his leadership. This seems to indicate that his leadership is not of the "primus inter pares" kind, not collegial but rather that his figure has a more important specific weight than that granted by the Socialist Party's statutes. Caciagli points out that "Felipe González has a great power emerging from the kind of situation charisma which is frequent in the period of a party's (re)construction." In this case, Caciagli adds, such power has been consecrated by the Conferences and the election of 1982. Although not all the party identifies with him, it is González who gives the party its external image, who serves as its "electoral engine," and who provides a meeting and balance-point of different forces within the party." But when a monocratic leadership enters into crisis, the effects are described as follows by Schonfeld

(1980): "because of the essential role played by the leader and the organization's tendency to identify with the leader, succession always implies a crisis. The monocrat's replacement always causes an important and brutal change of the staff and leadership as well as of the party's strategy and maybe style. With a new leader, a new organization is born."

The two leadership crises (1972–1974 and 1979) provoked a deep change in the party strategy and status. In 1972, the crisis led only to a change in the balance of the forces and the "dominant coalition"—at the benefit of the Gonzàlez faction—but did not break the party. What did change was the nature of the General Secretariat which became a collegial body, with Gonzàlez as First Secretary (López-Nieto and Colomè, 1989). The split between the two factions—"historic" and "renewed"—began at the XIIIth Conference held at Suresnes in 1974, which was not called by the appropriate person, (Rodolfo Llopis, General Secretary) but by Nicolás Redondo, an ally of Gonzàlez who had no official power to issue such a call. This coup succeeded, but instead of accepting the fact, Llopis called for an "orthodox" Conference, which took place in December. It is thus difficult to determine exactly who really split the PSOE, the "renewed" or the "historics." The latter counted on the party's legitimacy; the former on the legitimacy (conferred by) success.

The second crisis in the PSOE occurred in 1979, after the second defeat in the general elections. It was due to an ideological conflict: was Marxism still the primary reference for the party? The victory of the pro-Marxist group led to González's resignation. As the winning faction had not foreseen the need to offer alternative leadership, a new Conference was organized. Marxism was abandoned and González agreed to return to office. These two conferences were the "Bad-Godesberg" of Spanish Socialism.

We may talk of monocracy in parties where the leader is an unquestioned and unquestionable figure. Such power personalization is, however, induced by the media. One of the crucial elements of the PSOE strengthening was the González image among the voters. The media and particularly television are the mediators between politicians and parties and society; in a country like Spain, with extremely low reading levels, citizens have moved from the radio to television broadcasting without the critical view given by the daily written press. This fact has modified the forms of electoral campaigns and propaganda and particularly the identification of the parties through their image on television. In this respect, Puhle (1986) states that "it must be taken into account that post-Francoist Spain is one of the first cases (in the developed countries, at least) where the party system has stabilized after TV has conquered hegemony in the mass media market, thus being able to model the new mechanisms of political advertising and electoral campaigns. As far as we know, more traditional vehicles and instruments of political action have not had a relevant impact on voters' mobilization and choice, and has often been limited to distributive functions. The 1982 general election campaign, like previous ones, took place mainly on TV screens, where the leader incarnates the party, be it alone or with few collaborators. In the case of the PSOE, the party image, and specially its unity, resolution and steadiness, contributed to a large extent to victory. And this image was largely, and decisively, projected through TV by its leader, Felipe González."

Voters choose thus not on the basis of parties' manifestoes, but rather through the comparison of leaders' images which symbolize the basic programmatic messages as well as the parties they represent. Sani (1986), in this same line, states that "party leaders enjoy, in Spain and elsewhere, an enormous public visibility and, for many electors, they are the symbol of party and its policies. There are reasons to think that the images projected by parties' leaders and, even more, the comparative assessment made by voters, have become another dimension of the political component of the vote."

Television changes the type of leadership. It is clear that the PSOE was particularly turned toward voters and followed the trend described by Bartolini: "it cannot be doubted that social communication media have replaced membership as the key mean for transmitting the political messages of the parties to the broad masses of voters in today's highly educated and urbanized societies. The function of traditional activities of mobilization and campaigning, such as local assemblies, candidates meetings and canvassing, requiring a large investment in membership, seem to have entered into a period of decay, when faced with more efficient campaigning techniques."

It does not necessarily follow that the audiovisual impact of the party image, by itself, decides the outcome of elections, but, in any case, it can be an unvaluable help. "Lazarsfeld's analyses according to which radio broadcasting does not influence directly, but only through opinion leaders, does not diminish the importance of the fact. Mass media reach, indifferently, opinion leaders and followers, and the politician does not mind whether its speech has a direct or an indirect influence, as long as it has one" (Lòpez Guerra, 1976: 90).

It must not be forgotten that electoral campaigning aims to mobilize "undecided" voters, and to reinforce the favorable orientation of a party's own voters. Electoral campaigning has, everywhere, individualized leadership, which has come to symbolize the party and its ideas. The PSOE has the kind of undisputed and undisputable leader such a situation requires. As pointed out by Satrustegui (1992), "in effect, Felipe González's leadership doubtlessly constitutes an important factor in the cohesion of the PSOE. But it would be interesting to point out that this leadership has been consolidated not only because it is identified with the overall party objectives, but also because of its contribution to the efficiency of the entire social system. The fact that Gonzàlez has become a national leader capable of eliciting an ample social consensus (as reflected in the high-rating image received constantly in opinion polls) has at the same time strengthened the party's internal consensus based on his leadership. Yet this phenomenon is not unusual, but rather, according to Kirchheimer, is "typical of party leadership in the catch-all model" (Satrustegui, 1992).

CONCLUSIONS

In the 1970s, the PSOE undertook the integration of all the different Socialist options that were present in the first general election in 1977. This is the only example of such a process being carried out satisfactorily in the Spanish political system.

Second, both hierarchy and inner cohesion were imposed in the PSOE. González managed to unify the different factions and generations: in particular, historical leaders, leftists and newcomers joined the PSOE because of its ability to be a governing party. The highest point of this process was the XXVIIIth Party Conference and the 1979 Extraordinary Conference.

Third, as a result of the two factors already mentioned, Felipe González remains the indisputable and hegemonic Socialist leader since his election in 1974. This role was positive both internally and externally (Blondel, 1987).

The party's long term in government from 1982 to 1996 reinforced the leadership of González, but it also contributed to change in the PSOE. The predominance of the PSOE in terms of electoral influence, the exercise of national power and the following occupation of large areas in the public administration brought a decrease of inner tensions and a renewal of the party elite. Ministers, presidents of Autonomous Governments and mayors entered the Federal Committee. However, the PSOE became more and more organized around its elected officials. Membership and militants are now of little importance.

REFERENCES

Aguila, R. and Jose Montero (1984). *El Discurso Político de la Transición Española.* Madrid: CIS.

Barnes, Mc. (1986). "Volatile Parties and Stable Votes in Spain." *Government and Opposition* 21: 32–61.

Blondel, Jean (1987). *Political Leadership.* London: Sage.

Botella, Juan (1980). "Partis, parlamentaris i societat catalana." In Ismael Pilatch et al., *Partis i parlamentaris a Catalunya d'ayui.* Barcelona: Ediciones 62.

Caciagli, Mario (1986). *Elecciones Partidos en la Transición Española.* Madrid: CIS.

Caciagli, Mario and Piergiorgio Corbetta (1987). *Elezioni Regionali e Sistema Politico Nazionale.* Bologna: Il Mulino.

Cayrol, Roland and Colette Ysmal (1982). "Les Militants du PS, Originalité et Diversité." *Projet* 165: 572–586.

Colomé, Gabriel (1989). *El Partit dels Socialistes de Catalunya.* Barcelona: Ediciones 62.

Colomé, Gabriel (1992). *Socialist Parties in Europe II: Of Class, Populars, Catch-all.* Barcelona: ICPS.

De Esteban, Goige and Luis Lòpez Guerra (1982). *Los Partidos Políticos en la España Actual.* Barcelona: Planeta.

Duverger, Maurice (1981). *Los Partidos Políticos.* México: FCE.

Gillespie, Richard (1992). *El Partido Socialista Obrero Español.* Madrid: Alianza.

Guerra, A. and J.F. Tezanos (eds.) (1992). *La Decada del Cambio.* Madrid: Sistema.

Gunther, R., Giacomo Sani and G. Shabad (1986). *El Sistema de Partidos Políticos en España. Génesis y Evolución.* Madrid: CIS.

Linz, Juan and Jose Montero (1986). *Crisis y Cambio: Electores y Partidos en la España de los Años Ochenta.* Madrid: EC.

Lòpez Guerra, Luis (1976). "Sobre la Evolución de las Campañas Electorales y la Decadencia de los Partidos de Masas." *Revista Española Opinión Pública* 45: 91–110.

Lòpez-Nieto, Lourdes and Gabriel Colomé (1989). *Leadership Selection in the Spanish Political Parties.* Barcelona: ICPS.

Maravall, J.M. et al. (1991). *The Socialist Parties in Europe.* Barcelona: ICPS.

Montero, Jose (1981). "Partidos y Participación Política: Algunas Notas Sobre la Afiliación Política en la Etapa Inicial de la Transición Política." *Revista de Estudios Políticos* 23: 33–73.

Montero, Jose (1992). "Las Elecciones Legislativas." In Ramon Cotarelo (ed.), *Transicion Política y Consolidaciòn Democràtica en Espana.* Madrid: CIS.

Montero, Jose and M. Torcal (1990). "La Cultura Política de los Españoles: Pautas de Continuidad y Cambio." *Sistema* 99: 50–72.

Montero, Jose and M. Torcal (1992). "Autonomías y Comunidades Autónomas en España." *Revista de Estudios Políticos* 70: 7–34.

Morodor, R. (ed.) (1979). *Los Partidos Políticos en España,* Barcelona: Labor.

O'Donnell, Guillermo and Philippe Schmitter (1986). *Transitions from Authoritarian Rule. Tentative Conclusions about Uncertain Democracies.* Baltimore: Johns Hopkins University Press.

Pitarchi, E. et al. (1980). *Partits i Parlamentaris a la Catalunya d'avui, 1977–1979.* Barcelona: Ediciones 62.

Puhle, Hans (1986). "Un partido predominante y heterogeneo." In Juan Linz and José Ramòn Montero (eds.), *Crisis y Cambio: Electores y Partidos en la España de los Años Ochenta.* Madrid: Centro de Estudios Constitucionales.

Satori, Giovanni (1980). *Partidos y sistemas de partidos.* Madrid: Alianza.

Satrustegui, M. (1992). "PSOE: A New Catch-all Party." In Gabriel Colomé (ed.), *Socialist Parties in Europe II: Of Class, Populars, Catch-all?* Barcelona: ICPS.

Schonfeld, William (1980). "La Stabilité des Dirigeants des Partis Politiques." *Revue Française de Science Politique* 3: 477–505; and *Revue Française de Science Politique* 4: 846–866.

Tezanos, J.F. (1980). "Radiografía de Dos Congresos. Una Aportación al Estudio Sociológico de los Cuadros Políticos del Socialismo Español." *Sistema* 35: 79–99.

Tezanos, J.F. (1981). "Estructura y Dinámica de la Afiliación Socialista en España." *Revista Estudios Políticos* 23: 117–152.

Conclusion: Party Organization and Power—A Southern European Model?

—————————— *Piero Ignazi and Colette Ysmal*

FROM MASS TO CATCH-ALL PARTIES: EVOLUTION OF PARTY ORGANIZATION AND FUNCTIONS

The Apparent Success of the Mass Party

Southern European parties have basically accomplished Duverger's (1951) prescription of the mass-party model. The characteristics highlighted by Duverger in his analysis of Socialist and religious parties fit well with the left-wing organizations such as the Italian PCI, transformed into the Democratic Party of the Left (PDS) in 1991, the French PS and the Spanish PSOE; it was also adopted in 1974 by the Greek PASOK which emerged, after the military dictatorship period, in a country where there had never been any tradition of mass parties. As pointed out by Spourdalakis, "the PASOK is the first party in Greek political history to resemble a mass party with wide mass membership and a network of local committees." While the former PCI, and to a large extent the PDS too, match the requirements of the mass party (large and open membership, territorial penetration, bottom-top decision-making process, control over the elected official, accountability of leaders to representative organs, militantism, network of flanking organizations), the other Socialist parties are less accountable. The newcomers, in particular the PSOE and the PASOK, present a weaker version of the mass party. The PASOK, after its initial effort in setting up a solid organization, when entered the government in 1981, was "voided" of its internal resources as it relied on public officials and the personnel employed in the public economic sector that the party in government developed. Analogously, the PSOE, thanks to its monopolistic control of government and the adoption of a patronage practice, had "no real need to build a large party organization" (Morlino 1995: 356).

The mass-party standard imposed itself on all the other parties. Duverger's forecast of "contagion from the left" (Duverger, 1951: 25) seems to have been at work. The Greek ND moved from an assembly of notables (with a charismatic-like leader), as it was at the time of its creation in 1974, to an organized party with large membership, grassroots organizations at the district level, election of the leader not only by the parliamentary party but by a special body including representatives of the party's district units (Chapter 11, this volume). The French RPR, formed in 1976, was an attempt to transform the Gaullist cadre-parties of the beginning of the Fifth Republic into a "machine" with an appeal for members, activism, local organizations, strong national bodies and an attempt to secure a greater call for the membership in the leaders' selection process (Chapter 2, this volume). Although weak until the early 1950s, the Italian DC tried to implement a network of sections all around the country, to increase its membership and to tie up leader and members allowing more members influence over the leaders and at the same time requiring more loyalty and discipline of the members (Chapter 6, this volume). The Spanish AP/PP also emphasized open membership and set up a nationwide organization based on the Spanish regions. Its "refoundation" in the 1990s led to a higher integration of members and elected officials in the party and to more institutionalized organization: after the resignation of its historical leader (Manuel Fraga) and the emergence of José-Maria Aznar, the statutes became more precise "in defining the responsibilities, authority and functions of the various organisms making up the party organization and governing the party" (Lòpez-Nieto, Chapter 13, this volume).

Even the extreme Right parties such as the MSI/AN in Italy and the French FN followed the same path. The MSI established itself in 1948 with a formal structure derived from the mass party model: "the local branch was depicted as the basic unit of the organization and the decision-making process for the definition of the party platform followed the bottom-up flow of decision through section (local), federation (provincial) and then national Congresses" Chapter 8, this volume). Moreover, it favored (while with some ambiguities) mass recruitment and promoted a network of flanking organizations. As far as the French FN is concerned, before its first electoral successes in the mid-1980s, it was just a mere rallying point for the various extreme Right chapels. After its take-off, it succeeded in implementing an organization by largely copying the French Communist Party's model. In the last ten years, the FN has dramatically increased its membership and it has created an articulated national apparatus with executive (Executive Committee, Political Bureau) and representative organs (Central Committee and National Council) which have been adopted at regional or local levels as well. A large part of the new FN membership was not only attracted by the legitimacy attained by the party in the electoral arena but also as a consequence of the FN conscious effort to encapsulate citizens into the party organization (Chapter 3, this volume).

The accomplishment of the mass-party model of organization in all the southern European countries is not, however, complete. Some of Duverger's other requisites for a mass party are missing or have faded away in some or all the parties under consideration: these concern the functional structures (the cell or similar workplace organization); the activity of political education; and the ancillary or flanking organizations.

First, a feature of a mass party is its capacity to organize workers (salaried people in more modern terms) in their factories or bureaus. This workplace structure is not characterized by its territorial anchorage (even if territorial cell did exist at a lower level than the branch: district, hamlet, street and "block") rather than by its presence in the factories where workers are "exploited" and therefore particularly interested in changing the economic and social order. In practice, only Communist parties in France, Italy and Spain succeeded in organizing and maintaining "workplace cells" yet they represented less than 30 percent of the parties' cells. After a long decline, the PCI cell organization was dismantled when the party transformed itself into PDS in 1991. Neither the PASOK nor the PSOE really attempted to build such links between the party and its working base. The PASOK was mainly concerned with establishing clientelistic links with its electoral base through the local party "committees of solidarity" (Chapter 10, this volume); the PSOE was rather confident in its strong but conflictual relations with the unions and, in particular the Socialist General Union of Workers (UGT) (Chapter 14, this volume). The French PS made, at the end of the 1970s, some efforts to implement party sections or groups in the factories (Chapter 4, this volume). However, these groups were established only in the public sector (universities; civil servants; gas and electricity services; nationalized banks or factories) and had a very short life span. Generally speaking, the right-wing parties have always been reluctant to introduce political issues into the workplace. When trying to imitate the leftist organizations, they failed to establish the party at this level: this was the case for the DC's GIP (*Gruppi di Iniziativa politica*—Groups for Political Promotion) or for the RPR's AOP (*Association ouvrière et professionnelle*—Association for Workers and Salaried). As a consequence, they preferred to create, within the parties and at a national level, "commissions," "associations," "groups" or "sectors" as meeting points for various categories (farmers; managers; professionals; employees and sometimes blue-collar workers) belonging to the party.

Second, a mass party should perform a function of political education for people who are marginalized by both the political and the social systems. The underprivileged can make up their "handicap" if the party provides efficient means to increase their level of political awareness and competence. Traditionally, both Communist and Socialist parties organized schools that provided some knowledge about the party program, history and ideology values. This kind of activity was questioned for its dogmatic tendency and few parties, in the 1990s, are actually now interested in the formation of their membership. If existing in party organigrams, "formation sectors" are devoted to party cadres or to elected officeholders (at local or national level) and are centerd either on specific issues or on how to communicate with the electorate through the media.[1] The only exceptions are the former Communist PDS (to an increasingly limited extent) and the extreme Right French FN, cautious to maintain its strong ideological control over its membership.

Third, and last, flanking organizations established by a mass party under its control achieve a double function: they are not only a channel of participation and a means to improve parties' links with civil society but also a sort of "counter-society," organizing their members along the party's values.[2] Many southern European parties have never designed their organization along this pattern. This is the case of the French PS and RPR, the Greek PASOK and ND, the Spanish PSOE and AP/PP, which never developed an extensive network of organizations, associations, unions covering all the dimensions of the social spectrum (young and retired; workers and shopkeepers, small and middle entrepreneurs and managers, veterans and alumna, and so on) or acting in different domains as culture, leisure and sport. In those parties, only youth and women associations still exist. However, their function is less to mobilize members than to promote an appealing image of parties. Where such a network exists, as in Italy, it tends to decrease in terms of membership, linkage between the party and the citizenry or as a way to encapsulating some particular social/political categories as well.

The long tradition of flanking organizations that have been the basis of the widening influence of the PCI/PDS in the civil society was weakened when the flanking organizations obtained autonomous resources, both political and organizational (Chapter 7, this volume). In an other vein, the Italian DC, long before its collapse in the 1990s, had lost support from both the catholic world (associations; unions) and from some economic sectors organized by it (farmers, small shopkeepers or small and middle entrepreneurs) (Chapter 6, this volume). The MSI developed a large network of flanking organizations with a particular emphasis on the youth sector. In recent years, some traditionally important associations such as the veterans decreased in relevance to the benefit of new, less ideological associations such as the new ecological association (GRE, *Fare verde*) or the loosely tied youth and student groups (*Fare Fronte*). The MSI transformation into AN further developed the network of associations especially along occupational lines but, at the same time, their influence in the internal balance of power decreased (Chapter 8, this volume). The French FN seems to escape from this general trend. In its attempt to create a strong organization, during the 1990s, it has reinforced its youth sector, creating two students unions; it has set up a teachers' association; it has organized the veterans (primarily those of the Algerian war), the military and the police, the professional sectors and the business groups as well (Chapter 3, this volume). This peculiar organizational trait seems to be a consequence of, on one hand, the marginal position of the FN in the French political system and, on the other hand, of its limited access to elective positions due to the nature of the French electoral system.

The Dominant Catch-All Party Model

The reason why the current southern European parties have adopted a sort of relaxed mass-party model, different from Duverger's ideal type and from the reality of mass parties of the first half of the century, is largely linked to a change in parties' functions. Even if Duverger focused his analysis on party structures, he nevertheless suggested that the main function of a mass party was to empower the participation of the "masses" (workers generally excluded by the bourgeois political elites and the "notables") into the democratic process. Elections are a channel for participation but they are neither the only nor perhaps the best. The cadre party, stemming from electoral committees, is naturally oriented toward elections and parliamentary action while Socialist and, moreover, Communist parties introduce a wider scope to their activity.[3] The mass party "is not devoted to conquest votes, to link together party elected officials and to maintain links between party elected officials and their electorate. . . . *For it, elections and parliamentary debates are but a channel for political action among others and, even, a minor channel*" (Duverger, 1951: 54–55, emphasis added).

Such a perspective was radically questioned by Kirchheimer (1966), who analyzed the transformation that the mass party had undergone since the end of World War II and suggested the catch-all model. In contrast to what was stated recently by Peter Mair (1990), who emphazised the *organizational* innovations introduced by the catch-all party, one can contend that Kirchheimer was more interested in the functional evolution of the parties than in structural changes. In fact, only two of the five features of the catch-all party regard the organizational profile: the decreasing role of the membership and the corresponding increase in freedom of action and visibility of the leadership groups.[4] In addition, those organizational modifications are subordinated to the other three features: appeal to the electorate rather than to a specific clientele (*classe gardée*); de-ideologization abandoning *Weltanshaaungen* and universal principles in favor of pragmatism and more specific issues; attention given to more diversified interest groups. These three features compound the "catchallism" property. The affirmation of such catchallism entails the abandonment of the function of "integration/disintegration"[5] in favor of an office-seeking strategy: "The nomination of candidates for popular legitimation as officeholders, this emerges as the most important function of the present day catch-all party" (Kirchheimer, 1966:

198). Therefore, the party moved its emphasis from the function of channelling or expression to the electoral and office-seeking one.

Are these transformations—concerning overcoming the class barrier "embracing a variety of other clienteles" (Kirchheimer, 1966: 185) and reducing the ideological temper—perceptible in the southern European parties?

The appeal to the citizenry at large rather than to a specific electorate has become a common characteristic of the parties under consideration. The new parties in Greece and Spain, with no difference between leftist and rightist organizations, immediately established themselves as "governing parties" (Morlino, 1995). During the period of transition as well as during the period of consolidation of Democracy, they did not organize their electoral support on class-based issues but on an appeal to the general electorate by focusing on the key issue of the time, the furthering of the democratization process. Also the Socialist parties—PASOK and PSOE—were molded by their immediate access to power in the early 1980s. On the other hand, moderate-bourgeois parties such as the DC and the RPR have *always* been "voter-oriented" and have denied the relevance of social cleavages in their electoral strategies. Left-wing parties, on the contrary, had to face a deeper transformation since they had to move from a model whose primary aim was organizing the "masses" rather than enlarging the electorate. Nevertheless, in the case of the PCI/PDS, at the end of the 1980s, the relationship between the party and the electorate changed: "the party public office-holders were no longer the mere mandatory of party decisions, but became more responsive to the electorate" (Pamini, Chapter 7, this volume). The new relationship between party-elected members and voters was partly due both to the PCI/PDS aim to become a government party and to the increasing candidate-centered campaign which allowed a greater role for the elected members. Even the French PS, which in the 1970s theorized its electoral appeal in terms of social classes, later did not escape from the general trend. Its *"front de classes"* attempted to widen its electoral support by attracting other social groups (employees, managers and executives) beyond the traditional base of a Socialist Party (the blue-collar workers). Such a rally did not rest on general principles or ideological framework, instead it relied on specific issues linked to the social groups which made up the *front de classes*. Finally, the two far-Right parties—the MSI/AN and the FN—had somewhat followed the same path as the mass leftist parties. The MSI, created along the model of the classical mass party, nevertheless always appealed to a wide sociological spectrum thanks to its cross-cutting ideological profile (provided by fascism). On the other hand, it recently abandoned a specific call to underprivileged groups such as unemployed and southern young people who had a high protest potential, in favor of more mainstream social groups. When created in 1972, the FN was a tiny and loose organization for militants attracted by and socialized by anti-parliamentarism and political violence. With the electoral successes of the 1980s, the party developed an articulated apparatus for mobilizing a larger electoral support. The FN's aim, in the 1990s, went even further in this direction and it attempted to play the role of an ultimate arbiter in the elections' ballots, a key partner in right-wing coalitions and a main challenger to the Left. Consequently, the 1995 FN's manifesto stressed this new "majoritarian vocation" (Chapter 3, this volume).

The appeal to voters and the necessity to widen the social base in order to offer themselves as a "governing party" have pushed political parties toward a general softening of ideology.

The southern European leftist parties have all moved in this direction, but at different paces. The most profound ideological change involved the Italian Communist Party which, after 1989, became progressively like a Social Democrat Party: first it lost its class character; second, claiming that the party was not an "ideological organization," it unequivocally stated that "democracy is the way to socialism"; third, at the economic level, it attenuated the statist conception inherited from the Marxist tradition (Chapter 7, this volume). The path was longer for the French PS. More than a decade after its refounding (from 1971 until the early 1980s) the PS allied itself with the French Communist Party and promoted a "French Socialism," a national variant differing from all the other experiences. Afterward, since 1983, either in government and in opposition as well, the party (partially) withdrew its program of economic and social reforms concerning nationalizations or extension of the public sector, development of welfare, social and economic rights for workers, and moved to a more mainstream, pro-market policy. The marginalization of the leftist factions (CERES) and the presidential profile of the party contributed to diluting the Socialist element within the party. The PSOE altered its ideological standings in the 1979 Extraordinary Conference that established the definitive break with Marxism. Later on, the traditional pacifist and anti-NATO positions were also abandoned and, in the referendum held in 1986 about Spain's continued membership in the Atlantic Alliance, the party was in favor of not leaving the organization.

A transformation similar to that experienced by leftist parties occurred, *mutatis mutandis*, in another ideologically intense party, the Italian MSI. The transformation of the MSI into AN, in January 1995, did not imply a "substitution of ends" as was the case for the passage of the PCI to the PDS. The manifest ideology was skillfully articulated and fascism was diluted into the mainstream of the Right ("before, during and after fascism"): fascism was not rejected but "sent back to history." At any rate, the toning down of the founders' ideological reference is uncontested. On the other hand, the French FN shows no clear trend toward softening its ideology. In recent years the party seems to be more radicalized on some political topics (immigration, violence and crime in particular), while, on the other hand, it has watered down its economic positions from "conservative liberalism" to a more pro-welfare and social-minded program (maintenance of social security provisions, increase of salaries and wages) in accordance with the demands of its voters.

Less dramatic changes can be observed for the bourgeois camp. The Italian DC in fact did not experience any significant turning point in its ideological position. It maintained a clear catholic imprint attempting to confront (quite unsuccessfully) the widespreading secularization. The changes involved policies (for example, the minor emphasis on state intervention in the economy) rather than ideology or *Weltanshaaungen*. The 1981 defeat suffered by the French RPR led the party to adopt more conservative and neo-liberal positions and a more adversarial style of competition. After Chirac's defeat in his second bid for the presidency in 1988, the RPR moved from the "neoconservatism" championed in the 1981–1986 period to more moderate positions concerning either the role of the state in the economy or social deregulation. The Greek ND experienced a process similar to that of the French RPR. The passage into the opposition in 1981 led the party to elect a "staunch right-winger" leader (Evangelos Averoff) moving to "ultra-Conservative positions" and therefore "alienating many liberal politicians of the party." This radicalization ended in 1985 with the more traditional and mainstream leadership of Constantine Mitsotakis (Chapter 11, this volume). The Spanish AP, when it transformed itself into PP in the late 1980s, gave up all references to Spain's former *caudillo* Francisco Franco and turned into a moderate right-wing party.

The general evolution toward a catch-all party focusing on elections is also highlighted by the strict link between parties' internal organizational change and electoral results. In the case of the PCI/PDS, "the main external factor which influenced, since the mid-1980s, the beginning of the renewal of the leadership was the negative electoral trend": since 1979 the PCI lost votes in local and general elections. Within the AP/PP the various electoral defeats increased the likelihood of internal changes and the necessity of a "refoundation" of the party under Aznar's leadership. The RPR was created in 1976 because the previous Gaullist organization had lost the presidency in 1974 and then the prime minister's office in 1976. The reorganization of the PS in 1969 and in 1971 was a consequence of the decrease in the electoral influence of the SFIO. The Greek ND reinforced its structures and turned into a nationwide party only when it was sent into opposition in 1981. In other cases the relationship is a positive one. The PASOK created *ex nihilo* its organization at the time of its victory; the same had occurred, many decades before, to the DC when it had become the largest Italian party by far (while recently, electoral decline was *only one* of the reasons for its collapse). In the case of the FN, electoral successes pushed the party toward the development of the party in order to encapsulate the voters and to prevent it from future defeats. The MSI implemented its embryonic project to modify its political profile (leading to AN) thanks to the electoral success in the 1994 general elections and the subsequent participation in the Berlusconi government.

In sum, southern European parties exhibit, irrespective of political alignment, size and country, a general trend toward the abandoning of the tra-ditional mass-party profile—especially in terms of political education and penetration into the civil society through flanking organizations. Even if they are still formally designed along these lines in terms of formal rules, the empirical observation tells a different story. Parties have moved toward the catch-all model as they have generally appealed beyond their traditional *classe gardée* and/or clienteles and because they have softened their ideological tempers.

POWER CONFLICTS WITHIN POLITICAL PARTIES

Both Duverger and Kirchheimer depicted the party ideal type in a sort of evolutionary process where the mass party and the catch-all party represented the final stage.[6] Southern European parties demonstrate how widespread the formal adoption of the mass party general structure and the movement toward the "catchallism" have been.

The passage to the catch-all model has been highlighted in the previous paragraph focusing on the modified *expressive function* the party has begun to perform: the broadening of the channelling of the demand appealing to larger sectors of the society and different interest groups through the de-ideologization. The incoming "catchallism" of parties has an impact on the party organization: the diminishing role of the membership and the increasing freedom of action and external relevance of the leadership groups are the more relevant structural changes. In other terms, the leadership acquires more and more power vis-à-vis members. Leaders are not totally free, however. They are constrained by "organizational imperatives." On the one hand, the constraints involve "decentralization of intraparty policy decisions, restrictions of recruitment to party offices in favor of existing activists and officers, leadership accountability to activists and members." This bottom-top relationship could be seen also as a set of vertical power conflicts within parties. On the other hand, another set of conflicts inside parties involves competing elites: these are horizontal power conflicts among party elites.

All these conflicts, both horizontal and vertical, introduce the notion of party internal power. Panebianco (1982) has offered a highly articulated interpretation of how parties are shaped by the internal power relationship. In a nutshell, his theory, heavily derived by organizational studies, sees the party organization as an arena where "exchanges" among different actors are carried out for the control of the organization. As power cannot be held by a single leader (with the exception of charismatic leadership) a coalition of actors—the "dominant coalition"—will run the party. The dominant coalition takes shape when some "political entrepreneurs" get control of crucial "zones of uncertainty" or, in other terms, of crucial resources. As already said, this horizontal power conflict among competing coalitions is paralleled by a vertical power relationship between leaders and followers or members.

The latter type of conflict involves the problem of internal party democracy and of the changing role of the party member. The former one analyses the turnover in the dominant coalition, the degree of factionalization and the style of leadership, in order to assess which kind of linkage emerges among these elements.

The Enduring Role of the Membership and the Destiny of Party's Inner Democracy

The most relevant constraints faced by party leaders in dealing with their members occur when leaders have "to put some attention" to them. As pointed out by Panebianco (1982) and Offerlé (1987) (long after Mosca, Pareto, Michels or Weber), leaders and members do not have the same resources at their disposal since the former have (or are credited to have) more competence, skills and appeal—that is, qualities that the rank-and-file are convinced not to have. Offerlé (1987: 60) highlighted the unbalanced power relations within the party and underlined "the unequal distribution of social (social origin and status, education, gender), political (seniority in the political arena certified by the success in the internal party organization and the external political market) and symbolic resources (authority that such resources confer and belief that the political leader really holds the power which he is the formal representative of)." Leaders, however, have to act to maintain the membership's loyalty to the party and to the leadership, and to distribute, consequently, some benefits to the followers.

"Members still matter," Katz and Mair (1994) insisted. They are valuable because they assess the "strength" of the organization vis-à-vis the other parties; they provide money and free labor force for campaigning and diffusion of the party programs; they mobilize for and participate in mass rallies, mass demonstrations, open meetings, public conferences; moreover, they perform the "mythical" functions of linkage with the society (Lawson, 1976; Lawson and Merkl, 1988) and of internal party democracy through selection of leaders and program approval.

The last point is quite sensitive. In liberal democratic systems, parties are forced to adopt (at least formally) democratic rules which legitimize them. All parties are founded on the premises that members are welcome and that they are entitled—like voters in the electoral arena—to give their consent to policies and leaders' selection. Among the means used to organize this *mise en scène* of participatory democracy, local and national Party Congresses appear to fulfill a central role. The Congress can be described as "the festival of the activists" since it works as an occasion of personal interaction between the grass roots and the top hierarchy of the party; leaders pay particular attention to members' demands, pay tribute to their important role in party life and make great efforts to arouse their enthusiasm—that is, their loyalty. These elements of sociability, often highly rewarding for the militants, are common to all parties. On the other hand, if one considers the different parties' statutes, party conferences do not have the same powers.

Formal or ritual democracy seems to be more secured by the Socialist parties (PASOK, PSOE and PS[7]) and by the Italian PCI/PDS, in which delegates are entitled to elect all the executive bodies and the leader and to vote for the programs and the political strategy of the organization. A similar concern for the members' role in the decision-making process is perceptible in other established, mass-like parties such as the Italian DC and MSI. In both parties the process of nomination of party Conference delgates follows a bottom-top flow. However, the space allotted to ex officio members (MPs, representative of flanking organizations, local public officials, etc.) and the internal electoral rules—plus the inevitable maneuvering by the leadership in order to influence the delegates' selection and the members' orientation—reduce the real members' role. MSI delegates were in fact allowed to elect party officeholders (and since 1987 directly, the Party Secretary); however, congresses were filled—close to 40–45 percent—by ex officio members who enable the leadership to heavily influence the outcomes. The recent MSI move to AN has strengthened the concentration of power in the hands of the leadership: it now *nominates* the National Executive body, depriving party members of a substantial amount of power.

Among the weakly institutionalized parties ND is the only one to have moved toward a strengthening of the power of its rank-and-file. Since 1984, ND members influence party decision-making and make up a part (besides sitting deputies) of the special body in charge to elect the president. The other non-Socialist and nonestablished parties allow less room for their membership in the decision-making process. Despite the great number of congresses the AP/PP do not encourage members' effective participation. Only when its institutionalization process developed, were more clear and well-defined duties and rights established; however, this better role definition did not entail a larger voice for the membership. As far as the RPR is concerned, the so-called "Assises" have a limited function in party life: while the delegates elect the president of the party, they appoint only a minority of members to the national representative organ of the party (the National Council) which has no power; and they do not intervene in the elaboration of party programs generally published before the Congress. Similarly, although the FN congress elects the president, the delegates are "just expected to applaud" (Chapter 3, this volume). Neither the party manifestos nor the party strategy are questioned by the delegates since these subjects are not submitted for comments or to a vote.

The Control over Party and Public Offices Selection

Since Michels, we have learned that the most formal democratic rules do not prevent political parties from oligarchic tendencies and that participatory democracy is a myth. Once members are rewarded with more or less short-lived and symbolic benefits, they are left out and marginalized. Accountability to membership is, for the leadership, a less important issue than establishing its power vis-à-vis other potential contenders. In this horizontal conflict among competing elites, what is more crucial, for the leadership, is to get control of "zones of uncertainty," that is, of highly relevant resources, such as members' recruitment and selection to the most important national organs and to public offices.

As far as these aspects are concerned, one can distinguish two features among southern European parties. First, parties where control is high and concentrated in the hands of a sole leader; second, parties where the power is held by a coalition of actors—a "dominant coalition"—and where the shaping of such a coalition is made through a conflict between competing coalitions in order to acquire "dominance." The FN and, to some extent, the RPR, the AP/PP, the ND and the PCI belong to the first "model." For the FN, Ivaldi stresses that: first, the national bodies nominated by the president, "ensure Le Pen's monopoly and control with places virtually all reserved for apparatchiks"; second, candidates to national or European elective offices are selected at the top of the party with no participation by the local structures; third, elective officeholders have no autonomy vis-à-vis the party and its president. If conflicts appear, the opponents are immediately expelled from the organization, if they do not choose to leave. If within the RPR, the AP/PP and the ND, parliamentarians have more power in the decision-making process (since they are generally ex officio members of the largest bodies) and more freedom in expressing their views, the leader maintains the greatest control over the more politically significant committees or bureaus. Pappas indicates that "the ND's president makes the selection and appoints the top personnel to the . . . secretariats and special offices responsible for vital issues as political planning and party programming, training of party cadres, party briefing, electoral mobilization." Lòpez-Nieto stresses the fact that "under the leadership of Aznar, most of the members of the AP/PP executive organs were co-opted or appointed ex-officio by the president." While pointing out that three selection procedures co-exist (nomination; election and representation ex officio) within the RPR, Haegel recognizes that "the principle of election grants a decisive role to co-optation" and that, when bodies are particularly important, nomination is the rule. In a similar vein, the statutes state that candidates to national elected offices are selected by the department committee; in practice the procedure seems to be more centralized since the designation is made by an *ad hoc* "commission" convened by the party president and the Secretary-General. The centralized characteristics of the PCI organization and the formal ban of tendencies allowed the leadership to exercise full control over internal careers, candidatures to public offices and, last but not the least, over the parliamentary group. In the late 1980s, however, and especially after the transformation into the PDS, the party relaxed its control over the parliamentary group; with the legitimation of factions, the process of leader selection appeared less controlled but candidate selection is still in the hands of the National Executives (even if local branches can now suggest candidates).

When parties have to cope with recognized and long-lived factions or tendencies, such as in the French PS or the Italian DC and MSI, "entrepreneurial" leaders and subleaders try and generally succeed in establishing their dominance. All the DC's organs, including the Party Secretary, were selected on the basis of the factional representation criteria. Therefore, the designation of the leader is the result of an agreement among the different factions. As Baldini noted, examining the DC leadership in the 1980s, "De Mita's main aim was to achieve the greatest benefits possible for his faction and more generally for the left of the party. In order to avoid the representation of hostile factions, he managed to have on the nominations (to the more important executive committees) a greater weight than his predecessors" and to secure posts for members of his faction or from his region. The leader's power was, however, limited by the other factions and their subleaders that could not be totally eliminated from the party Executive Committee, and kept control over the candidatures to elected offices, each of them sponsoring their own candidates. A similar situation exists within the French PS. In the 1970s, Mitterrand promoted his own entourage or his closest backers as members of a personal cabinet not really controlled by the party; moreover, he supervised very closely candidatures to the party executive bodies, not only choosing his own tendency's candidates but also those of the other tendencies. His ability to design the party bodies was, however, strictly linked to his position as leader of the most important faction. That is to say that Mitterrand's apparent "freedom of action" was a consequence of the attitudes of the different tendencies which chose not to contest the leadership and attempted to enter the Mitterrand's "dominant coalition." The factions and their leaders were always free to oppose the leader as they did in 1979. On the other hand, even after they were integrated into the party majority, they always contained the leadership and the candidate selection process as well. Once Mitterrand was elected to the presidency in 1981, the factions rearranged their relationship in order to gain the leadership and to consolidate their control over the "zones of uncertainty."

Since the MSI adopted the mass-party model of organization, the executive bodies exercised control over the elected officials and especially over MPs. Second, since it was highly factionalized, the access to the top levels of party hierarchy involved a strong degree of conflict. Since the 1970s, those conflicts have been managed by the leadership, thanks to the increasing power of the General Secretary which increasingly freed itself from the control of the National Executive (to the point that, since 1995, the AN leader nominates the National Executive). At the same time, the candidate selection process involved the party's bodies at all levels: the provincial organ had the right to select candidates at the municipal level; the regional organ at the provincial level, and so on. However, the National Executive and the General Secretary kept the right to intervene for "nationally salient candidates." This power dramatically increased after the transformation into AN.

Finally, the PASOK and the PSOE occupy an intermediate position between the two models of internal power concentration. Both parties have been divided along ideological alignments but the founding or re-founding leader acted as a unifying element and portrayed himself as the essential and vital center of the party. The mix of personal qualities and of contextual factors elevated Andreas Papandreou and Felipe Gonzáles, leaders of the PASOK and the PSOE, respectively, to unchallenged positions. In many respects, theses two cases are similar to that of the French PS ,except for two elements. First, the PSOE and the PASOK were "built" almost from *nihilo* by Papandreou and Gonzáles, in contrast to the long history of the PS, which was already somewhat institutionalized and highly factionalized. Second, Mitterrand had to wait for a decade before attaining success (i.e., winning the presidency contest and bringing the PS to power with an absolute majority in the Parliament) while the other leaders obtained access to government more quickly. Both circumstances strengthened the position of the PSOE and PASOK party leaders (and prime ministers) enabling them to locate themselves above the internal tendencies and to rule unconstested.

The problem of the degree of concentration of power within parties—in the hands of one leader or in a dominant coalition—could be analyzed by also focusing on the different "style" of leadership. This approach implements and refines the above-sketched distinction by introducing three "classical" types of leadership: "charismatic-like," "monocratic" and "transactional."[8]

A charismatic-like type of leadership seems to characterize, in ascending order, the RPR, the PASOK and the FN. Papandreou's charisma was "situational" since "it served as the most important factor for unifying the party" and to avoid potential conflicts due "to the tacit development of the three tendencies within the party" (Chapter 10, this volume). As far as the RPR and the FN are concerned, charismatic-like leadership appears to be linked to a political culture based on the reverence of hierarchical and authoritarian values. In both parties, the election of the leadership by an overwhelming majority testifies, among other elements, of a sort of "cult of the leader." However, while the FN leader and founder, Jean-Marie Le Pen, shares some elements of "pure" charisma (in Weberian sense) since the relationship with their followers is one of absolute loyalty and the party is totally identified with him, the RPR case is rather different as its leadership, while absolute, is far less than charismatic. In this latter case a "routinization of charisma" seems at work.

A "monocratic structure of power" (Schonfeld, 1980) could be applied to the PSOE, the AP/PP and the ND (with the exception of the Karamanlis period characterized by a charismatic-like leadership). In the PSOE, "the power is in the hands of one person who controls the party. Gonzales is not the *primus inter pares* and his figure has a more important weight than granted by the party statutes. The leader became a real resource for the PSOE not only in electoral terms but also as the balance point of the different forces acting within the party" (Chapter 14, this volume). Fraga and Aznar (AP/PP) as well as Mitsotakis (ND), despite their lack of appeal, succeeded in imposing themselves over their respective parties by strict control over their organization and by elimination of internal dissent.

A "transactional" (Burns, 1978) style of leadership prevails in the French PS, the Italian DC and MSI/AN, thanks to the presence of well-structured factions. The party leader is the head of the dominant faction, either able to win the majority alone or to aggregate different groups into the "dominant coalition." Whatever the type of internal majority, the leader always governs under the control of the other factions, however, and it is forced to "bargain" constantly.

Finally, the PCI/PDS represents a peculiar case. Until the mid-1980s the party secretaries were uncontested and unanimously esteemed (with a taint of cult of personality) by all the members. After Berlinguer's death in 1984, the progressive factionalization of the party led to a new type of leadership: the secretary was no longer an "absolute leader" but rather "a leader guaranteeing pluralism." With the transformation of the PCI into the PDS, "the higher turnover (political and generational) has caused a high 'amalgamation' of the party elite. . . . The higher permeability of the leadership, together with its lower inner cohesion due, above all, to the strengthening of the internal factions, gave rise to a more widespread and fragmented distribution of power" (Chapter 7, this volume).

PARTY IN THE EXTERNAL ENVIRONMENT

The relationship between parties and the external environment is double-faced: it concerns the degree of "interpenetration" between party and the state, on the one hand, and the extent and pervasiveness of party control over the society (or civil society), on the other. The first aspect could be analyzed referring to the "party government" frame (Katz, 1986). The capacity of parties to appoint members of government—"the partyness of government"—is the first indicator of the party's power. Other factors define the party–state relationship. As stressed by Blondel (1995: 130ff), government appointments, policy and patronage are the means by which the parties manage this relationship. Where parties dominate government in all apects, a "fusion" between party and government occurs to the benefit of parties themselves (Blondel, 1995: 135). For parties in opposition, power is *a priori* less. They are never totally deprived of power, however. In fact, they can share power at the local level, control organized pressure groups (workers, industrialists, particular issue groups), be able to mobilize a large number of citizens and control the media as well.

The second aspect of the parties' interaction with the external environment concerns the degree of party patronage. Patronage could be defined as a power relationship between individuals or groups in unequal positions based upon the use of public resources by political leaders for the benefit of their parties. The capacity of parties to "colonize the society" is determined by the party presence in the centers of decision-making: this presence is linked to the expansion of the public sector at the national and local levels, and to the number of positions to be filled in by parties in government-controlled agencies, companies and in the bureacracy.

The Partyness of Government

The party–government relationship is first determined by the effectiveness of voters' influence on government formation. On the basis of the type of the electoral system and of the institutional constraints, parties are more or less free to negotiate alliances in the parliamentary arena irrespective of the voters' will. Majoritarian systems—where a bipartisan format does not exist—enforce parties to join large electoral and political coalitions: the winning bloc constitutes the government. Pure proportional representation favors high fragmentation in the party system and consequently the government majority is not directly issued by the polls but bargained in Parliament. On the other hand, proportional represention *with a low degree of proportionality* favors the major parties and leads to a majoritarian dynamic.

In southern Europe the electoral laws were intended to increase the links between voters' will at the polls and the composition of governments. In Greece and Spain, the democratic systems established in 1974 and 1977 are characterized by fewer national parties—representing three political families, Left, center-left and center-right—and electoral laws whose objective is to reinforce the two largest parties. France (from 1946 to 1958) and Italy (from 1946 to 1990) were characterized by pure proportional representation and a highly fragmented party system: the relationship between votes and offices was weak since the latter depended on the party position within the political system. Large parties with a high share of the vote could be excluded from government while small parties with poor electoral support and few seats in Parliament were given opportunities to enter into coalitions. The adoption of a majority system in France and of a mixed system (proportional and majoritarian) led the parties to enter into large electoral and political coalitions so that the winning bloc forms the government.

As to the partyness of government, Italy, Greece and Spain present a high degree of partisan appointments. DC ministers, who made up the largest part of all the governments from 1945 to 1992, were chosen by the party and according to the balance among party factions. Even the "extreme" parties which had been long excluded from power—MSI/AN and PCI/PDS—tended to follow the same pattern when participating, respectively, in the Berlusconi government (1994) or in the Prodi cabinet (1996). Greek and Spanish parties exhibited the same model of high partyness of government.

The direct power of appointment of ministers by parties was, in contrast, relatively low in France, under the Fifth Republic. Prime ministers and ministers were generally members and sometimes leaders of political parties (Morel, 1996). However, this transfer of party personnel into government is decided by the president *and* his Prime Minister in the case of a united government, the Prime Minister alone in the case of a divided government (cohabitation). Under the presidency of de Gaulle, Pompidou and Giscard d'Estaing as well as under Chirac, Gaullist and Giscardian parties did not really intervene in the government selection process. In the case of Socialist governments, the party's appointment capacity declined over time. The PS role weakened, moving from a form of "bargaining power" with the President (and the Prime Minister) which warranted party recognition (1981–1986) to an almost absolute exclusion from government appointments (1988–1993). As pointed out by Sawicki (Chapter 4, this volume), such a trend was one element of the PS crisis in the late 1980s and the early 1990s.

Patronage

As to the colonization of the state, southern European parties established a high level of control and penetration in the state and society. The Italian DC—an archetype of this tendency thanks to its dominant position in the governments for more than 40 years—began the colonization of the state in the 1950s through the expansion of the public sector of the economy. Despite different reforms and the loss of its hegemony within the government in the early 1990s, the DC maintained its dominant position in the public broadcasting system (which it monopolized until the mid-1970s), kept its hands on the direction of the main State holding companies and the management of the banks. Even the very recent privatizations of some public-owned companies did not abolish the party power since it ensured the appointment, as managers of those firms, of personnel close to the party.

The same approach involves the French governing parties, the PS and the RPR. Sawicki, in his analysis of the PS as a "government party," emphasizes the "multiplication of positions the PS had to offer directly or indirectly": in particular it adopted co-optation or *de jure* members in the higher administration and appointment of managers in state-owned companies, whose number increased dramatically with the process of nationalization initiated by the Socialists in 1981–1982. In the case of the RPR, Haegel suggested that, deprived of national governmental resources, Chirac, as mayor of Paris (1979–1983), "became the head of a staff of 40,000 civil servants which, from a financial and administrative but also from a symbolic point of view, was able to rival the State administration." In other terms, the mechanisms through which the Gaullist Party had insured its power at the national level in the past were reproduced at the local level. The power of both the RPR and the PS was established on the same principles: as far as the high administration is concerned, a spoils system, which led to changes in the personnel according to political affiliation, was enforced. One can add that the public broadcasting system has always been a means for ensuring party power. As the former French President of the Republic George Pompidou (1969–1974) said, "it is the voice of France," that is, the voice for parties in power. All in all, the managers of the television channels as well as people responsible for the news were always in the hands of the government and the parties. Reforms initiated by Mitterrand (free radios and private television channels; creation of an "independent" body to guarantee the freedom of the television and the radios) as well as the privatization of the oldest and more popular TV channels by the right-wing government in 1986, did not really alter the relations between parties in government and the broadcasting public sector. The "independent" body in charge of appointing the "independent" managers always chose "the right men in key positions"—that is, candidates backed by the government and parties in power.

In Greece too, both parties, ND and PASOK, "have inflated the political component of bureaucracy by creating inter-ministerial committees of political appointment and councils of advisers to ministers as well as some new ministries out of former public agencies or secretariats." According to Spourdalakis, the PASOK was, in the late 1970s, "the party through which clientelism resurfaced in Greece." A true "mass clientelism" or a "machine clientelism" was developed ensuring that the incentives were provided by the organizations, and no longer by the notables. The PASOK, in government during the 1980s, appointed 300,000 people in the civil service, 100,000 of those during pre-election periods, bypassing the standard procedure of recruitment. Moreover, in 1986, two-thirds of the PASOK's Central Committee occupied important positions in government or in offices at the government's disposal. The expansion of the state economic sector enforced by the PASOK and the high number of public offices to be filled by the party after its electoral success deprived the PASOK of its own organization which suddenly became far less relevant.

In Spain, state occupation by the PSOE during its rule seems to have become increasingly penetrating and widespread. Gillespie (1989: 132), emphasized "the big increase in the use of political appointments and co-optation to ensure the implementation of (its) policies, developing in this way a clientelist network": for example, between 1984 and 1987 about 25,000 administrative posts had been filled according to the "free choice" of the government (Gillespie, 1989). Moreover, the PSOE managed to establish a firm grip on the state-owned television channels via the nomination of their managers by the government.

Parties of the opposition control limited sectors of the state and society, especially at the local level. Since 1946, the PCI had had control of local government in the center of Italy. It expanded its presence within the local bureaucracy as well as its economic interests by creating and supporting cooperatives. Moreover, since the 1970s, the party had been gradually included in the general spoils system (*lottizzazione*) though it gained rather marginal benefits. On the other hand, the MSI/AN, while it was the fourth largest party in the Italian party system, given its extreme position on the political spectrum, never controlled local government or represented socioeconomic interest groups. Nevertheless, after its success in the 1993 local elections and in the 1994 general elections—which saw the party enter the Berlusconi government—it attempted to develop a hold of the state economic sectors. The FN, which never participated in French national or local governments, had consequently no opportunities to colonize the state. Its marginality in the political system makes the FN the least involved party of the southern European countries in the spoils system.

CONCLUSION

What similarities can be seen among southern European parties? What differences emerge? Do they differ along national or ideological lines?

The basic assumption of a generalization of the mass-party model is somewhat sustained while the conservative parties, in particular in France and Spain, present a more "relaxed" form. At least in a formal way—that is, in their statutes—all parties have structured themselves along the prescription of Duverger's mass model. On the other hand, some features of the mass parties appear to have vanished. First, the reference to a functional structure in the workplace as an imitation of the Communists' cell, after a series of attempts purported by non-Socialist parties, have been abandoned even by the PCI's successors, the PDS. Second, the political education function of the parties has almost completely disappeared with some exception (FN and PCI/PDS) and it has been substituted by more pragmatic and vote-seeking skills. Third, the flanking organizations have generally decreased in importance in terms of role and function yet they have not totally vanished (youth and women associations are still present in every party). The only exception to this trend is represented by the FN which has tried to build a "world apart" with an amazingly extensive network of associations.

Southern European parties are formally designed in terms of mass parties but they have all followed the catch-all schema. Every party softened its ideological appeal and tried to overcome the boundaries of its *classe guardée*. The increasing power of the leadership envisaged by Kirchheimer in his catch-all party is, however, far from absolute. All left-wing parties as well as some Conservatives (DC and ND) and extreme Right parties (MSI) pay homage to the rites of internal formal Democracy and therefore leave a role (or the appearance of a role) to the membership. But in reality the control is highly concentrated in the hands of a dominant coalition. In some cases (FN, PASOK, PSOE, RPR, AP/PP, ND and AN, the offspring of the Italian MSI) the dominant coalition is expressed by a single leader who exercises an overwhelming influence; and in the French FN and, to a lesser extent, in the PASOK, the leader has absolute power and could be rated as charismatic-like leader. In the other parties the high level of factionalism—which also characterized the late PCI and its offspring, the PDS—has led to rather unstable and noncohesive alliances among relevant actors within the party. Such instability and uncohesiveness was reflected by the struggle for the control over crucial resources such as the selection and the recruitment of the political personnel in party and public offices.

Finally, after having highlighted the parties' proximity or distance from the classical models provided by Duverger and Kirchheimer and the inner conflicts over the party's resources, the third part has dealt with the relationship of the party with the state and civil society. The first indicator of the party-government relationship concerns the degree of partyness of government—that is, the partisan appointment of members to cabinets. Some institutional constraints—the electoral system and the parliamentary versus presidential regime—determine the different profiles of southern European parties. Majoritarian or disrepresentative proportional electoral systems and/or presidential regimes, linking voters more directly with government formation, weaken the party power vis-à-vis cabinet appointments. This is the case for the French Fifth Republic, Spain and Greece. Appointment is independently determined by the party leader/Prime Minister with minor input by parties, particularly in France. On the other hand, in Italy parties have great influence over the choice of ministers.

The second aspect involves the party penetration into society and the state. The colonization of state and society by parties is also identified by the terms *partitocrazia, parteinstaat, partitocratie* or partitocracy that mean "a type of party government based on a large use of patronage" (De Winter, Della Porta, Donatella Deschower 1996: 219). The phenomenon of patronage and clientelism seems to be at work in the southern European countries, involving all governing parties and to a much lesser extent the traditional parties of opposition in Italy, PCI/PDS and MSI/AN, while only the French FN is totally extraneous to this practice.

In sum, what are the patterns of similarities in the parties under examination? The taxonomy along ideological lines finds some commonalities among leftist parties in terms of mass-party reminiscences in the organization, clear evolution toward catchallism, factionalism, high concern for formal Democracy and membership presence/activity, control over candidate selection. Many of these characteristics are, however, shared by the the extreme Right parties, especially the MSI/AN and, to some extent, also by the DC. On the other hand, conservative parties, while some of them experienced a strong party articulation, are more dependent on the leadership and have less concern for members and a greater concentration of the decison-making process and appointment procedures. However, this ideological distinction is too blurred: the DC and especially the extreme Right parties have many traits in common with the leftist parties; as well, within the leftist parties the newly formed Socialist parties—PSOE and PASOK—are distinct from the established parties—PS (referring to the SFIO experience) and PCI/PDS.

Nation-specific traits play a role. Two elements are nationally determined: the level of party institutionalization which differs mainly because of the nature of the regime (as two countries out of four did not experience democratic regimes until the mid-1970s); and the institutional constraints. The institutional contraints homogenize the French, Greek and Spanish parties, irrespective of ideological alignments; Greek and Spanish parties failed to become strongly institutionalized parties. First, their recent entry into the political arena, when the mass party was already declining, has inhibited the development of a strongly articulated structure; second, their quick access to government, thanks to rather disproportional electoral systems and majoritarian logics, has led parties to deemphasize the importance attached to traditional organizational means and to rely on public offices and patronage resources. When parties were in opposition they were concerned with organization: in Greece, the PASOK built its organization before entering the government in 1981 and then it relaxed it, while ND did not care so much for its structure until it was in power, but showed great concern when sent into opposition. In particular, these parties suffered from weak autonomy vis-à-vis the external environment: they became overwhelmingly dependent on the resources available to them when in government.

Patronage is an important resource for any party. The development of patronage activities by southern European political parties could be interpreted as the by-product of the well-rooted tradition of clientelism (called in Spain *caciquismo*) in the Mediterranean countries. The only difference would concern the evolution from an individualistic, dyadic relationship of patron-client to a collective dimension represented by political parties. Clientelism and patronage, however, are not limited to "traditional" societies nor a reminiscence of the past. In advanced societies, in fact, "the scope of private appropriation of public resources together with the network building it both requires and expresses—in short, the scope for patronage-type behaviour—is bound to increase" (Theobald, 1992: 191). The extension of the Quangos in Great Britain (Wilson, 1995), for example, which offer jobs selectively along partisan alignments, is one of the most clear demonstrations of the cross-country diffusion of this phenomenon. Therefore, the extension of the patronage system, even if it has found a fertile soil, is not specific to the Mediterranean countries but reflects a general tendency among contemporary parties.

In sum, which is the model for southern European parties? There is no special model. The parties under consideration have followed the same path experienced by their more institutionalized counterparts in continental and northern Europe: all moved toward the catch-all model first and then to the Katz and Mair (1995) cartel party. In fact, since the cartel party implies the "interpenetration between parties and the State," southern Europe provides a good opportunity for the development of such a party. But, again, this evolution reflects a general trend which is not specific to southern Europe. Mediterranean parties are fully integrated in Europe.

NOTES

1. Nowadays parties organize "sessions of formation" (term more or less inherited from the private sector). Such a kind of sessions concerns first, the parliamentarians, second, the local elective officeholders and sometimes the candidates to elections. The program is the same, however: how to answer a voter or an opponent with very simplified arguments and guide schedules, how to deal with the media, and so on.

2. See in the case of the PCF, Kriegel (1985); for the DC and the PCI, AAVV (1968); for the PCI/PDS, Ignazi (1992); for the MSI, Ignazi (1989).

3. If one considers the fascination of Duverger with the Communist parties, one can state that the organization of the Communist parties is the "ideal-type" of any mass party for Duverger himself.

4. Curiously, Kirchheimer never used, in his essay, the term "leader"; he used, rather, "leadership" and, preferably, "leadership groups." If this terminology is meaningful, one can conclude that Kirchheimer was conscious of the conflicts existing in political parties but not very interested in the distribution of the power within parties.

5. Kirchheimer emphasized the anti-system attitude of the early mass Socialist parties which integrated or encapsulated citizens for enforcing a system disruptive activity.

6. Other typologies have been presented by the scholars. See, for example, Leon Epstein's (1967) distinction between "electoral" and "nonelectoral" party; William Wright's (1971) hypothesis of a "rational-efficient" type of party opposed to the more traditional party-democracy type; Angelo Panebianco's (1982) typology of "electoral-professional" and "mass-bureaucratic" parties. Finally, the last model is Richard Katz and Peter Mair's (1995) "cartel party."

7. The PS First Secretary has been directly elected by the members since 1995. Previously, he was elected by the *Comité directeur* (Executive Committee) elected by the Congress. In the 1990s, strong conflicts between the different factions did not allow the different strata of the party to unanimously appoint the First Secretary. Many First Secretaries and dominant coalitions did not fit with the membership demands (see Sawicki). Therefore statutes were changed in order to weaken the power of the subleaders at the top of the party and to increase the participation of the followers.

8. The inflationary use of the term "charisma" leads us to adopt the expression "charismatic-like," as charismatic leaders are to be considered, following Weber, absolutely exceptional.

REFERENCES

AAVV (1968). *L'organizzazione del PCI e della DC.* Bologna: Il Mulino.

Blondel, Jean (1995). "Toward a Systematic Analysis of Government Party Relationships." *International Political Science Review* 16: 127–144.

Burns, James McGregor (1978). *Leadership.* New York: Harper and Row.

De Winter, Lieven, Donatella Della Porta, and Kris Deschower (1996). "Comparing Similar Countries: Italy and Belgium." *Res Publica* 37: 215–235.

Duverger, Maurice (1951). *Les Partis Politiques.* Paris: Seuil.

Epstein, Leon (1967). *Political Parties in Western Democracies.* Madison: University of Wisconsin Press.

Gillespie, Richard (1989). "Spanish Socialism in the 1980s." In Tom Gallangher and A.T. Williams (eds.), *Southern European Socialism*, pp. 59–85. Manchester: Manchester University Press.

Ignazi, Piero (1989). *Il Polo Escluso. Profilo del Movimento Sociale Italiano.* Bologna: Il Mulino.

Ignazi, Piero (1992). *Dal PCI al PDS.* Bologna: Il Mulino.

Katz, Richard (1986). "Party Government: A Realistic Conception." In Francis G. Castles and Rudolf Wildemann (eds.), *The Future of Party Government. Visions and Realities of Party Government*, vol. I. pp. 31–71. Berlin: De Gruyter.

Katz, Richard and Peter Mair (eds.) (1994). *How Parties Organize.* London: Sage.

Katz, Richard and Peter Mair (1995). "Changing Model of Party Organization and Party Democracy: The Emergence of the Cartel Party." *Party Politics.* 1: 5–28.

Kirchheimer, Otto (1966). "The Transformation of the Western European Party System." In Joseph La Palombara and Myron Weiner (eds.), *Political Parties and Political Development*, pp 177–200. Princeton: Princeton University Press.

Kriegel, Annie (1985). *Les Communistes Français.* Paris: Seuil.

Lawson, Kay (1976). *The Comparative Study of Political Parties.* New York: St. Martin's Press.

Lawson, Kay and Peter Merkl (eds.) (1988). *When Parties Fail: Emerging Alternative Political Organizations.* Princeton: Princeton University Press.

Mair, Peter (1990). "Introduction." In Peter Mair (ed.), *The West European Party System.* Oxford: Oxford University Press.

Morel, Laurent (1996). "France: Party Government at Last?" In Jean Blondel and Maurizio Cotta (eds.), *Party and Government*, pp. 40–60. New York: St. Martin's Press.

Morlino, Leonardo (1995). "Political Parties and Democratic Consolidation In Southern Europe." In Richard Gunther, Nikoforos Diamandouros and Hans Jurgen Puhle (eds.), *The Politics of Democratic Consolidation: Southern Europe in Comparative Perspective*, pp. 315–388. Baltimore and London: Johns Hopkins University Press.

Morlino, Leonardo (1996). *Which Democracies in Southern Europe?* ICPS Working Papers, no. 113.

Offerlé, Michel (1987). *Les parties politiques.* Paris: PUF.

Panebianco, Angelo (1982). *Modelli di partito.* Bologna: Il Mulino

Shonfield, William (1980). "La stabilité des dirigeants des partis politiques: Le personnel des directions nationales du parti Socialiste et du mouvement Gaulliste." *Revue Français de Science Politique* 30: 477–505.

Strøm, Kaare (1990). "A Behavioral Theory of Competitive Political Parties." *American Journal of Political Science* 34: 565–598.

Theobald, Robin (1992). "On the Survival of Patronage In Developed Societies." *Archives Européennes de Sociologie* 33: 183–191.

Wilson, David (1995). "Quangos in the Skeletal State." *Parliamentary Affairs* 48: 182–191.

Wright, William (1971). "Comparative Party Models: Rational-Efficient and Party Democracy." In William Wright (ed.), *A Comparative Study of Party Organization*, pp. 17–54. Columbus: Merrill.

Index

Action Française, 57
Agnelli, Giovanni, 96
Alianza Popular-Partido Demòcrata Popular-Partido Liberal (AP-PDP-PL), 255. *See also* Popular Party
Alliance for the Left and Progress, 188
Almirante, Giorgio, 158, 165, 166, 169, 171
Amendola, Giorgio, 140
Andreotti, Giulio, 95, 114, 116, 118, 121, 126, 129 n.13, 130 n.24, 131 n.32
Anti-Unemployment Front *(Front anti-chômage)*, 60
Antony, Bernard, 57
Area vasta, 174
Arrighi, Pascal, 62, 68 nn.12, 13
Association for the Research of Youth Employment (ARPEJ), 60
Association for Workers and Salaried (AOP), 283
Averoff, Evangelos, 226–227, 232, 235 nn.12, 13, 14, 288
Aznar, Jose-Maria, 245, 250, 262–263, 264, 265, 266 n.5, 268 nn.21, 23, 282, 288, 292, 295

Balladur, Edouard, 20, 23, 26, 34, 35, 36, 40

Bardi, Luciano, 118
Barre, Raymond, 20, 26
Bartolini, Stefano, 278
Basque Nationalist Party (PNV), 241, 243, 247, 262
Bérégovoy, Pierre, 83
Bergounioux, Alain, 70, 81
Berlinguer, Enrico, 135, 136, 140, 295
Berlusconi, Silvio, 99, 103, 104, 105, 172, 288, 297, 299
Bleu-Blanc-Rouge, 44
Blondel, Jean, 295
Blot, Jean, 56, 62
Bompard, Jacques, 55
Botella, Juan, 276
Bousquet, Pierre, 45, 46
Brigneau, François, 45, 57

Caciagli, Mario, 272, 274–275, 276
Cahiers Européens, 46
Cantiere Italia, 174
Carrillo, Santiago, 243, 246
Cartel des non saw, 14
Castellano, Pablo, 271
Castro, Fidel, 105
Catholic Action *(Azione Cattolica)*, 121
Cayrol, Roland, 276

Center for Democracy and Progress (CDP), 14, 16
Center of Social Democrats (CDS), 11, 16, 24 n.2
Center Union (EK), 182, 183, 206, 207
Center Union-New Forces (EK-ND), 182
Centre for Socialist Studies and Researches (CERES), 19, 73, 83, 287
Centre Union *(Unione di Centro)*, 103
Cercle national des rapatriés, 58
Chevènement, Jean-Pierre, 19, 79, 82
Chirac, Jacques, 16, 20, 23, 26, 27, 28, 30, 32, 34, 35, 36, 37, 38, 40, 62, 288, 297
Christian Democracy (DC): candidates' selection and, 117–118, 124; cartelization of, 111, 127–128; the Church and, 112, 121–122; clientelistic relationships of, 113, 119–120, 127; flanking organizations and, 121–122; inner factionalism of, 112–114, 115–118, 119, 125, 126, 128; institutionalization of, 111, 112–113, 121; local organization of, 118–119; national bodies, composition of, 115–116, 124; new parties from, 125; organizational reforms of, 110–111, 114, 118–119, 120, 124, 125–126; parliamentary groups of, 116–117; public broadcasting and, 122; public economy and, 119, 122–124; *Tangentopoli* inquiries and, 123, 124
Christian Democratic Centre (CCD), 101, 103, 105, 106, 131 n.31
Ciampi, Carlo Azeglio, 101, 104
Club de l'Horloge, 47, 56. *See also* Horlogers
Club 1989, 28
Colajanni, Napoleone, 140
Collinot, Michel, 46, 57
Collovald, Annie, 33
Committee for Christianism and Solidarity (CCS), 47, 60
Common Man Party *(Uomo Qualunque),* 159
Communion and Liberation (CL), 121
Communist and Internationalist Party (PCI), 10
Communist parties, 283–284, 285, 287.

See also Communist and Internationalist Party; Communist Party of Greece; Communist Party of Greece-Interior; Communist Refoundation; Communist and Revolutionary League; French Communist Party; Italian Communist Party; Spanish Communist Party
Communist Party of Greece (KKE), 182, 183, 193, 194, 211
Communist Party of Greece-Interior (KKE-Interior), 182, 183
Communist Refoundation (RC), 100, 103, 107, 140, 142
Communist and Revolutionary League (LCR), 10
Convention for Republican Institutions (CIR), 17, 19, 72
Convergence and Unity (CiU), 241, 246, 247, 255, 262
Cossutta, Armando, 140
Craxi, Bettino, 96, 100, 104, 131 n.32
Cresson, Edith, 83

D'Alema, Massimo, 141, 151, 152
Déat, Marcel, 57
De Beketch, Serge, 57
De Esteban, Goige, 272
De Gasperi, Alcide, 95, 112, 125
de Gaulle, Charles, 9, 13, 14, 16, 17, 31, 39, 297
Delors, Jacques, 83
De Mita, Ciriaco, 110, 111, 114, 115, 116, 118, 119, 121, 122, 125, 126, 127, 129 nn.11, 12, 14, 130 n.25, 293
Democratic Alliance (AD), 103
Democratic Center Union (UCD), 241, 243, 244, 247, 249, 256, 257, 260, 261, 262, 265 n.1, 266 n.7, 267 n.15, 268 n.20
Democratic Centre *(Centre démocrate),* 11, 16
Democratic Coalition (CD), 244, 255. *See also* Popular Party
Democratic Force (FD), 10, 11
Democratic and Social Center (CDS), 243, 249, 250, 265 n.1, 266 n.7
Dini, Lamberto, 105–106, 107

D'Ormesson, Olivier, 62
Dumont, René, 22
Duprat, François, 46, 68 nn.4, 9
Durand, Pierre, 57
Duverger, Maurice, 221, 274, 275, 281, 282, 283, 285, 289, 299, 300

Ecological Generation (GE), 10, 22–23
European Community, 195, 222, 224, 234 n.2. *See also* European Union
European Union, 189, 195
Eusko Alkartasuna (EA), 243
Evert, Miltiades, 230, 236 n.19

Fabius, Laurent, 41 n.15, 82, 83
Fanfani, Amintore, 110–111, 113, 114, 118, 119, 125
Farneti, Paolo, 94, 153 n.2
Federaciòn de Alianza Popular (FAP), 255, 260, 266 n.3. *See also* Popular Party
Federation for National and European Action (FANE), 46, 68 n.3
Fédération des socialistes et des chrétiens démocrates. See Large federation
Federation of the Democratic and Socialist Left (FGDS), 18, 71
Federation of Greek Industries (SEB), 197
Federation of Independent Republicans (FNRI), 11, 14, 16
Fini, Gianfranco, 165, 169, 171, 172, 173, 174, 175
Forlani, Arnaldo, 111, 114, 116, 118, 121, 124, 126, 130 n.23, 131 n.32
Fraga, Manuel, 242, 244, 245, 246, 249, 255, 256, 260, 261, 262, 265, 282, 295
Franco, Francisco, 247, 260, 267 nn.15, 16, 271, 272, 288
Fraternité Saint-Pie X, 60
Freedom Pole *(Polo delle Libertà)*, 103, 106, 125
French Communist Party (PCF), 10, 18, 19, 20, 21, 23, 56, 70, 77, 282, 287, 302 n.2
French Fraternity *(Fraternité française)*, 59, 60
French Jewish Circle (CJF), 60

French party system: ecologists and, 22–23; electoral laws and, 11–13, 23; fragmentation of, 10–11, 19–21; political families of, 10–13; the *Quadrille Bipolaire* and, 19–21; rise of National Front, 21–22; Union of the Left and, 18–19; UNR hegemony and, 13, 14–16
French Section of the Workers' International (SFIO), 9, 11, 13, 17, 18, 19, 24 nn.2, 3, 71, 73, 74, 75, 84 nn.2, 3, 6, 288, 301
Friends of the Earth *(Les amis de la Terre)*, 22
Fund for Southern Development *(Cassa per il Mezzogiorno)*, 113, 119

Galván, Enrique Tierno, 244, 271
Garaud, Marie-France, 35
Gardini, Raul, 100
Gaucher, Roland, 46, 57, 58
Gauchon, Pascal, 45
Gava, Antonio, 118
General Alliance Against Racism and for the Respect of the French and Christian Identity (AGRIF), 60
General Confederation of Greek Workers (GSEE), 197
General Workers' Union (UGT), 250, 270, 271, 283
Gillespie, Richard, 298
Giscard d'Estaing, Valery, 14, 16, 297
Go Italy! *(Forza Italia)*, 98, 103, 104, 105, 106, 107, 125, 172
Gollnisch, Bruno, 46, 54, 56, 63, 64, 65, 66
González, Felipe, 242, 244, 245, 246, 271, 274, 275, 277, 278, 279
Gramsci, Antonio, 139
Greek political system: anticommunism and, 182, 191–193; armed forces and, 191–192; catharsis and, 188; coalition governments and, 188; discriminatory system and, 191–192; electoral laws and, 182, 187–189; European Community and, 195–196; monarchy and, 191–192; parties' modernization and, 190, 191, 193, 194

The Greens *(I Verdi)*, 92, 98, 103, 106
The Greens *(Les Verts)*, 10, 22–23
Groups for Political Promotion (GIP), 283
Grunberg, Gérard, 70, 81
Guelf Movement *(Movimento Guelfo)*, 112
Guerra, Alfonso, 271, 274
Guerra, Luis Lopez, 272

Holeindre, Roger, 45, 51
Horlogers, 47, 63. *See also Club de l'Horloge*

Iglesias, Pablo, 270
Independent Republicans *(Républicains indépendants)*, 14
Ingrao, Pietro, 139, 149, 153 n.10
International Union of Socialist Youth (IUSY), 150
Italian Association of Catholic Workers (ACLI), 121, 126, 127
Italian Communist Party (PCI)/Democratic Party of the Left (PDS): center/periphery relationship in, 138; flanking organizations and, 147–150, 151–152; ideological changes of, 135, 139, 150–151; inner factionalism of, 139–141; national bodies, composition of, 141–145, 151; parliamentary group of, 145–146, 152; professional electoral party model and, 134, 143, 150–152; statutory changes of, 136–139
Italian Communist Young Federation (FGCI), 136, 147, 149–150, 154 nn.23, 24
Italian Confederation of Labour Unions (CISL), 121, 126
Italian Federation of the Catholic Universities (FUCI), 112, 127
Italian General Confederation of Labour (CGIL), 136, 147, 148–149, 152, 153 n.5, 154 nn.20, 21
Italian Liberal Party (PLI), 92, 95, 97, 100, 101, 103, 105
Italian party system: civil society and, 97–98; Clean Hands investigation and, 98, 99–101; dissatisfaction and, 100; fragmentation of, 92, 105, 106–107; governmental coalitions and, 92, 95–96, 104, 107; interest groups and, 96–97; mass media and, 98, 99, 104; new electoral system and, 100, 101, 105; *partitocrazia* and, 96, 97–98, 99; party finance and, 98; polarized pluralism of, 94, 106–107; stability of, 91–92
Italian Popular Party (PPI), 101, 103, 106, 110, 125
Italian Recreative Cultural Association (ARCI), 136, 147, 148, 152, 154 n.16
Italian Renewal (RI), 107
Italian Republican Party (PRI), 92, 95, 97, 100, 101, 105
Italian Social-Democratic Party (PSDI), 92, 95, 97, 100, 101, 105
Italian Social Movement (MSI)/National Alliance (AN): caesaristic features of, 165, 173–174; corporativism and, 166–167; DC and, 159; factional conflicts in, 158, 161, 168, 170–171, 172, 174; fascism and, 157–158, 159, 160–162, 166, 168, 169, 171, 172, 173, 174–175; flanking organizations of, 167–168; foundation of AN, 173–175; ideological debate in, 169, 171–172, 173; local organization of, 163–164, 173; membership of, 160, 162; national bodies of, 164–166, 173–174; parliamentary group of, 165, 166, 175
Italian Social Republic (RSI), 158, 161, 167
Italian Socialist Party (PSI), 92, 95, 96, 97, 99, 100, 101, 103, 104, 105, 114, 122, 123, 126, 148, 149
Italian Socialist Party Proletary Union (PSIUP), 100
Italian Union for Sports for All (UISP), 148

Jacob, Jean, 38
Jospin, Lionel, 20, 23, 78, 81, 82
Juillet, Pierre, 35
Juppé, Alain, 29, 33, 34, 35, 36, 41 n.12

Kanellopoulos, Athanasios, 230, 236
n.19
Karamanlis, Constantine, 181, 182, 183,
187, 193, 209, 222–225, 231, 232, 233,
294
Katz, Richard S., 118, 221, 290, 302, 302
n.6
Kirchheimer, Otto, 134, 221, 279, 285,
289, 299, 300, 302 nn.4, 5
Knapp, Andrew, 31, 38

Lalonde, Brice, 22, 23
Lambert, Hughes, 59, 68 n.11
Lang, Carl, 47, 50, 56, 63, 67, 68 n.7
Large federation *(Grande fédération)*,
17
Lavilla, Landelino, 243
Lazarsfeld, Paul F., 278
Le Chevallier, Jean-Marie, 55, 57
Le Gallou, Jean-Yves, 47, 56, 62
Leonardi, Robert, 122, 128 n.6, 130 n.22
Le Pen, Jean-Marie, 21, 43, 44, 45, 46,
47, 48, 49, 50, 51–52, 54, 55, 56, 57,
59, 60, 61, 62, 64, 65, 66, 67, 67 n.1,
68 nn.5, 11, 12, 13, 292, 294
Let Them Live *(Laissez-les vivre)*, 60
Llopis, Rodolfo, 271, 277
Longo, Luigi, 140

Madiran, Jean, 57, 68 n.9
Mair, Peter, 221, 285, 290, 302, 302 n.6
Makarios, Archbishop, 191
Making Front *(Fare Fronte)*, 168, 284
Making Green *(Fare Verde)*, 168, 284
Maréchal, Samuel, 60
Martinazzoli, Mino, 111, 124, 125, 126,
127, 131 n.29
Martinez, Serge, 57
Marx, Karl. *See* Marxism
Marxism, 76, 134, 135, 139, 140, 147,
150, 153 n.6, 212, 217 n.16, 245, 271,
277, 287
Mauroy, Pierre, 78, 82
Mégret, Bruno, 47, 50, 54, 56, 60, 62, 63–
64, 65, 66, 68 n.6
Michelini, Arturo, 169
Michels, Robert, 230, 290, 291
Militant, 45, 46

Minute-La France, 57
Mitsotakis, Constantine, 187, 227–228,
229, 230, 232, 233, 234, 236 n.19, 288,
295
Mitterrand, François, 16, 17, 18, 19, 20,
24 n.6, 62, 71, 72, 73, 76–77, 78–79,
81, 82–83, 84 n.6, 85 nn.12, 18, 293,
294, 298
Modern Enterprise and Freedom (EML),
59, 65
Monod, Jacques, 36
Mosca, Gaetano, 290
Movement for a National Teaching
(MEN), 58
Movement for Citizens (MDC), 10
Movement for reforms *(Mouvement ré-
formateur)*, 16
Movement of Catholic University Gradu-
ates *(Movimento Laureati)*, 112
Movement of Leftist Radicals (MRG), 11,
18–19, 20, 84 n.3
Movement of Young Socialists (MJS), 76,
85 n.10
Mussolini, Benito, 158, 159, 161, 172

Napolitano, Giorgio, 140, 153 n.10
National Center for Independents and
Farmers (CNIP), 9, 10, 11, 13, 14, 16
National Circle of Army Members
(CNGA), 58
National Circle of European Women
(CNFE), 59, 60
National Circle of Farmers (CNAF), 59
National Circle of Lieutenant Reserve
(CNOSOR), 58
National Circle of Retired and Pre-
Retired *(Cercle national des retraités
et préretraités)*, 60
National Democratic Union *(Ethniko
Demokratike Enosis)*, 182
National Front of Police (FNP), 59
National Front Party (FN): activists of,
58, 60–61; electoral success of, 48–49,
55–56, 64; elite recruitment of, 47–52;
executive bodies of, 48, 49, 52–54, 64,
65; flanking organizations of, 57–61;
ideology of, 45–47, 49–50, 56–57, 61,
64; inner factions of, 45–46, 50–51, 61–

65, 67; institutionalization of, 44–45, 56; internal turnover, 47; Le Pen, personal power and, 51–52, 65, 66–67; local organization of, 49, 51–52, 54–55, 64; membership of, 44, 48–49, 59–60; municipal elections and, 55–56, 63–64; relationship between office-holders and, 48–49, 51–52, 65; splits in, 46
National Front Youth (FNJ), 50, 58, 60, 64
National-Hebdo, 57
National Liberation Committee (CLN), 96
National Radical Union (ERE), 181, 204
National Revolutionary Group (GNR), 46
National University Union (UNI), 28
Natta, Alessandro, 134, 140–141, 153 nn.1, 3
The Network *(La Rete)*, 98, 103, 125, · 127, 130 n.24
New Democracy (ND): charismatic leadership and, 222, 225, 231–232; clientelism and patronage of, 223–224, 230; democratization process and, 222; external constraints on, 230; local organization of, 223–224; parliamentary group of, 223–225, 226, 227–230, 232, 234; process of institutionalization of, 222–223, 227; statutory changes of, 223–225, 228–229
New Order (ON), 45
New Right *(Nouvelle Droite)*, 46, 47, 56, 62, 168
North Atlantic Treaty Organization (NATO), 187, 249, 271
Northern League *(Lega Nord)*, 98, 100–101, 103, 105, 106, 107, 124, 125, 172
Nuevas Generaciones (NNGG), 259, 263

Occhetto, Achille, 134, 135, 140, 141, 144, 149, 151, 152, 153 nn.8, 10
Occident, 55, 60
Offerlé, Michel, 290
Olive Tree *(L'Ulivo)*, 106, 107, 125, 152
Orlando, Leoluca, 125, 130 n.24

Pacte Democràtic de Catalunya (PDC), 247
Panebianco, Angelo, 33, 38, 71, 110, 116, 121, 204, 221, 289, 290, 302 n.6
Panhellenic Socialist Movement (PASOK): charismatic leadership and, 205–208, 209, 215; clientelist relationships and, 209–210, 213–214; democratization process and, 204–206; electoralist strategy of, 204–205, 211; inner factionalism of, 204, 205–208, 212, 215; intra-party democracy of, 204–205, 207, 211, 212; periodization of, 213–214
Pannella, Marco, 101, 103
Papagos, Alexandros, 209
Papandreou, Andreas, 182, 183, 187, 188, 190, 193, 205, 207–208, 209, 211, 212, 214, 215, 216 nn.11, 12, 13, 14, 217 nn.16, 19, 227, 294
Papandreou, George, 182, 209, 216 n.12
Pareto, Vilfredo, 290
Parri, Ferruccio, 96
Partido Unido de Alianza Popular (PUAP), 255, 260, 266 nn.3, 4. *See also* Popular Party
Party of Democratic Renewal (DIANA), 228
Party of New Forces (PFN), 45
Pasqua, Charles, 36, 41 n.12
Peasants Newsletter *(Lettre aux Paysans)*, 59
Perdomo, Ronald, 55, 62
Piat, Yann, 47
Piccoli, Flaminio, 114
Pole of Good Government *(Polo del Buon governo)*, 103
Police Professional Independent Federation (FPIP), 59
Political Spring *(Politike Anixe)*, 189, 196
Pompidou, Georges, 14, 16, 26, 31, 297, 298
Pons, Bernard, 36, 41 n.12
Popular Alliance (AP)/Popular Party (PP): authoritarian political elite and, 260, 267 n.15; center/periphery, internal relation and, 255, 258, 263, 267

n.18, 268 n.20; electoral success of, 256, 264; foundation of, 254–255, 260, 266 n.3; institutionalization of, 257, 259–261, 264–265; membership of, 257–258, 262; national bodies of, 259, 261, 262–264, 268 n.23; renewal of, 261–264; renewal of elites in, 256, 257–258, 260, 262–263, 268 nn.20, 21; statutory changes of, 259–260, 263–264; UCD end and, 257, 260, 261; youth organization and, 259, 263

Popular Coalition (CP), 244

Popular Movement *(Movimento Popolare),* 121, 126, 127

Popular Party (PP), 112

Popular and Republican Movement (MRP), 9, 11, 13, 14, 16

Popular Socialist Party (PSP), 244, 271

Portelli, Hugues, 79

Présent, 47, 57, 65, 68 n.9

Présent-Militants, 65

Prodi, Romano, 106, 107, 297

Proletarian Democracy (DP), 92

Puhle, Hans-Jurgen, 250 n.1, 274, 276, 277

Pujol, Jord, 246

Radical party *(Parti radical),* 9, 10, 11, 13, 16, 17, 18, 24 n.2

Radical party (PR), 92, 98, 103

Radical-Socialist Party (PRS), 10

Rallis, George, 183, 187, 225, 226, 227, 232, 235 n.11

Rally for the Republic (RPR): activists of, 27, 30–31; candidates' selection in, 29–30; charismatic leadership and, 33, 38–40; governing bodies of, 32–33, 35–37; intra-party democracy of, 32–33; local organization of, 28–30, 32–33, 38; local leaders' recruitment in, 37–38; office holders/party leadership relationship in, 33–35, 38; membership of, 27, 30–31; presidential campaign of, 35–36; statutory changes of, 27, 31–32, 35; voters' party and, 30–31

Rally of the French People (RPF), 9, 10, 13, 39

Rauti, Pino, 165, 169, 171–172, 173, 174, 175, 176 nn.7, 8

Redondo, Nicolàs, 271, 277

Renaissance Circle *(Cercle Renaissance),* 60

Renault, Alain, 46

Renouveau étudiant (RE), 58

Renouveau lycéen (RL), 58

Renovators *(Rénovateurs),* 38

Republican Party (PR), 10, 11, 16, 24 n.2

Republican, Radical and Radical-Socialist Party *(Parti républicain radical et radical socialiste),* 9. *See also* Radical Party

Right and Freedom *(Droit et Liberté),* 59

Robert, Alain, 45

Rocard, Michel, 19, 72, 73, 78, 82

Sahagùn, Rodrìguez A., 243

Salò Republic. *See* Italian Social Republic

Samaras, Andonis, 189, 196, 230

Sani, Giacomo, 94, 278

Sartori, Giovanni, 94, 274

Satrusteghi, M., 278

Scalfaro, Oscar Luigi, 101

Schonfeld, William, 36, 276–277

Scotti, Vincenzo, 118

Il Secolo d'Italia, 169

Secrete Armed Organization (OAS), 45, 55, 57, 58, 68 n.4

Segni, Mario, 101, 125, 127

Segni Pact *(Patto Segni),* 101, 103, 105, 106

Seguin, Philippe, 36, 38, 41 n.12

Simites, Constantine, 214

Simonpieri, Daniel, 55

Small Farmers' Organisations *(Coldiretti),* 121, 126

Social Christians (CS), 103

Socialisme et République, 83

Socialist Action Party (PASOC), 271

Socialist Democratic Alliance (ASD), 244

Socialist parties, 281–282, 283–284, 286, 291, 301. *See also* Panhellenic Socialist Movement; Socialist Party; Spanish Socialist Workers Party

Socialist Party (PS): inner factionalism of, 71–73, 82–83; membership of, 71, 73–76, 80–82; office-holders and, 75, 77–78, 81; PCF and, 70, 77; presidential party and, 71, 77–78; professionalization of, 79–82; social composition of, 71, 76, 80; statutory changes of, 72, 75

Socialist Unified Party (PSU), 17, 19, 22, 24 n.3, 72

Solchaga, Carlos, 271

Solidaristes, 46, 61

SOS-Tout-Petits, 60

Sotelo, Calvo, 243

Spadolini, Giovanni, 96

Spanish Communist Party (PCE), 243–244, 247, 249, 270, 271

Spanish party system: crises in, 245, 249, 250; democratization process and, 241–242, 247–249; instability in, 244, 245; mass media and, 242, 246; PSOE as dominant party of, 249–250; renewal of elites in, 245–246

Spanish Socialist Workers Party (PSOE): charismatic leadership and, 276; federalism and, 272, 274; formal rules of, 272–273, 275; inner factionalism of, 274, 277; intra-party democracy of, 273–274, 275–276; membership and, 272–273, 278; national bodies of, 275–276

Stefanopoulos, Costis, 228

Stirbois, Jean-Pierre, 46, 48, 50, 54, 61, 62, 63, 64, 65, 67, 68 nn.4, 13

Stirbois, Marie-France, 46, 47, 68 n.8

Sturzo, Luigi, 125

Suàrez, Adolfo, 241, 243, 247, 249, 265 n.1, 267 n.15

Three-Colored Flame *(Fiamma Tricolore)*, 106

Tiersky, Ronald, 13

Tixier-Vignancour, Jean-Louis, 21

Togliatti, Palmiro, 139

Tomorrow France *(Demain La France)*, 36

Toubon, Jacques, 36, 41 n.15

Tristan, Anne, 61

Union de la Gauche (Union of the Left), 18, 71, 77

Union for the Defense of the Republic (UDR), 11, 14, 16, 21, 26, 27, 31, 36. *See also* Rally for the Republic

Union for the French Democracy (UDF), 16, 17, 19, 20, 21, 22, 23, 24, 24 n.2, 26, 27, 30, 32, 48, 55, 61

Union for the New Republic (UNR), 11, 13, 14, 26, 31, 39. *See also* Rally for the Republic

Union of Democrats for the Fifth Republic (UD Vè), 11

Union of Italian Women (UDI), 136, 147–148, 154 nn.14, 15

United Christian Democrats (CDU), 106, 107

United Democratic Left Party (EDA), 182, 204

United Left (IU), 244, 271

United Left *(Enomene Aristera)*, 182, 183

University Front of National Action (FUAN), 167

Veteran's National Circle (CNC), 58

Weber, Max, 38, 39, 233, 290

Wertman, Douglas A., 122, 128 n.6, 130 n.22

Women for the Future *(Femme-Avenir)*, 28

Workers' Struggle (LO), 10

Young Italy *(Giovane Italia)*, 167

Young Left in the PDS *(Sinistra Giovanile nel PDS)*, 150

Youth Front (FdG), 167

Youth grouping of students and workers *(Raggruppamento giovanile studenti e lavoratori)*, 167

Ysmal, Colette, 84 n.6, 276

Zaccagnini, Benigno, 114, 129 n.8

About the Contributors

GIANFRANCO BALDINI is Post-Doctoral Fellow in the Department of Politics, Institutions, History at the University of Bologna.

LUCIANO BARDI is Professor of Political Science in the Department of Politics, Institutions, History at the University of Bologna.

GABRIEL COLOMÉ is Professor of Political Science in the Faculty of Political Science and Sociology at the Autonomous University of Barcelona.

P. NIKOFOROS DIAMANDOUROS is Professor of Politics at the University of Athens and Director-Chairman of the Greek National Centre for Social Research (EKKE) of Athens.

FLORENCE HAEGEL is Researcher in the Research Centre on the French Political System at the National Foundation of Political Science of Paris.

PIERO IGNAZI is Professor of Comparative Politics in the Department of Politics, Institutions, History at the University of Bologna.

GILLES IVALDI is Researcher in the Institute of Political Studies of Grenoble.

LOURDES LÒPEZ-NIETO is Professor of Political Science in the Faculty of Political Science and Sociology at the Non-Resident National University of Madrid.

MARIA PAMINI is Graduate Researcher in the Department of Politics, Institutions, History at the University of Bologna.

TAKIS S. PAPPAS is Researcher in the Greek National Centre for Social Research (EKKE) of Athens.

FRÉDÉRIC SAWICKI is Professor of Political Science in the Faculty of Law and Political Science at the University of Lille.

MICHALIS SPOURDALAKIS is Associate Professor in the Department of Political Science and Public Administration at the University of Athens.

COLETTE YSMAL is Director for Research at the National Foundation of Political Science in Paris.

Lightning Source UK Ltd.
Milton Keynes UK
UKOW04n0941130817
307184UK00009B/88/P

9 780275 956127